SUCH DEVOTED SISTERS

Other Novels by Shena Mackay

A Bowl of Cherries
Dunedin

SUCH DEVOTED SISTERS

Shena Mackay, editor

MOYER BELL | Wakefield, Rhode Island & London

Published by Moyer Bell
First Edition 1994
Copyright © 1993 by Shena Mackay

**LIBRARY OF CONGRESS
CATALOGING-IN-PUBLICATION DATA**

Mackay, Shena.
Such devoted sisters/Shena Mackay

p. cm.

1. Title.

PR1111.W6S85   1993   93-44727
813'.0108352042—dc20   CIP
ISBN 1-55921-110-5

Printed in the United States of America
Distributed in North America by Publishers Group West, P.O.
Box 8843, Emeryville, CA 94662, 800-788-3123 (in California
510-658-3453), and in Europe by Gazelle Book Services Ltd.,
Falcon House, Queen Square, Lancaster LA1 1RN England.

Contents

Acknowledgements

Permission to reproduce stories by the following authors is gratefully acknowledged: *The New Yorker* for 'In the Zoo', Copyright © Jean Stafford; Weidenfeld & Nicholson for 'The Connor Girls', from *A Fanatic Heart* Copyright © Edna O'Brien 1985; Mary Flanagan for 'White Places' from *Bad Girls*, Jonathan Cape, Copyright © Mary Flanagan 1984; William Maxwell and Susanna Pinney, the Executors of Sylvia Townsend Warner, and Chatto & Windus for 'The Quality of Mercy', Copyright © Sylvia Townsend Warner; Marilyn Duckworth for 'A Game of Pretend', Copyright © Marilyn Duckworth 1993; Kali for Women and The Women's Press, for 'Aunty', from *The Slate of Life: An Anthology of Stories by Indian Women*, republished in Great Britain as *Truth Tales 2: The Slate of Life*, 1991, Copyright © Bani Basu; Curtis Brown Ltd., London, for 'Keel and Kool' from *You are Now Entering the Human Heart*, Copyright © Janet Frame 1983; Virago Press Ltd. and Anjana Appachana for 'Incantations' from *Incantations and Other Stories*, Copyright © Anjana Appachana 1991; Nann Morgenstern for 'Sorority', Copyright © Nann Morgenstern 1993; Cynthia Rich for 'My Sister's Marriage', Copyright © Cynthia Rich; Viking Penguin for 'Five Acre Virgin', Copyright © Elizabeth Jolley 1976; The Women's Press for 'My Sister Cherish' from *Rain Darling*, Copyright © Merle Collins 1990; Fiona Cooper for 'The Sisters Hood', Copyright © Fiona Cooper 1993; Dyan Sheldon for 'Day and Night', Copyright © Dyan Sheldon 1993; Kali for Women and The Women's Press for 'Hand-me-Downs', from *The Slate of Life: An Anthology of Stories by Indian Women*, republished in Great Britain as *Truth Tales 2: The Slate of Life*, 1991, Copyright © Wajida Tabussum; Georgina Hammick for 'Tales from the Spare Room' from *People for Lunch*, Copyright © Georgina Hammick 1987; Curtis Brown Ltd., London, for 'Habit' from *The Persimmon Tree and Other Stories*, Copyright © Marjorie Barnard 1945.

Every effort has been made to trace copyright holders in all copyright material in this book. The editor regrets if there has been any oversight and suggests the publisher is contacted in any such event.

The Author would like to thank David Miller for his generous help and advice.

Introduction

～～～

For there is no friend like a sister
In calm or stormy weather ...

In 'Goblin Market', a poem as erotic and exotic as the beautiful
tainted fruit of goblin men, where one sister risks moral and physical
corruption to save another, Christina Rossetti presents an ideal of
sisterhood. The bond is not so strong for some of the sisters in
this collection. For example, the devoted sisters of the song from
which the book takes its title, and which evokes a thousand amateur
drag queens camping it up in feathers and sock suspenders, agree
that sisterhood stops when Mr Right happens along: 'Lord help the
mister who comes between me and my sister, And Lord help the
sister who comes between me and My Man!!' *Holiday Inn* and its
remake *White Christmas* which featured the song were light-hearted
films, but what Hollywood in its heyday really liked was one sister
to be bad and preferably played by Bette Davis. One of its saddest
images and lines (the quotation may be an approximation but the
sentiment is the same) occurs in *Whatever Happened To Baby Jane*,
not her greatest film, but one in which Bette Davis gives a great
performance as Baby Jane, the grotesque ageing former child-star,
trapped in hatred with her crippled sister, Joan Crawford. When
Baby Jane, in her white frilly little-girl dress, like a ruined birthday
cake symbolizing two wasted lives, realizes that she was not after
all responsible for her sister's tragic accident, she turns melodrama
into tragedy as she says wonderingly, in her heartbreaking, cracked
doll's voice, 'To think that we might have been friends for all these
years.'

1

There are sisters who are friends in this collection and sisters who are not: Marjorie Barnard, a writer underrated except in her native Australia, has a woman who disproves the sentiment of the aforementioned song by choosing her sister rather than a husband, while the coldly virtuous sister in Sylvia Townsend Warner's brave, bleak little story shows less compassion than Lizzie in 'Goblin Market'. Fiona Cooper writes humorously about women who have made their own sisterhood and, letting her characters speak for themselves, reveals the tenderness beneath the tough exteriors of the *habituées* of a gay bar in Newcastle. Then there are the teenage girls in Nann Morgenstern's 'Sorority', who long for a sister of their own. The denouement of this poignant recollection of late-fifties America, told with stylistic grace and economy and vivid period detail, shows that Celeste's lifelong sense of the lack of a sister is rooted in actual loss, and yet the story transcends its acknowledged sadness to end on a note of optimism tempered by a newly adult awareness. It is significant that the girls there, adopting one another as sisters, take the names Jo and Meg, two of the March sisters in *Little Women*, and in the context of the story it is pitifully ironic that neither wants to be Beth. (Almost everybody identifies with Jo, and yet, as an adult, one can appreciate what a touching, well-drawn character Meg is.) An extract from *Little Women* seemed essential but it was difficult to select from this book, written in 1868, which has enthralled generations of, mostly, girls; amused, moved and inspired them to try to be better people. There are of course much jollier passages in *Good Wives* but I have opted for the account of Beth's death for its lasting portrayal of grief and its aftermath.

There has been much research into the influence of its position in a family on a child's character and development. Charlotte, in Mary Flanagan's 'White Places', is the youngest and fattest: 'Her shoes were always wet and untied with her socks sliding down into the heels. She had cold sores and was only in the fourth grade.' Charlotte, who is nicknamed Killer (there is a dreadful moment when the cruel name slips from Mummy's lips), has affinities with Elsie of *What Katy Did*, which like *Little Women* stands the test of time. 'Poor little Elsie!' Susan Coolidge wrote in 1872, in the first of the Katy books, 'In almost every family there is one of these unmated, left-out children.'

2

In Flanagan's brilliantly chilling exposition of victimization a game gets out of hand and threatens a tragic ending like that of *The Mistletoe Bough*, the story of the girl who hid in a chest on her wedding day and whose skeleton was discovered fifty years later.

The death of a child cannot be prevented in Merle Collins's haunting 'My Sister Cherish', a story taken from her collection *Rain Darling*, set in her native Grenada, which contains 'Rain', another marvellous, painful story about sisters. Janet Frame, who tells in her marvellous autobiographies how she suffered the unimaginable loss of two sisters in successive drowning accidents, brings an unbearable desolation to 'Keel and Kool' in recounting a seemingly arbitrary childish quarrel. Her fellow New Zealander Marilyn Duckworth, a prize-winning author whose work deserves to be better known in this country, contributes a wryly affectionate look at the sisterly bond, something she has explored in her novels, in 'A Game of Pretend'. And so, geographically, we come to Katherine Mansfield. 'The Daughters of the Late Colonel', is one of the best short stories ever written, and it was written 'as fast as possible for fear of dying before the story was sent'. It was acclaimed but widely misunderstood; Mansfield's own words describe best her intentions and its reception:

> While I was writing the story I lived for it but when it was finished, I confess I hoped very much that my readers would understand what I was trying to express. But very few did. They thought it was 'cruel'; they thought I was 'sneering' at Jug and Constantia; or they thought it was 'drab'. And in the last paragraph I was 'poking fun at the poor old things'. It's almost terrifying to be misunderstood. There was a moment when I first had 'the idea' when I saw the two sisters as *amusing*; but the moment I looked deeper (let me be quite frank) I bowed down to the beauty that was hidden in their lives and to discover that was all my desire ... All was meant, of course, to lead up to that last paragraph, when my two flowerless ones turned with that timid gesture, to the sun. 'Perhaps *now* ...'

Georgina Hammick's 'Tales from the Spare Room' has, on occasion, been misunderstood in a similar way. Like Mansfield's, hers 'just unfolds and opens', on the maids' sitting-room where the two little girls staying with their grandmother have been invited to play cards. Subtly, beautifully, Hammick exposes the unhappiness behind the façade of the Big House in post-war rural northern England, and

3

the insecurity of her 'privileged' children. There are four sisters here, for the maids are sisters too, and, not 'sneering' at the maids or their lives, Hammick presents them through the children's eyes with the same clarity of vision as that with which they perceive their one, saintly ally, and their monstrous grandmother, her spaniels, and the minutiae of their world. When the children step into the maids' world, as if through a looking-glass, and find themselves in a familiar High Street changed utterly, their experiences are devastating, their fear and disgrace almost tangible, but the maids' hurt perspective is there too.

'In the Zoo', an outstanding story written in the 1950s by Jean Stafford at the top of her excellent form, is another passionate, tragicomic account of children at the mercy of adults:

> And thus it was, in our grief for our parents, that we came cringing to the dry Western town and to the house where Mrs Placer lived, a house in which the square uncushioned furniture was cruel and the pictures on the walls were either dour or dire ... steeped in these mists of accusation and hidden plots and double meanings, Daisy and I grew up like worms.

The opening paragraph, describing a senile polar bear keening in the July heat in the zoo, gives notice that we are in the company of one of the greats, and although the tale of the orphaned worms ends on a wild fit of laughter, the reader's laughter will be close to tears.

It goes without saying that there are splendid stories and *novels* about sisters written by men (as there are novels by women which contain portraits of sisters, but I wanted to keep extracts to a minimum). And there is Shakespeare of course. There are also myths, ballads by the androgynous Anon, fairy-tales and the Bible – the story of Martha and Mary can still make a woman bristle like a scrubbing brush at the unfairness of it all. All the stories here are written by women about women but in several of them, not least in the Mansfield, there is a strong male presence. Cynthia Rich's skilfully understated 'My Sister's Marriage' has a manipulative father directing his daughters' lives and setting sister against sister, while Anjana Appachana, an impressive young Indian-born writer, tells a truly terrible tale of the fate of a young girl in a male-dominated society. If that is an indictment, Bani Basu's 'Aunty', set among a

Brahmin family in India, makes the plight of her abandoned old woman universal: when the family, in order to get their hands on some property, go in search of her in the old people's home where she has been dumped, they cannot pick her out from the macabre identity parade staged for their inspection: 'Actually, she had no identifying mark on her. In fact, she was just an aunt. One of innumerable aunts. Not anyone's mother or father, just an aunt.' In happier circumstances are Elizabeth Gaskell's Miss Jenkynses; with what acerbic wit and tenderness Elizabeth Gaskell wrote, and what an intriguing, masterly opening sentence: 'In the first place, Cranford is in possession of the Amazons; all the holders of houses, above a certain rent, are women.'

This collection boasts Edna O'Brien at her magnificent best, a fine characteristically edgy and funny new story of contrasts by Dyan Sheldon, 'Day and Night', full of angst and sisterly panic in the suburbs, Wajida Tabassum's neat tale of revenge in which resentment at wearing cast-off clothes is taken to extremes, and an introduction to Elizabeth Jolley's life-enhancing rackety Australian family. I hope that the choice will please many readers, my own sisters, daughters, nieces – and nephews – among them. There is one obvious categorical omission from what is a catholic selection but was intended to be a broader church: there is, *mea culpa*, no story about nuns. To make up for this, although it speaks of solitude rather than community, I should like to include here Gerard Manley Hopkins's perfect poem:

Heaven-Haven

A nun takes the veil

I have desired to go
Where springs not fail,
To fields where flies no sharp and sided hail
And a few lilies blow.

And I have asked to be
Where no storms come,
Where the green swell is in the havens dumb,
And out of the swing of the sea.

Shena Mackay, London, 1992

Jean Stafford

In the Zoo

Keening harshly in his senility, the blind polar bear slowly and ceaselessly shakes his head in the stark heat of the July and mountain noon. His open eyes are blue. No one stops to look at him; an old farmer, in passing, sums up the old bear's situation by observing, with a ruthless chuckle, that he is a 'back number'. Patient and despairing, he sits on his yellowed haunches on the central rock of his pool, his huge toy paws wearing short boots of mud.

The grizzlies to the right of him, a conventional family of father and mother and two spring cubs, alternately play the clown and sleep. There is a blustery, scoundrelly, half-likeable bravado in the manner of the black bear on the polar's left; his name, according to the legend on his cage, is Clancy, and he is a rough-and-tumble, brawling blowhard, thundering continually as he paces back and forth, or pauses to face his audience of children and mothers and release from his great, grey-tongued mouth a perfectly Vesuvian roar. If he were to be reincarnated in human form, he would be a man of action, possibly a football coach, probably a politician. One expects to see his black hat hanging from a branch of one of his trees; at any moment he will light a cigar.

The polar bear's next-door neighbours are not the only ones who offer so sharp and sad a contrast to him. Across a reach of scrappy grass and litter is the convocation of conceited monkeys, burrowing into each other's necks and chests for fleas, picking their noses with their long, black, finicky fingers, swinging by their gifted tails on the flying trapeze, screaming bloody murder. Even when they mourn – one would think the male orang-utan was on the very brink of suicide – they are comedians; they only fake depression, for they are firmly secure in their rambunctious tribalism and in their appalling insight and contempt. Their flibbertigibbet gambolling is a sham,

7

and, stealthily and shiftily, they are really watching the pitiful polar bear ('Back number,' they quote the farmer. 'That's *his* number all right,' they snigger), and the windy black bear ('Life of the party. Gasbag. Low IQ,' they note scornfully on his dossier) and the stupid, bourgeois grizzlies ('It's feed the face and hit the sack for them,' the monkeys say). And they are watching my sister and me, two middle-aged women, as we sit on a bench between the exhibits, eating popcorn, growing thirsty. We are thoughtful.

A chance remark of Daisy's a few minutes before has turned us to memory and meditation. 'I don't know why,' she said 'but that poor blind bear reminds me of Mr Murphy.' The name 'Mr Murphy' at once returned us both to childhood, and we were floated far and fast, our later lives diminished. So now we eat our popcorn in silence with the ritualistic appetite of childhood, which has little to do with hunger; it is not so much food as a sacrament, and in tribute to our sisterliness and our friendliness I break the silence to say that this is the best popcorn I have ever eaten in my life. The extravagance of my statement instantly makes me feel self-indulgent, and for some time I uneasily avoid looking at the blind bear. My sister does not agree or disagree; she simply says that popcorn is the only food she has ever really liked. For a long time, then, we eat without a word, but I know, because I know her well and know her similarity to me, that Daisy is thinking what I am thinking; both of us are mournfully remembering Mr Murphy, who, at one time in our lives, was our only friend.

This zoo is in Denver, a city that means nothing to my sister and me except as a place to take or meet trains. Daisy lives two hundred miles farther west, and it is her custom, when my every-other-year visit with her is over, to come across the mountains to see me off on my eastbound train. We know almost no one here, and because our stays are short, we have never bothered to learn the town in more than the most desultory way. We know the Burlington uptown office and the respectable hotels, a restaurant or two, the Union Station, and beginning today, the zoo in the city park.

But since the moment that Daisy named Mr Murphy by name our situation in Denver has been only corporeal; our minds and our hearts are in Adams, fifty miles north, and we are seeing, under the white sun at its pitiless meridian, the streets of that ugly town, its parks and trees and bridges, the bandstand in its dreary park, the roads that lead away from it, west to the mountains and east to the plains, its mongrel and multitudinous churches, its high school shaped like a loaf of bread, the campus of its college, an oasis of which we had no experience except to walk through it now and then, eyeing the woodbine on the impressive buildings. These things are engraved for ever on our minds with a legibility so insistent that you have only to say the name of the town aloud to us to rip the rinds from our nerves and leave us exposed in terror and humiliation.

We have supposed in later years that Adams was not so bad as all that, and we know that we magnified its ugliness because we looked upon it as the extension of the possessive, unloving, scornful, complacent foster mother, Mrs Placer, to whom, at the death of our parents within a month of each other, we were sent like Dickensian grotesqueries – cowardly, weak-stomached, given to tears, backward in school. Daisy was ten and I was eight when, unaccompanied, we made the long trip from Marblehead to our benefactress, whom we had never seen and, indeed, never heard of until the pastor of our church came to tell us of the arrangement our father had made on his deathbed, seconded by our mother on hers. This man, whose name and face I have forgotten and whose parting speeches to us I have not forgiven, tried to dry our tears with talk of Indians and of buffaloes; he spoke, however, at much greater length, and in preaching cadences, of the Christian goodness of Mrs Placer. She was, he said, childless and fond of children, and for many years she had been a widow, after the lingering demise of her tubercular husband, for whose sake she had moved to the Rocky Mountains. For his support and costly medical care, she had run a boarding house, and after his death, since he had left her nothing, she was obliged to continue running it. She had been a girlhood friend of our paternal grandmother, and our father, in the absence of responsible relatives, had made her the beneficiary of his life insurance on the condition that she lodge and rear us. The pastor, with a frankness remarkable considering that he was talking to children, explained to us that our father had left little more than a drop in the bucket for our care, and he enjoined us to give Mrs Placer, in return for her hospitality and sacrifice, courteous help and eternal thanks. 'Sacrifice' was a word we were never allowed to forget.

9

And thus it was, in grief for our parents, that we came cringing to the dry Western town and to the house where Mrs Placer lived, a house in which the square, uncushioned furniture was cruel and the pictures on the walls were either dour or dire and the lodgers, who lived in the upper floors among shadowy wardrobes and chiffoniers, had come through the years to resemble their landlady in appearance as well as in deportment.

After their ugly-coloured evening meal, Gran – as she bade us call her – and her paying guests would sit, rangey and aquiline, rocking on the front porch on spring and summer and autumn nights, tasting their delicious grievances: those slights delivered by ungrateful sons and daughters, those impudences committed by trolley-car conductors and uppity salesgirls in the ready-to-wear, all those slurs and calculated elbow-jostlings that were their daily crucifixion and their staff of life. We little girls, washing the dishes in the cavernous kitchen, listened to their even, martyred voices, fixed like leeches to their solitary subject and their solitary creed – that life was essentially a matter of being done in, let down, and swindled.

At regular intervals, Mrs Placer, chairwoman of the victims, would say, 'Of course, I don't care; I just have to laugh,' and then would tell a shocking tale of an intricate piece of skulduggery perpetrated against her by someone she did not even know. Sometimes, with her avid, partial jury sitting there on the porch behind the bitter hopvines in the heady mountain air, the cases she tried involved Daisy and me, and, listening, we travailed, hugging each other, whispering, 'I wish she wouldn't! Oh, how did she find out?' How *did* she? Certainly we never told her when we were snubbed or chosen last on teams, never admitted to a teacher's scolding or to the hoots of laughter that greeted us when we bit on silly, unfair jokes. But she knew. She knew about the slumber parties we were not invited to, the beefsteak fries at which we were pointedly left out; she knew that the singing teacher had said in so many words that I could not carry a tune in a basket and that the sewing superintendent had said that Daisy's fingers were all thumbs. With our teeth chattering in the cold of our isolation, we would hear her protestant, litigious voice defending our right to be orphans, paupers, wholly dependent on her – except for the really ridiculous pittance from our father's life insurance

10

– when it was all she could do to make ends meet. She did not care, but she had to laugh that people in general were so small-minded that they looked down on fatherless, motherless waifs like us and, by association, looked down on her. It seemed funny to her that people gave her no credit for taking on these sickly youngsters who were not even kin but only the grandchildren of a friend.

If a child with braces on her teeth came to play with us, she was, according to Gran, slyly lording it over us because our teeth were crooked, but there was no money to have them straightened. And what could be the meaning of our being asked to come for supper at the doctor's house? Were the doctor and his la-di-da New York wife and those pert girls with their solid-gold barrettes and their Shetland pony going to shame her poor darlings? Or shame their poor Gran by making them sorry to come home to the plain but honest life that was all she could provide for them?

There was no stratum of society not reeking with the effluvium of fraud and pettifoggery. And the school system was almost the worst of all: if we could not understand fractions, was that not our teacher's fault? And therefore what right had she to give us F? It was as plain as a pikestaff to Gran that the teacher was only covering up her own inability to teach. It was unlikely, too – highly unlikely – that it was by accident that time and time again the free medical clinic was closed for the day just as our names were about to be called out, so that nothing was done about our bad tonsils, which meant that we were repeatedly sick in the winter, with Gran fetching and carrying for us, climbing those stairs a jillion times a day with her game leg and her heart that was none too strong.

Steeped in these mists of accusation and hidden plots and double meanings, Daisy and I grew up like worms. I think no one could have withstood the atmosphere in that house where everyone trod on eggs that a little bird had told them were bad. They spied on one another, whispered behind doors, conjectured, drew parallels beginning 'With all due respect . . .' or 'It is a matter of indifference to *me* but . . .' The vigilantes patrolled our town by day, and by night returned to lay their goodies at their priestess's feet and wait for her oracular interpretation of the innards of the butcher, the baker, the candlestick maker, the soda jerk's girl, and the barber's unnatural deaf white cat.

11

Consequently, Daisy and I also became suspicious. But it was suspicion of ourselves that made us hope and weep and grimace with self-judgement. Why were we not happy when Gran had sacrificed herself to the bone for us? Why did we not cut dead the paper boy who had called her a filthy name? Why did we persist in our wilful friendliness with the grocer who had tried, unsuccessfully, to overcharge her on a case of pork and beans?

Our friendships were nervous and surreptitious; we sneaked and lied, and as our hungers sharpened, our debasement deepened; we were pitied; we were shifty-eyed, always on the look-out for Mrs Placer or one of her tattletale lodgers; we were hypocrites.

Nevertheless, one thin filament of instinct survived, and Daisy and I in time found asylum in a small menagerie down by the railroad tracks. It belonged to a gentle alcoholic ne'er-do-well, who did nothing all day long but drink bathtub gin in rickeys and play solitaire and smile to himself and talk to his animals. He had a little, stunted red vixen and a deodorized skunk, a parrot from Tahiti that spoke Parisian French, a woebegone coyote, and two capuchin monkeys, so serious and humanized, so small and sad and sweet, and so religious-looking with their tonsured heads that it was impossible not to think their gibberish was really an ordered language with a grammar that some day some philologist would understand.

Gran knew about our visits to Mr Murphy and she did not object, for it gave her keen pleasure to excoriate him when we came home. His vice was not a matter of guesswork; it was an established fact that he was half-seas over from dawn till midnight. 'With the black Irish,' said Gran, 'the taste for drink is taken in with the mother's milk and is never mastered. Oh, I know all about those promises to join the temperance movement and not to touch another drop. The way to Hell is paved with good intentions.'

We were still little girls when we discovered Mr Murphy, before the shattering disease of adolescence was to make our bones and brains ache even more painfully than before, and we loved him and we hoped to marry him when we grew up. We loved him, and we loved his monkeys to exactly the same degree and in exactly the same way; they were husbands and fathers and brothers, these little, ugly, dark, secret men who minded their own business and let us mind ours. If

12

we stuck our fingers through the bars of the cage, the monkeys would sometimes take them in their tight, tiny hands and look into our faces with a tentative, somehow absent-minded sorrow, as if they terribly regretted that they could not place us but were glad to see us all the same. Mr Murphy, playing a solitaire game of cards called 'once in a blue moon' on a kitchen table in his back yard beside the pens, would occasionally look up and blink his beautiful blue eyes and say, 'You're peaches to make over my wee friends. I love you for it.' There was nothing demanding in his voice, and nothing sticky; on his lips the word 'love' was jocose and forthright, it had no strings attached. We would sit on either side of him and watch him regiment his ranks of cards and stop to drink as deeply as if he were dying of thirst and wave to his animals and say to them, 'Yes, lads, you're dandies.'

Because Mr Murphy was as reserved with us as the capuchins were, as courteously noncommittal, we were surprised one spring day when he told us that he had a present for us, which he hoped Mrs Placer would let us keep; it was a puppy, for whom the owner had asked him to find a home – half collie and half Labrador retriever, blue-blooded on both sides.

'You might tell Mrs Placer –' he said, smiling at the name, for Gran was famous in the town. 'You might tell Mrs Placer,' said Mr Murphy, 'that this lad will make a fine watchdog. She'll never have to fear for her spoons again. Or her honour.' The last he said to himself, not laughing but tucking his chin into his collar; lines sprang to the corners of his eyes. He would not let us see the dog, whom we could hear yipping and squealing inside his shanty, for he said that our disappointment would weigh on his conscience if we lost our hearts to the fellow and then could not have him for our own.

That evening at supper, we told Gran about Mr Murphy's present. A dog? In the first place, why a dog? Was it possible that the news had reached Mr Murphy's ears that Gran had just this very day finished planting her spring garden, the very thing that a rampageous dog would have in his mind to destroy? What sex was it? A male! Females, she had heard, were more trustworthy; males roved and came home smelling of skunk; such a consideration as this, of course, would not have crossed Mr Murphy's fuddled mind. Was this young male dog housebroken? We had not asked? That was the limit!

13

Gran appealed to her followers, too raptly fascinated by Mr Murphy's machinations to eat their Harvard beets. 'Am I being far-fetched or does it strike you as decidedly queer that Mr Murphy is trying to fob off on my little girls a young cur that has not been trained?' she asked them. 'If it were housebroken, he would have said so, so I feel it is safe to assume that it is not. Perhaps cannot *be* housebroken. I've heard of such cases.'

The fantasy spun on, richly and rapidly, with all the skilled helping hands at work at once. The dog was tangibly in the room with us, shedding his hair, biting his fleas, shaking rain off himself to splatter the walls, dragging some dreadful carcass across the floor, chewing up slippers, knocking over chairs with his tail, gobbling the chops from the platter, barking, biting, fathering, fighting, smelling to high heaven of carrion, staining the rug with his muddy feet, scratching the floor with his claws. He developed rabies; he bit a child, two children! Three! Everyone in town! And Gran and her poor darlings went to gaol for harbouring this murderous, odoriferous, drunk, Roman Catholic dog.

And yet, astoundingly enough, she came around to agreeing to let us have the dog. It was, as Mr Murphy had predicted, the word 'watchdog' that deflected the course of the trial. The moment Daisy uttered it, Gran halted, marshalling her reverse march; while she rallied and tacked and reconnoitred, she sent us to the kitchen for the dessert. And by the time this course was under way, the uses of a dog, the enormous potentialities for investigation and law enforcement in a dog trained by Mrs Placer, were being minutely and passionately scrutinized by the eight upright bloodhounds sitting at the table wolfing their brown Betty as if it were fresh-killed rabbit. The dog now sat at attention beside his mistress, fiercely alert, ears cocked, nose aquiver, the protector of widows, of orphans, of lonely people who had no homes. He made short shrift of burglars, homicidal maniacs, Peeping Toms, gypsies, bogus missionaries, Fuller Brush men with a risqué spiel. He went to the store and brought back groceries, retrieved the evening paper from the awkward place the boy had meanly thrown it, rescued cripples from burning houses, saved children from drowning, heeled at command, begged, lay down, stood up, sat, jumped through a hoop, ratted.

Both times – when he was a ruffian of the blackest delinquency

14

and then a pillar of society – he was full-grown in his prefiguration, and when Laddy appeared on the following day, small, unsteady, and whimpering lonesomely, Gran and her lodgers were taken aback; his infant, clumsy paws embarrassed them, his melting eyes were unapropos. But it could never be said of Mrs Placer, as Mrs Placer her own self said, that she was a woman who went back on her word, and her darlings were going to have their dog, softheaded and feckless as he might be. All the first night, in his carton in the kitchen, he wailed for his mother, and in the morning, it was true, he had made a shambles of the room – fouled the floor, and pulled off the tablecloth together with a ketchup bottle, so that thick gore lay everywhere. At breakfast, the lodgers confessed they had had a most amusing night, for it had actually been funny the way the dog had been determined not to let anyone get a wink of sleep. After that first night, Laddy slept in our room, receiving from us, all through our delighted, sleepless nights, pats and embraces and kisses and whispers. He was our baby, our best friend, the smartest, prettiest, nicest dog in the entire wide world. Our soft and rapid blandishments excited him to yelp at us in pleased bewilderment, and then we would playfully grasp his muzzle, so that he would snarl, deep in his throat like an adult dog, and shake his head violently, and, when we freed him, nip us smartly with great good will.

He was an intelligent and genial dog and we trained him quickly. He steered clear of Gran's radishes and lettuce after she had several times given him a brisk come-uppance with a strap across the rump, and he soon left off chewing shoes and the laundry on the line, and he outgrew his babyish whining. He grew like a weed; he lost his spherical softness, and his coat, which had been sooty fluff, came in stiff and rusty black; his nose grew aristocratically long, and his clever, pointed ears stood at attention. He was all bronzy, lustrous black except for an Elizabethan ruff of white and a tip of white at the end of his perky tail. No one could deny that he was exceptionally handsome and that he had, as well, great personal charm and style. He escorted Daisy and me to school in the morning, laughing interiorly out of the enormous pleasure of his life as he gracefully cantered ahead of us, distracted occasionally by his private interest in smells or unfamiliar beings in the grass but, on the whole, engrossed in his role of chaperon. He made friends easily with other dogs, and

15

sometimes he went for a long hunting weekend into the mountains with a huge and bossy old red hound named Mess, who had been on the county most of his life and had made a good thing of it, particularly at the fire station.

It was after one of these three-day excursions into the high country that Gran took Laddy in hand. He had come back spent and filthy, his coat a mass of cockleburs and ticks, his eyes bloodshot, loud *râles* in his chest; for half a day he lay motionless before the front door like someone in a hangover, his groaning eyes explicitly saying 'Oh, for God's sake, leave me be' when we offered him food or bowls of water. Gran was disapproving, then affronted, and finally furious. Not, of course, with Laddy, since all inmates of her house enjoyed immunity, but with Mess, whose caddish character, together with that of his nominal masters, the firemen, she examined closely under a strong light, with an air of detachment, with her not caring but her having, all the same, to laugh. A lodger who occupied the back west room had something to say about the fire chief and his nocturnal visits to a certain house occupied by a certain group of young women, too near the same age to be sisters and too old to be the daughters of the woman who claimed to be their mother. What a story! The exophthalmic librarian – she lived in one of the front rooms – had some interesting insinuations to make about the deputy marshal, who had borrowed, significantly, she thought, a book on hypnotism. She also knew – she was, of course, in a most useful position in the town, and from her authoritative pen in the middle of the library her mammiform and azure eyes and her eager ears missed nothing – that the fire chief's wife was not as scrupulous as she might be when she was keeping score on bridge night at the Sorosis.

There was little at the moment that Mrs Placer and her disciples could do to save the souls of the Fire Department and their families, and therefore save the town from holocaust (a very timid boarder – a Mr Beaver, a newcomer who was not to linger long – had sniffed throughout this recitative as if he were smelling burning flesh), but at least the unwholesome bond between Mess and Laddy could and would be severed once and for all. Gran looked across the porch at Laddy, who lay stretched at full length in the darkest corner, shuddering and baying abortively in his throat as he chased jack rabbits in his dreams, and she said, 'A dog can have morals like a human.' With this declaration Laddy's randy, manly holidays were finished. It may have been telepathy that woke him; he lifted his heavy head from his paws, laboriously got up, hesitated for a moment, and then padded languidly across the porch to Gran. He stood docilely beside her chair, head down, tail drooping as if to say, 'OK, Mrs Placer, show me how and I'll walk the straight and narrow.'

The very next day, Gran changed Laddy's name to Caesar, as being more dignified, and a joke was made at the supper table that he had come, seen, and conquered Mrs Placer's heart – for within her circle, where the magnanimity she lavished upon her orphans was daily demonstrated, Mrs Placer's heart was highly thought of. On that day also, although we did not know it yet, Laddy ceased to be our dog. Before many weeks passed, indeed, he ceased to be anyone we had ever known. A week or so after he became Caesar, he took up residence in her room, sleeping alongside her bed. She broke him of the habit of taking us to school (temptation to low living was rife along those streets; there was a chow – well, never mind) by the simple expedient of chaining him to a tree as soon as she got up in the morning. This discipline, together with the stamina-building cuffs she gave his sensitive ears from time to time, gradually but certainly remade his character. From a sanguine, affectionate, easygoing Gael (with the fits of melancholy that alternated with the larkiness), he turned into an overbearing, military, efficient, loud-voiced Teuton. His bark, once wide of range, narrowed to one dark, glottal tone.

Soon the paper boy flatly refused to serve our house after Caesar efficiently removed the bicycle clip from his pants leg; the skin was not broken, or even bruised, but it was a matter of principle with the boy. The milkman approached the back door in a seizure of shakes like St Vitus's dance. The metermen, the coal men, and the garbage collector crossed themselves if they were Catholics and, if they were not, tried whistling in the dark. 'Good boy, good Caesar,' they carolled, and, unctuously lying, they said they knew his bark was worse than his bite, knowing full well that it was not, considering the very nasty nip, requiring stitches, he had given a representative of the Olson Rug Company, who had the folly to pat him on the head. Caesar did not molest the lodgers, but he disdained them and he did not brook being personally addressed by anyone except Gran. One

17

night, he wandered into the dining-room, appearing to be in search of something he had mislaid, and, for some reason that no one was ever able to divine, suddenly stood stock-still and gave the easily upset Mr Beaver a long and penetrating look. Mr Beaver, trembling from head to toe, stammered, 'Why – er, hello there, Caesar, old boy, old boy,' and Caesar charged. For a moment, it was touch and go, but Gran saved Mr Beaver, only to lose him an hour later when he departed, bag and baggage, for the YMCA. This rout and the consequent loss of revenue would more than likely have meant Caesar's downfall and his deportation to the pound if it had not been that a newly widowed druggist, very irascible and very much Gran's style, had applied for a room in her house a week or so before, and now he moved in delightedly, as if he were coming home.

Finally, the police demanded that Caesar be muzzled and they warned that if he committed any major crime again – they cited the case of the Olson man – he would be shot on sight. Mrs Placer, although she had no respect for the law, knowing as much as she did about its agents, obeyed. She obeyed, that is, in part; she put the muzzle on Caesar for a few hours a day, usually early in the morning when the traffic was light and before the deliveries had started, but the rest of the time his powerful jaws and dazzling white sabre teeth were free and snapping. There was between these two such preternatural rapport, such an impressive conjugation of suspicion, that he, sensing the approach of a policeman, could convey instantly to her the immediate necessity of clapping his nose cage on. And the policeman, sent out on the complaint of a terrorized neighbour, would be greeted by this law-abiding pair at the door.

Daisy and I wished we were dead. We were divided between hating Caesar and loving Laddy, and we could not give up the hope that something, some day, would change him back into the loving animal he had been before he was appointed vice-president of the Placerites. Now at the meetings after supper on the porch he took an active part, standing rigidly at Gran's side except when she sent him on an errand. He carried out these assignments not with the air of a servant but with that of an accomplice. 'Get me the paper, Caesar,' she would say to him, and he, dismayingly intelligent and a shade smart-alecky, would open the screen door by himself and in a minute come back with the *Bulletin*, from which Mrs Placer would then read

18

an item, like the Gospel of the day, and then read between the lines of it, scandalized.

In the deepening of our woe and our bereavement and humiliation, we mutely appealed to Mr Murphy. We did not speak outright to him, for Mr Murphy lived in a state of indirection, and often when he used the pronoun 'I,' he seemed to be speaking of someone standing a little to the left of him, but we went to see him and his animals each day during the sad summer, taking what comfort we could from the cosy, quiet indolence of his back yard, where small black eyes encountered ours politely and everyone was half asleep. When Mr Murphy inquired about Laddy in his bland, inattentive way, looking for a stratagem whereby to shift the queen of hearts into position by the king, we would say, 'Oh, he's fine,' or 'Laddy is a nifty dog.' And Mr Murphy, reverently slaking the thirst that was his talent and his concubine, would murmur, 'I'm glad.'

We wanted to tell him, we wanted his help, or at least his sympathy, but how could we cloud his sunny world? It was awful to see Mr Murphy ruffled. Up in the calm clouds as he generally was, he could occasionally be brought to earth with a thud, as we had seen and heard one day. Not far from his house, there lived a bad, troublemaking boy of twelve, who was forever hanging over the fence trying to teach the parrot obscene words. He got nowhere, for she spoke no English and she would flabbergast him with her cold eye and sneer, '*Tant pis.*' One day, this boorish fellow went too far; he suddenly shot his head over the fence like a jack-in-the-box and aimed a water pistol at the skunk's face. Mr Murphy leaped to his feet in a scarlet rage; he picked up a stone and threw it accurately, hitting the boy square in the back, so hard that he fell right down in a mud puddle and lay there kicking and squalling and, as it turned out, quite badly hurt. 'If you ever come back here again, I'll kill you!' roared Mr Murphy. I think he meant it, for I have seldom seen an anger so resolute, so brilliant, and so voluble. 'How dared he!' he cried, scrambling into Mallow's cage to hug and pet and soothe her. 'He must be absolutely mad! He must be the Devil!' He did not go back to his game after that but paced the yard, swearing a blue streak and only pausing to croon to his animals, now as frightened by him as they had been by the intruder, and to drink straight from the bottle,

19

not bothering with fixings. We were fascinated by this unfamiliar side of Mr Murphy, but we did not want to see it ever again, for his face had grown so dangerously purple and the veins of his forehead seemed ready to burst and his eyes looked scorched. He was the closest thing to a maniac we had ever seen. So we did not tell him about Laddy; what he did not know would not hurt him, although it was hurting us, throbbing in us like a great, bleating wound.

But eventually Mr Murphy heard about our dog's conversion, one night at the pool hall, which he visited from time to time when he was seized with a rare but compelling garrulity, and the next afternoon when he asked us how Laddy was and we replied that he was fine, he tranquilly told us, as he deliberated whether to move the jack of clubs now or to bide his time, that we were sweet girls but we were lying in our teeth. He did not seem at all angry but only interested, and all the while he questioned us, he went on about his business with the gin and the hearts and spades and diamonds and clubs. It rarely happened that he won the particular game he was playing, but that day he did, and when he saw all the cards laid out in their ideal pattern, he leaned back, looking disappointed, and he said, 'I'm damned.' He then scooped up the cards, in a gesture unusually quick and tidy for him, stacked them together, and bound them with a rubber band. Then he began to tell us what he thought of Gran. He grew as loud and apoplectic as he had been that other time, and though he kept repeating that he knew *we* were innocent and he put not a shred of the blame on us, we were afraid that he might suddenly change his mind, and, speechless, we cowered against the monkeys' cage. In dread, the monkeys clutched the fingers we offered to them and made soft, protesting noises, as if to say, 'Oh, stop it, Murphy! Our nerves!'

As quickly as it had started, the tantrum ended. Mr Murphy paled to his normal complexion and said calmly that the only practical thing was to go and have it out with Mrs Placer. 'At once,' he added, although he said he bitterly feared that it was too late and there would be no exorcizing the fiend from Laddy's misused spirit. And because he had given the dog to us and not to her, he required that we go along with him, stick up for our rights, stand on our mettle, get up our Irish, and give the old bitch something to put in her pipe and smoke.

*

Oh, it was hot that day! We walked in a kind of delirium through the simmer, where only the grasshoppers had the energy to move, and I remember wondering if ether smelled like the gin on Mr Murphy's breath. Daisy and I, in one way or another, were going to have our gizzards cut out along with our hearts and our souls and our pride, and I wished I were as drunk as Mr Murphy, who swam effortlessly through the heat, his lips parted comfortably, his eyes half closed. When we turned in to the path at Gran's house, my blood began to scald my veins. It was so futile and so dangerous and so absurd. Here we were on a high moral mission, two draggle-tailed, gumptionless little girls and a toper whom no one could take seriously, partly because he was little more than a gurgling bottle of booze and partly because of the clothes he wore. He was a sight, as he always was when he was out of his own yard. There, somehow, in the carefree disorder, his clothes did not look especially strange, but on the streets of the town, in the barber shop or the post office or on Gran's path, they were fantastic. He wore a pair of hound's-tooth pants, old but maintaining a vehement pattern, and with them he wore a collarless blue flannelette shirt. His hat was the silliest of all, because it was a derby three sizes too big. And as if Shannon, too, was a part of his funny-paper costume, the elder capuchin rode on his shoulder, tightly embracing his thin red neck.

Gran and Caesar were standing side by side behind the screen door, looking as if they had been expecting us all along. For a moment, Gran and Mr Murphy faced each other across the length of weedy brick between the gate and the front porch, and no one spoke. Gran took no notice at all of Daisy and me. She adjusted her eyeglasses, using both hands, and then looked down at Caesar and matter-of-factly asked, 'Do you want out?'

Caesar flung himself full-length upon the screen and it sprang open like a jaw. I ran to meet and head him off, and Daisy threw a library book at his head, but he was on Mr Murphy in one split second and had his monkey off his shoulder and had broken Shannon's neck in two shakes. He would have gone on nuzzling and mauling and growling over the corpse for hours if Gran had not marched out of the house and down the path and slapped him lightly on the flank and said, in a voice that could not have deceived an idiot, 'Why, Caesar, you scamp! You've hurt Mr Murphy's monkey! Aren't you ashamed?'

21

Hurt the monkey! In one final, apologetic shudder, the life was extinguished from the little fellow. Bloody and covered with slather, Shannon lay with his arms suppliantly stretched over his head, his leather fingers curled into loose, helpless fists. His hind legs and his tail lay limp and helter-skelter on the path. And Mr Murphy, all of a sudden reeling drunk, burst into the kind of tears that Daisy and I knew well – the kind that time alone could stop. We stood aghast in the darkened sunset, killed by our horror and our grief for Shannon and our unforgivable disgrace. We stood upright in a dead faint, and an eon passed before Mr Murphy picked up Shannon's body and wove away, sobbing, 'I don't believe it! I don't *believe* it!'

The very next day, again at morbid, heavy sunset, Caesar died in violent convulsions, knocking down two tall hollyhocks in his throes. Long after his heart had stopped, his right hind leg continued to jerk in aimless reflex. Madly methodical, Mr Murphy had poisoned some meat for him, had thoroughly envenomed a whole pound of hamburger, and early in the morning, before sun-up, when he must have been near collapse with his hangover, he had stolen up to Mrs Placer's house and put it by the kitchen door. He was so stealthy that Caesar never stirred in his fool's paradise there on the floor by Gran. We knew these to be the facts, for Mr Murphy made no bones about them. Afterwards, he had gone home and said a solemn Requiem for Shannon in so loud a voice that someone sent for the police, and they took him away in the Black Maria to sober him up on strong green tea. By the time he was in the lock-up and had confessed what he had done, it was far too late, for Caesar had already gulped down the meat. He suffered an undreamed-of agony in Gran's flower garden, and Daisy and I, unable to bear the sight of it, hiked up to the red rocks and shook there, wretchedly ripping to shreds the sand lilies that grew in the cracks. Flight was the only thing we could think of, but where could we go? We stared west at the mountains and quailed at the look of the stern white glacier; we wildly scanned the prairies for escape. 'If only we were something besides kids! Besides girls!' mourned Daisy. I could not speak at all; I huddled in a niche of the rocks and cried.

No one in town, except, of course, her lodgers, had the slightest sympathy for Gran. The townsfolk allowed that Mr Murphy was a drunk and was fighting Irish, but he had a heart and this was something that could never be said of Mrs Placer. The neighbour who had called the police when he was chanting the '*Dies Irae*' before breakfast in that deafening monotone had said, 'The poor guy is having some kind of spell, so don't be rough on him, hear?' Mr Murphy became, in fact, a kind of hero; some people, stretching a point, said he was a saint for the way that every day and twice on Sunday he sang a memorial Mass over Shannon's grave, now marked with a chipped, cheap plaster figure of Saint Francis. He withdrew from the world more and more, seldom venturing into the streets at all, except when he went to the bootlegger to get a new bottle to snuggle into. All summer, all fall, we saw him as we passed by his yard, sitting at his dilapidated table, enfeebled with gin, greying, withering, turning his head ever and ever more slowly as he manoeuvred the protocol of the kings and the queens and the knaves. Daisy and I could never stop to visit him again.

It went on like this, year after year. Daisy and I lived in a mesh of lies and evasions, baffled and mean, like rats in a maze. When we were old enough for beaux, we connived like sluts to see them, but we would never admit to their existence until Gran caught us out by some trick. Like this one, for example: Once, at the end of a long interrogation, she said to me, 'I'm more relieved than I can tell you that you *don't* have anything to do with Jimmy Gilmore, because I happen to know that he is after only one thing in a girl,' and then, off guard in the loving memory of sitting in the movies the night before with Jimmy, not even holding hands, I defended him and defeated myself, and Gran, smiling with success, said, 'I *thought* you knew him. It's a pretty safe rule of thumb that where there's smoke there's fire.' That finished Jimmy and me, for afterwards I was nervous with him and I confounded and alarmed and finally bored him by trying to convince him, although the subject had not come up, that I did not doubt his good intentions.

Daisy and I would come home from school, or, later, from our jobs, with a small triumph or an interesting piece of news and if we forgot ourselves and, in our exuberance, told Gran, we were hustled into court at once for cross-examination. Once, I remember, while I was still in high school, I told her about getting a part in a play. How very nice for me, she said, if that kind of make-believe seemed to me

23

worthwhile. But what was my role? An old woman! A widow woman believed to be a witch? She did not care a red cent, but she did have to laugh in view of the fact that Miss Eccles, in charge of dramatics, had almost run her down in her car. And I would forgive her, would I not, if she did not come to see the play, and would not think her eccentric for not wanting to see herself ridiculed in public?

My pleasure strangled, I crawled, joy-killed, to our third-floor room. The room was small and its monstrous furniture was too big and the rag rugs were repulsive, but it was bright. We would not hang a blind at the window, and on this day I stood there staring into the mountains that burned with the sun. I feared the mountains, but at times like this their massiveness consoled me; they, at least, could not be gossiped about.

Why did we stay until we were grown? Daisy and I ask ourselves this question as we sit here on the bench in the municipal zoo, reminded of Mr Murphy by the polar bear, reminded by the monkeys not of Shannon but of Mrs Placer's insatiable gossips at their postprandial feast.

'But how could we have left?' said Daisy, wringing her buttery hands. 'It was the depression. We had no money. We had nowhere to go.'

'All the same, we could have gone,' I say, resentful still of the waste of all those years. 'We could have come here and got jobs as waitresses. Or prostitutes, for that matter.'

'I wouldn't have wanted to be a prostitute,' says Daisy.

We agree that under the circumstances it would have been impossible for us to run away. The physical act would have been simple, for the city was not far and we could have stolen the bus fare or hitched a ride. Later, when we began to work as salesgirls in Kress's, it would have been no trick at all to vanish one Saturday afternoon with our week's pay, without so much as going home to say goodbye. But it had been infinitely harder than that, for Gran, as we now see, held us trapped by our sense of guilt. We were vitiated, and we had no choice but to wait, flaccidly, for her to die.

You may be sure we did not unlearn those years as soon as we put her out of sight in the cemetery and sold her house for a song to the first boob who would buy it. Nor did we forget when we left the town for another one, where we had jobs at a dude camp – the town where Daisy now lives with a happy husband

and two happy sons. The succubus did not relent for years, and I can still remember, in the beginning of our days at the Lazy S 3, overhearing an edgy millionaire say to his wife, naming my name, 'That girl gives me the cold shivers. One would think she had just seen a murder.' Well, I had. For years, whenever I woke in the night in fear or pain or loneliness, I would increase my suffering by the memory of Shannon, and my tears were as bitter as poor Mr Murphy's.

We have never been back to Adams. But we see that house plainly, with the hopvines straggling over the porch. The windows are hung with the cheapest grade of marquisette, dipped into coffee to impart to it an unwilling colour, neither white nor tan but individual and spitefully unattractive. We see the wicker rockers and the swing, and through the screen door we dimly make out the slightly veering corridor, along one wall of which stands a glass-doored bookcase; when we were children, it had contained not books but stale old cardboard boxes filled with such things as WCTU tracts and anti-cigarette literature and newspaper clippings related to sexual sin in the Christianized islands of the Pacific.

Even if we were able to close our minds' eyes to the past, Mr Murphy would still be before us in the apotheosis of the polar bear. My pain becomes intolerable, and I am relieved when Daisy rescues us. 'We've got to go,' she says in a sudden panic. 'I've got asthma coming on.' We rush to the nearest exit of the city park and hail a cab, and, once inside it, Daisy gives herself an injection of adrenalin and then leans back. We are heartbroken and infuriated, and we cannot speak.

Two hours later, beside my train, we clutch each other as if we were drowning. We ought to go out to the nearest policeman and say, 'We are not responsible women. You will have to take care of us because we cannot take care of ourselves.' But gradually the storm begins to lull.

'You're sure you've got your ticket?' says Daisy. 'You'll surely be able to get a roomette once you're on.'

'I don't know about that,' I say. 'If there are any VIPs on board, I won't have a chance. "Spinsters and Orphans Last" is the motto of this line.'

Daisy smiles. 'I didn't care,' she says, 'but I had to laugh when I saw that woman nab the redcap you had signalled to. I had a good notion to give her a piece of my mind.'

'It will be a miracle if I ever see my bags again,' I say, mounting the steps of the train. 'Do you suppose that blackguardly porter knows about the twenty-dollar gold piece in my little suitcase?'

'Anything's possible!' cries Daisy, and begins to laugh. She is so pretty, standing there in her bright-red linen suit and her black velvet hat. A solitary ray of sunshine comes through a broken pane in the domed vault of the train shed and lies on her shoulder like a silver arrow.

'So long, Daisy!' I call as the train begins to move.

She walks quickly along beside the train. 'Watch out for pick-pockets!' she calls.

'You, too!' My voice is thin and lost in the increasing noise of the speeding train wheels. 'Goodbye, old dear!'

I go at once to the club car and I appropriate the writing table, to the vexation of a harried priest, who snatches up the telegraph pad and gives me a sharp look. I write Daisy approximately the same letter I always write her under this particular set of circumstances, the burden of which is that nothing for either of us can ever be as bad as the past before Gran mercifully died. In a postscript I add: 'There is a Roman Catholic priest (that is to say, he is *dressed* like one) sitting behind me although all the chairs on the opposite side of the car are empty. I can only conclude that he is looking over my shoulder, and while I do not want to cause you any alarm, I think you would be advised to be on the look-out for any appearance of miraculous medals, scapulars, papist booklets, etc., in the shops of your town. It really makes me laugh to see the way he is pretending that all he wants is for me to finish this letter so that he can have the table.'

I sign my name and address the envelope, and I give up my place to the priest, who smiles nicely at me, and then I move across the car to watch the fields as they slip by. They are alfalfa fields, but you can bet your bottom dollar that they are chock-a-block with marijuana.

I begin to laugh. The fit is silent but it is devastating; it surges and rattles in my rib-cage, and I turn my face to the window to avoid the narrow gaze of the Filipino bar boy. I must think of something sad to stop this unholy giggle, and I think of the polar bear. But even his bleak tragedy does not sober me. Wildly I fling open the newspaper I have brought and I pretend to be reading something screamingly funny. The words I see are in a Hollywood gossip column: 'How a well-known starlet can get a divorce in Nevada without her crooner husband's consent, nobody knows. It won't be worth a plugged nickel here.'

26

Edna O'Brien

The Connor Girls

To know them would be to enter an exalted world. To open the stiff green iron gate, to go up their shaded avenue, and to knock on their white hall door was a journey I yearned to make. No one went there except the gardener, the postman, and a cleaning woman who told none of their secrets, merely boasted that the oil paintings on the walls were priceless and the furniture was all antique. They had a flower garden with fountains, a water-lily pond, a kitchen garden, and ornamental trees that they called monkey-puzzle trees. Mr Connor, the major, and his two daughters lived there. His only son had been killed in a car accident. It was said that the accident was due to his father's bullying of him, always urging him to drive faster since he had the most expensive car in the neighbourhood. Not even their tragedy brought them closer to the people in the town, partly because they were aloof, but being Protestants, the Catholics could not attend the service in the church or go to the Protestant graveyard, where they had a vault with steps leading down to it, just like a house. It was smothered in creeper. They never went into mourning and had a party about a month later to which their friends came.

The major had friends who owned a stud farm, and these were invited two or three times a year, along with a surgeon and his wife, from Dublin. The Connor girls were not beauties but they were distinguished, and they talked in an accent that made everyone else's seem flat and sprawling, like some familiar estuary or a puddle in a field. They were dark-haired, with dark eyes and leathery skin. Miss Amy wore her hair in plaits, which she folded over the crown of her head, and Miss Lucy's hair, being more bushy, was kept flattened with brown slides. If they as much as nodded to a local or stopped to admire a new baby in its pram, the news spread throughout the

27

parish and those who had never had a salute felt such a pang of envy, felt left out. We ourselves had been saluted and it was certain that we would become on better terms since they were under a sort of obligation to us. My father had given them permission to walk their dogs over our fields, so that most afternoons we saw the two girls in their white mackintoshes and biscuit-coloured walking sticks drawing these fawn unwieldy beasts on leashes. Once they had passed our house they used to let their dogs go, whereupon our own sheepdogs barked fiercely but kept inside our own paling, being, as I think, terrified of the thoroughbreds, who were beagles. Though they had been passing by for almost a year, they never stopped to talk to my mother if they met her returning from the hen house with an empty pail, or going there with the foodstuff. They merely saluted and passed on. They talked to my father, of course, and called him Mick, although his real name was Joseph, and they joked with him about his hunters, which had never won cup or medal. They ignored my mother and she resented this. She longed to bring them in so that they could admire our house with all its knick-knacks, and admire the thick wool rugs which she made in the winter nights and which she folded up when no visitors were expected.

'I'll ask them to tea this coming Friday,' she said to me. We planned to ask them impromptu, thinking that if we asked them ahead of time they were more likely to refuse. So we made cakes and sausage rolls and sandwiches of egg mayonnaise, some with onion, some without. The milk jelly we had made was whisked and seemed like a bowl of froth with a sweet confectionery smell. I was put on watch by the kitchen window, and as soon as I saw them coming in at the gate I called to Mama.

'They're coming, they're coming.'

She swept her hair back, pinned it with her brown tortoiseshell comb, and went out and leaned on the top rung of the gate as if she were posing for a photograph, or looking at a view. I heard her say, 'Excuse me, Miss Connor, or rather, Miss Connors,' in that exaggerated accent which she had picked up in America, and which she used when strangers came, or when she went to the city. It was like putting on new clothes or new shoes which did not fit her. I saw them shake their heads a couple of times, and long before she had come back into the house I knew that the Connor girls had refused our invitation and that the table which we had laid with such ceremony was a taunt and downright mockery.

Mama came back humming to herself as if to pretend that it hadn't mattered a jot. The Connor girls had walked on, and their dogs, which were off the leashes, were chasing our young turkeys into the woods.

'What will we do with this spread?' I asked Mama as she put on her overall.

'Give it to the men, I expect,' she said wearily.

You may know how downcast she was when she was prepared to give iced cake and dainty sandwiches to workmen who were ploughing and whose appetites were ferocious.

'They didn't come,' I said stupidly, being curious to know how the Connor girls had worded their refusal.

'They never eat between meals,' Mama said, quoting their exact phrase in an injured, sarcastic voice.

'Maybe they'll come later on,' I said.

'They're as odd as two left shoes,' she said, tearing a frayed tea towel in half. When in a temper, she resorted to doing something about the house. Either she took the curtains down, or got on her knees to scrub the floors and the legs and rungs of the wooden chairs.

'They see no one except that madman,' she said, mainly to herself.

The Connor girls kept very much to themselves and did most of their shopping in the city. They attended church on Sundays, four Protestant souls comprising the congregation in a stone church that was the oldest in our parish. Moss covered the stones, and various plants grew between the cracks, so that in the distance the side wall of the church was green from both verdure and centuries of rain. Their father did not attend each Sunday, but once a month the girls wheeled him down to the family vault, where his wife and son were interred. Local people who longed to be friends with them would rush out and offer their sympathy, as if the major were the only one to have suffered bereavement. Always he remained brusque and asked his daughters the name of the man or woman who happened to be talking to him. He was known to be crotchety, but this was because of his rheumatism, which he had contracted years before. He could not be persuaded to go to any of the holy wells where other people went, to pray and seek a cure for their ailments. He was a large man with a very red face and he always wore grey mittens. The rector visited him twice a month and in the dapping season sent up two fresh trout on the mail car. Soon after, the Connor girls invited the rector for dinner and some of the toffs who had come for the dapping.

Otherwise they entertained rarely, except for the madman, who visited them every Sunday. He was a retired captain from the next town and he had a brown moustache with a red tint in it and very large bloodshot eyes. People said that he slept with the Connor girls and hence he had been given the nickname of Stallion. It was him my mother referred to as the madman. On Sundays he drove over in his sports car, in time for afternoon tea, which in summertime they had outdoors on an iron table. We children used to go over there to look at them through the trees, and though we could not clearly see them, we could hear their voices, hear the girls' laughter and then the tap of a croquet mallet when they played a game. Their house was approached from the road by a winding avenue that was dense with evergreen trees. Those trees were hundreds of years old, but also there were younger trees that the major had planted for the important occasions in his life – the Coronation, the birth of his children, England's victory in the last war. For his daughters he had planted quinces. What were quinces, we wondered, and never found out. Nailed to the blue cedar, near the gate, was a sign which said BEWARE OF DOGS, and the white pebble-dashed walls that surrounded their acres of garden were topped with broken glass so that children could not climb over and steal from the orchard.

Everyone vetted them when they came out of their stronghold on Sunday evening. Their escort, the Stallion, walked the girls to the Greyhound Hotel. Miss Amy, who was younger, wore brighter clothes, but they both wore tweed costumes and flat shoes with ornamental tongues that came over the insteps and hid the laces. Miss Amy favoured red or maroon, while Miss Lucy wore dark brown with a matching dark-brown beret. In the hotel they had the exclusive use of the sitting-room, and sometimes when they were a little intoxicated Miss Lucy played the piano while her sister and the Stallion sang. It was a saucy song, a duet in which the man asked

30

the pretty maid where she was going to, and eventually asked for her hand in marriage. Refusing him, she said, 'I will not marry, marry, marry you,' and then stamped her feet to emphasize it, whereupon the men in the bar would start laughing and saying Miss Amy was 'bucking'. There was much speculation about their lives, because the Stallion always spent Sunday night in their house. Hickey, our hired help, said they were all so drunk that they probably tumbled into bed together. Walking home on the frosty nights, Hickey said it was a question of the blind leading the blind, as they slithered all over the road and, according to Hickey, used language that was not ladylike. He would report these things in the morning to my mother, and since they had rebuffed her, she was pleased, and emphasized the fact that they had no breeding. Naturally she thought the very worst of the Stallion and could never bring herself to pronounce his Christian name. To her he was 'that madman'.

The Stallion was their sole escort until fate sent another man in the form of a temporary bank clerk. We reckoned that he was a Protestant because he didn't go to Mass on the first Sunday. He was most dashing. He had brown hair, he too had a moustache, but it was fuller than the Stallion's and was a soft dark brown. Mostly he wore a tweed jacket and matching plus-fours. Also he had a motorcycle, and when he rode it, he wore goggles. Within two weeks he was walking Miss Amy out and escorting her to the Greyhound Hotel. She began to pay more attention to her clothes, she got two new accordion-pleated skirts and some tight-fitting jumpers that made her bust more pronounced. They were called Sloppy Joes, but although they were long and sloppy, they were also sleek, and they flattered the figure. Formerly her hair was wound in a staid plait around her head, but now it was allowed to tumble down in thick coils over her shoulders, and she toned down the colour in her cheeks with pale powder. No one ever said she was pretty, but certainly she looked handsome when she cycled to the village to collect the morning paper, and hummed to herself as she went freewheel down the hill that led to the town.

The bank clerk and she were in love. Hickey saw them embrace in the porch of the Greyhound Hotel when Miss Lucy had gone back in to get a pack of cigarettes. Later they kissed shamelessly when walking along the towpath, and people said that Miss Amy used to nibble the hairs of his luxurious moustache. One night she took off her sandal in the Greyhound Hotel and put her bare foot into the pocket of his sports jacket, and the two of them giggled at her proceedings. Her sister and the Stallion often tagged along, but Miss Amy and the bank clerk would set off on his motorcycle, down the Shannon Road, for fun. It was said that they swam naked, but no one could verify that, and it was possible that they just paddled their feet.

As it happened, someone brought mischievous news about the bank clerk. A commercial traveller who was familiar with other parts told it on good authority that the bank clerk was a lapsed Catholic and had previously disgraced himself in a seaside town. People were left to guess the nature of the mistake, and most concluded that it concerned a girl or a woman. Instantly the parish turned against him. The next evening when he came out from the bank he found that both wheels of his bicycle had been ripped and punctured, and on the saddle there was an anonymous letter which read 'Go to Mass or we'll kill you.' His persecutors won. He attended the last Mass the following Sunday, and knelt in the back pew with no beads and no prayer book, with only his fingers to pray on.

However, it did not blight the romance. Those who had predicted that Miss Amy would ditch him because he was a Catholic were proven wrong. Most evenings they went down the Shannon Road, a couple full of glee, her hair and her headscarf flying, and chuckles of laughter from both of them as they frightened a dog or hens that strayed onto the roadside. Much later he saw her home, and the lights were on in their front parlour until all hours. A local person (the undertaker actually) thought of fitting up a telescope to try to see into the parlour, but as soon as he went inside their front gate to reconnoitre, the dogs came rearing down the avenue and he ran for his life.

'Can it be serious, I wonder.' So at last my mother admitted to knowing about the romance. She could not abide it, she said that Catholics and Protestants just could not mix. She recalled a grievance held for many years from a time in her girlhood when she and all the others from the national school were invited to the big house to a garden party, and were made to make fools of themselves by doing running jumps and sack races and were then given watery lemonade in which wasps floated. Her mind was firmly made up about the incompatibility of Catholics and Protestants. That very night Miss Amy sported an engagement ring in the Greyhound Hotel and the following morning the engagement was announced in the paper. The ring was star-shaped and comprised of tiny blue stones that sparkled and trembled under the beam of the hanging lamp. People gasped when told that it was insured for a hundred pounds.

'Do we have to give Miss Amy some sort of present?' my mother said grudgingly that evening. She had not forgotten how they snubbed her and how they barely thanked her for the fillets of pork that she gave them every time we killed a pig.

'Indeed we do, and a good present,' my father said, so they went to Limerick some time after and got a carving knife and fork that were packed in a velvet-lined box. We presented it to Miss Amy the next time she was walking her dogs past our house.

'It *is* kind of you, thanks awfully,' she said, as she smiled at each one of us, and told my father coyly that as she was soon to be hitched up, they ought to have that night out. She was not serious, of course, yet we all laughed and my mother did a *tch tch* in mock disapproval. Miss Amy looked ravishing that day. Her skin was soft and her brown eyes had caught the reflection of her orange neck scarf and gave her a warm theatrical glow. Also she was amiable. It was a damp day, with shreds of mist on the mountains, and the trees dripped quietly as we spoke. Miss Amy held out the palms of her hands to take the drips from the walnut tree and announced to the heavens what a 'lucky gal' she was. My mother enquired about her trousseau and was told that she had four pairs of court shoes, two camel-hair coats, a saxe-blue going-away suit, and a bridal dress in voile that was a cross between peach and champagne colour. I loved her then, and wanted to know her and wished with all my heart that I could have gone across the fields with her and become her confidante, but I was ten and she was thirty or thirty-five.

There was much speculation about the wedding. No one from the village had been invited, but then that was to be expected. Some said that it was to be in a registry office in Dublin, but others said that the bank clerk had assured the parish priest that he would be married in a Catholic church, and had guaranteed a huge sum of money in order to get his letter of freedom. It was even said that Miss Amy was going to take instruction so as to be converted, but that was only wishful thinking. People were stunned the day the bank clerk suddenly left. He left the bank at lunchtime, after a private talk with the manager. Miss Amy drove him to the little railway station ten miles away, and they kissed several times before he jumped on to the moving train. The story was that he had gone ahead to make the plans and that the Connor girls and their father would travel shortly after. But the postman, who was a Protestant, said that the major would not travel one inch to see his daughter marry a Papist.

We watched the house and gate carefully but we did not see Miss Amy emerge throughout the week. No one knows when she left, or what she wore, or in what frame of mind. All we knew was that suddenly Miss Lucy was out walking with the Stallion and Miss Amy was not to be seen.

'And where's the bride-to-be tonight?' enquired Mrs O'Shea, the hotel proprietor. Miss Lucy's reply was clipped and haughty.

'My sister's gone away, for a change,' she said.

The frozen voice made everyone pause, and Mrs O'Shea gave some sort of untoward gasp that seemed to detect catastrophe.

'Is there anything else you would care to know, Mrs O'Shea?' Miss Lucy asked, and then turned on her heel and left with the Stallion. Never again did they drink in the Greyhound Hotel but moved to a public house up the street, where several of the locals soon followed them.

The mystery of Miss Amy was sending people into frenzies of conjecture and curiosity. Everyone thought that everyone else knew something. The postman was asked but he would just nod his head and say, 'Time will tell', although it was plain to see that he was pleased with the outcome. The priest, when asked in confidence by my mother, said that the most Christian thing to do would be to go down on one's knees and say a prayer for Miss Amy. The phrase 'star-crossed lovers' was used by many of the women, and for a while it even was suggested that Miss Amy had gone berserk and was shut up in an asylum. At last the suspense was ended, as each wedding present was returned, with an obscure but polite note from Miss Lucy. My mother took ours back to the shop and got some dinner plates in exchange. The reason given was that there had been a clash of family interests. Miss Lucy came to the village scarcely at all. The major had got more ill and she was busy nursing him. A night nurse cycled up their avenue every evening at five to nine, and the house itself, without so much coming and going, began to look forlorn. In the summer evenings I used to walk up the road and gaze in at it, admiring the green jalousies, the bird table nailed to the tree, the tall, important flowers and shrubs, which for want of tending had grown rampant. I used to wish that I could unlock the gate and go up and be admitted there and find the clue to Miss Amy's whereabouts and her secret.

We did in fact visit the house the following winter, when the major died. It was much more simply furnished than I had imagined, and the loose linen covers on the armchairs were a bit frayed. I was studying the portraits of glum, puffy, grave ancestors when suddenly there was a hush and into the parlour came Miss Amy, wearing a fur coat, looking quite different. She looked older and her face was coarse.

'Miss Amy, Miss Amy,' several people said aloud, and flinching she turned to tell the driver to please leave her trunk on the landing upstairs. She had got much fatter and was wearing no engagement ring. When the people sympathized with her, her eyes became cloudy with tears, and then she ran out of the room and up the stairs to sit with the remains.

It did not take long for everyone to realize that Miss Amy had become a drinker. As the coffin was laid in the vault she tried to talk to her father, which everyone knew was irrational. She did not just drink at night in the bar, but drank in the daytime, and would take a miniature bottle out of her bag when she queued in the butcher's shop to get chops and a sheep's head for the dogs. She drank with my father when he was on a drinking bout. In fact, she drank with anyone that would sit with her, and had lost all her snootiness. She sometimes referred to her engagement as 'my flutter'. Soon after, she was arrested in Limerick for drunken driving, but was not charged, because the superintendent had been a close friend of her father's. Her driving became calamitous. People were afraid to let their children play in the street in case Miss Amy might run them over in her Peugeot car. No one had forgotten that her brother had killed himself driving, and even her sister began to confide to my mother, telling her worries in tense whispers, spelling the words that were the most incriminating.

'It must be a broken heart,' my mother said.

'Of course, with Dad gone, there is no one to raise any objections now to the wedding.'

'So why don't they marry?' my mother asked, and in one fell swoop surrendered all her prejudices.

'Too late, too late,' Miss Lucy said, and then added that Miss Amy could not get the bank clerk out of her system, that she sat in the breakfast room staring at photographs they had taken the day of her engagement and was always looking for an excuse to use his name.

One night the new curate found Miss Amy drunk in a hedge under her bicycle. By then her driving licence had been taken away for a year. He picked her up, brought her home in his car, and the next day called on her because he had found a brooch stuck to the fuchsia hedge where she came a cropper. Furthermore, he had put her bicycle in to be repaired. This gesture worked wonders. He was asked to stay to tea, and invited again the following Sunday. Due to his influence, or perhaps secretly due to his prayers, Miss Amy began to drink less. To everyone's amazement the curate went there most Sunday nights and played bridge with the two girls and the Stallion. In no time Miss Amy was overcome with resolve and industry. The garden, which had been neglected, began to look bright and trim again, and she bought bulbs in the hardware shop, whereas formerly she used to send away to a nursery for them. Everyone remarked on how civil she had become. She and my mother exchanged recipes for apple jelly and lemon curd, and just before I went away to boarding school she gave me a present of a bound volume of *Aesop's Fables*. The print was so small that I could not read it, but it was the present that mattered. She handed it to me in the field and then asked if I would like to accompany her to gather some flowers. We went to the swamp to get the yellow irises. It was a close day, the air was thick with midges, and they lay in hosts over the murky water. Holding a small bunch to her chest, she said that she was going to post them to somebody, somebody special.

'Won't they wither?' I said, though what I really wanted to know was who they were meant for.

'Not if I pack them in damp moss,' she said, and it seemed that the thought of dispatching this little gift was bringing joy to her, though there was no telling who the recipient would be. She asked me if I'd fallen in love yet or had a 'beau'. I said that I had liked an actor who had come with the travelling players and had in fact got his autograph.

'Dreams,' she said, 'dreams', and then, using the flowers as a bat, swatted some midges away. In September I went to boarding school and got involved with nuns and various girlfriends, and in time the people in our parish, even the Connor girls, almost disappeared from my memory. I never dreamed of them anymore, and I had no ambitions to go cycling with them or to visit their house. Later when I went to university in Dublin I learned quite by chance that Miss Amy had worked in a beauty parlour in Stephens Green, had drunk heavily, and had joined a golf club. By then the stories of how she teetered on high heels, or wore unmatching stockings or smiled idiotically and took ages to say what she intended to say, had no interest for me.

Somewhat precipitately and unknown to my parents I had become engaged to a man who was not of our religion. Defying threats of severing bonds, I married him and incurred the wrath of family and relatives, just as Miss Amy had done, except that I was not there to bear the brunt of it. Horrible letters, some signed and some anonymous, used to reach me, and my mother had penned an oath that we would never meet again this side of the grave. I did not see my family for a few years, until long after my son was born, and having some change of heart they proposed by letter that my husband, my son, and I pay them a visit. We drove down one blowy autumn afternoon and I read stories aloud as much to distract myself as to pacify my son. I was quaking. The sky was watery and there were pale-green patches like holes or voids in it. I shall never forget the sense of awkwardness, sadness, and dismay when I stepped out of my husband's car and saw the large gaunt cut-stone house with thistles in the front garden. The thistle seed was blowing wildly, as were the leaves, and even those that had already fallen were rising and scattering about. I introduced my husband to my parents and very proudly I asked my little son to shake hands with his grandfather and his grandmother. They admired his gold hair, but he ignored them and ran to cuddle the two sheepdogs. He was going to be the one that would make our visit bearable.

In the best room my mother had laid the table for tea, and we sat and spoke to one another in thin, strained, unforgiving voices. The tea was too strong for my husband, who usually drank China tea anyhow, and instantly my mother jumped to get some hot water. I followed her out to apologize for the inconvenience.

'The house looks lovely and clean,' I said.

She had polished everywhere and she had even dusted the artificial flowers, which I remembered as being clogged with dust.

'You'll stay a month,' she said in a warm commandeering voice, and she put her arms around me in an embrace.

'We'll see,' I said prudently, knowing my husband's restlessness.

'You have a lot of friends to see,' she said.

'Not really,' I said, with a coldness that I could not conceal.

'Do you know who is going to ask you to tea – the Connor girls.' Her voice was urgent and grateful. It meant a victory for her, for me, and an acknowledgement of my husband's non-religion. In her eyes Protestants and atheists were one and the same thing.

'How are they?' I asked.

'They've got very sensible, and aren't half as stuck up,' she said, and then ran, as my father was calling for her to cut the iced cake. Next afternoon there was a gymkhana over in the village and my parents insisted that we go.

'I don't want to go to this thing,' my husband said to me. He had intended to do some trout fishing in one of the many mountain rivers, and to pass his few days, as he said, without being assailed by barbarians.

'Just for this once,' I begged, and I knew that he had consented because he put on his tie, but there was no affability in him. After lunch my father, my husband, my little son, and I set out. My mother did not come, as she had to guard her small chickens. She had told us in the most graphic detail of her immense sorrow one morning upon finding sixty week-old chicks laid out on the flagstone dead, with their necks wrung by weasels.

In the field where the gymkhana was held there were a few caravans, strains of accordion music, a gaudy sign announcing a Welsh clairvoyant, wild restless horses, and groups of self-conscious people in drab clothes, shivering as they waited for the events to begin. It was still windy and the horses looked unmanageable. They were being held in some sort of order by youngsters who had little power over them. I saw people stare in my direction and a few of them gave reluctant half smiles. I felt uneasy and awkward and superior all at once.

38

'There's the Connor girls,' my father said. They were perched on their walking sticks, which opened up to serve as little seats.

'Come on, come on,' he said excitedly, and as we approached them, they hailed me and said my name. They were older but still healthy and handsome, and Miss Amy showed no signs of her past despair. They shook my hand, shook my husband's hand, and were quick to flirt with him, to show him what spirited girls they were.

'And what do you think of this young man?' my father said proudly as he presented his grandson.

'What a sweet little chap,' they said together, and I saw my husband wince. Then from the pocket of her fawn coat Miss Amy took two unwrapped jelly sweets and handed them to the little boy. He was on the point of eating them when my husband bent down until their faces were level and said very calmly, 'But you don't eat sweets, now give them back.' The little boy pouted, then blushed, and held out the palm of his hand, on which rested these absurd two jellies that were dusted over with granular sugar. My father protested, the Connor girls let out exclamations of horror, and I said to my husband, 'Let him have them, it's a day out.' He gave me a menacing look, and very firmly he repeated to the little boy what he had already said. The sweets were handed back, and with scorn in her eyes Miss Amy looked at my husband and said, 'Hasn't the mummy got any say over her own child?'

There was a moment's strain, a moment's silence, and then my father produced a pack of cigarettes and gave them one each. Since we didn't smoke we were totally out of things.

'No vices,' Miss Lucy said, and my husband ignored her.

He suggested to me that we take the child across to where a man had a performing monkey clinging to a stick. He raised his cap slightly to say his farewell and I smiled as best I could. My father stayed behind with the Connor girls.

'They were going to ask us to tea,' I said to my husband as we walked downhill. I could hear the suction of his galoshes in the soggy ground.

'Don't think we missed much,' he said, and at that moment I realized that by choosing his world I had said goodbye to my own and to those in it. By such choices we gradually become exiles, until at last we are quite alone.

Mary Flanagan

White Places

C eleste was first cousin to Cissy and Killer. Peachey was Celeste's Best, meaning her best friend. They always said 'Bests' to keep their true relationship a secret, and to be able to talk about the secret without hurting anyone else's feelings. That was the important thing, Celeste said, that no one know and that no one get their feelings hurt. Of course Cissy and Killer knew, but that was all right because they were first cousins to Celeste and so practically first cousins to Peachey.

The four of them had a club. The name and nature of this club was changed every three or four weeks, depending on what Celeste was reading. Celeste talked like a book and was fond of titles. She liked being President, Secretary, Madam Chairman and Grand Duchess Genevra Samantha Roberta della Rocca of Upper Vernocopium, a place even more important than Oz. The others let her be. But everyone knew it was Cissy who ruled.

Killer was the youngest and the fattest. Her shoes were always wet and untied with her socks sliding down into the heels. She had cold sores and was only in fourth grade. Her name was not really Killer. It was Charlotte Mundy Fletcher Doyle (mixed marriage: Roman Catholic and Presbyterian). Like just about every awful thing, the nickname was an invention of Cissy's. It came from one of their earliest games in which she and Celeste, starlets sharing an apartment in Beverly Hills, were stalked by a dangerous maniac known simply as The Killer. Their pretend boyfriends, a producer and his brother, the world's most daring stunt man, came over and over again to their rescue. Over and over they carried off Killer, bound and gagged, to a lunatic asylum. That was how it began – a crude game by later standards, but the name stuck. Cissy's and Celeste's parents tried, without success, to stop the children calling her by it.

'Chaaaaarrrrrrrrlotte,' Cissy would sneer across the dinner table, 'pass the potatoes, Chaaaarrrrrrrlotte.' Cissy wasn't afraid of anything. Eventually though, when she behaved like this, she would be sent off to bed where she would lie awake, waiting to pinch her sister's fingers with the nutcracker as soon as she fell asleep, which was usually within three minutes.

Mrs Doyle insisted the others be nice to Killer, share with her. Once she even had cried when her youngest daughter came home wet, though uncomplaining, from the swamp. They had been on a Royal Expedition up the Nile, led by Robert Redford and Cissy in a sedan chair. Killer had been thrown to the crocodiles after attempting to kidnap the baby Moses. Later, Killer had listened with her ear to the door as her mother reprimanded Cissy.

'Cissy, why are you so mean to Killer –' She stopped impatiently. 'Oh for heaven's sake, you know I mean *Charlotte*.' It was too late. Mummy had said it and that made it true for ever.

Killer was six then, and Cissy was eight. By now the Pretends were much more complicated, and included a wide range of malice and glamour. (Cissy was maddeningly inventive.) But they were still variants on a single theme, and always ended with the Finding Out, the unmasking, at which everyone ran shrieking from Killer. Why the others liked pretending to be weak and frightened and in danger when really they were so strong, stronger than she would ever be, Killer could not understand.

A tried and true Pretend, used when all else had ended in boredom or hair-pulling, was The Crazy Doctor. Killer, in disguise, would come to the grown-ups' bedroom – it had to begin in there – to prescribe for one of the three, who were always orphaned sisters. Eventually, they would guess her wicked intentions and race, screaming and laughing, to the attic, down again, through the upstairs rooms and out on to the lawn, pursued by Killer who was well-versed in the terrifying snorts and snarls she was required to make. Once outside, she would be caught, rolled up in a blanket, tied and taken off to be burnt at the stake, then released and made to play her part all over again until parents put a stop to the game.

They spent school vacations at each other's houses. Easter at the Doyles' and Christmas at Celeste's. This time, Peachey would be with them. Peachey was too small for her age, but very energetic. She was called Peachey because she once had been taught by her father to respond, at the top of her chipmunk voice to all enquiries after her condition with the answer 'Peachey Keeno!'

Celeste's father and mother were very indulgent. Even when the girls kept them awake until four in the morning, they did not complain very much. Killer always fell asleep first. The others ate crackers in bed and pushed the crumbs on to her side. They made raids to the kitchen for peanut butter sandwiches at 2.00 a.m. They came back and covered Killer's face with toothpaste. By the beam of a flashlight, they held a club meeting and read comic books under the covers. Peachey wrapped all their apple cores in paper and put the bundle down the toilet. The next morning the plumbing was blocked, and Killer stood, serious-eyed (she had been banished by the girls until three), watching Aunty Lillian mop up the bathroom on her hands and knees. She was given a jelly doughnut and allowed to watch *Tom and Jerry* until called to come and be a werewolf.

There was a blizzard. Killer was frightened by the silence and by the way the snow climbed the window panes. When she pressed her face against them, she imagined that she had gone blind, but that her blindness was white instead of black. It seemed hard to breathe, and she wondered if everyone were going to be buried alive. She thought she might like to go home. It would be nice to be tucked in by her mother and to watch her baby brother kicking his feet like a small fat bug or dribbling breakfast down his pyjamas. But she was too scared to tell Aunty Lillian any of these things. Besides, she had to stay here and be a Body Snatcher.

Celeste said that they should make puppets and a theatre and put on a puppet show. They thought of nothing else for the three days the blizzard lasted. Cissy and Celeste wrote a play and made posters to advertise the event, while Peachey and Killer worked happily and messily with balloons, cardboard tubes and papier mâché. Aunt Lillian was very patient. She and Uncle Raymond, along with all of Celeste's and Peachey's dolls, were forced to attend three performances, and to applaud, exclaim and congratulate on each occasion.

They experimented with the left-over flour and water paste, and invented, by the addition of sugar, milk, vanilla, corn syrup and a dash of laundry starch, a drink which they called Plush and which they forced Killer to taste after the addition of each new ingredient. That evening Killer threw up her supper. Cissy said that she thought it was disgusting, and that Killer was not mature enough to have been allowed to come.

When the storm ended, they put up signs and tried to sell Plush from a snow fort which they built at the end of the driveway. The snow was very high there, nearly six feet, because the blizzard had been such a long one and the snow-plough had had to come around so many times. No one bought the drink but Uncle Raymond who tasted it, tried to smile, and said he would finish the rest in the house, if that was all right with 'you girls'. They lost interest in Plush. It turned sour, stank and Aunty Lillian carefully asked permission to throw it out.

They decided to enlarge the snow fort. They built half a dozen each winter and knew everything about their construction. This was to be the biggest they had ever made. To celebrate its completion, Cissy said, they must make up a brand new Pretend. Celeste agreed. Then Peachey and Killer agreed. They worked even harder on the snow fort than they had on the puppet show, talking and planning every minute for the Important Celebration Pretend. They were very excited, Killer could tell. She saw how much it thrilled them to make believe. To her, inside, it seemed almost frightening, the way they were always at it, never never getting tired of it. Why did they want to be something they weren't, to change everything into what it wasn't? Killer liked everything as it was – just plain with no Pretend, no titles, no talking like books, no ruling, no dressing up, no punishments, no Madam Chairman or Grand Duchesses or Cleopatras. But that was her secret. She knew that somehow it was wrong to like everything as it was, just plain. So she didn't dare tell them what she really liked.

What she liked was what they were doing now: sitting on top of their snow fort, watching people go by on the street – slipping and sliding, it was so funny – smelling the snow and sucking silently on the long icicles that hung from the maple trees and that tasted so sweet. Killer sat and sucked and felt happy to be with the others, happy about not having to do fractions, happy about the graham crackers and marshmallow they would be eating at four when Pretend was over.

Peachey, in a burst of Peachey energy, put snow down the back of her neck. Killer was soaked through anyway. They all were. But they hardly noticed, they were so warm with activity.

43

'Now this is the game,' Cissy announced, 'and you have to remember it. We've decided, so no changing the rules. Me and Celeste and Peachey are sisters and we're of noble birth. Our *real* mother dies and our father the Duke marries this woman Elvira, who pretends to be nice but who isn't – who's evil really. That's you Killer. You have to *seem* nice at first, remember that, otherwise you'll spoil everything. Then we find out that Elvira has killed our *real* mother and is plotting to kill our father and steal our inheritance and make us homeless orphans. Then – this is Celeste's part, she invented it, she says I have to say so – a prince saves us! He catches Elvira making a cowardly escape. Then he marries Celeste and introduces me and Peachey to his two brothers who are Paul Newman and Steve McQueen. Elvira goes to prison. Do you hear that, Killer? Are you listening? You're going to be shut up in the snow fort – don't interrupt me, you *have* to be. Do you want to spoil the game for everyone else? That *would* be something you'd do. Anyway, my word is law, so you're going to prison. We'll come back for you after we've been to the palace to recover our gold and attend the banquet.'

'But – what about my graham crackers?' Killer knew she mustn't cry.

'You can have them later – if you do everything you're supposed to.'

'OK.'

Now they were carrying out the dolls to be the Duke's courtiers. Dolls and dolls – Celeste's dolls. Peachey's dolls, vacationing at Celeste's to visit their friends and relations. Killer didn't really like dolls, not even Dorothy, the most beautiful, with her long brown hair and bridal gown. She played with them, but they were not her friends. She preferred real things like babies and kittens and beach balls and toads and desserts.

Under Cissy's direction the Pretend went off perfectly. The arrival of the prince and his brothers was very exciting. With their invisible help, Elvira was tied and gagged and dragged off to prison. To make sure she would never again be free to plot against them, the three sisters and the three brothers placed pieces of cardboard (they had not told Killer this part) over the front and back entrances of the snow fort. These they covered with packed snow over which they dribbled a little boiling water. It froze almost immediately, making a nice smooth surface. Then they went off to the palace.

Of course they were not going to the palace. They were going to eat graham crackers with marshmallow and watch cartoons. They were going to tell Aunty Lil that Killer had run off to play with some children and didn't want her snack. They would be warm and giggling and eating her graham crackers. Afterwards they might take their sleds to McLin's field and have a snowball fight with the Dewhurst boys or go with them to the housing project and tip over the garbage cans.

Killer was cold and lonely. Her wet snow suit was no longer made warm by the heat of her body. They had tied her so tightly that she could not move. She looked round at her small prison of white. She could see, feel, hear the white, the whiteness of crazy nothing that scared her so much. She longed for Celeste and Cissy and Peachey. She wanted them to come and get her. She would play any game they liked, be any terrible person, she was so lonely here in the white.

They had walled her up with her accomplices in the plot – the three least loved of Celeste's dolls. They were no help. They had bad characters and did not care what became of her. Buster was a villain like she was – always trying to wreck plans, to spoil balls and ceremonies, to kidnap Dorothy. And June. June would do anything to attract men's attention. She was spiteful with short hair and told lies. She was also stupid and got the lowest marks at school. No one would ever marry June. Jackie, the dirty yellow and white rabbit, had been good at first when he arrived four years ago as an Easter Bunny. But he had allowed himself to be corrupted by Buster. Celeste said Jackie was a failure. His many crimes had made him unhappy, but it was too late for him to change his ways. Killer knew that she and Jackie and June and Buster were what Peachey's mother called Lost Souls.

Killer rubbed her tongue over her cold sore. It tasted like metal and tomatoes. She could never let it alone. Tomatoes made her think of last summer: picnics at Lake Acushnet, then fights in the car, after which she would cringe under the glare of Cissy's green eyes; Cissy and Peachey throwing jelly doughnuts at her and her throwing them back – the only time she had ever defended herself; Celeste covering her face with Ipana toothpaste in the middle of the night; Cissy and Celeste frightening her with ghost stories and tales of torture so that she lay quaking in the dark as she was quaking now in the white; Quaker Meetings on the lawn ('Quaker Meeting has begun, no more laughing, no more fun, if you show your teeth or tongue, you will have to pay a forfeit'); the Mermaid game on the beach and Cissy whipping her with one of those long flat strips of seaweed. 'Peachey, you may take one giant step. Killer, you may take one baby step.' Oh the games, the endless games she could not resist. She must always play, never say no, never complain, please them by letting them hate her and be afraid of her. It was such a funny thing. Why was it like that? She couldn't really understand Pretend. And Pretend was so important. Pretend was everything, because without it you were only yourself.

How come Cissy and Celeste could make things up? They could think so fast. If she could think fast too, she almost realized before her thoughts slid back into simply people and things and events, she might not have to be always The Crazy Doctor. Not only could Cissy and Peachey and Celeste think faster and eat faster and run faster; they seemed to need less sleep, less food, less love than she did. They seemed, with the exception of jelly doughnuts, not even to *want* any of those things. Killer longed for them. She longed for them now. But if she tried to get out of the snow fort before supper, they'd be sure to call her a spoilsport and to torment her all night long.

Better stay here a little longer and freeze. They would have to come back for her, because sooner or later they would need her for the games. They would not be able to have any of the good ones without her. She tried to feel very certain that they would come, but her heart was tightening, tightening and sinking. Her crime had been so terrible this time. No one could forgive her. Perhaps not even God could forgive her. She had broken the third commandment. She had killed the Duchess and tried to steal the inheritance. No, there was no chance of God forgiving her. He was going to let her freeze to death with Jackie and June and Buster, the Lost Souls. He would make the others forget her. He would make Aunty Lil and Uncle Raymond forget her, even her own mother and father probably. He *could* make everyone forget her. That kind of thing was easy for him. They probably had forgotten already. Or maybe it wasn't God at all. Maybe *they* wanted her to die, to freeze to death with Buster and June and Jackie. Get rid of the trouble-makers, the wicked ones, all at once. What about Mummy? She was always so kind, but that might be a Pretend too. She might really have been plotting with Cissy and the rest of them all along to wall up her little girl in a snow fort. Killer couldn't help it, she cried.

She cried until she had no more strength to cry. She began to give up, to fall asleep, to float away to a place where there was no more cold, where nothing was white, but all nice greens and reds and blues. Something was carrying her up to the sky, like Ragged Robin in the orange tree – up and up, away from the white. It was Uncle Raymond. He was pulling her out of the snow fort, he was untying her, he was picking her up in his arms, taking her to the house, muttering over her.

'Oh my God, poor Killer.' She could not open her eyes, she was so tired. 'My God, poor little Killer.' She liked Uncle Raymond. He was a nice man.

The hospital where Killer spent the next two weeks was very white. When she first awoke, she was frightened and thought that the snow fort had grown larger and cleaner and more occupied. It was warm in the hospital (she saw quite quickly that it *was* a hospital) and there were lots of people, mainly kind, who leaned over her, gave her things, asked her questions in quiet tones, took things away, moved her about – sometimes hurting her, though not meaning to – and gazed at her for long stretches of time through her plastic tent. Their expressions were of worry, sorrow or silly cheerfulness, if grown-ups, and of questioning uncomfortableness, if children.

Killer hardly spoke. She *could* speak, she knew that, but she did not want to. She looked back through her plastic tent at all those queer expressions. Sometimes she smiled at them a little. Mostly she slept. Slept and dreamt. She dreamed they played the Mermaid game, and that she chased Cissy and Celeste and Peachey for ever along an empty beach.

When she was very much better, they took the plastic tent away and let the children come near her. Cissy's green eyes were still defiant, but she spoke nicely to her sister and called her Charlotte. Killer understood that Cissy and Celeste had had some kind of punishment, but that now everyone was pretending that nothing had ever really happened.

Peachey held her hand and leaned over her. 'Bests,' Peachey whispered. Killer blinked at her. Did she mean it, was she making believe? Killer didn't understand, but smiled to let Peachey know that she was pretending she did.

Celeste even offered her Dorothy to keep for ever and be her very own. Dorothy with her bridal gown and long brown hair.

Killer hesitated. Then she spoke for the first time since the day in the snow fort.

'Can I have June instead?' she asked.

Sylvia Townsend Warner

~~

The Quality of Mercy

On an impulse, the boy got up, and saying to his friends, 'Back presently', crossed the room and sat down at the table to which the young woman had just returned, walking unsteadily from the bar counter with her fourth whisky. He supposed the impulse to be sudden; in fact, it was the crest of a compulsion which had been gathering force in him during the last quarter of an hour. Now he curled his hand round the glass and pulled it toward him.

'Excuse me.'

She started. Seeing her glass on his side of the table, she paled with rage. But mastering herself, she replied, 'That's all right. Your necessity's greater than mine.'

Her speech was thick but she spoke in an educated voice. She was, what he hadn't expected, a lady. Further, and this too he had not expected, she was considerably older than he. Studying her from a distance, he had taken her to be no more than a kid. The untidy tendrils of soft pale hair, the air of inconsequence, poverty, and recklessness, were youthful; and to be wearing a coat so much too large for her slender frame, a coat that might have been passed on to her by a rich aunt, that was youthful, too. But actually, she was quite an age – thirty or forty, he supposed.

Having committed himself, he could only go on.

'Johnnie! A tomato juice for the lady.'

The barman brought it and pocketed the money without comment. The El Dorado was a place where any one might get off with any one. Every English provincial town has such an establishment, showy in a back street, decorated with some degree of sophistication, licensed for drinks and light refreshments, and frequented by the young because it is at once more refined and more raffish than the public

48

houses their parents go to. He knew the boy, a young tough called Danny, and the group he came with. The woman he had never seen before and wouldn't be sorry if he never saw again. She was a misfit; and the El Dorado wasn't geared for misfits.

Impaled on the same reflection, the boy said, 'Have I seen you here before?'

'No, I've been away. But this is my native town.'

'Is it really?'

She did not answer.

'Born here, and all that?'

'Born and bred in a briar patch.'

God alone knew what she meant. Her glance hovered on the whisky, and he tightened his hand round the glass.

'Why did you take away my whisky?'

'Reasons of my own.'

'Hypothetical reasons.'

Confusing hypothetical with highfalutin, he frowned. Answering the frown, she continued; 'Obviously hypothetical since it's still there. The only practical reason would be that you wanted to drink it yourself.'

And do I want to, he thought, evading its limpid hazel eye.

'So you've been going round the town celebrating your return?'

'Till you spoilt my little game.'

Her laugh bared her teeth, she looked ready to bite him. He could feel the grins at the table he had quitted burning into his back. Her hand flashed out, quick as a viper. Just in time, he withdrew the glass, and since there seemed no alternative, he drank off the whisky.

'Danny's in! Danny falls for the umpteenth time.' He heard his friends sniggering, and their grins burned deeper into his back. This was what you let yourself in for, fancying you can be a Good Samaritan. You go off the drink, for more than three weeks you keep off it – and because of a soppy impulse to salvage a poor kid who turns out to be nothing of the sort, you're landed with having to drink her whisky.

Rage made him speak insultingly. 'And where have you been hiding yourself, all this long time?'

'I had a job in London – but it came to an end.'

Easy to see why.

'A puppet theatre – I played the guitar and kept the accounts. But we couldn't keep going. And then . . .' She rambled on as though talking to the wind, how this went wrong and that became impossible. In spite of the fortuity of her narrative it was always easy to see why.

'And the doctor, such a kind man, I found out he was a Zen Buddhist, said I must have a quiet country life. So I came down on Friday – my sister's taken me in. But I mean to get back!'

The last words came out in a squawk, propelled by her tears. In desperation, she gulped some tomato juice, commenting, 'Any port in a storm.'

'That's right. Like a smoke?'

'Dying for one.'

As he leant forward to light the cigarette, he noticed how the tears on her cheeks reflected minute tinsel images of the flame.

'That's enough about me. Now tell me about yourself.'

'Soon told. I'm nineteen. I've got a good clean home, I work for a builder, and I booze. Actually, I haven't lost my job yet. But I've been up three times for being drunk and disorderly, and next time it won't be so good.'

'Oh. Was that why you came over to my table?'

'Sort of.'

'Alcoholics Anonymous.'

Now her voice was cold and her manner detached. She was retreating behind the barrier of her class, and if he had chosen, he could have got away. But he did not choose.

He said, 'Nothing to laugh at. They're good people. They've got the right idea, anyhow.'

'That we can help one another?'

'That no one else can.'

She nodded; but immediately her face took on a repelling expression, and she enquired, almost derisively and yet beguilingly, 'Were you very drunk? And *very* disorderly?'

'Blind drunk. Killing drunk.'

She flinched.

'That's how I am, when I'm drunk. That's what it will come to, one of these days.'

Like the moon coming out of a cloud, he thought, like a face on the screen fading out and another looking through it. For she had dropped all her airs and disguises, and the real woman (he had no doubt it was the real woman) had emerged and declared herself and was looking at him with the childish sternness of somebody by nature very timid.

'You oughtn't to say that, even to me. It's not true. You only say it to bolster yourself up, because you are young, and so lonely. But it's not true. Not yet.'

'Not yet.'

'Exactly. Not yet. Well, that's a foothold, isn't it? Instead of saying, "It will come to killing, one of these days," you should say to yourself, every night, "Thank God I haven't killed." It would be much more in harmony with your feelings, for you're a kind person by nature. I could see that, when you came to sit with me, and ordered the tomato juice. Not many people would have troubled to do that. What made you do it?'

'Well, I thought you'd had about enough, and that probably you weren't –'

He broke off, appalled. He had so nearly said, old enough.

'Go on.'

'. . . that you didn't –'

'Go on.'

'Well, that you hadn't – that you hadn't been at it long enough to know much about it.'

'That I was young enough to be worth helping, that I might still pull up. No. But you, you are young enough. Can't you try? You've been so kind to me, I really would like to be a warning to you. Do try!'

The barman was going to and fro, collecting glasses and emptying ash trays. Reaching their table, he picked up the emptied whisky glass, hesitated disdainfully over the half-finished tomato juice.

'Done with it?'

'I'm not preaching,' she said, disregarding the enquiry. The humility in her voice released Danny from thinking, 'Now she'll want us to try together.'

'Well, actually, I don't mind telling you I have been trying. It's three weeks and two days since I touched a drop – barring putting away your rightful . . .'

'O my God!'

The exclamation was so rapid, so furtive, that if he had not

51

seen her stricken countenance he might not have known he had heard it.

'Don't worry yourself about that. It won't make any difference.'

'No difference!'

'I swear it shan't,' he said vehemently.

It was closing time. All round them people were getting up, and shafts of cold air drove in as the door opened and shut. She made no move.

'Have you far to go?'

'Not really very far. Edgecombe Road, the farther end.'

She rose, her coat straggling from her shoulders.

'I'll help you in. You'll want it, it's a cold night.' He took hold of the coat, and at the same moment she vanished from within it, and was sitting down once more.

'I can't stand very well. Oh! There's my bag.'

He turned to the group of his friends who were watching from the doorway.

'Here, Louis! Lend me a hand. The rest of you can get out.'

Together, he and Louis shoved her into her coat and hauled her through the doorway.

'She'll be better, once she feels the air,' he said, knowing too well that this was a fallacy.

'Oh, will she? Where are we taking her to?'

'Far end of Edgecombe Road.'

'Whew! Nice sight we'll make in that respectable neighbourhood. I say, Danny! Won't do for us to meet the cops. We'll have to go roundabout.'

They went by alleys and byways, twice making a detour to avoid a policeman on his beat, often crossing the road to forestall a face-to-face meeting with other belated walkers. Whenever they stopped to debate which way to turn next, she regained a hold on her consciousness, apologized for having such silly legs, and thanked them with a rambling graciousness for being so kind to her. This made them hurry on, for when they walked she fell silent, and seemed in a stupor – so that at intervals they conversed about her as though it were a straw dummy they dragged along between them, a badly made straw dummy, bits of which were flapping and threatening to come loose.

'She must have put away a lot before ever she came to the El, that's my opinion. Look out! We don't want no dogs after us.'

'Tiger, Tiger! Come here at once!' The lady taking out her terrier saw with relief that they were disappearing down Meeting House Lane.

'You know, Danny, I'm beginning to think we'd better turn back and take her to the hospital. We can't knock at every door in Edgecombe Road and say, "Excuse me, does this lady belong here?" '

'We haven't got there yet.'

This truth was unexpectedly reinforced by a voice interpolating, 'But my sister doesn't live anywhere near the gasworks.'

'Where does she live?' enquired Louis, who was the quick-witted one.

'Edgecombe Road.'

'Any particular number?'

'A hundred and thirteen. But on the gate it's Lilliesleaf. A place we used to go to when we were children. Nowhere near the gasworks.'

'She's slipped off again,' said Louis, 'But she's coming round. She'll be more or less herself before we hit Lilyleaf. Pretty voice she's got too. You wouldn't think it, really.'

The pretty voice remarked, 'I'm going to be sick.'

When they had tidied her up and assured her that now she'd do fine, they set on once more, but had to go back to look for her bag which she dropped during her vomit, and which they had overlooked. It had been splashed, and while Danny was rubbing it on a grass verge, the town clock told midnight.

'Oh heavens! Was that twelve?'

'Don't worry. We won't turn into pumpkins. Here's your bag.'

'I know what you will turn into. You'll turn into angels.' Her spirits were rising, and she had got back some use of her legs, though she still could not walk straight. Once more they left the gasworks behind them. Ten minutes later they came to the railway bridge, where the wind whined in the cutting.

'One of our puppet turns was a porter, and the trunk was on a wire of its own, so whenever he tried to lift it – Wait a minute, I think the quickest way to Edgecombe Road is on the right.'

'Hush! So's the cop. Sorry to take you out of your way, but it won't do for our Danny to cause remark. Turning cold, isn't it?'

Presently they were in the politer part of the town, where the houses stood separately and afforded less shelter from the wind. When they rounded the corner into Edgecombe Road, they met the full force of it, and drew closer together.

'And your place is right at the top?'

'Yes. Look. I'm feeling so much better, let me go the rest of the way by myself.'

'This isn't a road where I'm what you might call on my native heath in,' said Louis. 'So I'd like to see more of it. Same for Danny, I'm sure.'

The houses at the lower end of the Edgecombe Road were Victorian, tall and massive, with spectral conservatories attached, and standing each in its large garden. It took a long time to go from one to the next. Some were for sale, with house-agents' boards rearing out of unpruned laurels; all were lightless, morose, implacably respectable. Ahead was a church with an ornamental spire and a plain-faced clock in it. By the time they drew level the hands stood at 12:28. Soon after the church, the Victorian houses were succeeded by a variety of Edwardian villas. These were smaller, and gave an illusion of ground gained; but the gardens were almost equally large so the illusion soon faded. Then came an open space, laid out in tennis courts and lawns. Then, after a dozen more villas, and a petrol station fronting a cemetery, the houses became contemporary, of meaner proportions and placed near to the road. All were lightless, spruce, and implacably respectable; but their respectability was alerter and more tight-lipped.

'Not far now,' said Louis consolingly. He sensed that consolation was needed. There was no answer. Danny was thinking how much better it would have been to have fallen in with the suggestion of the hospital. The woman's faculties were concentrated in her gaze, that searched ahead to where a chink of light had momentarily appeared in a ground-floor window. Where the chink had been there presently loomed a faint curtained glow. Margaret was sitting up.

'This is it.'

Danny unlatched the gate.

'I shall never be able to tell you how grateful –'

A bright light was switched on in the hall, the door was flung open.

'Fanny! Where on earth have you been? Do you know what time it is?'

'O Margaret, I'm so sorry. We came as fast –'

'We?'

Margaret stood on the top step, blinking angrily into the darkness. The light delineated her small trim figure and shone down on her rigidly waved yellow hair.

'We?'

Danny came forward.

'We brought the lady back. She wasn't feeling too good.'

'O Margaret, they've been so kind to me, especially this one. He's Danny, the other's Louis. They've come all this way, and it's so horribly cold, and I'm sure you've got a kettle on, you'd never be without a kettle –'

'What's that on your skirt?'

'– so can my guardian angels have some tea?'

'You're drunk. You filthy, stinking, drunken beast, you stand there gabbling about guardian angels, when you ought to be ashamed to show your face. All these hours I've been waiting for you! Little you care! I took you in when nobody else would; I washed your filthy clothes; I listened to your excuses and your repentances. And the first moment I take my eye off you, you rush out for another wallow, and disgrace yourself in front of half the town. Oh, you're worthless, worthless, worthless! The gutter's too good for you.'

She raged, and her hair remained in its rigid undulations, placid as a wig. 'And then, as if that wasn't enough, you trail home with these two sots, and have the effrontery –'

'No! How dare you speak like that? It's not right, it's not just. They're good, they're kind, they've done everything they can to help me. Danny even drank my whisky.'

'That I can well believe.'

'But Margaret – Oh, it's hopeless, you'll never understand. Oh, I wish I were dead!'

'I wish I had a pair of tongs.'

She was dragged up the steps. On the top step she tripped and fell on her knees. Still on her knees, she shuffled round and said into the darkness, 'I'm sorry my sister doesn't know how to behave.'

'In with you! And as for you two, I'm going to report you to the police.'

The door was slammed. They heard the noise of furious altercation behind it, and then, from the curtained room, the clicking of a telephone dial.

Marilyn Duckworth

~~~

A Game of Pretend

I can't name the exact year when my sister and I learned that babies 'came out of Mummy's tummy'. At an early age we seemed to know that giving birth took place in a bed. The knowledge provided us with a simple game of pretend played usually on a Sunday morning when no one was hurrying us out of the bed we shared – no doubt our parents had games of their own to play. One of us would burrow down under the blankets and make herself small while the other spouted a self-conscious monologue.

'Look at the time. I should be getting up and going to clean my kitchen.' This was the signal for the burrowed one to wriggle and emerge, quite slowly and dramatically, mewing like a kitten. 'Why whatever's this? My goodness me – it's a *baby*!'

We reversed the roles from time to time but usually I was the mewing baby and I would be clasped against Hester's small bony chest while she cooed and comforted me and I sucked my thumb.

Our knowledge of childbirth had extended considerably by the time we were sent to stay with relations in Leicestershire to avoid wartime bombing. We made a 'house' at the top of a haystack behind a tall hedge. Hester relayed the latest information she had gleaned on the subject. We remembered our game and laughed at our younger selves. Then she told me a story about a girl who was still at school but who secretly gave birth to her soldier boyfriend's baby and as secretly raised it. She kept the baby in a summerhouse at the bottom of the garden where presumably it never cried.

'But what about milk?' Because of wartime rationing I could never get enough milk – we had to mix it with water to put on our Weetabix. I was aware that babies had to be registered at the Food Office to have their special needs filled.

'She fed it herself. From her bosoms. You know – like the sow we saw in the pig-sty.'

'Oh yes.' But I was still sceptical. 'Anyway in school holidays she could go to the school and borrow what was left over in the crate.'

'If you like.'

We were entranced with this story. There were pauses in the narrative while Hester was solving some practical problem for the young mother and during these gaps I submerged myself gleefully into the fantasy. I was the young mother, and so was Hester. Our eyes glazed with maternal fervour.

That night I woke in our double bed racked with frustrated maternal instinct. I woke up Hester.

'Why can't little girls have babies? I want one now. I hope Rosie's all right.' Rosie was the only one of my motley doll collection who could be called a 'baby doll'. Her plaster limbs were dimpled and fixed in a cradled position.

'Of course she's all right. Mummy put her in the cabin trunk under the stairs.'

'But the doodlebugs!'

'Under the stairs,' Hester reminded me. The safest place in an air raid, we'd been told.

'I need her to cuddle,' I said, feeling desperate.

Hester was unsympathetic. 'Look,' she said. 'I can bite my toenails.' Cranking her knee up sideways and reaching down with her teeth. It was a distraction.

At my new school I felt small and out of place. I had no real friends. I tried but it was too late in the year; the friendships were all fixed and I was unnecessary. There was a girl called Alison whose popularity I envied. One Monday when she had been absent for a whole week I dared to ask her – 'Why were you away?'

She rolled her eyes at me, then snapped – 'I was having kittens.'

My own eyes rolled. I believed her. We had heard rumours about a woman who had taken her dog into bed while her husband was away at the war and had given birth to alsatian puppies. Still, I didn't think Alison needed to be so grumpy about my question. I wondered if the kittens' claws had scratched in her tummy. It was such a horridly interesting story I didn't repeat it even to Hester until years later.

At sixteen I had given up longing for babies. I did have a kitten. But not for long. Soon after we brought Fluppence home he developed neat round bald patches. Ringworm. It was in the days before there was any easy cure for the disease. Mother painted him a dotty orange with iodine, but the ringworm progressed. He was not to be stroked or petted. His arm's-length mewing was puzzled and pitiful. The sound tugged at me.

I went to a friend's house for the weekend and when I returned two things had happened. I learned about one of them travelling back home in my father's car.

'We had to have Fluppence put to sleep. I'm sorry, dear.'

'They stuff them in a black bag then stick a big needle right through so the cat doesn't see it coming,' my friend offered.

'They don't – do they?'

'What?' My father wasn't listening. 'We're going to lose your sister,' he confided, leaning sideways from the steering wheel.

I saw Hester in a black bag with a big needle sticking right through her. 'What do you *mean?*'

'She'll tell you about it. It's all right – it's something good.'

We were going to lose Hester and it was *good*? I couldn't begin to imagine what he was talking about.

In the living-room the chairs had been arranged in a new close huddle which I didn't recognize. It reminded me of a stage set. When we came into the room three serious faces turned half-heartedly. There was a sort of hush. The radio had been turned off and Hester and her university friend held tiny glasses in their hands, glinting with something I guessed was alcohol. We were a non-drinking family in those days. I was bemused. It looked to me like some sort of ritual ceremony and I was still in the black bag with my dead kitten. But it was all right. Hester was only engaged, not dying.

By the time the wedding happened there had been months – plenty of time for me to understand. But I didn't. I studied the surprising boxes of sherry and spirits as they were delivered to the house. I read the wedding invitations, and the lists of what Hester and her husband would need in their new home. But the future was well buried under all this paraphernalia and excitement. For the time being I was shut out of Hester's bedroom while she and her fiancé filled the room with smoke and other fuggy smells. I was shy about making noises in the next-door bathroom and learned how to spit toothpaste foam soundlessly.

On the day of the wedding the house was cluttered with visiting relations and I was transferred to a camp bed in a small space. I didn't mind. It wasn't until all the relations were departed and the camp bed folded up in the cupboard that I noticed what had happened. Hester had gone. Not just for a holiday. Gone. And I had forgotten to prepare myself for it. Her clothes had gone from her wardrobe. I could spit as noisily as I liked. I don't remember crying. It was worse than that. There is a phrase – 'My belly thinks my throat's been cut.' Yes – that describes the feeling well enough I think. Emptied out. Closed off.

Two years later I was at university myself. Time had taken care of my empty belly. I had new friends, new obsessions. I quarrelled with my boyfriend and suggested we see nothing of each other for a whole week. We had been devouring each other's time and apart from anything else could do with a few night's sleep. We were also struggling not to risk pregnancy.

I was sleeping soundly, catching up on dreams, when I heard someone moving about my bedroom. It was my father.

'Go back to sleep. Ssh. I'm getting some blankets to make up a bed for Brian. He just took Hester in to have the baby.'

I woke up with a jerk. 'Is she all right?'

'She's fine.'

'Oh poor Hes!' It was astonishing and awful. She had to go through all that stuff we'd read about in novels. Supposing she changed her mind and didn't want to go through with it? But she had to – even Hester, who could bite her own toenails, couldn't choose now. Didn't the doctors and nurses know she was just little Hester, my sister, not a real grown-up at all? Or perhaps she was? I couldn't go back to sleep.

In the morning I rang my boyfriend. I had to share this with him. A truce was called in our quarrel and we travelled together to visit the maternity ward.

Hester had another more talkative visitor but we pulled up chairs alongside and I stared at her. My boyfriend took my hand and held on to it. Earlier we had been to the nursery and stared at the baby. Hester's baby. It was more real, more incredible than kittens. I remembered our game as children, giving birth to each other. 'Whatever can it be? Goodness, it's a baby!' And this time it really was. She'd done it. I was filled with envy, and with a kind of outrage.

Later I sat with my boyfriend and said – 'I wish I had a baby now. I need a baby *now*. But I'm too scared. It's not sex – it's the whole thing. The hospital, and what people expect of you. I think I'll always be too scared.'

And he said – 'I'll hold your hand the whole time it's happening and I won't let go. All right?' He was a romantic. He was nearly crying. I could see he was visualizing a domestic idyll, a white-draped bassinet, me in a frilly housecoat, flowing with milk. His eyes were brim full of it.

I was moved. I would have been more moved if I'd known he would in fact die young, like my kitten, and never father anyone's child, let alone mine. But my own eyes were filled up at the time with another picture – Hester, her arms laden with a new life I was no part of, walking away from me. Smiling above her grown-up breasts and walking away.

Bani Basu

Aunty

The feast for the Brahmins was over yesterday. The arrangements were sumptuous. Today was the last day of mourning. No one knew how, but there were around two hundred and fifty guests. Over fifty of them just belonged to the clan. In addition there were the families related by marriage. And then the neighbours.

'Where would our father's prestige be, leave alone our own, if we hadn't fed them fish and rice?' said Anish.

Deepika or Dipu said, 'Absolutely. Father was totally helpless. You men had escaped long ago. These boys of the neighbourhood – Keshta, Bishtu, Gonu, Bhodor – if they hadn't been there, there probably would have been no doctor when he needed one. After all, Aunty is only a woman.'

Midstream, her words hit a raw spot in Anish. Dipu was always good at being unpleasant. Hadn't he admitted already that he had done nothing? He couldn't afford to. If a man works in Hoshiarpur in Punjab, he certainly can't keep running across to Rishi Bankim Sarani in Srirampore every once in a while to look after his father. Those staying closer home should have been the ones to come to some arrangement among themselves on this matter. The reply to Deepika's snide comment, however, came from Anish's wife, Deepika's sister-in-law. Coming from Comilla, she had a way with words. 'Well, Didi,' she said, 'your elder brother fled a long time ago, thinking of what would be best for the family. But these days even daughters get a share of the property. Should only the sons do the looking after?'

Abashed, Deepika replied, 'If only you had a charming son like mine! You would have understood then, Boudi, whatever few hours ride it is between Asansol and Srirampore, why I didn't have the opportunity to visit my father's home more often.'

Atish's wife, Shukla, was the cheerful sort who didn't like quarrels and conflicts. She laughed and said, 'Ever since you came, Didi, you've been concentrating your attack on Bubulram. Why? What has he done?'

'What can he possibly do? Nothing at all. Only his daily routine is written in letters of gore. Today a fishbone plants itself on his brow. Tomorrow a deuce ball hits his groin. The day after his hand falls on the kitchen knife and out flows a river of blood. And then there is a stream of complaints – from the neighbourhood, from the school. It's just that he comes first in class every year, so they don't throw him out in spite of all his devilish pranks.' Dipu's face shone with pride.

'Is he that naughty? He doesn't look it though!'

Dipu was happy to have turned the course of the conversation. She hadn't really wanted to quarrel with her elder brother. Although she enjoyed making a biting comment once in a while. 'What do you mean, naughty?' she said. 'Didn't I tell you he is an absolute devil? Keeps punching a sandbag twice a day. Then makes me squat and dashes off over my head. Says he is learning karate. And the club is an additional nuisance.'

Dipu's sister Anita, or Anu, could share her elder sister's pride in her son. Usually in these matters sisters feel a sense of empathy. 'Mejoboudi,' she said, 'did you know that Bubul was the all-Bengal champion in yoga last year? He can do such difficult asanas, you'll go crazy watching him. Worse than the circus contortionists.'

Shukla opened her eyes wide, 'Really, Anu! Such a young boy and so much talent! We only knew that he was good at his studies.'

As the ladies had, as usual, got around to extolling the virtues of their offspring, Anish was about to leave the room in disgust. Atish came in to say, 'Dada, what are you doing here? Father's boss, Das Sahib, and quite a few others from the office have been waiting a long time. Remember Das Sahib?'

'What are you saying, Rontu? How can I not remember him? He is the man who guided me in my youth. I sat for the competitive exam only because he said so. You should have called me.'

The two brothers, looking like hermits with their shaven heads, immediately bustled out of the room, holding on to the flowing ends of their dhotis*.

* Loincloths.

Out in the verandah they bumped into their youngest sister Ishita or Itu. Up the flight of stairs was the large hall of the first floor, where the guests had gathered. Itu was looking after them. Seeing her elder brothers, she waved her arms and said, 'There you are, Gaur-Nitai, alias Jagai-Madhai. Where are you off to in such a hurry? Do you realize that the first batch of guests must be fed now?'

Atish said, 'You're the expert. Why don't you call Dipu, Anu and Boudi? Don't ask Shukla, she'll end up doing everything wrong.'

'Is that the truth or are you protecting your wife?' Itu made an eloquent face.

'Stop trying to be too smart. Why don't you call her and see the fun? She wouldn't know one aunt from another; she'd mix up the uncles and cousins and make such a mess that you'll be taught a lesson.'

Atish didn't stop any longer. Anish had gone ahead, so he too lifted the end of his dhoti and advanced towards the stairs.

Das Sahib and the others had been there quite a while. When Anish, the eldest son of the family, got a first class with Honours in BSc, Das Sahib had driven down in his impressive car all the way from Theatre Road to Srirampore, carrying a box of cakes. He had filled the corridors of the old house with the resonance of his deep voice and said, 'Rakhaharibabu, don't you send your son into the university now. Let him sit for the competitive examination.'

'But with such good results! Shouldn't he study further?'

'Why? To become a clerk? Or to take a seventy-five rupee job as a school-teacher? This is an order – Anish will sit for the administrative services examination. Forget about his MSc. Bengali boys are increasingly being left behind in the competitive examinations, Rakhaharibabu. Boys from the South, UP and even Bihar get into the administrative services these days. And these Bengali bookworms, driven by the ghosts of Faraday and Edison, manage nothing more than their daily bread.'

At the time when Anish had joined the IPS, sons of middle-class families did not think on these lines at all. Certainly not his middle-class father. Touching the feet of an octogenarian Das Sahib, Anish remembered those early days.

'Enough, enough. May you have a long life, son.' Having lost his hair and teeth, the erstwhile Sahib had become a homely old Bengali gentleman. In the empty cave of his loose, hanging mouth he seemed to be perpetually chewing something. There was a walking-stick in his hand. It was easy to doubt whether there was a human body at all inside the shell of the sparkling dhoti and kurta.

'Your revered father was a hundred per cent honest man, honest citizen, my son. Dutiful, unselfish, concerned about the well-being of others. Who knows why he had to survive ten long years in this way after his wife's death. It's all God's will.'

Anish's father-in-law was present. He said, 'Their mother had produced gems, Radhamohanbabu. With her blessings, all the children are well settled. Wherever they were placed, there must they stay.' He added a Sanskrit shloka* to that effect. 'But the boys took turns to do the looking after. And over and above them all was my other sister by marriage, their aunt. She kept her elder brother confined within the shelter of her arms, and never let the children feel the absence of their mother. I was quite a regular visitor, you see. The paan was ready in time, so were the fruit juice, tea, sherbat†, sweetened bel fruit, flea-seed husks; all set to a rhythm from which there was no departure.'

'Really! Is that so?' The mobile mouth of Das Sahib became more agitated. 'Rakhaharibabu must have indeed been a man of great virtue. As for me, having married off my only daughter in Canada, I keep counting my days, so that I don't have to suffer the loss of my wife. It's my prayer night and day. You know how it is – even a dog would shed tears for a widower. So where is this pious sister of ours? Let us bless our eyes with a glimpse of her!'

Both Atish and Anish realized that Das Sahib had become somewhat senile. But recalling that this tiger sans claws and teeth was once a man of immense power and a guardian angel to this family, Anish said, 'Rontu, go and fetch Aunty.'

Das Sahib had come on the day of the funeral ceremony, driving his old Morris Minor. But that day the brothers had been busy with the ceremony. All the elaborate rites were performed exactly according to the scriptures. The priest, a university professor, wouldn't tolerate any compromise. Consequently there was little time for social intercourse. Having listened to the devotional songs, rewarded the

* Verse or couplet.
† Sweetened soft drink.

singers, sat at the ceremony for ten minutes, and had his share of sweets and a cold drink, the old man had departed along with the rest of them.

Atish was getting into quite a state bringing Aunty out of the ladies sitting-room upstairs, down the steps and across the big verandah. If only Das Sahib had asked for his wife Shukla instead, it would have been a more pleasing and easier chore. Shukla is sociable, witty and pleasant-looking. Not just pleasant, she is downright beautiful. After twelve days of mourning, she was looking gorgeous in her golden silk Tangail sari, her nails painted, her hair shampooed and vermilion on her forehead. She would have come smartly, talked sweetly. But escorting Aunty was making him gasp for air. As it is she was over seventy-three. In a stiffly starched plain white sari which her nieces and the wives of her nephews had made her wear, she looked just like a pod that had outgrown the fruit. With her rheumatic legs, she suddenly looked eighty, now that her brother was dead. Helpless, immobile, like a bundle. With eyes that didn't see, feet that couldn't move. Annoyed, Atish said, 'Do you have legs made of straw, Aunty? And who put you in these stylish clothes? It's standing up around you like Queen Elizabeth's gown! God help me!'

Other than a few missing molars, at her age Aunty still had most of her teeth. She said, 'I can do so little nowadays, my child, my sweet. Now all of you are my eyes, my legs. If you can take me along, well and good. If not, I'll just sit down here.'

Atish said, 'Help! Why did you have to stop? Don't you know, Das Sahib wants to meet you?'

The last batch to be fed had only the members of the family and the helpers. Seeing that Aunty was still willing to wait, Anish's wife Pratima insisted, 'That can't be, Aunty. You must go and lie down now.'

Aunty said, 'You come from East Bengal, darling; how can you possibly talk of lying down in the afternoon? I don't need to rest.'

'You haven't even eaten anything.'

'What? Two fat bananas, a fistful of wet flattened rice, sweets! Enough to drown in. I've crossed seventy-three – in my seventy-fourth year – just a bite once a day and my body carries on as usual.

I last out on the strength of my mind, not of my body any longer, my sweets.'

Pulling a low stool towards her, she settled down on one side.

'Have a little of the smoked fish, darlings, Shukla, Mejobouma, don't throw it away. Just swallow it with the rice, as you would the banana on Dashara.'*

Anish remarked, 'These old customs are not there any more, Aunty. Forget about them.'

Shukla asked Atish, 'What is all this about swallowing bananas on the tenth day?'

'How do I know?' Atish replied.

Deepika was sitting on the other side. She said, 'Why! Don't you remember, Mejda, Mother used to stuff a banana with bitter gourd and make us swallow it? Supposed to be a great antidote. It's true, we hardly ever fell ill. Twice a week the bitter *chireta* herb, twice a week the equally bitter *kalmegh*. Those were the days! Loud wails, thrashing limbs – what drama!'

By three in the afternoon the house was more or less empty. The relatives departed one by one. As it was a Sunday, all those invited had managed to come. They met each other after so long that much time was spent in getting the latest news. The members of the older generation are all going – the lamps are going out one by one, they said as they left. The children of the family were either playing around with the furniture brought by the decorators, or falling off to sleep.

Anu came in to say, 'I couldn't control your son, Didi. He has defeated me. Put away three-fourths of the chairs all by himself. The men from the decorators are sitting idle, smoking their bidis and grinding away. He has started on the tables now – those long wooden planks, that is.'

Chewing a paan, Dipu asked in a lazy voice, 'What are Dada and Mejda doing then?'

'You think they are anywhere around? Dada went to see off his father-in-law at the station. And Mejda too . . .'

---

* Tenth day of the lunar fortnight of the second month of the Bengali calendar, Jaishtha; the date of the descent of the river Ganga upon earth. On this day a bath in the Ganga relieves one of ten kinds of sin, hence 'Dashara'.

Shukla said, 'Hey, Mejdi! Watch out, I'm right here. Don't you say anything nasty about him!'

Anu turned to look at her. Itu was smiling. She said, 'We three sisters say whatever we have to in public. We don't say it behind anyone's back, Mejoboudi.'

Shukla laughed, 'We had actually started on Bubulram.'

Dipu said, 'Oh yes, he is removing the furniture. Let him. It is better to start early with whatever one is going to do in later life.'

'Is your son going to be a decorator or a caterer?' asked Anu.

'He'll be a Class IV government employee,' replied Dipu. 'What else can he be?'

Shukla commented, 'How can you worry so much about a boy who comes first in class every time?'

Dipu said, 'Do you think the Class IV employee has any less of an IQ? With the right guidance, some of them could have taken over from doctors and engineers. It is really a matter of inclination, Boudi. If someone is inclined towards cleaning up after other people, he will do just that in life. Aren't there other children here? Dada's Rai may have grown up. But what about your Kishen, or Anu's Sampi, Mampi? Are they picking up empty chairs, dirty tables or dirty dishes?'

'Why leave out the activities of my son, Didi?' said Itu, 'just see what he is rehearsing for the future.'

Itu's son was only seven months old. He had just woken up from sleep, produced some waste matter, and was looking grumpy. Itu rolled with laughter, 'Look at that! According to your formula, that's all my son's going to do all his life.'

Dipu hit her sister playfully. Shukla had tears of laughter in her eyes. She said, 'Really, Itu, you're the limit. Let's find out where your elder brothers and sisters have gone.'

Itu shouted out to her, 'Leave the others out of it. We all know who you're going to look for.'

Everyone laughed. But after a while, Shukla actually appeared with four of them. Anu's husband hadn't managed to come today at all. Dipu's husband had attended the funeral ceremony and returned to Asansol. The only son-in-law present was the youngest – Itu's husband.

Atish folded the end of his dhoti and settled down in the middle of the group. 'All right, say what you want to say to

67

me,' he said. 'I hear everyone has been looking for me for a long time?'

Dipu said, 'Actually it was only Shukla. But now that you are here, you may as well believe that it was all of us. It's really been a long time since the brothers and sisters got together. They say kings might meet often, but sisters never do. But in our case, we never even meet our brothers.'

Anish asked, 'Where are the children? I saw Dipu's son having a great argument with Ismail. Ismail claims that there is a doddering old man in his village who is two hundred and seventy-three years old. Dipu's son says, that is impossible. He has read the name of a Chinese or a Russian in the Guinness Book of Records.'

Anu said, 'Really, it's so sad to be old, isn't it? How old was Father?'

'Eighty-three. He couldn't hear, couldn't see. No teeth to eat his favourite food with,' replied Dipu.

Anish said, 'But he had his dentures!'

Pratima said, 'So what? Father wouldn't use them regularly. They used to hurt him a bit in the beginning as they usually do. My father had false teeth by the time he was in his sixties. But someone had got it into your father's head that dentures can cause cancer. So that was that.'

'We'd been telling him to go through a cataract operation right from the time he was seventy,' said Itu. 'Mother was alive then and I wasn't married. All he said was he wasn't going to live for long and he could carry on with his eyes as they were till then.'

Atish said, 'From seventy, he reached eighty-three. Nowadays these operations are nothing at all; they let you go after two hours. If he had given me permission, I would have arranged for it. But he wouldn't allow it.'

Dipu said, 'It was only because of Aunty that he didn't become an invalid, didn't have bedsores. The two of them would shuffle up to the terrace together twice a day and look after the plants. Father went while he was still in reasonable shape. He didn't like to eat anything but vegetarian food lately.'

Itu said, 'But whenever we came, Aunty would get meat and fish.'

Anu said, 'Itu, do you remember Aunty's potato curry? And her fried *notay* leaves?'

'Of course I do!' replied Itu. 'It's a funny story. I didn't used to have spinach and all those leaves. Didn't even like potatoes then. At my in-laws', in Bhagalpur, they have a Bihari Brahmin; you can't imagine how bad his cooking is. He has no idea of Bengali food. My mother-in-law, being an advocate, doesn't pay any attention to the kitchen. I came back home after three months and peeped into Aunty's kitchen. Aunty said, "Go and sit down, I'll get your lunch." I said, "Give me a little of whatever you have made yourself, Aunty." Aunty said, "You'll eat fried *notay* leaves?" "Definitely." Oh Didi, oh Boudi, you don't know how lovely it was! The taste lingered. In the evening she made soft, white parathas and potato curry. Not steamed potatoes. Just curry. But what a taste!'

Anu said, 'She sends a basket full of home-made flour sweets every year to my in-laws' home. We have other sections of the family as our neighbours; we share the sweets with them. Now every year from the sixth day of the Durga Puja, they all come and ask me whether Aunty will send the sweets this year! Greedy pigs.'

Atish said, 'That's nothing. When I was first posted to Durgapur, I took Aunty there. She soon became a popular figure. My students and colleagues knew Aunty more than they knew me. In fact I was being introduced to people as "Aunty's nephew" – all because of all those home-made sweets and pickles and what have you. In desperation I told her one day, "Aunty, I brought you to solve my meal problems. And there you are, feeding all Durgapur. If you go on in this way, I'll soon be out on the street." She laughed, "Why, does someone want to have my cooking?" You know, P.R. Sen was an absolute glutton. He was badgering me. Aunty said soothingly, "Let me see what I can do." That evening, when P.R. Sen arrived, she offered him a plate of her sweets and said, "Pinaki dear, I've been wanting to do something with your help." P.R. Sen said, "This nephew is always at your command. Just tell me how many times I'll have to go to the market." Aunty replied, "Well, yes, dear, that's just it. I very much want to feed your family at your home." Put him on the spot. But he loved Aunty so much, he just picked her up in his arms and danced around the room. I didn't have to do a thing. He arranged for Aunty to feed all our colleagues on the campus. The applause was deafening.'

Dipu said, 'Aunty must be very clever. I'm sure an IQ test will place her above the average.'

'Very possible,' said Atish. 'Even Mother had a terrific memory. She could recall the year and the day of any incident. When Itu had said something funny, where Rontu had picked up his Asiatic cholera, what I had been discussing with my friends – Mother could repeat everything exactly. What an intellect. A lot of our old people in this country are like that. They all retain their original brain-power. But where is Aunty now?'

'Forced her to go and lie down a bit,' said Anu and Itu.

Anish said, 'There is something important to discuss. We may as well get it over with now. It would have been better if the brothers-in-law had been present as well. As they are not here, we'll have to sort this out among ourselves.'

Anu was slightly apprehensive at Anish's tone of voice. 'Why are you so serious, Dada? Say whatever you want to say with a smile. The way you're going on, it's giving me palpitations.'

Anish lowered his voice, 'In this huge house, Aunty will be alone now. Have you thought of that? Totally alone. Is it right to allow an old woman of seventy-three to live this way?'

'That's true! What do we do? There's not even a reliable servant in the house,' said Dipu.

Atish said, 'Forget it. You can't leave such a large house and an old woman in the hands of any servant, reliable or no. The only solution is for one of us to be here. Anu, you could do that!'

Anu or Anita lived in Ballygunj Place, her husband had his own firm of auditors somewhere near Garia. Her in-laws stayed with her. Anita said, 'I could come and visit. But I can't live here. My father-in-law is seventy-four, my mother-in-law, sixty-nine. I have to look after them too all the time. Sampi and Mampi are studying in Modern High. We had to make a lot of effort to get them admitted there.'

Anish said, 'Anu is the only one who lives in Calcutta. If she can't come and stay here, there is no question of the others. In that case the solution is to take Aunty with one of us. Just now everything is uncertain for me. Having been three years at one place I can get transferred anywhere any minute. Wherever it is, I'll get good enough accommodation all right. But I work in the danger zone. That's why I've sent Rai to a hostel. Even Pratima should not be with me. If I take a totally dependent old lady like Aunty with me, in a week's time Pratima or I will get a stroke just worrying. What do you say, Rontu?'

Atish said, 'You know that I'm to leave for Germany in three months' time, Dada. I was planning to send Kishen to boarding school and take Shukla with me. Wives are allowed there. She won't get another chance such as this in her life. If I take Aunty, it won't be possible. Dipu, can't you? Anu and Itu both have their in-laws with them as well as other relatives. It wouldn't be right to take Aunty there.'

Dipu hemmed and hawed, 'He isn't here. I can't really decide anything without taking his opinion. Also, he is terribly bad-tempered. I never hide that fact. All of you chose him for me, he is your brother-in-law. But when the man throws a tantrum at the drop of a hat, I can't take the risk of bringing Aunty into his home without asking his permission. And I know that he intensely dislikes having a third person in the house.'

Anish sounded hopeless, 'Then what?'

Atish said, 'There's only one solution left. There are many good old people's homes available these days. Find a place for her in one of them.'

Anish asked, 'And the house?'

'Sell it and divide it among the five of us. Nobody will come to live in Srirampore. I've bought some land already in Durgapur. I can start building there if I get my share.'

Anish looked thoughtful, 'I too need a house. I'll probably settle in Delhi finally. The money would certainly come in handy. But there'll be little left after dividing it by five.'

Deepu and Anu silently exchanged glances. Dipu said, 'If it's a question of relinquishing our shares, your brothers-in-law should be present.'

'Don't talk rubbish!' said Atish. 'The shares will belong to you, not to our brothers-in-law. You can easily say whatever you want to yourselves.'

Itu said, 'We share a house with my in-laws; it's a large family. Whatever he earns, every paisa has to be handed to his father. Only I know what it is to have no money of one's own.'

Anu said, 'You're absolutely right. I too feel the same way. The keys are kept by the mother-in-law. The authority is hers and the labour is mine. If she ever gives any pocket money, you have to submit a debit-credit report, maintain a journal of accounts.'

Dipu said, 'You see, the house in Bhadreswar is their ancestral home, divided among seven brothers. You can imagine what it's like. Three of the brothers live elsewhere. The rest are all hanging on to the property. Whenever I've been back, I've stayed with Father. It will take us more than one lifetime to extract our share of my in-laws' property, buy some land and build a house. If I get my share from this property, we could think of a roof over our heads somewhere, whether in Bhadreswar or in Asansol.'

Anish said, 'All right, all right. That's final then. Start looking for an old people's home. I'm here another week, we must make some arrangement within that time.'

Just then there was a noise at the door. Aunty's close-cropped head became visible. She opened the door wide and said, 'Dinu, my sweet, all my darlings are gathered here. Boro Bouma, my love, just pour out the tea for everyone from Dinu's tray, please.'

Pratima and Itu both stood up. Pratima poured the tea and Itu passed on the cups. 'What have you done, Aunty?' she exclaimed. 'Fried fish, pompadoms, sweets! After that huge lunch?'

'Keep your mouth shut, silly girl,' admonished Aunty. 'You want to eat the tops of the puris alone and look like a rope to tie corpses with, that's up to you. Don't I know how many bites all of you took after feeding the guests to the gills in the afternoon? I didn't allow the cook to add all the fish to the gravy. Now go on eat, enjoy the hot food. Montu, don't you dare say no. Mejobouma, see that Rontu eats. He won't be able to say no to you. Dipu darling, I know you couldn't eat anything in the afternoon with that naughty son of yours around.'

Anu said, 'You didn't call me darling or love, Aunty. Didn't even ask me to eat. So I won't. There. Familiarity breeds contempt, doesn't it?'

Aunty's face broke into a wide grin, 'I'll feed you myself, I'll place you on my knees, darling. You are very special. The Lord Shiva has daughters like Lakshmi and Saraswati. But his very own and dearest is Mother Manasa. She sits on the Lord's knees.'

It is true that when Anu was born, her mother nearly died. For a long time she was not allowed to feed the baby, or even pick her up in her arms. Anu was brought up almost entirely by Aunty.

Shukla said, 'Why don't you sit down, Aunty? Here, on this stool.'

72

'Of course I will,' said Aunty. 'How can I resist being here, where all happiness has gathered? As God has still left me with my eyes, let me see all of you and fill my heart.'

Atish said, 'We have gathered here only to mark the end of the mourning for Father. And you call it a happy occasion, Aunty?'

'Why shouldn't I? Dada too must be saying the same thing up there – and laughing as he says it to Boudi. Unless we die, you don't come together, my loves. He has gone the best way. God willing, I too will go that way. And then all of you will gather like this, laugh and be happy, tease each other . . .'

Aunty wiped the tears from her eyes with the edge of her sari.

About three days later, after making enquiries, Atish came and told Anish, 'Dada, there's a big problem.'

'What is it?'

'The old people's homes are all right, but the better ones want large sums of money. Some of them even want it in advance.'

'Did you check up with the missionary organizations?'

'I did, but you know what a strict Brahmin she is. If we leave her in one of those places, Aunty might starve herself to death.'

'Problematic.' Anish looked thoughtful, 'All right, let me tap the sources I have.'

Finally, Anu's husband, Ranjit, brought news of a social service organization. It was run entirely by Hindus. But they looked after old people from all castes and creeds, free of cost. You could take a train there from Sealdah station. One day Anish and Atish went with Ranjit to check out the place. It seemed quite all right. They received secret donations from some big people, so they didn't charge anything. If anyone insisted, they might agree to a small donation. Next, the news had to be broken to Aunty.

Dipu said, 'What will you do now, Aunty?'

'Do about what?'

'I mean, where will you live and how? Have you thought about that?'

Surprised, Aunty looked at all of them and said, 'I have five children, not just one or two. At the age of seventy-three, do I have to worry about my own future?'

All the children remained silent. Ultimately, Atish said, 'All right, we should do the worrying for you, then. You have given us permission to do so. Now listen. We have located a very good institution for you in Shyamnagar. You will stay there. They will look after you. We'll come and visit you whenever we can. It is an entirely Hindu set-up. No Christians, no non-Hindus at all. You'll be able to live the way you want.'

Aunty was staring in amazement. The end of her sari had fallen off her head in sheer surprise. Looking blankly at him she said, 'Institution? What will an institution do for me, Rontu? Can't I stay here? In this Dash Gal?' The house was named Grace Dale. Aunty had always called it by a strange name, but that odd name had always remained her favourite.

Looking uncomfortable, Atish replied, 'Of course you can stay here. But who will look after you? That's the problem. You're not getting any younger, are you? Is it easy to look after this huge house and keep it habitable? And where will we find such a reliable servant?'

'Why? Dinu will be here, Rontu. At the end of the month you can send a hundred or two, whatever you can, just as you did when your father was alive. It's been more than enough for me. You'll all visit me when you come this way. You'll stay, have your meals here.'

'And what if you fall ill?'

'Nothing will happen to me, love. I'll go in my sleep. And Dinu is here.'

'We can't trust or depend upon Dinu that much, Aunty. He will go to his village the moment it is harvest season. Won't turn up for two or three months. Ultimately the house will be taken over by squatters, you'll see. And that Dinu will help them to settle down.'

'What will I do then?'

'You'll do what I said. You'll live in a beautiful place. When I come back from Germany, I'll take you with me. When Dada can, he will fetch you too. Just for now this seems to be the only possible way out.'

Aunty said nothing. Anish and Atish had some work. They went out. The house agent was outside. Then they would have to go to the office of the municipality to find out what must be done about the mutation of the property. Everything had to be done in a short time. Pratima had gone to visit the neighbours with Rai. Rai had hair with a golden tinge, a fair complexion and a face that was attractive if not beautiful.

74

She studied in Miranda House. Seeing that little girl so grown up and so lovely at the funeral, the neighbours were all highly impressed. The social visits were a result of many invitations. Shukla sat for a while, then suddenly remembered that she hadn't seen Kishen in a while. Who knew what mischief he was up to with that naughty Bubul. She got up and left, calling for Kishen. Dipu was fiddling with her nails. The three sisters cautiously left Aunty's room one by one. Aunty went on sitting on the small stool. Evening fell on her face, then night. In just a few hours, Aunty became ten years older.

After all the papers were signed, Deepika said, 'Could you tell us your visiting days and the hours, Mataji, we'll note them down.'

Mataji lifted her head, 'You're making a mistake. The people who come here have nobody in the world to call their own, nobody who can take their financial responsibility. So we don't have any visiting hours.'

Taken aback, Anita asked, 'No visiting hours?'

'No, we only keep those who have no one of their own.' Anita recovered quickly, 'That's true, of course. Aunty really has no one of her own. No children, no grandchildren, nobody.'

Dipu said, 'We are not her blood relations. Not her own family at all. Did you know that she was Father's stepsister?'

Itu said, 'None of us knew that while Mother was alive.'

'It was Mother's generosity. After all she came from a different family,' added Anu.

Dipu said, 'It was Father's generosity too.'

This story would have ended here. That is the way it should have been. But it didn't happen like that. Late one night, Dipu started howling in her sleep. The noise woke up Asamanja, her bad-tempered husband. It woke her naughty son. Asamanja said, 'What's the matter? Why are you raising the roof in the middle of the night?'

Dipu kept crying like a child, saying, 'Tell me first whether you will allow me to keep Aunty with me, tell me! I'll be your slave for life. After Anu was born, I wouldn't eat anything unless she fed me with her own hands. I would place my hand on her breast, think her my mother, when I went to sleep. And that Aunty . . . Oh, I would have

75

died without Aunty. I had the rickets. You wouldn't have had me at all. Some other witch would have come to make your home.'

Asamanja said, 'Why start this in the middle of the night? You never told me you wanted to bring Aunty to stay with you?'

'How could I? You've such a temper! I wouldn't be as scared of Hitler as I am of you!'

'Then why blame me? It'll be wonderful if Aunty is here. She is a great cook. Go and fetch her. I won't have to suffer half-cooked food with too little salt, and too much sugar. And this is what's making you cry?'

'What if your mother says something?'

'She'll only say it in Bhadreswar. Wouldn't reach our ears here. And if she does, she is my mother, I'll handle her. Oh! You women are so crafty.'

'Not crafty, just cowards.'

'All right, accepted. Now go to sleep.'

Dipu came across Anu right at the station. All five of them now had a key to the collapsible inner gate of the Srirampore house. Dinu had the key to the outer door. Till the house was sold, he would stay as the caretaker.

Astonished, Anu said, 'Didi?'

Dipu said, 'Anu?'

Anu was looking tearful, 'I dreamt last night of a thin, emaciated kitten whom Sampi was throwing across the wall. Suddenly the kitten cried out in a pathetic tone. And then I saw it was not a kitten at all, but Aunty! Didi, I can't leave Aunty in an old people's home. God will never forgive me then. When Mother was ill after giving birth to me, Aunty saved my life. It is she who is my real mother.' Anu started weeping.

The two sisters shared a rickshaw and had a heart-to-heart on their way home. Dipu said, 'I swear Anu, I've only been scared of my husband all this time. Terribly scared. If the socks aren't darned, he throws them away. If there's less salt in the dal, he throws that out, too. I had been summoned to Bubul's school and got late coming home. He just walked out of the house. God! That man! Today for the first time I respect him, perhaps love him too.'

Anu said, 'I thought a lot and decided that I'll come and stay here

76

till the house gets sold. I've looked after my mother-in-law's son all this while. Let her look after my daughters for a change. Sampi and Mampi will come to this house Friday nights and go back with their father on Sundays. It's good for them to be a little self-reliant. Then when the house is sold, I'll take my share and keep Aunty as a paying guest in a South Indian home very near us. They would give a room, a bath and a small kitchen, so she can cook for herself. Aunty will manage quite well, and I'll be able to look after her all the time.'

The door of the house was opened by Atish himself. 'What brings the two of you here?' he said in surprise.

'And what about you, Mejda?'

'Don't ask. Ever since we reached Durgapur, Shukla has been sulking. Yesterday she started making a terrible racket. Said, "I won't go to Germany. If it is in my fate, I'll get another chance. If not, I don't care. I'm not greedy for anything foreign. You go. I'll stay here with Aunty and Kishen." And then there was another incident.'

'What incident?'

'Come inside. I'll show you.'

On their way in, Atish shouted instructions to Dinu, 'Make some good tea with soaked bay leaves. And start a curry or something. Two of the sisters are here.'

Dinu came and said, 'Give me some money, I'll go to the market. There's no kerosene either. I'll have to buy that too.'

Suddenly the lights went off – load-shedding. The courtyard was covered with moss, the basil plant had become a little jungle. It wasn't looking like anything divine at all. More like a dishevelled demon.

Atish said, 'Be careful when you go to the bathroom, Dipu. The courtyard especially. I took such a toss . . . ugh!'

Dipu said, 'We wouldn't have had to worry about such things if Aunty were here. The larder was always full, as if the generous goddess Annapurna had set up her store here. The house shone as if with the presence of Lakshmi herself. The courtyard slippery with moss, the house in darkness. Never in all my life have I seen it looking like this.'

Atish scolded her, 'Go on, do something about it quickly. Stop lecturing me. All your life, indeed! How long have you lived in this house? Five years or seven?'

77

Dinu said, 'Whatever's five, could be taken to be seven as well. Not much difference, Dababu.'

When the electricity came back, Atish handed a telegram and an aerogramme sent by fast mail to the sisters.

It was from Anish, to Atish at Durgapur. 'Am transferred to Delhi. Send Aunty sharp by the next Rajdhani. Awaiting information – Dada.'

Itu's letter was also sent to Durgapur. She had written to both Atish and Shukla.

Dear Mejda and Mejoboudi,

Right from the beginning we did not like the idea of sending Aunty to an old people's home. But I am after all the youngest, and also have a large household at my in-laws'. Your brother-in-law is not only shy, he is also the youngest in the family. For me it is unfortunately quite impossible to do anything about Aunty. But ever since I heard that they don't even allow anyone to visit her, I've been extremely unhappy. Discussing it at length with your brother-in-law, I discovered a legal point. Although Aunty was Father's stepsister, they shared the same father. And although Father had added to it a bit, Grace Dale in Srirampore was built by Grandfather. As such, Aunty should get a half share of the property. The other half we can divide up among ourselves. Aunty, therefore, is not as helpless as we believe. After selling the house, use her share of the money to put her in a really good place where we can go and visit her and bring her over when necessary. And if that is not possible, if you are going to deprive her after all, I would like to surrender my share. With that money, too, something similar could be arranged. Our ancestral property is built on about seven hundred square yards of land. One-fifth of that should be worth at least a lakh of rupees. With love.

Yours,
Itu

After reading the letter, Dipu said, 'That's true, Mejda. According to the laws of today, Aunty should have a share in the property. None of us thought of that. Did you?'

Atish said, 'Honestly, I didn't, Dipu.'

They carried on their consultations late into the night. In the middle, Dinu went and got them some inedible roti and vegetable.

There was no kerosene in the shops and Dinu didn't seem terribly keen on cooking for the four of them. Finally it was decided that they would fetch Aunty at once from Asha Niketan. The attempt to sell the house at Srirampore would be shelved for the moment. As long as Aunty was there, she should enjoy the house. Dinu would be there. If necessary, they'd look for another servant. Anu would supervise and come and spend the weekends here. Later, after Aunty's death, they could decide on what was to be done with the house. Next morning, the three of them sent off telegrams to Anish and Itu, telling them about the new arrangements, and made their way towards Sealdah.

As the train moved, the three kept impatiently reading the name of each station.

Atish said, 'You know, actually, for us, there has never been any difference between Aunty and our parents. Mother and Father looked at it that way.'

Dipu said, 'You've realized it a little late in the day, Mejda. In Aunty we had our father's blood and our mother's affection.'

Anu said, 'Do you remember how Mother used to call her Didimani? That tone of her voice? It was as if Mother and Father protected her with all their might because she was a child-widow.'

Dipu said, 'Last time I heard Father say, "Ruchi, you must go before me", Aunty said, "Don't ever say such a thing, Dada. You go first. I'll come after you. Who'll look after you if I am not there?" "And who'll look after you when I am gone?" asked Father. Aunty said, "Don't worry about me. For a woman just a little bit goes a very long way." '

The Mataji now in charge of Asha Niketan was not the one they had met earlier. Though it was difficult to tell at first sight. The same white clothes, the edge of the sari drawn behind the ears and round the head. She listened to them carefully and said, 'You made a mistake, a terrible mistake. We don't take in anyone here who has any family. Society demands that people look after each other. Anyone who has someone to care for her wouldn't come to a charitable institution. It is the moral responsibility of her near and dear ones to look after her somehow. Why did you keep her here? Do you see the problem? We have branches of our institution all over India. We try to do whatever we can, not just for old people, but also

79

for anybody who is alone and totally helpless. They all work for the institution as well. We don't keep the inmates too long in one place. Every few months they are taken to a new place. This is our rule. We never take any address for them. We don't even call them by their names. Besides a number, a new name is added for each member. We try to help them wipe out their past and build a new life here. As far as I remember, though, there haven't been any recent transfers. This name you gave me, Ruchishila Bhattacharya – I can't go inside and ask anyone about it. Here we are named after light, water, air, fire – Alo, Salil, Banhi, Varun, Pavan, Agun. I don't know who among them would be Ruchidevi, and cannot let you know either.'

Seeing Anu in tears, Mataji relented, 'All right. I'll do something for you. Stay in here; I'll darken the room. You see that square window – behind it is a verandah. I'll take the women inmates down the verandah. Keep count of them and tell me the number when you recognize her. After that I'll arrange to fetch her.'

She shut the windows that looked outside, kept only the inner one open and left the room.

A little while later the identity parade began outside the open window. The first woman had close-cropped hair, salt and pepper, a somewhat wrinkled face, not quite fair, not dark either. The second had shoulder-length hair, salt and pepper, a somewhat wrinkled face, not quite fair, not dark either. The third had close-cropped hair, all grey, a somewhat wrinkled face, not quite fair, not dark either. The procession ended after the thirteenth woman inmate. Mataji came in a little later, 'Did you see them? Which one is she?'

Dipu said, 'Who else? The first one.'

'Never!' said Atish, 'The third one. You didn't realize she has gone all grey.'

Anu said, 'I'm sure she's the fifth one.'

Mataji said, 'What? You say she is a close relative, your aunt, and you can't recognize her? All right, I'll go and ask these three ladies separately if one of them is Ruchishila Devi. Although, once again I must point out that this is against our rules.'

Five minutes later Mataji returned to say, 'None of them is called Ruchishila. The first one is Janakibai, a Bihari. The third one is Fatima Begum – obviously a Bengali Muslim. And the fifth one's name is just Butia. She used to live in a beggars' slum and never had a proper name. Even if she had one, she has forgotten it now. We call her Dharitri – earth. Why don't you do something – give us a recent photograph of your aunt, some identification mark and a proper description. After that we'll see what can be done.'

Then Atish, Dipu and Anu talked it over at length among themselves and discovered that in the last ten years Aunty had never been photographed on any occasion. Also, that she was not too thin, nor fat; neither dark, nor fair; her hair was not all grey, nor all black; she hadn't lost all her teeth, nor did she have all of them; she was not too old, but certainly nothing less than old. Actually, she had no identifying mark on her. In fact, she was just an aunt. One of innumerable aunts. Not anyone's mother or father, just an aunt.

Translated by Shampa Bannerjee

Janet Frame

~~~

Keel and Kool

Father shook the bidi-bids off the big red and grey rug and then he spread it out again in the grass.

'There you are,' he said. 'Mother here, and Winnie here, and Joan you stay beside Winnie. We'll put the biscuit tin out of the way so it won't come into the photo. Now say cheese.'

He stepped back and cupped his hand over the front of the camera, and then he looked over his shoulder – 'to see if the sun's looking too', he told the children who were saying cheese. And then he clicked the shiny thing at the side of the camera.

'There you are,' he said. 'It's taken. A happy family.'

'Oh,' said Mother. 'Were we all right? Because I want to show the photo to Elsie. It's the first we've taken since Eva – went.'

Mother always said went or passed away or passed beyond when she talked of death. As if it were not death really, only pretend.

'We were good weren't we Dad,' said Winnie. 'And now are you going fishing?'

'Yes,' said Father. 'I'm going fishing. I'll put this in a safe place and then I'm off up the river for salmon.'

He carried the camera over to where the coats were piled, and he stowed it in one of the bags carefully, for photos were precious things.

And then he stooped and fastened the top strap of his gumboots to his belt.

'Cheerio,' he said, kissing Mother. He always kissed everyone when he went away anywhere, even for a little while. And then he kissed Winnie and pulled her hair, and he pulled Joan's hair too but he didn't kiss her because she was the girl over the road and no relation.

'I'll come back with a salmon or I'll go butcher's hook.'

They watched him walking towards the river, a funny clumpy walk

82

because he had his gumboots on. He was leaning to one side, with his right shoulder lower than his left, as if he were trying to dodge a blow that might come from the sky or the trees or the air. They watched him going and going, like someone on the films, who grows smaller and smaller and then The End is printed across the screen, and music plays and the lights go up. He was like a man in a story walking away from them. Winnie hoped he wouldn't go too far away because the river was deep and wild and made a roaring noise that could be heard even above the willow trees and pine trees. It was the greyest river Winnie had ever seen. And the sky was grey too with a tiny dot of sun. The grey of the sky seemed to swim into the grey of the river.

Then Father turned and waved.

Winnie and Joan waved back.

'And now we're going to play by the pine tree Mrs Todd, aren't we Winnie,' said Joan.

'We'll play ladies,' said Winnie.

Mother sighed. The children were such happy little things. They didn't realize . . .

'All right kiddies,' she said. 'You can run away and play. Don't go near the river and mind the stinging nettle.'

Then she opened her *Woman's Weekly* and put it on her knee. She knew that she would read only as far as 'Over the Teacups' and then she would think all over again about Eva passing away, her first baby. A sad blow, people said, to lose your first, just when she was growing up to be a help to you. But it's all for the best and you have Wonderful Faith Mrs Todd, she's happier in another sphere, you wouldn't have wished it otherwise, and you've got her photo, it's always nice to have their photos. Bear up Mrs Todd.

Mrs Todd shut her eyes and tried to forget and then she started to read 'Over the Teacups'. It was better to forget and not think about it.

Winnie and Joan raced each other through the grass to the pine tree by the fence, Joan's dark hair bobbing up and down and getting in her eyes. 'Bother,' she said. Winnie stared enviously. She wished her own hair was long enough to hang over her eyes and be brushed away. How nice to say bother, and brush your hair out of your eyes. Eva's hair had been long. It was so funny about Eva, and the flowers and telegrams and Aunty May coming and bringing sugar buns and custard squares. It was so funny at home with Eva's dresses hanging up and her shoes under the wardrobe and no Eva to wear them, and the yellow quilt spread unruffled over her bed, and staying unruffled all night. But it was good wearing Eva's blue pyjamas. They had pink round the bottom of the legs and pink round the neck and sleeves. Winnie liked to walk round the bedroom in them and see herself in the mirror and then get into bed and yawn, stretching her arms above her head like a lady. But it would have been better if Eva were there to see.

And what fun if Eva were there at the picnic!

'Come on,' said Joan. 'We'll play ladies in fur coats. I know because my Mother's got a fur coat.'

'I'm a lady going to bed,' said Winnie. 'I'm wearing some beautiful blue pyjamas and I'm yawning, and my maid's just brought my coffee to me.' She lay under the pine tree. She could smell the pine and hear the hush-hush of its branches and beyond that the rainy sound of the river, and see the shrivelled-up cones like little brown claws, and the grey sky like a tent with the wind blowing under it and puffing it out. And there was Joan walking up and down in her fur coat, and smiling at all the ladies and gentlemen and saying oh no, I've got heaps of fur coats. Bother, my hair does get in my eyes so.

Joan had been Eva's best friend. She was so beautiful. She was Spanish she said, a little bit anyway. She had secrets with Eva. They used to whisper together and giggle and talk in code.

'I'm tired of wearing my fur coat,' said Joan, suddenly. 'And you can't go on yawning for ever.'

'I can go on yawning for ever if I like,' said Winnie, remembering the giggles and the secrets and the code she couldn't understand. And she yawned and said thank you to the maid for her coffee. And then she yawned again.

'I can do what I like,' she said.

'You can't always,' said Joan. 'Your Mother wouldn't let you. Anyway I'm tired of wearing my fur coat, I want to make something.'

She turned her back on Winnie and sat down in the grass away from the pine tree, and began to pick stalks of feathery grass. Winnie stopped yawning. She heard the rainy-wind sound of the river and she wondered where her Father was. And what was Mother doing? And what was Joan making with the feathery grass?

'What are you making, Joan?'

'I'm making Christmas trees,' answered Joan graciously. 'Eva showed me. Didn't Eva show you?'

And she held up a Christmas tree.

'Yes,' lied Winnie, 'Eva showed me Christmas trees.'

She stared at the tiny tree in Joan's hand. The grass was wet with last night's dew and the tree sparkled, catching the tiny drop of sunlight that fell from the high grey and white air. It was like a fairy tree or like the song they sang at school – Little fir tree neat and green. Winnie had never seen such a lovely thing to make.

'And Eva showed me some new bits to Tinker Tailor,' said Joan, biting off a piece of grass with her teeth. 'Boots, shoes, slippers, clodhoppers, silk, satin, cotton, rags – it's what you're married in.'

'She showed me too,' lied Winnie. 'Eva showed me lots of things.'

'She showed me things too,' said Joan tenaciously.

Winnie didn't say anything to that. She looked up in the sky and watched a seagull flying over. I'm Keel, I'm Keel it seemed to say. Come home Kool come home Kool. Keel Keel. Winnie felt lonely staring up into the sky. Why was the pine tree so big and dark and old? Why was the seagull crying out I'm Keel I'm Keel as if it were calling for somebody who wouldn't come. Keel Keel, come home Kool, come home Kool it cried.

Winnie wished her Mother would call out to them. She wished her Father were back from the river, and they were all sitting on the rug, drinking billy tea and eating water biscuits that crackled in your mouth. She wished Joan were away and there were just Father and Mother and Winnie, and no Joan. She wished she had long hair and could make Christmas trees out of feathery grass. She wished she knew more bits to Tinker Tailor. What was it Joan had said? 'Boots shoes slippers clodhoppers.' Why hadn't Eva told her?

'You're going to sleep,' said Joan suddenly. 'I've made three Christmas trees. Look.'

'I'm not going to sleep. I'm hungry,' said Winnie. 'And I think Joan Mason that some people tell lies.'

Joan flushed. 'I *have* made three Christmas trees.'

85

'It's not that,' said Winnie, taking up a pine needle and making pine-needle writing in the air.

'I just think that some people tell lies.'

'But I'm not a liar, Winnie,' protested Joan anxiously. 'I'm not honestly.'

'Some people,' Winnie murmured, writing with her pine needle.

'You're not fair Winnie Todd,' quivered Joan throwing down her Christmas trees. 'I know you mean me.'

'Nobody said I did. I just said – some people.'

'Well you looked at me.'

'Did I?'

Winnie crushed her pine needle and smelt it. She wanted to cry. She wished she had never come for a picnic. She was cold too with just her print dress on. She wished she were somewhere far far away from the river and the pine tree and Joan Mason and the Christmas trees, somewhere far far away, she didn't know where.

Perhaps there was no place. Perhaps she would never find anywhere to go. Her Mother would die and her Father would die and Joan Mason would go on flicking the hair from her eyes and saying bother and wearing her fur coat and not knowing what it was like to have a mother and father dead.

'Yes,' said Winnie. 'You're a liar. Eva told me things about you. Your uncle was eaten by cannibals and your father shot an albatross and had a curse put on him and your hair went green when you went for a swim in Christchurch and you had to be fed on pineapple for three weeks before it turned black again. Eva told me. You're a liar. She didn't believe you either. And take your Christmas trees.' She picked up one of the trees and tore it to pieces.

Joan started to cry.

'Cry baby, liar, so there.'

Winnie reached forward and gave Joan a push, and then she turned to the pine tree and, catching hold of the lowest branches, she pulled herself up into the tree. Soon she was over halfway up. The branches rocked up and down, sighing and sighing. Winnie peered down on to the ground and saw Joan running away through the grass, her hair bobbing up and down as she ran. She would be going back to where Winnie's mother was. Perhaps she would tell. Winnie pushed me over and called me names. And then when Winnie got down from the tree and went to join the others her Mother would look at her with a hurt expression in her eyes and say blessed are the peacemakers. And her Father would be sitting there telling them all about the salmon, but he would stop when she came up, hours and hours later, and say sternly I hoped you would behave yourself. And then he would look at Mother, and Winnie would know they were thinking of Eva and the flowers and telegrams and Aunty May saying bear up, you have Wonderful Faith. And then Mother would say have one of these chocolate biscuits, Joan. And Mother and Father and Joan would be together, sharing things.

Winnie's eyes filled with tears of pity for herself. She wished Eva were there. They would both sit up the pine tree with their hands clutching hold of the sticky branches, and they would ride up and down, like two birds on the waves, and then they would turn into princesses and sleep at night in blue pyjamas with pink round the edges, and in the daytime they would make Christmas trees out of feathery grass and play Tinker Tailor – boots, shoes, slippers, clodhoppers.

'Boots, shoes, slippers, clodhoppers,' whispered Winnie. But there was no one to answer her. Only up in the sky there was a seagull as white as chalk, circling and crying Keel Keel Come home Kool, come home Kool. And Kool would never come, ever.

Anjana Appachana

~~~

Incantations

One hot summer night, when I was twelve and tear-deep in Victorian fiction, dreaming in bed beside my sister that I was Jane Eyre and Agnes wooed by Rochester and David, I felt my sister shuddering. It was the eve of her wedding, and I, with all the wisdom of my twelve years, turned to her, and putting my arm around her heaving body, assured her that there was no need for pre-wedding nerves, for wasn't Nikhil, her husband-to-be, kind and tender and handsome, and she, beautiful to boot? Turning to me then, she held my hand in a painful grip and said that two days ago she had been raped by Nikhil's brother, Abhinay. As she put the back of her hand to her mouth to stifle a moan, I moved over to her bed, lay beside her and held her. But the sounds from her throat could not be controlled. Our parents would hear. I helped Sangeeta out of bed to the bathroom, pulled the flush, turned on both taps and shut the bathroom door. She sat on the pot, I on the damp floor, and after ten uncontrolled minutes, she laid her head against the wall, and, turning away from me, spoke.

Nikhil's mother had taken her shopping for sarees two days ago and Abhinay, his younger brother, decided to join them. 'You'll make someone a good husband,' his mother had teased, 'if you have so much patience with women shopping.' And patient he had been. After the shopping he had told his mother that he would drop her, then Sangeeta, home. He dropped his mother and then asked Sangeeta if they could stop briefly at the barsati where he lived, as he had to pick up something. He insisted she didn't stay alone in the car, so she went up with him. Once inside, he locked the door.

My sister, who had been staring at the wall as she spoke, now looked at me. I try now to imagine how I looked to her then, pyjama-clad, thin, hair in a tight plait, my face like the photograph she

88

once took of me, guileless, adoring. My sister turned away from me and said, 'Then he raped me.' I put my hands around her bare feet and held them tightly, leaning my face against her thighs. 'I didn't fight,' she said. 'He said he'd deny it and tell everyone I wanted it. He said no one would believe me. And he took so long over it, so long.' She turned to me and felt my cheek. 'Do you know what rape is?' I made a sound of assent and felt my cheeks wet against her nightie. Yes, I knew what rape was. I wasn't supposed to know, I wasn't even supposed to know what sex is. Relentlessly my friend and I had proceeded to find out, our only source being the books we were not supposed to read. The *Reader's Digest*, though not forbidden, gave us a vague idea, for there was always something about the do's and don'ts of marital strife, the musts and must nots of sexual convolutions. Add excitement to marriage, the *Digest* instructed, do it under the dining-table, on the dining-table, under the bed, in the bathtub. My friend and I sighed with excitement. Oh to be married! Light candles, the *Digest* urged, use perfume, open the door for your husband one evening, naked! My friend and I shivered. Could the excitement in marriage ever cease? Never! Could one ever be done with all these experiments? Impossible! But with all this going on how did married people look so calm, so matter of fact, so unlike the exuberance of the Daily Act? One historic day, my friend discovered a much-thumbed paperback in her parents' room, which, when they were out she read swiftly, terror-stricken at the prospect of their arrival, enthralled at the discoveries she was making. It was rather complicated, she told me later in hushed tones. Sex apparently, was divided into four stages – foreplay, meaning kissing; intercourse, meaning intercourse; climax, meaning some height; and orgasm, meaning some release. The art of kissing, one we had always thought so simple, seemed almost as fraught with complications as the act that followed. The book said it was not confined to the lips and required great expertise. The rest was hazy. We could not put action to any of the words. We pondered over the question of time. Ten minutes? Half an hour? One hour? Furtively we tried to imagine our parents doing it. But no, that was not possible. Parents were beyond such experiments, beyond such desires, beyond any heights, any releases. Mystified, frustrated, delighted, we stared at each other. It was a far more complex and lengthy process than we had anticipated and, therefore, certainly far more to be desired. Sex was something that one day would happen to the likes of us and then lightning would crack and the heavens would change colour. We would have our Rochesters and our Rhett Butlers, it was only a question of time. A question of time when our noses would become finer, our lips more sensual, our eyes large and liquid, our hair thick and luxurious, the kind men loved to run their fingers through. A question of time before the pimples would vanish gracefully, the breasts appear mysteriously, the hair on our arms and legs fall off quietly, our eyebrows arch and distance themselves silently. Only a question of time, of time. Not the times our mothers were subject to, who slept with bedroom doors wide open on beds three feet away from our fathers, who had slept that way ever since we could remember. No, not the time our mothers were subject to, who as brides, were even more ignorant than we were as children. I think now of these multitudes of mothers, once silent brides entering yellow and white flower-bedecked bedrooms after the wedding, against which their bridal sarees burnt red and gold. How did our fathers undress these women, so many of whom did not even know the reason for such a ritual? Did our mothers then protest, silently, silently? Or quietly, unprotestingly acquiesce to what some instinct told them had to be endured, hearing during the act, like incantations, the distant refrain of their mothers' voices, chanting, do what your husband tells you to, accept, endure. Or perhaps, stricken with shyness and the strangeness of it all, did our fathers speak falteringly to their brides, initiate them slowly, gently, assuming an experience they never had? Was there the possibility for love? And their stories lay untold, swollen like rivers after the monsoon rains. Years later, untold stories still, and our mothers like the parched, cracked countryside, waiting for rain that will never come.

'After raping me,' Sangeeta said, 'he dropped me home.' I recalled that evening, recalled that my mother was busy getting everything arranged for the women's sangeet. The house was decorated with rangoli and the kitchen, redolent with the smell of cooking. Two hours before the sangeet, Sangeeta entered the house and I remembered how strange she looked, her eyes swollen, face pale, her saree more crumpled than the heat warranted. She told our mother that the heat was bothering her and Ma shepherded her to the bedroom and urged her to hurry and get ready. And I remembered that she took two hours over her bath. Then our relatives and friends arrived in a glitter of gold and Kanchivaram sarees. Sangeeta, exquisite in a yellow and silver Benarasi saree with pearls, her hair covered with jasmine, sat mutely as someone played the dholak and everyone sang. As the songs turned sentimental, lamenting the daughter leaving her mother's house, my mother, predictably, began to cry, but Sangeeta, playing with the gold bangles on her wrist, did not. I remember there were gulab jamuns, pedas and rasmalai after dinner, and I with my passion for sweets and without my mother's eagle eye on me, rapidly consumed a meal composed entirely of sweets. Then, overcome by the weight of my pimples, my oily skin, lanky hair and my intense shyness, I went to our bedroom and slept.

Now, twenty years later, I try and imagine what would have happened had my sister told my parents about the rape. They would, of course, have called it off. And Sangeeta, with her lost virginity would have continued to live with our parents, a fallen woman, as people would say. Despoiled, she would have faded quietly away into the greyness of eternal spinsterhood, while my parents prayed that some nice man would come along and love her in spite of it all, not questing the unbroken hymen. Had I been older, I would have told my parents and watched them shrivel away with barely a rustle, accepting this as their karma for sins committed in their last births, cradling their first-born, bearing forever the burden of an unmarried and deflowered daughter. And the people, oh the people would have talked and talked and the fault would have been entirely hers.

And what of Nikhil, the groom-to-be? Twenty-five to Sangeeta's twenty, he was a man so tall, so attractive, so charming, that he put to shame Darcy, Rochester and almost, but not quite, Rhett Butler. Theirs was an arranged marriage and as is inevitably the case, they fell violently in love. What romance! What courtship! What a profusion of roses for Sangeeta, what an exchange of love letters! Though they lived in the same city, they wrote to each other every day, went out with parental approval every other day. A romantic though I was, I could not imagine what they could write about after meeting so often. Didn't they talk? If I received vicarious pleasure from my books, it was nothing to that which I received from their romance. But, consumed by shyness, I could barely talk to Nikhil or

91

his brother Abhinay who was Sangeeta's age and almost as handsome as Nikhil. Their parents were kind to me. They would pat my head and declare that I was a polite and good girl. Which was true, for being shy, I could be nothing if not good and polite. Besides, what else could they say about me? I had neither looks nor charm nor poise. Sangeeta had all three. She made me giggle with her chatter, let me use her old lipsticks, feel her silk sarees. She cooked me my favourite dishes, told me stories about the excitement and adventure in her world – the grown-up world. She bought me books, usually ones I had long outgrown, but it didn't matter. She was wildly extravagant and almost always happy. She believed that money was meant to be spent and life was meant to be enjoyed, and she did both with abandon. When she was at home I didn't mind not reading; instead I watched her and listened to her. I thought her the most beautiful woman I had ever seen and her eyes were always brimming with laughter. Unlike mine which were always sad and lost, God knows why, for then I had nothing to be sad about.

That night Sangeeta and I put each other to sleep. I don't think she slept, but I did, deeply, the sleep of the young. When I awoke she was locking her six suitcases.

And so they were married late that night, on the auspicious time the pandit had augured. The pandit chanted the shlokas that nobody understood and my sister and Nikhil, under a mandap decorated with marigolds and surrounded by matkas painted green and red and white, went seven times around the holy fire. Abhinay was sitting behind Nikhil, I behind Sangeeta, and, as I cried, Abhinay patted my hand. I found myself holding his finger and bending it back and I think I would have broken it if he hadn't, in shock and pain, snatched it away. No one noticed and I continued sobbing with all the other weeping women.

The day after the wedding, Sangeeta and Nikhil came home, she in a green Kanchivaram saree with a magenta border, ruby drops in her ears, he in a spotless white silk pyjama-kurta. 'Made for each other', as the cigarette ad said, and I thought, 'It's all right, it's all right now,' relief washing over me in waves. Then I saw her eyes, blank, listless. We all sat in the puja room and my mother performed a short puja. After it was over we ate and as my parents talked to Nikhil, my sister took me to the bedroom, sat on the bed, sat me at her feet, and, looking away from me at the wall, began to talk, her voice flat, expressionless, compulsive. Nikhil hadn't done anything last night. She had recoiled and he had attributed it to natural shyness and apprehension. He had soothed her forehead and said, take your time. And she, shivering with distaste, lay awake all night. Nikhil sickened her, nauseated her. 'Didi,' I said, 'Didi, please don't.' Still looking away from me, Sangeeta said, 'Do you know what Abhinay did?' 'No,' I said, rising, but she pushed me back to the floor, then described at length the rape and I listened, nausea rising, till the very end when I saw her lying bleeding on the cool floor. Then my mother came into the room, Sangeeta's expression changed to the sister I knew and she hugged me.

The following month Abhinay moved in with them. He needed coaching for his chartered accountancy exams and Nikhil, being a chartered accountant, would coach him. Their mother was pleased and fondly said that now Abhinay had a bhabi who would cook and look after him. When my sister told us this at her next visit, my mother's face grew grim with disapproval. It was unhealthy, she told my father after Sangeeta left. When Nikhil went to work Sangeeta and Abhinay would be together all day – it was unhealthy. My father, disturbed, cleared his throat.

Fear for my sister, coupled with guilt at my own behaviour, engulfed me. I had avoided being alone with her on the occasions she came home and refused to visit her in her house with my parents. When she came home I would sit in the living-room with everyone else, ignoring Sangeeta's plea that I should show her my books. Now, terrified at the new development, I went to the nearby temple and prayed. I told the Gods that if they made things all right for my sister I would never marry, sacrifice forever my Rochesterlike husband. Not enough, not enough. I prayed that if things had to change, and in order to effect the change if I had to sacrifice what I most loved, I would sacrifice books, not all books (I was still in school), but fiction. I would stop reading fiction now, today. I prostrated myself before Ganesh, Lakshmi, Saraswati and Hanuman, and having appeased them all with coconuts, I came home.

Time stopped. Not being able to read, there was nothing to do. School was closed for the summer holiday and my only friend had gone to visit her grandparents. By the next evening I was in a ferment of boredom. I could not live without my books but I could not break my vow to the Gods. What to do? I finished a box of sweets in the fridge, stared hungrily at *Jane Eyre* which I had been reading for the third time (why hadn't I finished it before making my vow?) and fantasized about spending a day in the library. I stood for a long time before the bookshelf in my bedroom, closed my eyes, took out a book at random and opening it, smelled it deeply, the smell that still makes my stomach tighten with excitement and anticipation. Smelling wasn't breaking a vow. Then I thrust the book back. I took a walk to the nearby library, assured myself that I had read most of the books and that none were worth rereading. Craving, tearful, I walked back home. There my father presented me with a heavy cardboard box. I opened it. Books, books, books. 'All second-hand,' my father said happily. 'I couldn't resist the bargain for my little girl.' 'But,' said my mother the disciplinarian, 'One at a time, *not* more than *one* a day, or else you'll get mental indigestion. Choose one,' she told me, 'and you lock the rest away,' she told my father. She knew too well my ability to drug myself with books and prescribed as low a dose as she possibly could, irritated by my state of stupor during my reading spells.

Watery-eyed, I looked away and said, 'No, I don't want to read, I've outgrown books.'

'You're learning to be sarcastic, aren't you?' my mother retorted. 'Talking this way won't get you more than one.'

'Don't want any,' I said and went to my bedroom, bereft, broken. My father followed me and sat beside me apprehensively. 'Are you unwell? Do you miss your sister?'

My sister. My sister. I had forgotten my sister. My sister. I began to wail and miraculously, Sangeeta entered the room. I caught hold of her saree palla. 'Come back home,' I cried, 'don't go back. Come back home.' I pulled her palla till the saree tore at her shoulders, screaming, 'I won't let you go back, I won't let you go back.' My mother, books forgotten, rocked me in her arms. Then Sangeeta cradled me in hers, whispering in my ear, 'If you tell anyone I'll deny it, I'll never talk to you, I'm finished.'

When I finally emerged from the room, a confused Nikhil patted me awkwardly and gave me a chocolate. Dinner was a quiet affair; my parents still shocked by my unprecedented behaviour. I went

94

to bed immediately after dinner. Sangeeta followed me and sat on the bed. 'No,' I said, 'Didi, no.' Her head turned away from me, she told me that every morning when Nikhil was away on work, Abhinay raped her and at night Nikhil did.

'No, didi, don't.'

'Abhinay does it every single day. And, at night, after coaching him for his exams, Nikhil does the same thing. Only, Nikhil takes ten times as long because he thinks he's being patient, but it always hurts me, always, it doesn't matter how you do it . . . it's the same thing. Nikhil's patience only prolongs the pain, I detest them, I . . .'

I put my fingers in my ears. Sangeeta turned to me and removed them. She held both her hands over mine and hissed, 'Listen, *listen.*' Then, still holding my hands, she continued, 'Nikhil thinks I've changed. He says I've lost my spontaneity, my warmth, lost it all, all of it. He doesn't understand me, he says.' And she became quiet, and almost wistful. I got out of bed and went to the living-room.

After they left I asked my mother how long one had to sacrifice something to the Gods in order for one's wish to be fulfilled. 'At least a year,' she said, then sighed, 'and sometimes, never.' My mother kept innumerable fasts and was forever giving up sweets or meat or something she loved as part of the many bargains she struck with God. If never, I asked, why didn't she stop? 'How can I?' she answered. 'After all these years.'

And so I took *Jane Eyre* and ravenously finished it for the third time. I asked my father for the books he had got for me, and frenzied, finished fourteen in a week. 'It's the summer holiday, so do what you want,' my mother snapped in exasperation.

Sangeeta came home on three occasions after that, each time in a saree brighter than the last, and each time I sat glued in my chair in the living-room with the rest of the family, ignoring her pleas to talk in the bedroom. 'Bad girl,' she said once, pouting. 'You don't love your sister.' My mother said, 'Go and talk to your sister, you don't have to sit with us.' I burst into tears. 'Everyone bosses me around,' I said inadequately. And Nikhil, dear Nikhil produced a chocolate, and, giving it to me, said, 'For heaven's sake, let her be'. I could see unhappiness writ large on his face and when I caught him looking at my sister, he looked bewildered. She talked non-stop when she came home, her hands moving, bangles tinkling and she wouldn't listen

95

to anyone else. My parents obviously found nothing wrong and my mother once commented that she had become even more talkative after her marriage.

Then for some time, I think two weeks, Sangeeta didn't come home. One night I woke up screaming in my sleep, emerging from a nightmare where the sound of the shehenai mingled with the sound of Sangeeta moaning and I saw her covered with marigolds and Nikhil and Abhinay on either side of my dead sister. I woke to find my parents bending over me and in anguish I called out my sister's name. 'Didi's dead,' I told my parents. 'Didi's dead.' My mother held me as my body was racked with sobs and my father in his striped pyjamas looked bewildered.

The next morning my parents called my mother's youngest sister home for lunch. Mala Mousi was a gynaecologist and my parents no doubt attributed my hysteria to some vague, ill-defined, ill-articulated problem, thought perhaps, that my hormones were going awry, my periods on their way, imagined that in some obscure fashion I was jealous of my sister's fairy-tale marriage, wished her dead, that beneath my quiet exterior lay suppressed violence and anger. They had seen the change occurring after Sangeeta's marriage and, typically, refused to question me on matters so explosive, and handed me over to Mala Mousi. At thirty, Mala Mousi was twelve years younger than my mother. She was slim, attractive with pert, sharp features and short, dark hair, direct brown eyes and a nose so small and straight that I almost died of envy every time I saw it. She was brisk, sharp and cutting and everyone including my mother was a little scared of her. Sangeeta found her most intimidating – too direct, too crisp, too outspoken, too independent. Mala Mousi, she felt, had too many sharp edges and not enough of the softness and oozing affection she associated with our Aunts. She found Mala Mousi's remarks too penetrating, her views shocking and her attitude to the world too serious to justify a life that was meant to be enjoyed. 'She thinks too much,' Sangeeta would tell our mother. 'There's no point philosophizing on life and all that rubbish. She doesn't know how to have fun. And what's the point of all her philosophy and reading if she still isn't married?' For Mala Mousi at thirty was single and, to my horror and admiration, seemed none the worse for it. Mala Mousi did love life, but her love for life was of a different nature from Sangeeta's. It was serious, contemplative, silent. I found her optimism impossible to understand in the light of her two broken engagements, her constant fighting for her privacy and independence, the fact that she lived alone and that her family pitied her unmarried state and constantly reminded her of it. None of this seemed to affect Mala Mousi, who was quite ruthless with her six sisters and reminded them at regular intervals that she was the only one who wasn't using her education to cook. I could share my love of books with her since she too was a voracious reader. She listened to me quite seriously, never babied me, and on my questioning, was perfectly willing to talk to me about issues like God and the universe and what we were doing in it. She told me that she didn't believe in God and certainly not in Heaven and Hell, a revelation I tried hard to swallow with equanimity. According to her Heaven and Hell only existed on earth and as hard as I tried, I could never figure this out. In the convent where I studied, Heaven and Hell were realities you could not ignore, and I was sure Purgatory was the place for me, since I sinned by reading books that were forbidden. In school we had our Christian God, at home our Hindu ones, and I had no trouble in believing in both. When the nuns told us about the miracles Christ performed, I would chime in with the miracles Krishna performed, for I truly loved them both, and the nuns would listen, patient, amused, disbelieving. I loved the Bible almost as much as I loved the *Ramayana* and the *Mahabharata*, for they were all stories that stirred me deeply, moved me to inevitable tears. I wept when Lord Rama abandoned his pregnant wife in the forest. Unfair, unjust. All because he had overheard a conversation where one of his subjects questioned Sita's purity. All because Lord Rama wanted to show his subjects that he did care what they thought. And so, without telling Sita, and she pregnant, he sent his brother, Lakshmana to escort her to the forest and leave her there, alone, unprotected. '*How* could he, Ma, how *could* he?' I cried every time she told me this story. Once, my father, overhearing this, said, 'Such are the Gods we worship.' I wept too for Draupadi, gambled away by her five husbands, the Pandavas, along with their kingdom, to their enemies, the Kauravas. I wept as Duryodhana ordered Dussasana to strip Draupadi naked, as Dussasana began pulling at her saree before the entire court, and Draupadi's five husbands,

97

helpless, watched. 'How could they, Ma?' I cried. 'How could her husbands do it?' And my mother told me how Draupadi vowed that one day she would wash her hair in Duryodhana's blood and till then her hair would lie loose and uncombed. Then I sighed with anger and anticipation. And my father, listening again, reaffirmed his disgust with the men in our mythology. The *Ramayana* and the *Mahabharata* abounded in passion, intrigue, vengeance and retribution – stories within stories within stories, and ultimately, of course, Good always triumphed over Evil. They had to be true, I reasoned, they absolutely had to, for how could anyone possibly have the imagination to make it all up?

Mala Mousi, in addition to her apocalyptic views, also smoked, to my parents' disapproval and embarrassment. 'Decent women don't smoke,' my father would tell my mother, and my mother, torn between her assent and her love for her baby sister, would not reply. She even drank occasionally, and she did both with such grace and style that, in my bedroom, I would often go over each gesture, the elegant lift of her slim hand, the leisurely movement of her long fingers holding the cigarette, her magenta lips coolly exhaling smoke. I longed both to impress her and impress upon her that I too had views to express that were radical. But I did not. I didn't even argue with my parents, for, besides wanting to read more, there was nothing to argue about.

Yes, Mala Mousi fascinated me. But I didn't aspire to be like her because to do so would mean no marriage and no babies and I wanted both. However, not to be like her would mean to be like my mother who had marriage and babies and was fat, comforting, unexciting, exacting, loving, practical, oozing security and discontentment. And every woman I saw around me who was married was like my mother – totally, completely unromantic. Was there no in-between?

Before lunch Ma and Mala Mousi were closeted in my parents' bedroom and many years later I was told that the conversation went something like this:

Ma: Geeti's seriously disturbed. I don't know what to do.
Mousi: Talk to her. Find out.
Ma: Perhaps she's had her periods and doesn't know what do to?

Mousi: Ask her.

Ma: You're a gynaecologist. Check her up.

Mousi: What do you mean, check her up! She's your daughter for heaven's sake, and having her periods isn't a disease. The poor child.

Ma: Mala, beti, please talk to her.

Mousi: Didi, you're being totally irresponsible. The poor child needs you, not me.

Ma: Mala, beti, I think she's seriously disturbed about Sangeeta's marriage.

Mousi: Why?

Ma: She's behaving in such a strange manner – she cries for no reason and yesterday she dreamt that Sangeeta was dead – do you think she wants her dead?

At this point my mother burst into tears. Then Mala Mousi lectured her on her repression, her stupidity, her utter blindness to my loneliness.

'But I wasn't lonely,' I tell her now, twenty years later. 'I can't recall ever having been lonely.'

'Rubbish,' Mala Mousi says. 'You were a solitary child with practically no friends. You were so lost in your world of books that the real world eluded you completely. And you were totally, horribly oblivious to the terrible burden placed on you by your selfish sister.'

'She had no one else,' I say. 'No one.'

'She had your parents,' Mala Mousi says. 'She had a choice. She chose to stay in that masochistic set-up and use you.' Suddenly her eyes fill and she murmurs, 'The poor child, poor, poor Geeti.'

I persist. 'She was terrified that no one would believe or understand. She wasn't even aware that a choice existed.' Things are so cut and dried for Mala Mousi. Mala Mousi says, 'Your beloved sister was weak. She accepted every bit of her suffering and that made her a masochist.'

But of that day, twenty years ago, Mala Mousi's lecture to my mother, the strained lunch ... After lunch Mala Mousi asked me to tell her about the books I was reading. We went to my bedroom, and in the middle of my talk on Jane Eyre's sad childhood, I faltered.

'Something is bothering you, Geeti,' Mala Mousi said.

99

'No,' I replied, for if I spoke my sister would die.

'Have you had your periods?'

I blushed. 'No.'

'Do you know why women have them?'

'Oh yes,' I said airily. 'If women have periods, then they can have babies.'

'Yes,' she answered and then told me about a woman's anatomy and reproductive organs, and then about a man's. After this, to my acute embarrassment, she told me about the sexual act, mixing it nicely with biology.

When she finished I said, 'I bet you don't know how *much* it hurts.'

'Rubbish,' said my aunt.

'*I* know,' I said. '*You* don't know.'

'Actually,' Mala Mousi said, 'I don't know. Why don't you tell me?'

'You'll know when you get married,' I said sadly.

'But you're not married, Geeti. How do you know?'

'I know people who are married, Mousi, friends,' I clarified hastily.

'And what do your married friends tell you?'

'I have one married friend,' I said, 'whose brother-in-law raped her two days before the wedding.'

'And then?'

'Then her brother-in-law came to stay with them and now he rapes her in the morning and her husband rapes her at night.'

I noticed that Mala Mousi's hands were shaking. She said, 'Geeti, my child, is that woman your sister?'

I did not answer. I felt my throat was paralysed. My frightened face was answer enough. 'Don't tell Ma,' I said.

Mala Mousi took my hands in hers. 'Geeti, baby, trust me. Do you believe I'll never harm your sister?'

'Yes,' I whispered, the tears flowing.

She wiped my tears and said, 'We'll have to tell your mother and your father.'

'No.'

'Yes. They'll get your sister back home. She'll be safe. No one will harm her. They'll never let her go back. And *whatever* happens, I'll be with you.'

100

'Promise? Cross your heart and promise.'

'I cross my heart,' she echoed, doing it, 'and I promise.'

'Ma can't take it,' I said. 'She'll become hysterical.' Mala Mousi pressed my hand. 'But Daddy,' I said, 'will be brave and strong. He is,' I struggled for the word, 'an invulnerable man.'

For some time we sat together quietly, Mala Mousi, her arm around me, stroking my forehead. I was filled with a sense of peace and comfort I had never known before and have never known since. Then I looked up and saw that Mala Mousi, my strong, no-nonsense Mala Mousi, was crying quietly. The fear rushed back, making me dizzy and I looked at her with such terror that she covered my eyes with her wet fingers. She said, 'Nothing will happen to Sangeeta. I'm crying for you.'

I sighed deeply, then smiled. '*I'm* all right.' I looked up at her. 'See, I'm all right.'

I really believed I was.

And so Mala Mousi called my parents to my bedroom and told them. I waited for Ma's loud tears and lamentations, but there were none. She sat limply against her chair, the faint lines around her mouth suddenly darker, her large eyes unfocused. It was my father who wept, not silently and soundlessly as I believed men cried, but in spasms of uncontrolled sounds, a sight so impossible, so unbearable, that I then felt the complete and irrevocable collapse of my world.

Mala Mousi helped me pack my suitcase and then we went to her apartment to stay for a week. She told me that my parents would get my sister back home and it would be better for me to stay with her for a short time.

That evening she told me with infinite gentleness, that my sister had died in her sleep.

After the first storm of grief, I lay in her arms and said, 'She must have died of a broken heart.' They didn't let me attend the cremation and Mala Mousi didn't either, but stayed with me, holding me during my periodic bursts of weeping.

Sangeeta did not die in her sleep and of course, she did not die of a broken heart. I discovered this four years after the event, and then only because my kid cousin, an irritating girl of great precocity, wanted me to tell her a story. I, absorbed in my book, had no intention of, or interest in indulging her. So she said, 'I bet

101

no one told you that Sangeeta didi died because she hung herself from the fan.'

I put down my book.

'I knew I could stop you reading your stupid book,' she crowed.

I stared at her.

She grinned. 'And before she killed herself she cut off Abhinay's . . . *thing* and he died bleeding.' And overcome with embarrassment at mentioning Abhinay's 'thing', she covered her mouth and giggled.

They all knew, all, all of them, our relatives, neighbours and the entire city where we had lived, and which we moved out of a month after her death. They all knew, since of course, it made headlines in the local newspapers and there were the police, the journalists and curious people like tidal waves against our door. During that entire period I was at Mala Mousi's, kept away from newspapers and people, and soon after I left with my parents for another city, a place too distant for our relatives to descend as regularly. They all knew that when my parents entered Sangeeta's house (the front door was unbolted), she was hanging from the fan, and Abhinay lay below, next to the door.

How did she do it? When he was sleeping, probably, the sleep of the satiated, the safe, knowing Nikhil was away on work for a week. After that she must have locked the bedroom door, watching and hearing him as he tried to crawl towards it, watching and hearing him collapse. In the note she left for me she wrote, 'Today Abhinay raped me for the fifty-second time. I am pregnant. I can hear him dying and I like the sound.' Did she then carefully place the note on the table, and hands folded, patiently watch Abhinay die? Or did she, as he screamed, trying to crawl towards the locked door, whisper to him about the fifty-two times?

There was a bottle of Ganga water on the side table, which she had drunk before stepping on to the chair.

It was Mala Mousi who finally told me all this. My parents, when I confronted them, were of no use. In the kitchen I held my mother and shook her, begging for the truth. My mother, leaning against the kitchen wall, shook her head, her face wet. I held her face in both my hands then, and forced her to look at me; but her eyes, streaming, looked at the ceiling. Then I went to my father who was sitting in the verandah. He had heard me. Face averted, he said hoarsely, 'Don't ask me anything.' 'Tell me,' I shrieked, 'tell me!' The next-door neighbour peeped out from her door and my cousin cowered in the corner of the verandah. Then I went to my parents' bedroom, opened my mother's saree trunk, rummaged in the folds of her sarees till I found the money carefully tucked away, my mother's only savings put away each month from the household money. I counted four hundred rupees in ten and five rupee notes. The next day I took the train to the city where Mala Mousi lived, the city we had left four years ago. My parents, unprotesting, let me go.

Mala Mousi also told me that my parents, ravaged with grief and shock, had broken down completely, and that Nikhil had looked after them for a week as a son would. Nikhil's parents, though mad with grief and remorse, accepted their son's fate as retribution. They too eventually left the city. Mala Mousi showed me some of the women's magazines that had written about Sangeeta, making the case an issue. One compared her to Draupadi on the battlefield after the war had been won by the Pandavas, washing her hair in the blood of the man who had humiliated her, fulfilling her vow like a woman possessed.

'But she was no Draupadi,' Mala Mousi tells me today, twenty years after the event. 'She had no courage, no endurance, no ability to sustain herself or others.' My aunt, so kind and compassionate with me, does not spare my sister or my mother. She tells me that my mother has been irresponsible at each stage. 'First she hands you over to me to find out what you're disturbed about, then she turns to religion after Sangeeta's death, then she refuses to tell you anything, leaving you to find out from that precocious cousin of yours.'

I defend my mother. 'You can't expect her to discuss it with any equilibrium.'

Mala Mousi grunts. 'No, I can't. So I do it for your parents both times.' She pauses. 'She lets her children find out through a series of inopportune accidents, as she herself did when she got married. One would think her own experience would sensitize her to her children, but no. Did you know that the first time your mother was in labour, she took medicine for stomach-ache?' She notes my aghast expression with satisfaction. She rubs it in. 'Sangeeta's conception was one big accidental discovery, her birth another.' Mala Mousi has virtually stopped seeing my parents. 'My sister depresses me,' she says.

'You're not one for euphemisms, Mousi,' I murmur, and she smiles reluctantly. My mother doesn't merely depress Mala Mousi, she infuriates her, enrages her. My mother is now fanatically religious, praying and meditating for six hours a day. On my visits home (and they are increasingly briefer now), I hear her bed creak at 4 every morning, listen to the sounds of her entering her bathroom, bathing, emerging and getting dressed. Then the smell of incense drifts into my room. If I arrive unexpectedly at my parents' home and she is in the middle of her prayers, she does not come out to greet me, and I sit in my bedroom and await the end of her puja, while my father, still unable to make tea, hovers around me and says I've become thin. My mother is practising detachment, believing completely that attachments only bring sorrow. When she isn't praying, she asks about my work as a surgeon and about my separation in a desultory manner, not always listening to my response. My father, always a believer of sorts, is still, strangely, one. Once in a while he shakes his head and says, 'Nothing is understandable', then follows this with, 'God has His ways'. Mala Mousi says that in the process of my mother's prayers and my father's sighs they have lost whatever little ability they had to be responsible and make decisions. She sees the whole affair as the inevitable result of their attitudes and choices, rather than the act of a God who has His ways, as my father says, or as retribution for sins committed in the last birth, as my mother believes. But for all her raving, all her intolerance, Mala Mousi is a woman of great optimism, and, therefore, I feel, of great courage. She has no complaints about a cruel fate or a malevolent God, believing, of course, in neither, accepts it when things go wrong in her life, and for the rest, goes about delivering babies, tending to her garden and reading with great zest.

Was there no in-between, I asked at twelve. Yes, there is. I am the in-between; it was only a question of time. A question of time when my nose became finer, my eyes with kajal, larger, my hair actually thicker and longer. A question of time when the pimples vanished gracefully, the breasts appeared mysteriously, the hair on my arms and legs disappeared – waxed determinedly, my eyebrows arched and distanced themselves, having been plucked painstakingly. It was only a question of time ... a time not still and stagnant like my mother's, but one entirely my own. Time passed as I waited for the man who would be my Rochester, my Rhett Butler, my Darcy, my David, my Sanjeevani, my life-giver, my healer. I foisted all these attributes on the man I eventually married, waited for his eyes to turn dark with compassion and understanding as I told him the story of my life. Mad, obsessed, he said of me. Crazy, he said of my sister. The less he listened, the shriller I became. As I eventually turned away from him in bed, he said, it must be running in the family.

And so I went back to Mala Mousi. She listened. No questions here, no judgements. I spoke of Sangeeta, my parents, my husband, sobbed out my dreams and fantasies, my illusions and the reality. And when I stopped my outpouring, she began hers.

Yes, I am the in-between; not married, fat, discontented and accepting like my mother, or unmarried, uncompromising and independent like Mala Mousi, but separated for the time being from my uncomprehending, angry husband, having shed my old fantasies for another – that of empathy, tenderness and companionship. In my dreams I foist this on my resisting husband, unwilling to believe that he is as unlikely my Sanjeevani as I am his Gopi.

And like women possessed, Mala Mousi and I come back to Sangeeta every time we meet. Mala Mousi still hasn't got over the stricken twelve-year-old or the traumatized sixteen-year-old she looked after and counselled. When talking of it she speaks as though the child were not me but another girl in another time. She says she couldn't bear it then and can hardly bear it now. Sometimes, unconsciously, she talks of me in the third person. 'The poor child,' she tells me. 'The poor, poor child.' It is as though Mala Mousi has become twelve-year-old Geeti, recapitulating her experience for me, her thirty-two-year-old friend, articulating all that the twelve-year-old never did. Then it is my turn, and I become Sangeeta, living every day and every night of my sister's marriage, recreating it to the last bloody day. Then, groaning, I tell Mala Mousi that perhaps I should be thankful for my husband. A statement that she promptly tears to shreds, berating me for acting out the wifely resignation epitaph of 'others have it worse'.

Mala Mousi's aphorisms, while sensible, were too practical for me, her philosophy of life – for her, solid and flourishing and protecting like a Banyan tree, was for me too frail a branch to hold. I wanted to believe my mother when she told me, 'It is all a delusion, everything. To think this is the real world, that is what leads us all astray.' Her eyes were bleak as she looked out of the kitchen window.

'Rubbish,' Mala Mousi said when I repeated this to her. 'It is your mother who is deluded.' Her expression softened as she saw my face. 'I know. It allows her to continue living.'

Caught between my longing to believe my mother and my longing for Mala Mousi's approval, I alternated between hope and guilt. How did Mala Mousi cope? Where did she get her optimism from, how could she be so cheerful about her future, all alone, always alone? And I, how could I even begin freeing myself from the past, desperately loving all that I remembered of my sister, quietly loving Mala Mousi, and even against my will loving my husband, in spite of his Rhett Butlerish, Rochesterlike qualities, seeing in his bewilderment, some hope?

And Nikhil. My chocolate-bearer, blind unwitting rapist, big, kind brother-in-law. Many years after Sangeeta's death he came to see me at Mala Mousi's house and for the first five minutes, so shocked was I at the change in him that I couldn't talk. He had greyed prematurely, had a slight stoop and had lost forever the charm that was so much part of him. He came to find out what Sangeeta had told me. All these years it had obsessed him, knowing that Sangeeta had talked to me, not knowing what she had said. Year after year he had visited Mala Mousi but she had refused to betray my confidence. My parents had refused to let him see me. Mala Mousi had told me of his visits but not the reason for them. 'I thought it would be too hard on you,' she said defensively. Dear Mala Mousi. All these years, Nikhil told me, he had waited to talk to me. What had Sangeeta told me? Why, how had she borne it? When had it begun? So I told him and his face shrivelled. Shuddering, he said, 'I thought she was inhibited. O God, I was no better than my brother.' Looking down, he whispered, 'Now I understand.' There was a long silence, then Nikhil looked at me, his eyes crazed with pain, and said, 'I thought you would tell me that she loved me. I came feeling that hearing this I could go away bearing it at last. But this, oh Geeti, this is beyond bearing, beyond going away from.' After that he could not speak. We sat mutely for fifteen minutes, he looking blindly out of the window. Finally, when he left he said, 'I will have to pray. I will go to Amarnath next month to pray that I can atone to her in my next birth.' As he turned to walk away he said, 'Before I met you I had hope.'

I went back to the living-room and sat on the divan, shaking with the old grief. Even today it takes me by surprise, this feeling, and I'm twelve again and uncomprehending once more. Ah the promise of our next births where we can atone for the sins committed in this one, accept our suffering in this birth, believing all our pain is our karma for the sins committed in the last one. There is much to say for Hindu philosophy, for belief brings with it acceptance and hope. It denies the eternal damnation of Hell, makes explicable the inexplicable, is the only logical answer to the tormented why. By that logic, my parents, my sister, Nikhil and I must have sinned voluptuously, horribly, in our last births. I too, like Nikhil, pray; like my mother, I make promises to the Gods, but I do it surreptitiously. Mala Mousi would disown me if she knew, for she relegates the cycle of births to the same category as Heaven and Hell. I pray that Sangeeta's soul is resting, that if there is another birth, we will know each other again. What a ritual of secrecy and guilt my prayers are! There are times when I long for Mala Mousi's conviction of one life and one death and nothing before or after, long too, for her optimism and faith in herself. But if I had her conviction, I would not have her optimism, and could I then continue living, knowing that this is the end, that this is all? I pray, just in case.

Nann Morgenstern

Sorority

'Resolved: Agricultural Parity as a Policy is a Trick rather than a Treat for US Farmers' was the zappy title of the debate. It was going badly. Celeste stared down at the printed index cards, now so damp and running with sweat that they were scarcely legible, and awaited her time to take the lectern again. She attempted to slow down her breathing; if she'd been at home now her mother would be forcing her to breathe into a brown paper bag. But she was not home, she was on a godamned stage, making a total fool of herself in front of an audience of twenty or more, including her own (mercifully bagless) mother and her four best friends. Just as she had been on the Junior Varsity Lacrosse Team for only half a game until thrown off it, now she was demonstrating a similar lack of talent for debate. Celeste thought, for what? Just to add 'Debating Society' next to 'JV Lacrosse' on her college application forms to look so well-rounded she couldn't fail to get into one of the star-studded Seven Sisters, the Ivy League. Well-rounded, hah; complete asshole, more like.

Howard Stern, already chosen to be the Class Valedictorian in six months' time, was delivering his rebuttal in his highly imitable silver-tongued Victorian orator style and Celeste had already guessed that her con side had lost. Howard was emoting away about the inalienable rights of Oakies to endless rows of waving wheat after their long trek to the heart, soul and breadbowl of our Great American nation. What did it matter if they overproduced until the cows came home, or didn't, in this case? Celeste could almost see the chorus from the Rogers and Hammerstein hit De Milling about and hunkering down fondling inalienable corn and dared a scarcely focused glance into the audience in order to pass an invisible but complicit sneer to the Sisterhood in the second row. The steely whispering sounds of their hyperactive knitting needles had ceased and almost all she could hear above Howard's soprano profundo and her own blood coursing through her veins was the occasional detection-proof crump of bubblegum imploding in closed mouths. Lo, instead of the eye-rolling smirks she expected, all five of them were staring gulled, cow-eyed and damp-cheeked at Howard Stern as though he was Ricky Nelson. Defeat *and* betrayal! Hyperventilation lurched into fourth gear and Celeste tipped over backward, chair, notes and all.

She came to with her head between her knees, her mother pushing her wringing wet hair out of her eyes. She inadvertently blinked a few times, willing herself not to move and just feign death for as long as it took to clear the room. Howard stood above her with an empty glass and the water pitcher which had been on the lectern.

'Howard *is* a quick thinker,' Celeste's mother trilled. The Sisterhood, huddled together tragically, dangling half-knitted argyll socks and handbags at the side of the stage, were not slow in agreeing. Celeste grimaced.

'If you don't mind me saying, Mrs Coleman,' Miss Stromberg said, 'I think it would be better all round if Celeste were seen by a doctor; given a complete check-up, you know. This is such an important year for her that we have to make sure she's in tip-top condition to cope with all the stress of the examinations and interviews.'

The MMs gathered Celeste's notes, her coat and other belongings together as her mother and Howard helped her struggle to her weak and still-tingling feet. They all bundled her into the car and ensconced her in the front passenger seat, from which she glared stonily ahead as her mother's fulsome gratitude flowed over Howard. The Sisterhood waved and blew kisses as they drove off to the doctor's.

The hospital room was more pleasant and homey than Celeste's dread at the thought of it had allowed her to imagine. There were cabbage rosy chintz curtains at the louvred windows, Redouté rose prints on the lemony neutral walls, a TV tuned in to *American Bandstand* on a wheeled base, a couple of upholstered armchairs and two beds, one of which was empty.

The other was occupied by a pale, wispy-haired, sharp-featured blonde girl with deep circles under her eyes.

'Welcome to Dracula City,' she said. 'I'm Emily.'

'Celeste. Why "Dracula City"?' She picked up the starched backless gown on the other bed and looked at it with distaste.

'You just wait and see,' Emily laughed softly, showing one bruised and bandaged arm above her bedclothes then started singing along with Sam Cooke's 'You Send Me', minding her own business while Celeste rigged herself out in the scratchy, shapeless gown and put her street clothes away. As instructed, she sat down on the still-made bed.

'I love Sam Cooke,' she said.

Emily nodded, still humming softly.

'How long have you been in here?' Celeste asked.

'Ten days so far, this time,' Emily shrugged. 'What are you in for? You look OK to me.'

'Oh, you know, tests and things. I fainted at school and they all got over-excited. The doctor mentioned mono, maybe; glands and things up where they shouldn't be. Who knows? And you?'

Emily shrugged again. 'They never tell me anything, actually. I'm some sort of leper. Maybe I godda a Social Disease . . .' she said, Officer Krupke-style.

The sight of a nurse entering the room with what looked like a horse syringe stopped Celeste's laughter. The nurse drew a curtain around Celeste's bed. Emily stopped singing and 'Why do Fools Fall in Love' blared out alone.

After a few days of a thorough going-over, Celeste knew more than she wanted to about Dracula City. Each day her mother would grow more and more grim-faced and distrait. Each time the MMs came in variations of two, they spoke in ever-more-quiet tones, handing her items like *Seventeen* magazine, Persian Melon Nail Polish or her favourite Russell Stover Chocolate-Covered Mint Whips from the 'real world'. This time it was a quart of Rocky Road ice-cream, which Natalie handed to Celeste with a tentative hug and an air kiss.

'Today's little treat from the MMs,' Margot said.

'Why in the world do you call yourselves that anyway?' Emily,

110

already dubbed an honorary MM herself, asked. 'Minnie Mice? Mean Mamas? Mystifying Maniacs?'

'Close. It's short for *"Messhugena Maidlich"*,' Margot explained as she handed round plastic bowls and spoons. 'That's Yiddish for "Crazy Girls", Arline's mother gave us that name about three years ago. We were always laughing together and fooling around. We really got on everybody's nerves all the time,' she bragged.

Celeste's mind's eye flashed back to that sun-moated November afternoon in Arline's kitchen. She'd known the other three girls only since September, after they'd had to move into the new apartment in Queens. She'd felt almost overwhelmed with pleasure to be counted as one of the group, like part of a family again. The moment had stuck with her since as though framed and frozen on a TV screen. 'Yeah, I remember,' she said. 'Arline's mother said, "You five girls can be *Messhugena Maidlich* now, but just you wait until you're wives and mothers yourselves and then you'll be laughing out of the other side of your mouths." '

'Personally, I can't wait to be married,' Margot sighed and licked her spoon.

'Me neither,' said Natalie. 'I'm so sick of all of this college crap. What's it all for, anyway?'

'You know what it's for, darling; don't you want to marry a doctor or a lawyer or an accountant? Someone with a *future*?' Margot imitated her own mother's loaded intonation.

'Is that really why you're going to college? You've got to be kidding.' Emily said in amazement.

'Yup,' Margot and Natalie agreed.

'Not me,' Celeste said.

'Nah,' the other two MMs looked at each other and said in tandem. 'She's an egghead. She even wants to go to a women-only college so she can study ...' Natalie rolled her eyes to the ceiling. 'I ask you ...'

'So, what's wrong with that?' asked Emily. 'God knows I've missed enough school over these past two years, but when I make it up, I want to go to college, to an all-girls school, too; Vassar, probably, if I make it. My Aunt Thalia went there. She's a doctor.'

'What's her husband do?' Margot asked.

'She hasn't got one,' Emily answered, perplexed.

'See?' Margot arched her eyebrows and pointed at Celeste.

'You guys make me sick,' Celeste snorted.

Emily laughed and said, 'So *that's* your problem . . .'

Celeste laughed too, appreciating Emily's quick retort. After Margot and Natalie cleared away the remains of the ice-cream orgy and left, Celeste told Emily about that feeling she'd had when Arline's mother had inadvertently dubbed them the MMs. Even though she didn't think that the closeness of the group would last much beyond school, she said, it was as close as she'd ever got to feeling like she belonged *somewhere*.

'I guess I know what you mean,' Emily nodded, 'Actually, I've always longed for a sister, or even a brother, God forbid, for sort of that reason. You're the only other only child I know, you know.'

'I know.'

'You know.' They laughed together and Emily sputtered, 'Well, I know you know', which started Celeste off again.

'Yeah, me too.' Celeste wiped her eyes on a tissue from the box on her bedside table. 'My mother had a hysterectomy when I was five or so, but even when I was a little kid I used to day-dream about her having another baby, somehow. Barf-making, but I used to think that maybe her insides could reconstruct themselves, like out of food, and I'd get my wish. Then my dad died and that was the end of that.'

Emily tortured the petals from a drooping tulip in the glass vase on her own bedside table and said, 'Let's pretend we're sisters, OK?'

Celeste said, 'Right. Like Meg and Jo in *Little Women*. I always wanted to be Jo. Meg's all right, but Beth and Amy are just so . . . blah.'

'Give Amy a break; she's the youngest and she's cute, but, OK, I'll be Meg.' As Emily reached out her hand to clasp Celeste's the red tulip petals rained down on the vinyl-tiled floor.

Arline and Chickie sat in the armchairs near Celeste's bed, knitting their socks, each resplendent with a veritable catherine wheel of needles and dangling bobbins of multicoloured wool. Celeste had never been able to master the intricacies of the art of sock-knitting, argyll or other, and, having neither father, brother nor boyfriend steady and long-suffering enough to hang around the two months or so argyll sock-knitting by the MMs took, had felt no need to compete in this area with her sisters. She preferred reading or the ballet as leisure activities, especially as 'gratuitous argyll sock-knitting' was not, in any case, a pursuit that would look good on those college application forms.

Arline held up her three-quarters finished brown, black, grey with a hint of red job for Celeste and Emily to admire.

'Look how far I've got already! A couple more days and the whole pair will be finished.'

'Who are you going to give them to?' Emily asked, propping herself up on one elbow to admire Arline's handiwork more closely.

'I don't know,' Arline demurred and blushed. 'I was going to give them to Alan, my brother, but now ... I may give them to my new boyfriend.'

'What's that I hear? You've been keeping something from me? So, who's the new man in your life this time?' Celeste enquired archly.

Arline and Chickie exchanged glances. Arline nodded and Chickie said, 'She didn't want to upset you in your condition, you know, but it's Howard Stern.'

'Feh,' Celeste sneered and glanced at Emily, who had already been treated to Celeste's opinion on the person in question.

'The valley-*dick*-taurean, Jo?' Emily whispered to her.

'None other, Meg.' Celeste snorted back.

Chickie changed the subject. 'So when are they letting you guys out of this dump, anyway?'

'I'm going under the knife tomorrow and then home in a day or two, depending on what they find.' Celeste felt under her left breast and stroked the lump in the fold of skin gingerly. The 'thing' was so familiar to her after having discovered it four years ago that she had dismissed it from her mind as it hadn't developed into the freaky third boob its nippled appearance had threatened. She'd never even thought to mention it to her mother or anyone else. 'All the tests are fine, but I've got this cyst thing under my boob they want to look at more closely.'

Again Arline and Chickie exchanged glances, this time of scared repulsion, Celeste noted.

Emily said, 'I think I'm off home in a couple of days, too. I feel so much better really and Mom and Dad told Dr Schwartz they'd rather have me at home now than hanging around here. Anyway, I couldn't bear to stay here after Celeste goes.'

Arline, Chickie and Celeste stared in some bewilderment at Emily, who most certainly didn't look well enough to leave her bed, let alone the hospital. They said nothing and the sock-knitters returned to their craft. Celeste looked at her watch and leapt out of bed to switch on *American Bandstand*. They all began to sing along to 'Two Silhouettes on the Shade'.

'Aren't you scared, Celeste?' Emily asked after their parents had gone that evening and the nurse had put the sign 'NIL BY MOUTH' on Celeste's headboard. 'About what they might find, I mean.'

'A little, I suppose. Not much. I've grown accustomed to my lump,' she intoned. 'I kind of like it in a strange, familiar way. It hasn't grown any bigger or anything in four years. How serious could it be, for God's sake; I'm only sixteen ... Sorry,' she winced at her own clumsiness.

'I'm always scared,' Em admitted when Celeste had switched off their bedside lamps. Celeste stared at her friend in the dark but could think of nothing at all that wasn't too stupid to say.

'Break a leg,' Emily murmured to Celeste as she was being trundled out from their room to the operating theatre. 'I really love you, you know, Jo.'

Celeste attempted a suitable rejoinder but failed, too high from her pre-op to be able to form a coherent sentence. If this is what drugs do, gimme more, her brain said to itself, while all her mouth could manage was, 'See you. Bye. Wow.'

She waved a floppy wrist in Em's direction.

Celeste regained a foggy consciousness, retching from the ether. Clutching the kidney bowl her mother hastily proffered, Celeste aimed and retched again.

'It's OK, Cookie. You're OK, just fine, really OK,' her mother kept repeating the litany as Celeste heaved up stringy bile into the bowl.

Laying her head back against the pillows, Celeste said, 'Yuk. I really, really, really have got to brush my teeth.' She glanced over

114

the high cotlike restraining sides of the bed in the direction of the bathroom where her washbag was, taking in the made-up, unoccupied bed with a headbanging shock.

'Ma, where's Emily?' Celeste started to shake.

'Gone home,' her mother said tersely and shrugged. 'Her parents thought it would be better this way.'

'We didn't even say goodbye, for shit sake.' Celeste's mother hugged her fetid daughter. 'Did they give you their address? Phone number?' she mumbled into her mother's bosom. She could feel her mother shaking her head and burst into desolate tears, savouring the actual physical pain that seared through her chest as she flailed about in her mother's embrace.

Nurse O'Connor checked the bandage under Celeste's breast.

'That's fine; just grand. Only eleven small sutures and it won't even leave a scar. You can wear a two-piece bathing suit again by the time summer rolls around.

'Make an appointment for next Tuesday with Dr Fisher, will you, Mrs Coleman? He'll whip out those stitches and she'll be good as new.'

Mrs Coleman beamed at her daughter and began to place her street clothes on the armchair.

'You can get dressed now and go home, you lucky young lady,' the nurse affirmed. 'And you can go back to school on Thursday, but no PE for a month, mind you.'

The lucky young lady breathed a shaky sigh of relief as she stepped into her underpants.

The late January light seemed almost too silver, the cars too garish, the sky too blue to belong to the real 'real world' Celeste remembered. She drew down the passenger seat sunshade and rolled the window more tightly closed against the glare and blare of it all, feeling dizzy, dislocated and clammy but freezing cold.

'Aren't you ever going to tell me what was wrong with me, Ma? I *am* sixteen years old: I can take it.' She heard herself whine and wrinkled her nose in self-disgust.

Her mother took a deep breath and cleared her throat. 'As they thought, it was just a simple cyst, Celeste; nothing to write home

115

about, easily excised and never going to recur.' Her words were nearly lost above the blast of the car's fan heater.

'I don't believe you, Ma,' Celeste put her hand over her mother's, preventing her from turning the ignition key. Something sounded fishy, over-rehearsed. 'You've got to tell me the truth or I'm going to think that something as bad as what's happening to Emily is going to happen to me . . .'

'Nothing bad's going to happen to you, Celeste, I swear,' Celeste's mother said too loudly. 'Nothing!' She paused then in a softer tone conceded, 'I wasn't going to tell you this because it's, well, a little weird, to say the least, for a highly strung kid like you to take, maybe, but here goes . . .' An inadvertent burble of embarrassed laughter erupted from her mother's mouth.

'Really! I am *not* a child, Ma!' Celeste interrupted through gritted teeth.

'I know you're not, Celeste, but you always will be my child, my only child . . .' Celeste's mother sighed and strangled another burst of nervous laughter.

'I know, I know; get on with it.'

'Well, to put it bluntly, without beating around the bush, the "lump" they removed was full of, uh, hair and bone and teeth.'

'?,' Celeste boggled, crossing her arms over her breasts protectively.

'A "witch's tit", they call it vulgarly. Dr Fisher did give me some Latin name for it, but I forgot it. You can ask him next week; anyway, it's not at all that uncommon, he says. Apparently, sometimes two embryos form in one egg in the womb, identical twins, only just one manages to thrive and the other is absorbed into the growing body of the remaining embryo or foetus or whatever,' Celeste's mother floundered, shrugging. 'I can't . . .'

Celeste got the point. 'You mean that lump was my *sister?*'

'You could say that, I suppose. Kind of a gruesome way to put it, though.'

'No, it's not,' Celeste said calmly, placated. It was not the sort of thing she'd want to share with the MMs, that was for sure, but Emily would have appreciated it: sisters beneath the skin.

Cynthia Rich

〜〜〜

My Sister's Marriage

When my mother died she left just Olive and me to take care of Father. Yesterday when I burned the package of Olive's letters that left only me. I know that you'll side with my sister in all of this because you're only outsiders, and strangers can afford to sympathize with young love, and with whatever sounds daring and romantic, without thinking what it does to all the other people involved. I don't want you to hate my sister – I don't hate her – but I do want you to see that we're happier this way, Father and I, and as for Olive, she made her choice.

But if you weren't strangers, all of you, I wouldn't be able to tell you about this. 'Keep yourself to yourself,' my father has always said. 'If you ever have worries, Sarah Ann, you come to me and don't go sharing your problems around town.' And that's what I've always done. So if I knew you I certainly wouldn't ever tell you about Olive throwing the hairbrush, or about finding the letters buried in the back of the drawer.

I don't know what made Olive the way she is. We grew up together like twins – there were people who thought we were – and every morning before we went to school she plaited my hair and I plaited hers before the same mirror, in the same little twist of ribbons and braids behind our head. We wore the same dresses and there was never a stain on the hem or a rip in our stockings to say to a stranger that we had lost our mother. And although we have never been well-to-do – my father is a doctor and his patients often can't pay – I know there are people here in Conkling today who think we're rich, just because of little things like candlelight at dinner and my father's cigarette holder and the piano lessons that Olive and I had and the reproduction of *The Anatomy Lesson* that hangs above the mantelpiece instead of botanical prints. 'You

117

don't have to be rich to be a gentleman,' my father says, 'or to live like one.'

My father is a gentleman and he raised Olive and myself as ladies. I can hear you laughing, because people like to make fun of words like 'gentleman' and 'lady', but they are words with ideals and standards behind them, and I hope that I will always hold to those ideals as my father taught me to. If Olive has renounced them, at least we did all we could.

Perhaps the reason that I can't understand Olive is that I have never been in love. I know that if I had ever fallen in love it would not have been, like Olive, at first sight but only after a long acquaintance. My father knew my mother for seven years before he proposed – it is much the safest way. Nowadays people make fun of that too, and the magazines are full of stories about people meeting in the moonlight and marrying the next morning, but if you read those stories you know that they are not the sort of people you would want to be like.

Even today Olive wouldn't deny that we had a happy childhood. She used to be very proud of being the lady of the house, of sitting across the candlelight from my father at dinner like a little wife. Sometimes my father would hold his carving knife poised above the roast to stand smiling at her and say: 'Olive, every day you remind me more of your mother.'

I think that although she liked the smile, she minded the compliment, because she didn't like to hear about Mother. Once when my father spoke of her she said: 'Papa, you're missing Mother again. I can't bear it when you miss Mother. Don't I take care of you all right? Don't I make things happy for you?' It wasn't that she hadn't loved Mother but that she wanted my father to be completely happy.

To tell the truth, it was Olive Father loved best. There was a time when I couldn't have said that, it would have hurt me too much. Taking care of our father was like playing a long game of 'let's pretend', and when little girls play family nobody wants to be the children. I thought it wasn't fair, just because Olive was three years older, that she should always be the mother. I wanted to sit opposite my father at dinner and have him smile at me like that.

I was glad when Olive first began walking out with young men in the summer evenings. Then I would make lemonade for my father

('Is it as good as Olive's?') and we would sit out on the screened porch together watching the fireflies. I asked him about the patients he had seen that day, trying to think of questions as intelligent as Olive's. I knew that he was missing her and frowning into the long twilight for the swing of her white skirts. When she came up the steps he said, 'I missed my housewife tonight,' just as though I hadn't made the lemonade right after all. She knew, too, that it wasn't the same for him in the evenings without her and for a while, instead of going out, she brought the young men to the house. But soon she stopped even that ('I never realized how silly and shallow they were until I saw them with Papa,' she said. 'I was ashamed to have him talk to them.'). I know that he was glad, and when my turn came I didn't want to go out because I hated leaving them alone together. It all seems a very long time ago. I used to hate it when Olive 'mothered' me. Now I feel a little like Olive's mother, and she is like my rebellious child.

In spite of everything, I loved Olive. When we were children we used to play together. The other children disliked us because we talked like grown-ups and didn't like to get dirty, but we were happy playing by ourselves on the front lawn where my father, if he were home, could watch us from his study window. So it wasn't surprising that when we grew older we were still best friends. I loved Olive and I see now how she took advantage of that love. Sometimes I think she felt that if she were to betray my father she wanted me to betray him too.

I still believe that it all began, not really with Mr Dixon, but with the foreign stamps. She didn't see many of them, those years after high school when she was working in the post office, because not very many people in Conkling have friends abroad, but the ones she saw – and even the postmarks from Chicago or California – made her dream. She told her dreams to Father, and of course he understood and said that perhaps some summer we could take a trip to New England as far as Boston. My father hasn't lived in Conkling all of his life. He went to Harvard, and that is one reason he is different from the other men here. He is a scholar and not bound to provincial ideas. People here respect him and come to him for advice.

Olive wasn't satisfied and she began to rebel. Even she admitted that there wasn't anything for her to rebel against. She told me about

119

it, sitting on the window sill in her long white nightgown, braiding and unbraiding the hair that she had never cut.

'It's not, don't you see, that I don't love Father. And it certainly isn't that I'm not happy here. But what I mean is, how can I ever know whether or not I'm really happy here unless I go somewhere else? When you graduate from school you'll feel the same way. You'll want – you'll want to know.'

'I like it here,' I said from the darkness of the room, but she didn't hear me.

'You know what I'm going to do, Sarah Ann? Do you know what I'm going to do? I'm going to save some money and go on a little trip – it wouldn't have to be expensive, I could go by bus – and I'll just see things, and then maybe I'll know.'

'Father promised he'd take us to New England.'

'No,' said Olive, 'you don't understand. Anyhow, I'll save the money.'

And still she wasn't satisfied. She began to read. Olive and I always did well in school, and our names were called out for Special Recognition on Class Day. Miss Singleton wanted Olive to go to drama school after she played the part of Miranda in *The Tempest*, but my father talked to her, and when he told her what an actress's life is like she realized it wasn't what she wanted. Aside from books for school, though, we never read very much. We didn't need to because my father has read everything you've heard of, and people in town have said that talking to him about anything is better than reading three books.

Still, Olive decided to read. She would choose a book from my father's library and go into the kitchen, where the air was still heavy and hot from dinner, and sit on the very edge of the tall, hard three-legged stool. She had an idea that if she sat in a comfortable chair in the parlour she would not be attentive or would skip the difficult passages. So she would sit like that for hours, under the hard light of the unshaded bulb that hangs from the ceiling, until her arms ached from holding the book.

'What do you want to find out about?' my father would ask.

'Nothing,' Olive said. 'I'm just reading.'

My father hates evasion.

'Now, Olive, nobody reads without a purpose. If you're interested

120

in something, maybe I can help you. I might even know something about it myself.'

When she came into our bedroom she threw the book on the quilt and said: 'Why does he have to pry, Sarah Ann? It's so simple – just wanting to read a book. Why does he have to make a fuss about it as though I were trying to hide something from him?'

That was the first time I felt a little like Olive's mother.

'But he's only taking an interest,' I said. 'He just wants us to share things with him. Lots of fathers wouldn't even care. You don't know how lucky we are.'

'You don't understand, Sarah Ann. You're too young to understand.'

'Of course I understand,' I said shortly. 'Only I've outgrown feelings like that.'

It was true. When I was a little girl I wrote something on a piece of paper, something that didn't matter much, but it mattered to me because it was a private thought. My father came into my room and saw me shove the paper under the blotter, and he wanted me to show it to him. So I quickly said, 'No, it's private. I wrote it to myself, I didn't write it to be seen,' but he said he wanted to see it. And I said, 'No, no, no, it was silly anyway,' and he said, 'Sarah Ann, nothing you have to say would seem silly to me, you never give me credit for understanding, I can understand a great deal,' but I said it wasn't just him, really it wasn't, because I hadn't written it for anyone at all to see. Then he was all sad and hurt and said this wasn't a family where we keep things hidden and there I was hiding this from him. I heard his voice, and it went on and on, and he said I had no faith in him and that I shouldn't keep things from him – and I said it wasn't anything big or special, it was just some silly nonsense, but if it was nonsense, he said, why wouldn't I let him read it, since it would make him happy? And I cried and cried, because it was only a very little piece of paper and why did he have to see it anyway, but he was very solemn and said if you held back little things soon you would be holding back bigger things and the gap would grow wider and wider. So I gave him the paper. He read it and said nothing except that I was a good girl and he couldn't see what all the fuss had been about.

Of course now I know that he was only taking an interest and I shouldn't have minded that. But I was a little girl then and minded

121

dreadfully, and that is why I understood how Olive felt, although she was grown-up then and should have known better.

She must have understood that she was being childish, because when my father came in a few minutes later and said, 'Olive, you're our little mother. We mustn't quarrel. There should be only love between us,' she rose and kissed him. She told him about the book she had been reading, and he said: 'Well, as it happens, I do know something about that.' They sat for a long time discussing the book, and I think he loved Olive better than ever. The next evening, instead of shutting herself in the bright, hot kitchen, Olive sat with us in the cool of the parlour until bedtime, hemming a slip. And it was just as always.

But I suppose that these things really had made a difference in Olive. For we had always been alike, and I cannot imagine allowing a perfect stranger to ask me personal questions before we had even been introduced. She told me about it afterward, how he had bought a book of three-cent stamps and stayed to chat through the half-open grilled window. Suddenly he said, quite seriously: 'Why do you wear your hair like that?'

'Pardon me?' said Olive.

'Why do you wear your hair like that? You ought to shake it loose around your shoulders. It must be yards long.'

That is when I would have remembered – if I had forgotten – that I was a lady. I would have closed the grill, not rudely but just firmly enough to show my displeasure, and gone back to my desk. Olive told me she thought of doing that but she looked at him and knew, she said, that he didn't mean to be impolite, that he really wanted to know.

And instead she said: 'I only wear it down at night.'

That afternoon he walked her home from the post office.

Olive told me everything long before my father knew anything. It was the beginning of an unwholesome deceit in her. And it was nearly a week later that she told even me. By that time he was meeting her every afternoon and they took long walks together, as far as Merton's Pond, before she came home to set the dinner-table.

'Only don't tell Father,' she said.

'Why not?'

'I think I'm afraid of him. I don't know why. I'm afraid of what he might say.'

'He won't say anything,' I said. 'Unless there's something wrong. And if there's something wrong, wouldn't you want to know?'

Of course, I should have told Father myself right away. But that was how she played upon my love for her.

'I'm telling you,' she said, 'because I want so much to share it with you. I'm so happy, Sarah Ann, and I feel so free, don't you see. We've always been so close – I've been closer to you than to Father, I think – or at least differently.' She had to qualify it, you see, because it wasn't true. But it still made me happy and I promised not to tell, and I was even glad for her because, as I've told you, I've always loved Olive.

I saw them together one day when I was coming home from school. They were walking together in the rain, holding hands like schoolchildren, and when Olive saw me from a distance she dropped his hand suddenly and then just as suddenly took it again.

'Hullo!' he said when she introduced us. 'She does look like you!'

I want to be fair and honest with you – it is Olive's dishonesty that still shocks me – and so I will say that I liked Mr Dixon that day. But I thought even then how different he was from my father, and that should have warned me. He was a big man with a square face and sun-bleached hair. I could see a glimpse of his bright, speckled tie under his tan raincoat, and his laugh sounded warm and easy in the rain. I liked him, I suppose, for the very things I should have distrusted in him. I liked his ease and the way that he accepted me immediately, spontaneously and freely, without waiting – waiting for whatever people wait for when they hold themselves back (as I should have done) to find out more about you. I could almost understand what had made Olive, after five minutes, tell him how she wore her hair at night.

I am glad, at least, that I begged Olive to tell my father about him. I couldn't understand why at first she refused. I think now that she was afraid of seeing them together, that she was afraid of seeing the difference. I have told you that my father is a gentleman. Even now you must be able to tell what sort of man Mr Dixon was. My father knew at once, without even meeting him.

The weeks had passed and Olive told me that Mr Dixon's business was completed but that his vacation was coming and he planned to spend it in Conkling. She said she would tell my father. We were sitting on the porch after dinner. The evening had just begun to thicken and some children had wandered down the road, playing a game of pirates at the very edge of our lawn. One of them had a long paper sword and the others were waving tall sticks, and they were screaming. My father had to raise his voice to be heard.

'So this man whom you have been seeing behind my back is a travelling salesman for Miracle-wear soles.'

'*Surrender in the name of the King.*'

'I am more than surprised at you, Olive. That hardly sounds like the kind of man you would want to be associated with.'

'Why not?' said Olive. 'Why not?'

'It's notorious, my dear. Men like that have no respect for a girl. They'll flatter her with slick words but it doesn't mean anything. Just take my word for it, dear. It may seem hard, but I know the world.'

'*Fight to the death! Fight to the death!*'

'I can't hear you, my dear. Sarah Ann, ask those children to play their games somewhere else.'

I went down the steps and across the lawn.

'Dr Landis is trying to rest after a long day,' I explained. They nodded and vanished down the dusky road, brandishing their silent swords.

'I am saying nothing of the extraordinary manner of your meeting, not even of the deceitful way in which he has carried on this – friendship.'

It was dark on the porch. I switched on the yellow overhead light, and the three of us blinked for a moment, rediscovering each other as the shadows leaped back.

'The cheapness of it is so apparent it amazes me that even in your innocence of the world –'

My father was fitting a cigarette into its black holder. He turned it slowly to and fro until it was firm before he struck a match and lit it. It is beautiful to watch him do even the most trivial things. He is always in control of himself and he never makes a useless gesture or thinks a useless thought. If you met him you might believe at first that he was totally relaxed, but because I have lived with him so long I know that there is at all times a tension controlling his body; you can feel it

124

when you touch his hand. Tension, I think, is the wrong word. It is rather a self-awareness, as though not a muscle contracted without his conscious knowledge.

'You know it very well yourself, Olive. Could anything but shame have kept you from bringing this man to your home?'

His voice is like the way he moves. It is clear and considered and each word exists by itself. However common it may be, when he speaks it, it has become his, it has dignity because he has chosen it.

'Father, all I ask is that you'll have him here – that you will meet him. Surely that's not too much to ask before you – judge him.'

Olive sat on the step at my father's feet. Her hands had been moving across her skirt, smoothing the folds over her knees, but when she spoke she clasped them tightly in her lap. She was trying to speak as he spoke, in that calm, certain voice, but it was a poor imitation.

'I'm afraid that it is too much to ask, Olive. I have seen too many of his kind to take any interest in seeing another.'

'I think you should see him, Father.' She spoke very softly. 'I think I am in love with him.'

'Olive!' I said. I had known it all along, of course, but when she spoke it, in that voice trying so childishly to sound sure, I knew its absurdity. How could she say it after Father had made it so clear? As soon as he had repeated after her, 'A salesman for Miracle-wear soles,' even the inflections of his voice showed me that it was ludicrous; I realized what I had known all along, the cheapness of it all for Olive – for Olive with her ideals.

I looked across at my father but he had not stirred. The moths brushed their wings against the light bulb. He flicked a long grey ash.

'Don't use that word lightly, Olive,' he said. 'That is a sacred word. Love is the word for what I felt for your mother – what I hope you feel for me and for your sister. You mustn't confuse it with innocent infatuation.'

'But I do love him – how can you know? How can you know anything about it? I do love him.' Her voice was shrill and not pleasant.

'Olive,' said my father. 'I must ask you not to use that word.'

She sat looking up at his face and from his chair he looked back at her. Then she rose and went into the house. He did not follow her, even with his eyes. We sat for a long time before I went over to him and took his hand. I think he had forgotten me. He started and said nothing and his hand did not acknowledge mine. I would rather he had slapped me. I left him and went into the house.

In our bedroom Olive was sitting before the dressing-table in her nightgown, brushing her hair. You mustn't think I don't love her, that I didn't love her then. As I say, we were like twins, and when I saw her reflection in the tall, gilded mirror I might have been seeing my own eyes filled with tears. I tell you, I wanted to put my arms around her, but you must see that it was for her own sake that I didn't. She had done wrong, she had deceived my father and she had made me deceive him. It would have been wicked to give her sympathy then.

'It's hard, of course, Olive,' I said gently. 'But you know that Father's right.'

She didn't answer. She brushed her hair in long strokes and it rose on the air. She did not turn even when the doorknob rattled and my father stood in the doorway and quietly spoke her name.

'Olive,' he repeated. 'Of course I must ask you not to see this – this man again.'

Olive turned suddenly with her dark hair whirling about her head. She hurled the silver hairbrush at my father, and in that single moment when it leaped from her hand I felt an elation I have never known before. Then I heard it clatter to the floor a few feet from where he stood, and I knew that he was unhurt and that it was I, and not Olive, who had for that single moment meant it to strike him. I longed to throw my arms about him and beg his forgiveness.

He went over and picked up the brush and gave it to Olive. Then he left the room.

'How could you, Olive?' I whispered.

She sat with the brush in her hand. Her hair had fallen all about her face and her eyes were dark and bright. The next morning at breakfast she did not speak to my father and he did not speak to her, although he sat looking at her so intensely that if I had been Olive I would have blushed. I thought, He loves her more now, this morning, than when he used to smile and say she was like Mother. I remember thinking, Why couldn't he love me like that? I would never hurt him.

126

Just before she left for work he went over to her and brushed her arm lightly with his hand.

'We'll talk it all over tonight, Olive,' he said. 'I know you will understand that this is best.'

She looked down at his hand as though it were a strange animal and shook her head and hurried down the steps.

That night she called from a little town outside Richmond to say that she was married. I stood behind my father in the shadowy little hallway as he spoke to her. I could hear her voice, higher-pitched than usual over the static of the wires, and I heard her say that they would come, that very evening, if he would see them.

I almost thought he hadn't understood her, his voice was so calm.

'I suppose you want my blessings. I cannot give them to deceit and cowardice. You will have to find them elsewhere if you can, my dear. If you can.'

After he had replaced the receiver he still stood before the mouthpiece, talking into it.

'That she would give up all she has had – that she would stoop to a – for a – physical attraction –'

Then he turned to me. His eyes were dark.

'Why are you crying?' he said suddenly. 'What are you crying for? She's made her choice. Am I crying? Do you think I would want to see her – now? If she – when she comes to see what she has done – but it's not a question of forgiveness. Even then it wouldn't be the same. She has made her choice.'

He stood looking at me and I thought at first that what he saw was distasteful to him, but his voice was gentle when he spoke.

'Would you have done this to me, Sarah Ann? Would you have done it?'

'No,' I said, and I was almost joyful, knowing it was true. 'Oh, no.'

That was a year ago. We never speak of Olive any more. At first letters used to come from her, long letters from New York and then from Chicago. Always she asked me about Father and whether he would read a letter if she wrote one. I wrote her long letters back and said that I would talk to him. But he wasn't well – even now he has to stay in bed for days at a time – and I knew that he didn't want to hear her name.

One morning he came into my room while I was writing to her. He saw me thrust the package of letters into a cubbyhole and I knew I had betrayed him again.

'Don't ally yourself with deception, Sarah Ann,' he said quietly. 'You did that once and you see what came of it.'

'But if she writes to me –' I said. 'What do you want me to do?'

He stood in the doorway in his long bathrobe. He had been in bed and his hair was slightly awry from the pillows and his face was a little pale. I have taken good care of him and he still looks young – not more than forty – but his cheekbones worry me. They are sharp and white.

'I want you to give me her letters,' he said. 'To burn.'

'Won't you read them, Father? I know that what she did was wrong, but she sounds happy –'

I don't know what made me say that except that, you see, I did love Olive.

He stared at me and came into the room

'And you believe her? Do you think that happiness can come from deception?'

'But she's my sister,' I said, and although I knew that he was right I began to cry. 'And she's your daughter. And you love her so.'

He came and stood beside my chair. This time he didn't ask me why I was crying.

'We'll keep each other company, Sarah Ann, just the two of us. We can be happy that way, can't we? We'll always have each other, don't you know?' He put his hand on my hair.

I knew then that was the way it should be. I leaned my head on his shoulder, and when I had finished crying I smiled at him and gave him Olive's letters.

'You take them,' I said. 'I can't –'

He nodded and took them and then took my hand.

I know that when he took them he meant to burn them. I found them by chance yesterday in the back of his desk drawer, under a pile of old medical reports. They lay there like love letters from someone who had died or moved away. They were tied in a slim green hair ribbon – it was one of mine, but I suppose he had found it and thought it was Olive's.

I didn't wonder what to do. It wasn't fair, don't you see? He hadn't any right to keep those letters after he told me I was the only daughter he had left. He would always be secretly reading them and fingering them, and it wouldn't do him any good. I took them to the incinerator in the back yard and burned them carefully, one by one. His bed is by the window and I know that he was watching me, but of course he couldn't say anything.

Maybe you feel sorry for Father, maybe you think I was cruel. But I did it for his sake and I don't care what you think because you're all of you strangers, anyway, and you can't understand that there couldn't be two of us. As I said before, I don't hate Olive. But sometimes I think this is the way it was meant to be. First Mother died and left just the two of us to take care of Father. And yesterday when I burned Olive's letters I thought, Now there is only me.

Elizabeth Jolley

Five Acre Virgin

'There's a five acre virgin for sale.' Mother scooped up her avocado pear and drank her cocoa quickly. She pushed the country towns and properties into her shopping bag. 'We'll have a look later,' she said. 'Might be just right for Mr Hodgetts.' She looked at the clock. 'We'll have to hurry if we're going to get all the rooms done today.' Some days I helped Mother like today when I had a half day from the toy shop where she had got me this little job to keep me occupied, as she said, during the long summer holidays. I was screaming mad in that shop, it was so quiet in there. Like yesterday I only had two people in all day, just two little boys who looked at everything, opened all the boxes and took things off the shelves, spilled all the marbles and kept asking me, 'What's this?' and 'How much is this?' And then in the end they just bought themselves a plastic dagger each. I preferred to go with Mother on her cleaning jobs. She had all these luxury apartments in South Heights to do. We got a taste of the pleasures of the rich there and it had the advantage that Mother could let people from down our street in at times to enjoy some of the things which rich people take for granted like rubbish chutes and so much hot water that you could have showers and do all your washing and wash your hair every day if you wanted to. Old Mrs Myer was always first in to Baldpate's penthouse to soak her poor painful feet.

Just now Mother was terribly concerned over Mr Hodgetts our lodger. He was a surgeon in the City and District Hospital; he worked such long and odd hours Mother felt sure a piece of land was what he needed to relax him.

'He don't get no pleasure poor man,' Mother said. 'There's nothing like having a piece of land to conquer,' she said. 'It makes a man feel better to clear the scrub and have a good burning off.' All doctors had

130

yachts or horses or farms and it would be quite fitting for Mr Hodgetts to have some acres of his own.

Mr Hodgetts never stopped working. He used to come home clomping his boots across the verandah. Mother said his firm heavy step was Authority walking. She said it was the measured tread of a clever man pondering over an appendix.

His room opened off the end of the verandah so we had to pass it going in and out of our own place. He needed privacy, Mother said, and she put a lace curtain over the glass part of the door and she got my brother to fix up a little plate with his name on. The plate had to be right at the bottom of the door as this was the only part they could make holes in for the screws.

'Who ever heard of a surgeon being a lodger,' my brother said.

'Well anyone might be a lodger temporarily,' Mother said. 'If the Queen came she'd have to stay somewhere till the council got a palace built for her.'

'Not in a crappy place like this.' My brother shoved at the window to open it and the whole thing fell into the yard.

'Well Mr Hodgetts hasn't said he's the Queen, has he.' Mother had to go out to get something for tea then. Thinking what to get Mr Hodgetts and my brother for their tea was a real worry.

'What about lamb's fry and bacon,' I said, but Mother said she thought she had better prepare something elegant like sardines. She was always on about the elegance of sardines and brown bread and butter.

'You'll be giving us celery and yogurt next!' My brother looked disgusted. 'You know I can't stand fish,' he said, 'and tell your surgeon he can take off his cycle clips in the house.' With that he slammed off out. Sometimes he was in a terrible mood, Mother said it was because he couldn't tolerate the false values of society and didn't know how to say so.

'I'll have to hurry,' Mother said. 'It's Mr Hodgetts' ear nose and throat clinic tonight.'

Mother always assisted Mr Hodgetts. He just presumed she would wash and iron his white coat and every night he stood with his arms out waiting for her to help him into it. The first time I saw them dressed in white with bits of cloth tied over their faces

I nearly died laughing. I had to lean against the door post it was killing me laughing so much. Mother gave me such a kind look.

'Just you sit down on that chair,' she said to me, 'and you can be first in, Mr Hodgetts will see you first.'

'But I don't want to see Doctor Hodgetts, there's nothing wrong with me.'

'It's *Mr* Hodgetts,' Mother said ever so gently. 'Surgeons is always Mr not Doctor.'

That shut me up I can tell you. So every Friday I had my throat examined and Mr Hodgetts sat there with a little mirror fixed to a band round his head. He peered into my ears too and made notes on a card. Mother fixed up his medical book between the cruet and the tomato sauce on the sideboard. The whole thing was covered with a cloth. Every day we had to bake cloths in the stove to make them sterile for Mr Hodgetts. And Mother made and changed appointments for the people down our street in the back of my old home science notebook.

When Mr Hodgetts went on the night shift Mother took the opportunity to suggest we go to have a look at the five acres.

'We can go on the eight o'clock bus,' she said to him, 'and come back on the one o'clock and you can have time for your sleep after that. We could have a nice outing and take Mrs Myer, it's been a while since she was taken anywhere.'

Mr Hodgetts pondered and then said, 'That's right. The lists don't start till 8.00 p.m.'

'The list', Mother explained to us, was the operations.

'Who ever heard of operations being done all night,' my brother was scornful. 'And they don't wear boiler suits in the operating theatre and who ever heard of a surgeon having his own vacuum polisher and taking it on the bus.'

'Well he can't take it on his bike can he,' Mother said.

It was true the wash line was heavy with grey boiler suits; every day Mother had this big wash, white coat and all.

'Just you hush!' Mother said as I was about to ask her something. 'And you mind what you're saying!' she said to my brother. Mr Hodgetts was clomping through the verandah.

'Oh!' I said very loud. 'I could have sworn I saw a cat hunched on the window.' Of course there was no cat there, I said it so Mr Hodgetts wouldn't think we were discussing him.

'Oh that's nothing,' Mother said, 'your Aunty Shovell once saw a black umbrella walk right round the room of itself.'

Just then there was a knock on the kitchen door and who should come in but our Aunty Shovell.

'Oh!' Mother had to sit down. 'Talk of angels!' she said white as a sheet. 'We just this minute said your name and you walk in through that door!'

'Nothing I wouldn't say about myself I hope.' Aunty Shovell dropped her parcels, lemons rolled from her full shopping bag, and she sank, out of breath, on to the kitchen chair. 'Got a kiss for me then?' My brother obediently gave her a little kiss and Aunty Shovell smiled at him lovingly. She had a special place in her heart for my brother, she always said. She even carried a photo of him as a little boy in her handbag. Mother would never look at it. She said there was too much shy hope and tenderness and expectation in his face.

'Who's our gentleman?' Aunty Shovell indicated the verandah with a toss of her head. The firm footstep was on its way back from the wash house.

'Anyways,' she said before Mother could explain, 'a man who walks like that could never be a thief.' She settled herself comfortably and didn't make any attempt to leave till she got Mother to ask her to tea the next day.

In the morning we nearly missed our bus, as my brother wouldn't get out of bed and Mr Hodgetts took so long writing up his kidneys and then old Mrs Myer was late too.

Mother was half under the bus.

'I think there's a big nail drove right into your tyre,' she called up to the impatient driver. 'You better come down and have a look.' Mrs Myer was waddling up the street as fast as she could. Everyone just made it into the front seats of the bus by the time the driver had climbed down and been under to check the tyre which seemed to be all right after all.

We found the piece of land but Mr Hodgetts did not seem very impressed.

'Look here's a few fencing posts, probably thrown in with the price.' Mother pointed out the advantages. 'And over there there's a little flat part where you could put your shed and I'm sure these rocks could be useful for something.' Her face was all flushed from the fresh air and her nose had gone red the way it does if she's excited about things.

'There's no money in wool,' Mr Hodgetts said slowly.

Mother agreed. 'Too right! There's nothing in wool these days and, in any case, if you put sheep here they'd break their necks in no time,' she said. 'And there's nothing for them to eat.'

It was a terrible piece of land, even if it was virgin. There was no shade and it was so steep we had to leave Mrs Myer at the bottom.

'Oh it's so fragrant!' Mother said. 'You know, land isn't just for sheep. It's for people to enjoy themselves.' She waved her arms. 'I'm sure there are masses of flowers here in the spring, you must agree it's a wonderful spot!'

Mr Hodgetts stroked his chin thoughtfully.

'I feel this land is very strong,' Mother urged, 'and what's more it's only two hundred dollars deposit.'

'Why pay two hundred dollars to kill yourself,' my brother said, 'when you could do it for nothing,' and he pretended to slip and fall down the steep rock.

'Halp! I'm falling!' he called and his thin white fingers clutched at the fragments of scrub. 'Halp!' His long thin body struggled on the rock face as he went on falling. He put on his idiot's face with his eyes up so only the whites showed. 'Haaalp!'

'Oh Donald be careful!' Mother called. As he fell and rolled we had to see the funny side and we both roared our heads off while Mr Hodgetts stood there in his good clothes and boots.

Suddenly we saw smoke curling up from below.

'Quick!' Mother cried. 'There's a fire down there, Mrs Myer will get burned to death!' She began to scramble down. 'Fire always goes uphill,' she said. 'Hurry! Hurry! We must stop it! Don't be afraid, there's my good girl!' she said to me and we got down that hill much faster than we got up it.

'I am josst boilink my kettle,' Mrs Myer explained from the middle of her fire. 'I sought ve vould all hev tea. I bring everylink in my begs,' she said. 'My leetle cookink is surprise for you!' I don't think I have ever seen Mrs Myer look so happy. My brother was already stamping out the little runs of flame and the rest of us quickly did the same while Mrs Myer busied herself with her teapot.

Mother had a lot on her mind on the way home. It was clear Mr Hodgetts had no feeling for the land.

'And another thing,' she said to me in a low voice. 'There isn't a soul for his outpatients clinic tonight. The street's all been. Wherever am I going to find someone else to come.' She seemed so tired and disappointed. And of course she would have extra to do at South Heights to make up for not being there today.

'What about Aunt Shovell?' I said. 'She's never been examined.' Mother shook her head.

'Shovell's never believed in doctors,' she said. And another burden settled on her. 'Whatever shall I get for *her* tea tonight?'

All through the meal Mr Hodgetts never took his eyes off Aunt Shovell. Mother had asked him into the kitchen as it seemed a shame for him to eat off his tray all alone.

'Mr Hodgetts, this is my sister Miss Shovell Hurst, Shovell this is Mr Hodgetts who lodges with us.'

'Pleased to meet you Cheryl.' Mr Hodgetts leaned over the table and shook hands and after that it was all Cheryl. He kept getting up to pass her the plate of brown bread and butter. He kept telling her things too, starting every remark with, 'Cheryl, I must tell you,' and 'Cheryl, have you heard this . . .' And then he asked her a riddle. 'Cheryl, what lies at the bottom of the ocean and shivers?'

'Oh,' she said, 'now let me see, what lies at the bottom of the ocean and shivers? I give up!'

'A nervous wreck.' Mr Hodgetts laughed his head off nearly, so did Aunt Shovell. And then she said, 'Pass your cup, I'll read your tea leaves and tell your fortune,' so we all listened while Aunt Shovell predicted a long life of prosperity and happiness for Mr Hodgetts.

'Romance is to be yours,' she said leaning right across the table. 'Miss Right is nearer to you than you think!' Mr Hodgetts sat there amazed.

'Is that so, Cheryl,' he said. 'Well I never,' and after tea he asked her if he could take her home before going to his own job.

'We never had the clinic,' I said to Mother when Mr Hodgetts had left for the hospital, walking Aunty Shovell to her bus on the way to his. 'Mr Hodgetts forgot about his clinic.'

'Never mind!' Mother said.

135

'I never knew Aunty Shovell's name was Cheryl.'

'Yes Shovell, like I said, Shovell,' Mother said.

'Is Aunty Shovell a virgin then?' I asked.

'Nice girls don't ask things like that,' Mother said.

'There's pretty near five acres of her whatever she is,' my brother said.

I thought Mother would go for him for saying that but she only asked him, 'Is my nose red?' as if he cared.

'Just a bit,' he said.

'I expect it's the fresh air,' Mother said and she began to sing,

'How do you feel when you marry your ideal . . .

it's a popular song from my youth,' she explained.

'How do you feel when you marry your ideal,
ever so goosey goosey goosey goosey,'

and she laughed so much we thought she must be really round the bend this time.

Merle Collins

~

My Sister Cherish

Whenever I think of my sister Cherish, I remember the bird. I saw it on the window-sill of the room a few days after she died. Or was it the day after she died? I was going into the room to get something. I don't remember what. But then I saw the bird, and backed towards the door. A white, long-legged bird, just standing there picking something off the window-sill. Or was it looking towards the bed where Cherish used to lie, looking at the window sometimes and laughing? The bird lifted its head towards the room. I watched it, and backed towards the kitchen. For the rest of that day, I kept as close to my mother as I could, but at fourteen it is not easy to find a reason to be always standing close to one's mother, so I tried to keep her in sight as much as possible. I sat in the dining-room and watched her working in the kitchen. When she hummed or sang, I closed my eyes a little. I stood at the window and watched her when she went to hang the kitchen towels on the line. Perhaps it was partly because it was Sunday that I felt like that, because Sunday was a logical sort of day for spirits to visit. For the whole of that day, the leaves of the trees seemed greener, the breeze blew more gently than usual; even the sun was softer. There was so much tenderness and uncertainty and fear around that even when my brother tried to start a quarrel, I just looked at him and smiled. Mom stopped her humming then and stared at me.

'What wrong with you today? Jumbie* got you tongue?'

'Don' say dat, non.'

My mother looked at me, the frown on her forehead reflecting my own. I knew she was watching the light fold of my bottom lip where the lower teeth were worrying the inside of my mouth. She laughed.

* Spirit.

137

My mother always did things like that, laughed when someone else was looking really serious about something and she couldn't quite figure out what there was to be so serious about.

'So is true, then? Jumbie have you tongue in truth?' She giggled.

I didn't answer, and my mother went back to her humming of 'How Great Thou Art'. It annoyed me, usually, this Sunday hymn-singing, or hymn-humming, really, since my mother often didn't know the words. She would sing out loud:

O Lord my God
When I in awesome wonder
Consider a-a-all
The things that thou hast made

And then would come a humming of this same tune again. Afterwards she would hold her head up high and look out of the window – it seemed that she was always near to a window for this part of the song – and sing out loud again, looking at the blue sky with the flecks of white clouds skidding across:

How great thou a-a-art

and then some more humming, followed by the slow, climactic

HOW GREAT THOU ART!

My mother would stand for a while after this, wringing the towel or wiping her hands or something and just looking out at the sky and the palm tree quiet in the distance. Then she would turn away to do something else in the kitchen, starting to hum again.

That Sunday the singing didn't annoy me. I just listened and felt kind of sad. It wasn't that I was afraid, really. Well, yes it was, in a way, because I tried not to remember what Cherish's face was like as she lay there on the bed day after day. And I looked behind me often. And I looked around the yard to see what sort of birds were there. But . . .

'Mammie, I saw a bird on the window in your room this morning.'

My mother looked at me and waited. When I said nothing further, she frowned, and her mouth opened slightly. I wanted to giggle then, because I could see that she was beginning to wonder if I was

138

going mad. Although I wanted to laugh, I knew it was something that worried my mother every so often. Some time, far back in the family, she had a great-great-grandparent who had gone mad because of worries. My mother was always afraid that this madness would suddenly appear again and claim someone who was having worries. I knew, because she had told me the story, and sometimes when things started to bother her, she would suddenly say, 'Anyway let me don't take on that, eh! We not a family with strong head.' This always sounded strange, because it seemed to me that my mother had the strongest head I knew. I think she worried more about me than anything. Sometimes, if we had just heard about someone who was ill, or sick, and I asked lots of questions about it, she would sound annoyed. Then soon afterwards she would say, 'Take that look outa you eye. Why you stand up there lookin like you in wonderland, so? I tell you already you don't have to take the troubles of the world put on you shoulders. Fix you face, girl!' I didn't say anything more now. I just waited. I knew that my mother would speak again.

'So?'

'It was a white bird, the ones with long, long legs.'

'Galain?'

'I dunno.'

'So what happen if a bird on the window in my room? You know somebody buy spot there?'

'It was a white, white bird, you know, and sometimes when people die . . .'

My mother chuckled. 'So you think might have been Cherish?'

I didn't really know what I thought, so I just stood biting my lip. My mother sat down in the living-room and hummed for a while again, as though she had forgotten about me. This time she was humming 'Jesus Gentlest Saviour'. Then the humming stopped. I watched her turning the pages of her hymn book. She lifted a hand and pushed the glasses further up her nose.

'So that is why you wouldn't go in the room all day?'

I frowned.

'For a person who grow up going to church every Sunday, you really superstitious.'

I just steupsed.

'Who you steupsing for? Don' make me give you one box, eh!'

139

I didn't say anything, and Mammie stopped looking fierce. She leaned back in the rocking chair and rubbed her feet together.

'But you know, if is you sister spirit, which I doubt,' she chuckled, 'you have nothing to fear. It wouldn't do you anything but good. She gone to the angels for sure. Never do a thing to hurt anybody in her life. For sure she gone to the angels. Spirit like that is good spirit.'

'Don' talk about that, non!'

'So is me that bring up the conversation, then? Girl behave yourself, eh!' My mother sucked her teeth and went back to her humming.

Later that evening, I heard her whispering to herself in the kitchen, 'Gone to the angels for sure, God rest her soul.' And then I heard her telling Daddy, 'You daughter think she see her sister spirit on the window in the room.'

Daddy gave an uncertain half-laugh at first. 'Why? What? What she see?'

'A bird.'

'A bird?'

'Yes. She see a white bird on the window. For the whole day she won't go in the room, and then just afterwards she come telling me about this bird.'

Daddy chuckled then, the laugh starting deep inside his throat. But I knew from the way he answered at first that he was wondering if I had seen Cherish for real. It sort of made me more frightened, because it meant that my father wasn't so sure that there weren't spirits. Besides, there were times when Mammie would say, 'Ah chuts,' when we talked about someone who had seen a spirit, and Daddy would look as if he agreed with her. But soon afterwards he would start a spirit story beginning, 'But in spite of that, there are things you can't explain, you know. Like I remember one time, eh ...' And Mammie would suck her teeth and say, 'Umm, now heself, he see spirit too.' But now they were laughing at me, so I tiptoed from the step for them not to see me out there and know that I had heard. It would make them laugh even more.

My sister Cherish was six years old when she died, and for most of those six years I had only ever seen her leave the bed when our father carried her. Through Cherish, I came to know a side of my father that I never knew existed. Usually he was impatient with us children, my brother and me, and we were very quiet when he was around. He hardly ever spoke directly to us, except to quarrel about something, or to give an order.

My mother said that from the time that Cherish was born, there was something special between the two of them. He looked at her lying next to my mother and chuckled deep inside his throat. His face crinkled up and he smiled. She said that she remembered him saying something like, 'Poor little thing,' not because he thought she was sick or anything, but as if just watching her there all small and defenceless-looking made him go all tender and loving. And to think that he had wanted a boy!

My mother said that when Cherish was born, she was lighter-skinned than any of us had been. She was always very light-skinned compared to us, but Mammie said that was because she wasn't always out in the sunshine like we were. Daddy felt it was because she hadn't come to stay in this world, so that her face was always kind of transparent, as if you could almost see through it to the world that she had come from and was going to. My father was fanciful sometimes. My mother made a kind of sound in her throat and then said, 'Is only because the child was sick. That is all there is to it. Not enough sunshine.' Then after a while she said in a softer voice, 'But she wasn't for this world in truth, poor little thing.'

'Well,' said my aunt, 'if she wasn't for this world, she must be richer than us in fact.' She was silent for a while too, then she said, 'The Lord giveth and the Lord taketh away.'

'Amen,' my mother said.

My father grunted. Then after a while, as if he thought perhaps the Lord might be listening, he cleared his throat and said, 'Well, God knows best.'

My mother said that it was when Cherish was about three months old that she began to worry about her. When she held her up, the baby's head drooped to her shoulder, and she seemed to make no effort to lift it, like a baby normally would.

'Is like something wrong with her,' my mother said to my father. But he answered that perhaps she was just a bit slow, and everything would be all right.

After a while my mother began to worry more and she went with Cherish to the doctor. The doctor said not to worry too much. The head was a little heavy but she would grow it out. There was no need for concern. But Cherish's head kept on growing faster than her body. The body stayed thin and long and the head got bigger, and rounder, and almost transparent, and very soft. My mother cried often. And my father looked as if he wanted to cry, too, but really couldn't. They took Cherish to many different doctors. The doctors said they knew something was wrong, but couldn't say what. When Cherish was about eight months old, with a big round head and a long, thin, tiny body, one doctor said that she had water on the brain. My mother cried and prayed. Was there no cure for it? she wanted to know. No way of getting the water out? Was it something she had done while pregnant? Had the water got in because she was careless while bathing the child? The doctors said that she shouldn't blame herself, that it wasn't her fault, but they couldn't say whose fault it was.

And that was when my brother and I started to feel guilty. We had often been warned by our parents not to take the baby off the bed. At six and seven, they told us, we were too young to control the child's weight. We used to go often to watch her when she was in her cradle, lying there kicking her legs and laughing her toothless laugh at the ceiling. We liked best to watch her when it rained. As the rain pounded on the roof of the house, her tiny hands would go up, the right held slightly higher than the left; her right foot would be drawn close to her body, the left held higher and slightly more stretched, her fists tight as her eyes remained fixed on some spot beyond the range of our vision.

'She listening. She listening to the rain.'

'What happen, Cherish? You like it? You fraid?'

And as we touched her tiny fist to draw her attention, Cherish would laugh and move both feet and hands vigorously, laughing and laughing as if it were wonderful to be alive when it rained. She made us laugh, too, and when we were with her, my brother and I were always good friends. We found it most difficult to resist her when she lay on our parents' bed surrounded by pillows.

I don't remember what happened exactly, but I know that one day we tried to lift her. Perhaps we couldn't control her properly and her head drooped forward in a way it never did when our parents held her. Perhaps she cried. I don't remember. Yes, I think she started to cry and then when Mammie came running, me and Joseph said

142

that we were just there watching her and playing with her and then she started to cry. And when Mammie asked if we had touched her or done something wicked like pinch her or anything, we said, 'No, Mammie, in truth, we were just there playing with her and then she started to cry.'

And then after that all I know is that when Mammie started to wonder if she might be responsible for Cherish's head being that size, my brother and I had the same thought about ourselves, remembering the one time that we had done the forbidden thing and lifted our sister off the bed. She didn't seem sick then. Suppose we had started it all by lifting her? Suppose we had knocked her head too hard when we put her down, so that the soft centre had started to expand? We only whispered to each other about it once and then were too afraid to talk with each other about it afterwards. We used to stand at our parents' bedside and watch her, looking at the big eyes in the long thin face, making her laugh and wondering if we were responsible. Joseph didn't say anything, but I knew that he was always thinking the same thing as me about that, especially because sometimes when we were standing near to her bed and I looked at him, he would frown and suck his teeth as if he was telling me to behave myself.

After Cherish died, whenever there was something on the news or in the newspaper about someone who had committed a murder, my brother and I would never have anything to say about if the person should be punished or not, and how. We would avoid each other's eyes and I know that we were both thinking about our terrible secret. I don't remember if we ever told our mother. I don't remember, but I know that in spite of everything I still feel guilty sometimes. That's why I know how my mother felt when she wondered if she was responsible.

After a while, our sister's head was so heavy that only our father could lift her right off the bed. And he did it with a tenderness that made us feel like crying.

'Cher? All right. Yes. Yes. You laughing, eh? A'right, a'right! Oops! Daddy wouldn' hurt you, non. Eh, Cher? Ye-e-es! Good girl. Look how she laughin!'

We used to stand watching as Daddy lifted Cherish off the bed, helping him with our eyes, with our half-lifted hands, with our half-opened mouths, as if we would make it softer and easier for her just by watching. Cherish's small body would stiffen as he lifted her and her large eyes would wander to the roof and around the room, as if she was trying to figure out what was happening.

'You just going to the drawing-room to sit down for a while, eh? A'right? A'right, Cher?'

Her eyes would continue to look around vacantly, wondering, afraid, but still kind of secure because we were there. You ever see somebody eyes talk? Well it was just as if Cherish used to talk with her eyes. And I always used to think she felt kind of safe because we were there, especially after she had to leave us. At times, when there was no one in the room with her she would really scream, and then get quiet when someone went in and sat by her bed.

Daddy often sat with her in the drawing-room. Sometimes she sat propped up in a specially-made chair that they had bought her. I don't remember if they bought it at the store, or if it was the carpenter down the road that they got to make it, but in any case they bought this kind of reclining chair for her. Occasionally Daddy carried her outside and we all sat watching her as she sat in the chair on the grass. Cherish loved this. She would roll her eyes trying to see the blue distance of the sky and the trees and she would laugh and laugh. Watching her, we laughed too, just smiled and showed our teeth watching Cherish laugh.

Our mother tried everything that she knew and found out about a lot that she didn't know. When the doctors agreed that it was water on the brain and that there was nothing we could do about it but watch and pray, we all prayed, but I think our mother prayed the hardest. She looked for God all around her and when she didn't find the answer she wanted, it was as if she went into every little corner looking for God.

'Sometimes you can't find the reason in things,' she said, 'is God alone that know.' She said this often, and each time she looked up at the sky, or at the roof if she was inside, and opened out her hands with the palms up.

'Lord, you self know I always say I baptize in the Anglican church and I have nowhere else to go to because is the same God that everywhere, but any church at all that could do something for this my child, Lord, I will follow them to the end of my days.

Lord, if it be Thy will, Thy will be done. But please, Lord, cure my child.'

Miss Magdalene helped our mother to find one way to talk to God. Miss Magdalene started to come to us when Cherish was two years old. It was the year that our younger sister Hope was born. Now that I am talking about it, another thing that I remember is that my aunt Cleopatra didn't like that name, Hope.

'When for you to give the child a ordinary name like Mary or something, and make sure that she under the guidance of some saint, you calling her Hope. Is this new-fangled names and all these people that not thinking of the church that causing all the trouble. You was all right with the first two. Martha and Joseph is proper name. But with this last two I don't know what do you at all. How is Hope you go by now dey? And before that was Cherish. Who know if is that that do the child? What Cherish mean? Cherish!'

My mother was hurt. 'So you saying is me that responsible for how Cherish is today?'

'I not saying that. But who know how God does show his vexation?'

My mother didn't say anything for a while, which was unusual for her. And when I looked at her I could see that her eyes were full of tears. I looked at Aunty but she was watching something in the prayer book and her lips were moving and she didn't see the tears in my mother's eyes. Then all of a sudden Mammie got up and went outside to the kitchen for something. When she came back her eyes were dry and she said kind of quiet like, 'Is because of Cherish self I call this one Hope.'

My aunt didn't say anything and although I was afraid of God and wondered if he would do a thing like that in truth, I suddenly remembered hearing somebody say that she was not a real aunt, just someone my father's mother had taken to stay with them. And I was so vexed with her for doing that to our mother that I thought, that is why she could say that. Because Cherish not really related to her. Daddy wouldn't say that. Nobody else wouldn't say that. But then I thought it wasn't that alone, because I knew a lot of people not related to us who wouldn't say a thing like that and hurt my mother so. But after that I never felt good about my aunt. And I told my brother, and sometimes when nobody was around, we would tear a leaf out of my aunt's prayer book and leave it in there all rumpled. Or one day we hid her slippers. And sometimes when she called we just wouldn't answer. But the worst, worst thing we did and never admitted to was to push down the kind of wooden cross that used to hang on the door inside my aunt's room. We just meant for it to fall on the floor so that she would have to pick it up, but when it fell it broke and my brother and I had another secret that we couldn't tell anybody. And later on when my aunt was talking about the cross and saying that she didn't know how this cross could fall and break so, and that she thought she had felt the house shake a little bit during the day, so perhaps there had been a slight earthquake, we looked at the cross too and said, 'Oh, oh, but look what happen!'

My mother gave Hope two names. She called her Anne, so that she was christened Hope Anne Chandler. When all the rest of us called her Hope, my aunt Cleopatra always called her Anne.

But anyway, after Hope was born, Mammie was always tired. Cherish cried a lot in the night when she wet herself and couldn't turn or anything, or when she was tired of lying on one side and couldn't move herself. And now Hope started crying in the night too. So my mother was always getting up to see after both of them and in the morning she was really tired. My father got up once or twice, but he used to fret a lot, and sometimes after Cherish was crying for a long time, I would hear him through the partition from the room where me and my brother slept saying to my mother in the night, 'You don't hear the child crying, then?' Then my mother got up. Sometimes again she just sucked her teeth and said, 'You get up. Is you that could turn her properly.' And then my father would get up and go to Cherish. Then at times Hope woke up and started crying too.

In the morning my father would be muttering and saying, 'Well these children cry whole night, you know. I so tired, eh, they could well fire me from work today.' And he would leave in a really bad temper for his job driving the truck at the Public Works Department in St George's. And Mammie would be in a bad temper too if we didn't want to drink the cocoa or the soursop tea before we went to school.

Then one night after Cherish had really cried a lot, Daddy hired a car from town to come up and take her and Mammie to the doctor. It was a Saturday, when Daddy wasn't working, because by this time Mammie couldn't lift Cherish, and anyway the car couldn't drive right in. Daddy had to hold her up careful, careful and walk one today, one tomorrow, up the gap.

Aunty Cleopatra walked in front of him, backing back up the gap and saying, 'Put down you foot careful, now, it have a rough patch there,' and 'that is a big stone you puttin you foot on, eh, Joseph, and it kind of smooth. Go easy. Oops, watch it. Hold up, hold up. Go careful, now.'

And then when they had walked up the track to the road, Mammie was already sitting inside the car at the back so that she could help take some of the weight as Daddy sat down inside with Cherish, saying all the time, 'Cher, you all right? Um? Daddy wouldn't hurt you, non.'

Joseph and I stood with Aunty Cleopatra and watched them go, feeling as if it was a death or a real going away or something. The car drove off and Aunty Cleopatra said, 'You children go inside now. Go and find something to do. Martha, make some tea for the other little one. You, Joseph, sweep up the leaves from the breadfruit tree that falling in the yard there. Come on, come on. Find something to do.' She walked up the steps saying, 'Trust in the Lord for all.'

The doctor said that it had reached a stage when he didn't think they could take care of Cherish at home like that. He said that with Hope young too, it was really too much and the whole house could have a breakdown if they continued like that; he thought it was best if they put her into the children's home in St George's. There were nurses there, he said, trained to do that, and it would take the pressure off the family.

When they came back home, our mother cried. And Daddy kept saying, 'Take it easy, non. So you want to start the family breakdown he talk about then? Take it easy, non.' He looked irritated and spoke kind of vexed-like to Mammie, sucking his teeth and everything, but later I saw him in the room kneeling next to Cher's bed and his face was hidden down on the bed, and I don't know if he was crying or just praying, but I got frightened and I didn't wait to see.

I asked my mother what the doctor meant when he said that the whole family could have a breakdown.

'He means it's too much for us,' my mother said.

'Yes, but he mean the *whole* family could . . . could . . . ?'

My mother just said steupes, and turned away from me. I don't

147

think I really believed that we could all go mad in the family because of Cherish, but I kept remembering that long-ago relative, and how bad it was to take on worries, and I began to be very nervous everytime she cried, and I would pray every night for her not to wake up and cry. And when she did, I woke up and stayed awake too until Mammie and Daddy settled down again. I listened to what they said, too, just to see if there were signs of a breakdown. It was after the visit to the doctor that Daddy talked about Miss Magdalene.

He came home one day, on a Saturday when he had to do some extra work, and said that his friend Vernon's mother, Magdalene, wouldn't mind having a little something to do that could bring in a few extra cents. It was one December, I remember, just before Christmas. Peas was in season and he was sitting there eating his pea soup. It was late, about half past five, and me and Joseph were sitting at the dining-table too doing our homework. Aunty Cleopatra and Aunty Genevieve, who were staying with us for a time because they were looking for work in the area, were sitting outside under the julie mango tree counting some story. I couldn't hear what they were saying but I remember that through the window I could see Aunty Genevieve's hand go up to her mouth and her eyes open wide. You could imagine that she was saying something like, 'Eh, my sister, you ever see a thing like that?' I was just about to touch Joe's knee under the table to get him to look out of the window and see her too so that we could laugh together when Daddy brought up the subject of Miss Magdalene, saying that she was looking for work helping out somebody. I remember it as clear as ever. You know how some things just stay in your mind? Mammie was sitting there nursing Hope. And she said, 'Um-hm. So what you thinking?'

Daddy said, 'Well,' in that way that sounded like, 'It should be kind of obvious what I'm thinking.' And he moved his hand as if to brush away the flies, only there weren't any flies around at the time. 'If we could manage to take her on, she could help you out in the house here, help a little bit in the garden around, taking care of the tomatoes and lettuce and things that getting so overgrown now, help you with the cooking sometimes, and to take care of the children. You know what I mean, anything that need doing.'

Mammie finished nursing Hope and put her up against her shoulder to burp. 'That would be a godsend,' she said. 'But where we going to get the money to pay her?'

Daddy put down his spoon and chewed on the peas, twisting his mouth to get at the really good bits.

'Hm. That is a question.' He looked outside to where Aunty Genevieve and Aunty Cleopatra were sitting. 'That is a question. But,' he took up the beef bone and started sucking at it, 'we have to try. Apparently,' he paused and cleared his throat, 'she wouldn't want what those big people and so could pay, you know; she would be satisfied with a small payment and whatever little peas and provision and tomatoes and so she could get from the garden here. Because as they living right in the heart of town there, those things expensive, so that would help out well.'

'Well yes,' said my mother, 'if she would agree to something that you think you could pay, and she would take whatever we could produce in the garden here, that sound good.'

'That is what I saying.' Daddy pushed back his chair a little bit, turned sideways and crossed his legs. 'And,' he put his head back and looked up at the rafters, the bone in his hand there waiting until he was ready, 'it going be an easy arrangement, you know; I talk to her already; she know how thing is, and she say that if one week things really bad, as long as we give her something to get by, she wouldn't make a fuss.'

'Well yes,' Mammie laughed, sounding excited. 'Well yes. That sound like it could be a godsend in truth.'

Daddy started sucking at the bone again and I giggled. Mammie looked at me cross-eyed, thinking that I was listening to big people conversation and laughing, but I was really laughing at the way Joseph was watching Daddy's bone and chewing with him. I knocked his knee under the table and he frowned at me, pulled his lips together and said, 'Girl, behave yourself, non.'

Mammie stopped patting Hope's back for a moment and looked at the two of us and said, 'If you two can't behave, clear out!' Joseph muttered something and I stifled a giggle. He poked at my knee under the table and I would have knocked him down then and there, but I knew it would cause trouble, so I just waited to get at him later. Daddy put down the bone.

149

'I was thinking,' he said, 'that perhaps we could have asked Cleopatra, but . . .'

'Forget about that,' said Mammie. 'While she here and she could give a help, we thankful, but let her look for her work because we can't afford to pay her what she need to look after these dozen and one children that waiting on her to feed them.'

'Well, yes, that is what I been thinking.' He stretched his hands high above his head, letting the food go down. 'Hm! This Godfrey, eh! He don't even look back.'

'Well, forget bout he, because that is the livin dead. All the responsibility is on Cleopatra shoulders. And Genevieve self dey holdin on to this other one that you could take and tie a bundle of wood, he so lazy.'

Joseph and I giggled. Daddy chuckled. Mammie looked at us and said, 'The two of you siddown dey takin the words right out of me mouth, but leave it right where you hear it. I don't give you no message for nobody.'

'Ay! I doin my homework, yes.'

'Yes, because you homework is to stay with you bottom lip drooping and drink up every word I say. Clear out; go and make up a bed for Hope.'

'But, Mammie, I not finish . . .'

'Clear out, ka dammit, make up the bed and come back and finish you homework. You go and help her, Joey.'

'But Mammie . . .'

'Clear out, ka dammit.'

By the time we were finished with Hope's bed, the conversation was over. Miss Magdalene started coming to our house the Monday after that. She was really nice. She was old like, older than Mammie and Daddy and sort of like a grandmother, and really, really nice. She used to tell all sorts of stories, and lots of people in her family had seen spirits and things. And she loved Cherish. She would sit on a chair near to Cherish's bed and tell her all sorts of stories. And I'm sure Cherish understood. She laughed a lot, too, when the juicy parts of the story came along. And she would move her hands up and down, her eyes would roll around, and then she would be quiet again, just her eyes moving, and listening to Magdie's voice.

It was Hope who started to call her Magdie when she couldn't say her name properly and was trying to say Magdalene. Sometimes we called her Magdie, too, but most times we just said Miss Magdalene – Mammie, Daddy, all of us. I remember one day Joseph stayed outside by under the mango tree and shout out, 'Magdalene!' I don't know what get into him. It was such a shock. I was in the kitchen with Mammie, and is just as if she didn't hear. She was there grating some coconut to boil oil, and humming a tune; she just raised her head a little bit and then bend down again over the grater and continue humming. I said to myself, if was me, she woulda turn me face wrongside with a box.

Mammie finish grating the piece of coconut and long, long after, she call quiet-like, 'Joseph!'

'Yes, Mammie.'

I don't know how Joseph didn't guess something, because from the time Mammie say, 'Joseph,' I thinking, 'Eh-heh! Something in the mortar besides the pestle.' But Joseph must have been real bazodee* that day, because he come running from outside, making a sound with his mouth like a truck driving, and steering with his hands. He reach by the kitchen door, pull brakes, park the truck outside, and come inside.

'Yes, Mammie?'

Mammie was filling a cup with water from the pipe to pour it into the big bowl of coconut and she looked up at Joseph standing by the door, stopped the humming for a moment and said, 'Come.'

Perhaps Joseph thought it was to help her with the coconut or something, but he not usually so stupid; he went right up near to her, and she well take her time and catch him. She put down the cup in the sink, and turn around and hold his left hand hard. Is only then Joseph realize something wrong and he start to pull away. Is only then! Imagine that!

'Ay, Mammie, what happen?'

'Stop pulling, because you not stronger than me, Mister Man.' Mammie just stand up there looking at Joseph, and I don't believe she did mean to beat him. She just say, quiet-like, 'Now listen to me, and listen well.'

Joseph frowned. You could see the fear of a beating and the wonder

---

* Foolish.

about what wrong in his face, but me, right away I know. And I believe Joseph knew too, but he just pretending, because both of us know you can't speak to big people like that. But because Mammie take so long before she call him, he thought he did get away with it.

'Ay, Mammie.'

'Stop "Ay Mammie-ing" me, before I turn you face wrongside.'

I couldn't help it; I giggled, and then remembering myself, I put the towel that I was wiping the wares with to my face. Mammie watched me one cross-eye.

'The towel is for wiping the wares, not stuffing in you mouth.' I tried to disappear into the wall. I wanted her attention to stay with Joseph. She looked at him. 'So you and Miss Magdalene same age?' Joseph was silent.

'Answer me!'

'No, Mammie.'

'You is Miss Magdalene grandfather?'

'No, Mammie.'

'Somebody did call you to stand for her in church?'

I keep my face well straight, because I know that if I did so much as let it go, anything could happen. Joseph looked across at me under his eyes to see if I was laughing. But I just opened my eyes wide. I was standing too near to Mammie.

'I ask you a question, Joseph.'

'No, Mammie.'

'Well, gentleman! Next time I hear you calling her like a lord you will swallow you tongue, you hear me?'

'Yes, Mammie.'

'Miss Magdalene worth you grandmother. You ever hear me or you father shouting her out *Magdalene*, like a grandmaster?'

'No, Mammie.'

'Well, watch yourself. And when you boots get too big to fit inside here, build you own shack outside, you hear me?'

'Yes, Mammie.'

'Or else you will find that you might have to swallow me cuff whole.'

I had to bite the insides of my cheeks that time, otherwise I would surely have taken the licks for Joseph. And even so a kind of sound knocked at my throat. But Mammie didn't hear. She let Joseph go. But

152

he really had the Devil with him that day, because before he could even reach by the kitchen door, he mutter, 'But ain't Miss Magdalene is a servant?'

Mammie moved so fast that the plate I was just picking up to wipe drop on the floor and mash up. Joseph didn't stand a chance to reach the door. She practically dragged him inside the house with her. Well at last Joseph sense return and he pulling away and bawling.

'I sorry, Mammie. I didn't mean that, Mammie. I know Miss Magdalene is not a servant, Mammie. Woy! Woy! Don't beat me, Mammie. I fraid licks, Mammie.'

By the time I clear up the big pieces of plate from the floor and reach inside by the drawing-room door, Mammie had Daddy's leather belt in her hand, and Joseph was dancing all around her. She lifted her hand.

'Woy!'

'Now Miss Magdalene is not your servant!'

'I know, Mammie!'

'Not today!'

'Don't beat me, Mammie. You don't have to beat me, Mammie. I know that, Mammie.'

'Not yesterday!'

'Yes, Mammie; yes, Mammie. I understand, Mammie.'

'Not anytime in the future!'

'Oh gosh, Mammie, it burnin, Mammie.'

'Leave him now, Miss Chandler. He didn't mean anything. He never rude with me. He just a little bit fresh, that is all. Leave him now.'

'Is the freshness I trying to get out of him. If he fresh he in the wrong place, because thing that fresh down in the sea.'

'Mammie I not fresh again, in truth, Mammie!'

'And if is so you think you have to talk about servants,' Mammie pulled Joseph from where he was wrapping himself behind her back, 'I hope you never have none.'

'Mammie, it hurtin in truth, Mammie.'

'Shut up! You smellin yourself! Talking bout servant! Who is servant with you?'

Mammie let him go, and Joseph rushed to the door.

'Where you going? Come back and sit you tail right inside here, and understand that Miss Magdalene is a old woman with great-grandchildren older than you. Sit down there and think about that. And don't let me hear no noise from you.'

Joseph sobbed loudly.

'Swallow them! Swallow them, I say.' Mammie moved closer to him, and Joseph's sobs quietened. After Mammie went back to the kitchen, I went and sat near to him, but he pushed me away. For the rest of that day, Joseph was king. When Daddy came home, I heard him and Mammie talking quietly in the kitchen. Daddy chuckled.

'Well what happen to this child at all?'

'And I don't like to beat him, you know. But you think is licks self? He full up the house with bawling, but is you little thin belt I take and half of those lash fall on he clothes.'

'Eh-eh! So he want servant, yes?'

'Is like he feel he is man, you know.'

That night Mammie even called Joseph to help her in the kitchen, because she knew he liked to make saltfish souse. She let him cut up the tomatoes and onions and everything. And afterwards Mammie and Daddy talking about how the souse so nice. But it was just to make Joseph feel good, because the souse wasn't no nicer than usual. The whole time, though, Joseph only looked at the tablecloth. Even when Daddy leaned across and kind of laughed and touched him on the side of the head, he didn't say anything. Just pulled his head away and continue eating his souse.

Miss Magdalene stayed with us a long time. But then she started to get tired too, and she couldn't be there all the time. She helped Mammie a lot with Cherish, though, and you could see that Cherish liked her. Things were getting really difficult after a time, because Cherish was getting big and by the time she was five years old, the head was so big that Daddy couldn't even lift her from the bed comfortable again. He could do it in a way, but it was very awkward for him. And Cherish started getting sores, too. Mammie said that those on her bottom were because she was always wetting herself and we had to keep turning her.

Sometimes she would be crying so much that Mammie would say, 'But, sweetheart, I can't turn you anywhere else; is only two sides you have, and I just turn you from the other one. OK, love? All right?' But Cherish would go right on crying, because she was hurting. You see, she couldn't eat any solid food, so she was always drinking milk and water and juice and things like that, and sometimes before she well finish drinking, it would come right back out again.

When I think about it now, I feel really bad, because in the afternoon, after Miss Magdalene went home, when we had come back from school, we would pretend not to hear Mammie when she was calling us to help with Cherish. Sometimes we would be sitting right there on the step, and as soon as Cherish started to cry, we would sneak away, because Mammie might be preparing something for Hope, and we knew that she was going to call us. So we would run far away where she couldn't find us. And at times Hope would see us running and tell Mammie. But then she stopped, because after she did that, we wouldn't let her play with us at all for a long time. Hope was a real little newsmonger that time. She's still like that sometimes, but she's a little better now that she's getting older. She was almost four when Cherish died, and she will soon be five, so she has more sense now.

But anyway, with all the sores on her body, Cherish was crying a lot night and day. And Mammie and Daddy were always arguing. And sometimes it was Miss Magdalene that had to part them.

Once, when Cherish started getting sores on her head, they called the doctor to come and see her. He said it was because of the water inside, and because the head needed to be turned often, too, but it was so heavy. And besides, sometimes when Daddy was turning it, it was as if it hurt her, so she would cry. And once after Daddy turned her, I believe he hurt her neck, and she screamed so much that Daddy sat there next to her and started to cry. And Mammie went and touched him and said, 'Is all right, is not your fault, Joe.' Joseph had the same name as our father, and when Mammie talked like this it sounded as if it wasn't Joseph my father but Joseph my brother she was talking to. But it was really our father, because he was so sad for Cherish. 'Is not your fault, Joe. You couldn't help it. Is because the head heavy. Is not your fault.'

And sometimes both of them would turn her together, or me and Mammie would turn her. Mammie would put her hands under the head on one side, turn it, and then tell me to ease the other side a little bit, and together we would turn her on the other side. Sometimes Mammie and Joseph would turn her, or sometimes

Mammie and Miss Magdalene, but Joseph and I never turned her together or alone. And whenever someone was turning her, Hope would stand a little way off with her head to one side and say, 'Oh, oh! Careful, now! Careful!' She was really nice sometimes, only that she was such a little newsmonger.

Hope liked to sit down and talk to Cherish. Sometimes, she would take a book, push a chair near to the bed, climb up and sit there and pretend to read to her, saying things like

One little piggy went to market
And one little piggy stayed home
And one little piggy had roasted beef
And one little piggy had none.

When she couldn't say it properly, it sounded like 'Awn ittu piddy ent to market, and awn ittu piddy stayed ome.' We would walk into the room and the two of them would be there laughing away. But one day after Cherish screamed out, Mammie said she believed that Hope had pinched her, because we had seen her do it once. And that day when Mammie went in after the scream, she was just standing there with the end of her dress in her mouth, sucking it and looking at Cherish without saying anything. So after that, we closed the door so that Hope couldn't go in there alone until she was old enough to understand that she shouldn't pinch her.

We used to leave the windows wide open in Mammie and Daddy's room, where Cherish used to be, and tie up the curtains, so that she could see the trees all of the time. She liked that. When the wind blew a little bit and the trees rustled, she laughed out loud and made sounds in her throat; it was almost as if she was talking to the wind. Sometimes when we went into the room she would be there just looking at the open window and laughing. Then she would be quiet and listening, and start laughing all of a sudden, as though someone else had said something to amuse her.

Once Mammie and I went in together and stood up watching her. While she was listening, I said, 'Cher?' and she jumped and started to cry.

Mammie said, 'Sh-h-h! Don't interrupt her like that! Sh-h! All right, Cher!' And Mammie just put the net over her, because we used to cover her with a net sometimes, especially during fly season; then she put her finger to her mouth to make me keep quiet, and motioned me towards the door.

'How you mean don't interrupt her, Mammie?'

'She was conversing.'

'Conversing? With who?'

'With people that we can't see. She in another world.'

'Um.' I was annoyed.

My mother laughed. She knew that I got annoyed about things that I couldn't understand but which scared me a little.

'You frightened?'

I sucked my teeth. 'You self always saying it don't have spirits.'

'There are more things in heaven and earth than we could understand.'

I was not satisfied, but my mother started humming, and I couldn't think of a suitable question to interrupt her with. Not one that would make her stop humming. But sometimes I think that this is partly why I felt that way when I saw the bird.

One night, after Hope was ill, and Cherish was crying, and none of us slept much for the night, Miss Magdalene told our mother that she should buy a candle and give to her to put on the altar in the Catholic church.

They were talking just outside the kitchen door, the place where I always imagined a truck was parked, because that day after Joseph got his beating, he never went back for the truck he had parked there. Anyway, they stood there talking and I remained very quiet in the kitchen, because I knew that if Mammie remembered I was there, she would move away, or motion to Miss Magdalene to leave the conversation for later.

'Buy a candle?' my mother asked.

'Yes, things getting really bad now with the little one, and it wearing you out, so you have to ask for the Lord's help, child.'

'I praying night and day. God self know I always bend me knee in prayer for that little girl. I even send off to *Daily Word* to get people to pray in fellowship with me.'

'That good. That good, Miss Chandler. But prayers never too much. And in the Catholic church, the prayers there good, good. Dem is the best. They prayers really strong. Barring going and see those other people that you say you don't like to go to there, dem is the best.'

'You not talking about . . .' my mother paused and I thought perhaps she had remembered me, so I tiptoed and stooped down behind the big barrel where we collected water for in case there was none in the pipe. I don't know if she peeped inside of the kitchen, but as I strained to hear from behind the barrel, I heard her say in a low, low voice, 'You mean like obeah, Miss Magdalene?'

'No, no,' said Miss Magdalene. 'I not talking about anything like that at all. A lot of the big, big people who does go to church every day does put a candle in front of the saints to ask for a special favour sometimes. Is the same thing.'

'But . . .'

'Is the same thing, I telling you, Miss Chandler. Is nothing to fraid. Is the same thing that people does do from time. They say is a good thing to put a candle in front of St Anne, especially, and to say a prayer for whatever it is you want. And a really good thing to do, besides putting a candle in the side-aisle by where St Anne does be, is to give another candle to the priest special, so that he could put it on the altar during the Mass, and ask him to offer up special prayers for a something private for you. You don' even have to say what.'

'Well, yes, I will try that. Anything that could help, Miss Magdalene. Anything at all, yes, with this child that on me hand dey.'

'All right then! If you give me two candles end of the week, I will bring them in the church for you.'

'OK. I will take it in the message from the shop this week.'

I tiptoed from behind the barrel after that, and went inside, so I don't know what else went on, but I was really excited. It was a good secret. I didn't even tell Joseph, because it felt so important, having to do with God and everything. The candle must have gone in to the church that Sunday, and believe me eh, for the whole of the next week, Cherish was really quiet, laughing all the time, and we could sleep in peace. I even heard Daddy commenting about how she improve. I hear Mammie saying is a miracle, but I don't know if she told him that it was a miracle in truth, because although I listened a lot to what they were saying, I never heard anything. They probably said it when I wasn't around. Because Mammie was always looking at me as if she felt I listened to her conversations, and one day she even asked me if I wanted to rent a spot inside of her mouth. It was at the dining-table, and all of the

158

others laughed, even Hope, and Joseph too, although I cut my eyes at him.

And Daddy looked at me as if he thought I deserved that. And he said, 'I hope you give as much attention to your school work.'

So I said, 'I don't want spot inside nobody mouth!'

'What is that?'

'Nothing, Daddy!'

'It better be nothing!'

I tried to talk to Miss Magdalene about the church, too, but she just looked at me and said, 'I see why Miss Chandler does say that the walls in this house have long ears!'

After that good week, Cherish started to get sores and cry again. I wanted to advise Mammie to try the candle again, but I didn't have the courage. I don't know if she ever tried it another time, but Cherish kept getting worse and crying more.

Once, some preachers came to Grenada. Everybody said that they were very good. They were preachers from the United States of America, Born Again Christians, and they were good. They called on the Lord and did healing; the talk was that lots of people who were very ill had been healed. They even said that one woman who hadn't walked for years threw away her chair when the preacher prayed and laid his hands upon her. Aunty Genevieve said that she leapt to her feet, threw away her chair, and walked, testifying that she was healed. 'God be praised,' said Aunty Genevieve.

'You know, I going to that meeting tent in Queen's Park, yes,' my mother said one day.

'For truth?' Our aunt – Aunty Cleopatra, that is, because she was the one who was usually with us – she sounded surprised. 'You would go there?'

'Go, yes.' Miss Magdalene was certain. 'Go, Miss Chandler. I telling you, eh, anything that could work, anything at all, at all, try it, yes! Perhaps is only a miracle that could cure her. Who know what wrong with the child? An we shouldn' take away she chances. Go, you hear, Ma. And they say the man good, you know. Pastor Johnson. They say when you see he cast out the spirits so, the people just jumpin' on the stage and shouting for joy!'

'Well, nobody will shout for joy more than me if he make Cherish walk! This is one time the world will hear me testify!'

159

'You right, yes. Go an see what he could do for you!'

Our mother went. Daddy went, too. He and his friend, Miss Magdalene's son, were carrying Cherish on a kind of stretcher like, and walking slow. Mammie said that she walked right to the front of that huge crowd and they sat with Cherish in the front row. Cherish was almost five years old at that time. Whatever goodness was there, Mammie wanted our Cherish to get all of it. Pastor Johnson prayed. Pastor Johnson prayed for the entire congregation. Mammie shouted, 'Amen dear Jesus,' as loudly as anybody else, and placed her right hand on Cherish's head, all the while watching her face. I didn't go with them, but Miss Magdalene went, and she told me all about it afterwards. Mammie looked at Pastor Johnson's face. He prayed. He asked for those who wanted special prayers and Mammie's hand went up before anybody else could put up their hand. Pastor Johnson walked to the front row, and Miss Magdalene said he asked, 'Sister, the prayers are for this little one here?'

And Mammie said, 'Yes, Pastor.'

And then the Pastor asked, 'What seems to be the matter, sister?'

And Miss Magdalene said it was really funny, because Mammie said something like, 'The head is growing, Doc . . . er, Pastor.'

And Pastor Johnson took the mistake right up, and he kind of smiled and said, 'You're right, my sister. I am God's chosen doctor. Do you believe?'

Miss Magdalene is something else. When she telling me and Joseph the story, she say, 'Look eh, the pastor so good he say, "Doctor, priest, whatever you want to give me, me is that."'

And afterwards we heard Mammie telling Daddy that when the pastor asked about believing, she wanted to ask him, 'What? Believe what? That you are God's chosen doctor, or that my child would be healed? To tell you the truth,' said Mammie, 'I couldn't care less whether he think he is God's chosen doctor or the Devil incarnate, but at that moment if is belief that could heal my child, how ah don' believe dey! Nobody inside there believe more than me. I believe anything they want me to believe.'

And so she said, 'Yes, Pastor, I believe.'

Pastor Johnson held up his hand high and Miss Magdalene really jokey yes. She say that he almost go to meet his maker; he was stretching up so much on his toes. He punched the air with his

160

fist and shouted 'Praise the Lord,' and all of them kept watching Cherish's face to see if any change was happening.

And Pastor Johnson asked Mammie, 'What is your name, sister?'

'Marybelle.'

'And the little one?'

'Cherish.'

'Oh yes, my sister. She is God's cherished one, too.' All of them who went, Miss Magdalene, Mammie and Daddy, said that just that made them feel better about the preacher.

But Miss Magdalene was the best one. I wish I could tell you the story and act it out like her. She told us the whole preacher's prayer, and when Joseph asked, 'Is so he say it?' she stopped and said it slow like, in a deep voice, not to mock, you understand, but because she could see we wanted to get the feel of everything that happened. And although I'm not sure I remember it exactly, Magdie's prayer from the preacher went something like, 'Oh Lord our God, look down upon this your servant Cherish. Suffer this child of your suffering, this child for whom you gave your pure and gentle life, to come right to you in health and beauty, Lord.'

And then the congregation said, 'True, Lord. Amen, dear Jesus. Isn't it true, Lord! You self see, Lord! Oh, yes!' And Mammie, too, was saying things like, 'Yes, Lord; we will serve you always, Lord.'

Well, Miss Magdalene said so, and knowing how much Mammie wanted Cherish to be cured, I know it's true, but I really can't picture it. Not Mammie. It just goes to show. Miss Magdalene said that Daddy sat next to her looking at Cherish's face, too, screwing his lips to one side and occasionally clearing his throat. We know that this is true, because Daddy often looks like that when he is thinking hard. And Magdie said that sometimes he leaned forward a little to peep into Cherish's face, just to see what was happening. Miss Magdalene didn't tell us what she herself said, but I could imagine she must have been muttering prayers, too. Because she loved Cherish. Even me would have mutter some deep prayers if I was there.

And then when Pastor Johnson rested his hand on Cherish's head, Magdie said that our sister's body stiffened. Her eyes moved quickly around like she was wondering what was happening. And the little hands stretched out stiff and straight in front of her. Cherish began to fret. Cranking up to cry, as Mammie would say.

161

And then our Dad got all soft and tender, running his fingers along the top of her head. Magdie said that he was saying, gentle like, 'All right, eh, Cher. Is nothing. Is all right.' And Cherish kind of relaxed a little bit. And Daddy said, 'Cher?' and leaned over, so that she could see his face. And Cherish actually opened her mouth and laughed out loud. 'That child really like the father, you know,' Magdie said.

The pastor prayed some more. Magdie said that he talked about the leper woman and the hem of Jesus's garment. This was very sad, because it sounded like church, and Magdie lowered her voice when she got to this part, and we were very quiet. And the preacher prayed his main prayer, and I'm almost sure I remember it exactly as Magdie said it. 'Lord, let your healing come through my fingers. You who healed the leper woman when she touched but the hem of your garment, heal, I say heal! I say heal this your innocent servant, Lord. Let your healing truth pass through my fingers onto the suffering spot. In the name of God who can cast away devils, *be healed!*' And the congregation moaned and chanted. 'Oh Jesus!' And through the whole prayer Cherish's eyes were searching Daddy's face. And then at the end of the prayer, when the pastor's voice stopped, she laughed again.

Magdie said that the pastor was sweating by the time he was finished. And he told Mammie that she should watch Cherish for a few days and see the Lord's healing work. I didn't hear Daddy saying how he felt, but I heard Mammie telling him that she tried hard the whole time not to listen to the doubting Thomas from the Bible. I know that our mother really wanted to believe, because she was baptized that day. She showed us the certificate when she came home. It was printed in Tennessee, USA. Towards the top part of the certificate was a drawing of the kind of scene that in my schoolbook was called lush green valleys, on either side of a meandering stream of blue water. I remember that word well, 'meandering', because Miss made us spell it once. It had little light-blue markings at the top of the scene, like a sky that was coming and going. Then right around the edge of the certificate was a kind of green criss-cross line like a chain around the words. The words at the bottom of the lush green valleys said:

*

Baptismal Certificate

This certifies that
In obedience to the command and in imitation of the
example of our Lord Jesus Christ
Marybelle Chandler
was 'buried with Him in baptism' on the
1st day of *August 1960*
at *St George's Grenada.*

Our mother left the certificate on the dressing-table. For days we would go to stand looking at it, my brother and I, thinking of a new mother buried with the Lord in baptism. Then we would look at Cherish lying on the bed, her eyes circling the room, her mouth opening into a welcome smile if we went closer. We would stand there and push our finger into her tightened fist. Cherish would move her hands and make sounds of pleasure. And my brother and I would laugh and watch the head closely to see if it was getting any smaller.

One day I saw our mother standing and watching the head, too. One day she said she thought it looked as if the growing had stopped. We were sitting at the table eating then and my father grunted, but he didn't say anything.

'Ah well,' my mother said, 'thy will be done.'

And then one day, I don't remember how long it was after the healing at Queen's Park, the certificate disappeared from the top of the dressing-table. And my mother never talked again about the healing.

And then some time afterwards Miss Magdalene started having really bad arthritis, and for weeks she didn't come to our house. Both Aunty Genevieve and Aunty Cleopatra were working, too, and we hardly saw them. And most of Mammie's relatives were living far up in the country, and working too, so that that they didn't visit us much. And then one day Joseph surprised me. We were sitting under the mango tree. It was drizzling kind of light, but the sun was shining really hot, so the Devil and his wife must have been fighting like hell. Anyway, we were sitting outside there, and hoping no one would look outside and tell us to get out of the rain.

'Mammie don't have time to think about us,' said Joseph, 'she wondering if is to put Cherish in a hospital.'

'What *sut* you talking, boy?'

'You always know who talking *sut*.'

'But why you say that?'

'I talking *sut*.'

He wouldn't tell me now. And if I tried to fight him, it would be worse. I sucked my teeth and yawned. I looked up at the branches of the mango tree. A leaf fell. I stretched out my hand so that it would touch me as it fell. It did. I was really pleased.

'The leaf fall on me, yes. I getting a letter, boy.'

Joseph sucked his teeth. I stood up and stretched. 'Like the drizzle getting stronger. I better go inside.' Joseph stopped whittling at the mango stick and looked up at me.

'I hear Mammie and Daddy talking this afternoon when you went to tie the sheep under the house. When they went in town yesterday, they went to see the children's hospital. Mammie say the children well taken care of, and perhaps it's best to put Cherish there.'

'But they can't do that. How they could do that to Cherish?'

'Well somebody have to look after her, you know. And now that Mammie pregnant again . . .'

'Never!'

'Don't talk loud so, girl!' We both looked towards the house, but it seemed that no one had heard us. I stared at Joseph. 'Is Daddy I hear saying that while they talkin' today. Mammie pregnant, Miss Magdalene sick, Hope still small, and it just too much for Mammie.'

'But I didn't know Mom . . .'

'Since when you calling her Mom? Nowadays I only hearing you with this Mom, Mom. Since when?'

I didn't say anything. It was because some of the girls at school said Mummy, but that sounded too strange in my mouth, so I kind of dragged the Mammie into a sort of half-Mummy, and so sometimes I said Mommy or Mom. I wasn't going to explain that to Joseph, because I knew he would just look at me with scorn and suck his teeth. Joseph was like that sometimes. He didn't like to change things. So I just sucked my teeth.

'Well, Mammie, then. I . . . well, I just don't know what to say.'

164

'I bet you they tell us that they will do that. Watch you gon see.'

They told us about two days later, when we came home from school. And they took us to see the hospital. The children looked clean and nice. Two of them didn't have anything wrong with them. Just that there was no one to take care of them. This was strange, because there was always someone to take care of children, some relative somewhere, but these two little children didn't have anyone who wanted them. But they looked happy in the hospital, talking and laughing to the nurses, and helping to carry things. They were twins, about five or six years old, and they came to talk to us. They asked us if we were coming to live there too. Joseph and I just shook our heads. There were children who couldn't talk, too. And a little boy with no hands. But there wasn't anyone like Cherish there.

'You sure she will be all right, Mammie?'

'Yes. Two nurses came to see her yesterday, while youall were at school. They say she will be all right.'

Joseph and I didn't say anything. But perhaps Mammie could see that we wanted to cry.

'You children understand that Cherish getting too much for me? That I really can't take care of her at home anymore?' Mammie sounded as if she wanted to cry, too.

Then Daddy said, 'Cherish getting too much for your mother. She can't manage anymore on her own. You understand?'

'Yes, Daddy.'

Cherish went to the hospital in September. I don't remember what time in September, exactly. But I remember that it was September. Joseph and I went to see her three times, because we had to wait until Mammie or Daddy took the bus and went with us. Both of them went all the time, but Mammie went sometimes while we were at school.

What Joseph had said was true too. I only knew because one day a lady up the road asked me if I was glad that I was going to get a new little sister or brother. Fancy that! I don't know how I felt, just kind of strange, and I didn't even tell Joseph, or Mammie, and not Daddy of course. Daddy went sometimes to see Cherish during his lunch-break when he went to work.

The last time I went to see Cherish it was some time in October. She had sores, still, and her bed was wet, and she was crying. Mammie said she wasn't always like that. She reminded me that Cherish used to be like that at home sometimes, and said it didn't mean that they weren't taking care of her at the hospital. I remember Joseph started crying. He was just standing there and clenching his teeth and a sobbing sound was coming from his throat.

I tried to stop him, saying, 'Is all right, Joseph. She not seeing trouble.' I put my arm around his shoulder, and he just continued sobbing quietly, looking at Cherish and crying. 'Joseph, if you don't stop that, Mammie will start crying, too, you know. And you know you don't want that to happen.' But I was crying too, now, and I couldn't help it, and when I looked at Mammie her lips were trembling. And Daddy just turned and walked out of the room. And then Mammie changed Cherish. We stayed with her a while. Daddy came back into the room afterwards, and by the time we left it was a little better, because Cherish was laughing.

When we were going home on the bus, Joseph asked Mammie if children couldn't go and stay for a night, sometimes. Mammie said it was a good idea, and she would ask the nurse, so that when we got holiday from school, we could probably stay a night sometimes. I was proud of Joseph. I looked at him different after that, like a person with sense. I thought it was such a good idea. But it never happened.

One morning early, about six o'clock, a little boy came running into the yard while I was brushing my teeth to get ready for school. He came with a message from the man in the shop out the road. The hospital had telephoned them to ask them to get a message to us. Cherish was dead. She had died in her sleep the night before. Mammie and Daddy left right away for the hospital and we didn't go to school that day.

Mammie said afterwards that she didn't want to tell us children anything, but she could see Cherish slipping away. *I* hadn't wanted to say anything, but I had noticed something strange, too. Because the last time we visited, Cherish's eyes didn't look secure any more when we touched her, or when we made her laugh, or when they were just wandering around the room. I think that is why I cried so much. Because I could see that she missed us, and missed the window through which she could see the trees, and missed hearing Daddy's voice all the time, and missed us touching her.

Mammie said that Cherish was happier now. And in a way I

believed her. The day that Cherish died, I went into the room and looked at the bed where she used to lie down before, and I said 'Cherish. You all right, eh?' And I just felt that she was all right. And in a way I felt as if she was back with us again, and that was better than being in the hospital. Joseph looked at the bed, too. I know that he cried, but I think he felt better, too. All of us cried at home, quiet-like. I mean I saw everybody crying, except Daddy. I know for certain sure that he cry too, because of the way he was with Cherish, but when we were crying, he just blinked a lot, and cleared his throat, and then he walk away. Perhaps that is when he cried, when he went into the bathroom.

And Miss Magdalene came home and she cried, too. And Mammie's relatives came, and Aunty Genevieve and Aunty Cleopatra came. And Mammie's sisters, two in Brooklyn and one in London, sent telegrams. And Aunt Cleopatra said, 'The Lord giveth and the Lord taketh away.' And Aunty Magdalene said, 'Yes, this one is his angel for sure. Never did a bad thing in her life.' Daddy said, 'She wasn't for this world. I never see a prettier child.'

None of us cried at the funeral. You could see people looking at us and wondering why we didn't cry, and thinking perhaps that we didn't care about Cherish. But in a way I think we were all happy that she wasn't suffering now, and that she was back with us at home again. At least that is how I felt. The organ played for the funeral, and Mammie said that was really good, the choir members turn out well, because is not all funerals they play the organ for. It was beautiful. And the choir sang 'Suffer the Little Children to Come Unto Me'.

When I saw the bird that morning, I remembered all of that, so it must have been like the day after the funeral, and the funeral was two days after Cherish died. And you know, I believe that Cherish is somewhere; I believe that she is listening to all of this. And I'd better stop this story, because I've told you the main things that I wanted to say, how we loved Cherish, and that she is happy now. And I'm always afraid of thinking about things like spirits and so, but Mammie is right, if Cherish *is* really a spirit, then she is a good spirit, but still, I don't want to see her, because I can't handle the idea of seeing any spirit, good or bad. So let me cross my fingers and stop this story.

And make the sign of the cross.

167

Fiona Cooper

The Sisters Hood

Rose pushed the stained-glass door wide open and slid into the room with the confidence of a sacred cobra. By the time she reached the bar, a hundred eyes had clocked her, every mouth was busy with the legendary facts and exaggerated fiction of her life.

The Howling Wolf was a modern day temple for Sapphic acolytes. There was not a garland or flowing white robe in sight, still less a distant blur of peacock-wing ocean. The air was wreathed with cigarette smoke, the sacred libations came in pint glasses and coins and growling banter were exchanged at the beer-matted altar. Everyone knew everyone and no new face could slide into the leather-and-denim mêlée without causing a ripple of speculation.

Absence made the gossip grow wilder and Rose Hood had not been on the scene for six months or more, following the ritual breaking of hearts, heads and windows that marked the end of an affair.

Rose didn't walk, she coiled. Her cheeks were twin clouds of soft rose clay. Her smile was fangs flickering to hypnotize as her neck swayed side to side and her eyes took it all in, everything and everyone, wherever she went.

Her fingers were scaled in gold, glittering with diamonds side by side with glass cut to spark like diamonds. Sparkle and dazzle every time she flicked her dangerous pink nails to her lips with a puff of smoke. Her neck carried golden links fine as gossamer, as thick as the chain a high-class whore might clip to a lap-fed chihuahua. Gold dust weighted her eyelids, sweeping to spikes of jet. Her eyes were a fairy-tale green, one of them mottled with bronze. Her eyes were dangerous pools where many have drowned.

'Jesus CHRIST! What's that?' said Venus, her pint frozen in midair.

'Trouble with a friggin' great T,' said Mighty Mo, reaching her leather arm up to clasp Venus's neck in her rough and loving gauntlet of a hand. They'd been together for three and a half years and it was still a love thing.

'I mean, I don't fancy her or anything,' said Venus, coughing through the beer. 'I just wondered . . .'

'Every bastard fancies her. Except the bastards who've been there,' said Mighty Mo, winking. 'Am I right, Esky?'

'Whey aye, pet,' Esky snorted. 'Cruella de Ville. You can tell the poor bastards been through there. They're drinking halves and they count their change twice.'

'What does she do?' said Venus.

Mighty Mo and Eskimo Nell cackled.

'Oh, what does she not do?' said Esky. 'She's a professional cleaner.'

'And the rest!' said Venus, 'I've never seen a cleaner flash that much metal.'

'That one cleans out bank accounts,' said Esky. 'She gets you writing cheques, begging her to let you spend your money on her. She's clever.'

'Esky had a spell in the spider's web,' said Mighty Mo. 'Didn't you, pet? I told you, she'll take the skin off your back and you'll buy her the knife to do it with . . .'

'Aye,' said Esky. 'I'd have walked over coals for that one and thanked her for the blisters.'

'What did you call her? Cruella?'

'She was raven black when I knew her, with a great streak of silver. She only wore silver then. Looks like it's her Goldfinger period these days.'

'Her name's Rose. The Rose with many a thorn. I can't believe we came out of the same pod,' said Mighty Mo. 'Knowing my mother, she did, but the two of us never got in the same way.'

Venus stared at her, then at Rose, the only woman in the bar with space enough to lounge, the only one sipping clear ice-jagged liquid, the only one wearing a skirt.

'She's never your sister!'

'Aye, that's another skeleton in my cupboard, pet,' said Mighty Mo. 'We're not speaking, like, not after what she did to Esky. Blood runs thin in our family. Family!'

Rose leaned on the bar, tapping her cigarette, then steadying the offered flame with a half handclasp. Her lips curved upwards into a perfect wistful smile and her eyelids drooped a little.

'Thank you,' she said, breathing smoke towards the young stranger beside her, gawping in her squeaky clean leather jacket, fiddling with her otter-slick hair.

That come-to-bed *thank you* was enough to make her blush, she was tongue-tied. A light can be offered wordlessly, or with a grunt. But what do you say to such a vision? Do you come here often? I haven't seen you before. Have you got a girlfriend? Do you fancy me, cuz I fancy you. Can I take you home? I love you. Rose's opalescent lips held her speechless.

'Can I get you a drink, like?' she said.

Rose looked surprised and pleased. By, she hadn't lost her touch. Whatever it was, it had been with her since she was fourteen years old. For the last thirty years it was only at home alone that she'd ever lit her own cigarettes or poured her own drink.

'Vodka and tonic. Thank you,' she said. This one was wet behind the ears. She'd do for the moment. When she ordered a large vodka, Rose leaned a little towards her. She'd maybe even do for most of the evening. There'd be tears and trauma at bedtime, but what the hell, the night and the stuttering admirer were both young enough to play with.

'I'm Rose,' she said, and arched the bow-string of one eyebrow.

'I'm Peggy,' said the young woman, trying to hand her a drink, hold a cigarette and shake hands all at once.

'Poor lass,' said Mo from two tables away. 'She's hooked.'

'Just like that?' Venus said.

'Just like that,' said Mighty Mo. 'Some people have the decency to stick a maggot on their line, but my dear sister – my ex-sister – she's the type to throw a stick of dynamite in the river and all the little fishies come up blown to bits or gasping for more. I thought she was the world's greatest lover, you know, got an inferiority complex, me. I could wear my fists out on her, after what she did to Esky. The glamour's only skin-deep.'

'She doesn't like sex,' said Esky, shaking her head. 'She likes you to do her decorating, like. Diven't work yourself, Mo, it was my mistake. She's a friggin' great iceberg.'

170

'She's cold as a witch's tit and hard as the hobs of hell,' said Mo.

Although the words were a dismissive sneer, her eyes held a wisp of anxiety, like smoke caught in a breeze. She sighed.

'Well, she's good with her bairns,' said Esky. 'Come on Mo, you've not spoken for four years, since she dumped me, but you'd be right in there if anyone was picking on her. You know it. You're soft as clarts.'

'No more than you,' said Mo, indignant. This was the bar where you could swear right down you'd put any bastard's lights out: the bar was for swagger and bullshit and feeling big.

Rose and her bairns! Rose and her life! She had every reason to be a bastard. But. But she shouldn't have treated Esky that way: Esky was decent.

Mo looked over at her sister, charming the pants off Peggy: old enough to know better? Old enough not to give a sheep's fart for anyone's opinion, leave alone her little sister's cold-shouldered disapproval. And they'd been so close for so long. She'd been there almost every day when Rose was married. Rose had said, don't show me up, Mo, he's good to me. She'd just stared and said, well, is it what you want, like? Oh yes, said Rose, ooh yes, he's different. Well, Mo said, I promise I'll behave.

But her heart sank when she met Barry. He was flash and nervous and brash and cruel. Just like their stepfather only twenty years younger so that cruel came and went in flashes and nervous could pass for caring. Flash and brash looked like generous. Whatever had supplied Barry's gold chains and rolex and BMW and hand-made shoes and leather jackets had the exotic scent of Jack the Lad one step ahead and better keep on your toes. Rose was totally loyal to him, and Mo found herself being offered dodgy videos, hot stereos and rummage-sale priced designer jeans. Who in their right mind would say no? It was all new gear, not as if it belonged to real people, anyway.

In terms of villains, Barry was a little bigger than small time: he handled goods and every copper knew it, but he was eel-smart and alibi-ed up to his greedy blue eyes. The police turned Rose's flat over every month or so and found nothing. To tell the truth, Rose liked it, thumbing her nose at warrants and summonses, eating and drinking from bone china and crystal in dim-lit restaurants, fingering her jewels. Mo had never seen her so confident and happy. She turned down her blowtorch of disapproval: the bastard made Rose laugh after all.

Barry behaved himself until they were married. He took her to Tenerife for a honeymoon and she had twelve of their holiday snaps blown up and framed. She was radiant. Barry took the piss out of Mo for being gay, but he wasn't nasty. Mo dropped by a lot until one day when:

'What the hell have you done to your face, Rose?'

Rose's fingers shook over a dark patch along her cheekbone. She was chain-smoking.

'Well, it was him, I won't lie to you, Mo,' she said, tears glistening. 'But I did push him. I think he's seeing someone else.'

'So how's that you pushing him?' Mo said, furious.

'Mo, who's perfect? I wouldn't leave it alone, you see. He's been late every night this week, but he said it was business and I believed him. You know me. I can't sit in and look at four walls for ever. I went out last night, just for a drink with Liz and Dell. I got a cab back and saw him on the way, kissing this blonde bit. When he came in, I went off it. He said it was a friendly kiss, she'd put a lot of work his way. I should have left it, but I didn't.'

'Bloody leave him more like,' Mo spluttered. 'Lying git. Once they hit you they don't stop, Rose. Throw the bugger out.'

'Oh no,' said Rose, 'He spent the night crying like a baby once he'd put his fists on me. He swears on his mother's life it'll never happen again.'

'Uh huh,' Mo said. 'And what about the blonde bit?'

'He said, yes, she fancied him, but nothing had happened. Last night was when he told her nothing would. That kiss was a goodbye.'

'You believe that?'

'Oh yes,' said Rose. 'Anyway, I'm pregnant. That always makes a difference. He's over the moon.'

Yes, being pregnant made a difference: Rose stopped being the glamorous mistress made legal for Barry to show off to his friends. Jack the Lad becomes a dad and it can make or break him. Mo put the word out and if she'd written a dossier on Barry and his 'birds', blonde, auburn, black-haired, permed, straight, bobbed – the bloody dossier would have been a foot thick. But you don't tell your sister about it when she's seven months gone and blooming like a peach. She'd tackled Barry and he just laughed and said, go on Mo, prove it and tell her, break her heart, you've got a very dirty mind, you know. You bent bitch.

Well, she never heard how he explained away the shiner she'd left him with.

The baby was a blue-eyed boy and Rose adored him. Barry bragged and got her pregnant again sooner than was decent. That was a girl, green-eyed like Rose. Rose collected bruises she swore were inflicted by stairs and doorways and Barry got nicked finally, small fish trying to be a shark and the nets wrapped him head to toe. He divorced her from Durham Gaol. Now he was bulging in the middle and thinning on top, married again and still putting himself about like Casanova.

Bugger him, thought Mo, draining her pint. Rose had cut herself off from the world after the divorce: she and her children were on a little island ten floors up. Mo felt excluded and awkward, everybody did. Rose and the children seemed to be waiting for her to leave from the moment she arrived. The children wanted for nothing and Rose was thin and demure. Now both had left home, but they were back most weeks going through Rose's fridge and handbag like jackals. The lad was already streetwise and known to the law, the lass was a moody heartbreaker with a bairn of her own. Rose worshipped the grandbairn and he spent most weekends with her. She spoilt him rotten just like all good grandmas do, and Mo had a sneaking suspicion that she'd wind up raising him as well.

Rose wouldn't hear a word against her children, although, just like Barry and his blonde bit, she knew. So she was tough and mean now and taking it out on anyone who fell for her. You couldn't blame her. Love doesn't die unless you kill it, and Barry had turned the knife so deep and so often that in unguarded moments, Rose looked like a dead woman. Even so, raged Mo, even so, she shouldn't treat women that way.

And Mo was hurt, too, although she blamed herself. When the bairns were teenagers, Rose started to come out drinking with her and she'd had to fight everyone off her big sister, just like when they were little. Until Rose had told her, quite simply, to leave her be, she could take care of herself.

'Are you gay, like?' she'd asked.

173

'I might be.'

Rose wouldn't say more. She turned from heartbreaker into emotional vampire and Mo had many an aching head use her shoulder for a tear-stained pillow. She'd been so proud of her sister, walking out of fourteen years of solitude and on to the scene with a big smile on her face. And now she was behaving just as badly as men were supposed to. She'd been hurt, but that was no reason to dish it out to other people. Especially Esky, her sister's best friend. That was the last straw.

Oh sod it, here she was thinking into Rose's mind again. It was her night out as well. She drowned her pint and ruffled Venus's hair. Women! Venus smiled at her and they hip-smooched and giggled.

'I like my beer cold and my woman hot and soft with it,' Mighty Mo snarled, clutching a beer mat to stop herself crashing off the bar stool. 'Swear to God they don't wash out those pumps, Esky, I've had a bad pint tonight.'

Eskimo Nell's thirteen-holed oxblood DMs ground the spent Piccadilly butt to extinction. One iron fist shot out and grabbed Mighty Mo's studded leather collar just in time to help her defy the laws of gravity and intemperance.

'Bad pint?' she growled. 'Which one was that, eh, Mo? You've got seven to choose from and that's only since you've been in here. You were in here for ten to, where d'you come from?'

'I wish you'd just go back, wherever it was,' said Venus, five foot nine of truck-driving muscle and nothing but mush when in love. She slung her arm round Mighty Mo.

'I cannot, man,' said Mo. 'Listen. I was out at seven, minding me own in the corner of Hades and that bouncer came in. You know the one? The Mexican Mafia? Him! I'm sipping a half, you know, take it easy after the night we had yesterday.'

'Not him!' said Venus. 'I'd like to take a fork-lift to him and his daft moustache. The bastard only works at Hades on a Tuesday.'

'You'd think,' said Mighty Mo, 'but he's Mister Never-Off-Duty, him. He looks at us and says OUT! I said to him, ah, leave us be man, I'm drinking my half. He says not here you're not, you're barred.'

'Never in God's world!' said Esky. 'That was three month since and you never started it.'

'Well, I didn't,' said Mighty Mo, 'but I'll not stand by and see my

174

mates being hassled by him nor any bugger else. He's got a right good scar off that night, we did him a favour. Makes him look hard.'

'He'd not see it that way.'

'Lucky he's still got eyes in his head,' said Mo, all bluster and bravado and beer-fuelled bullshit.

'Ah, shut it, little 'un,' said Venus.

'Now then,' said Esky, warningly. 'Mo, what bars *are* you let in these days?'

Mo shook her head.

'You know, Esky, there's that many thrown us out that I cannot remember where and for how long. Hades is out, like I said.'

'Martina's?'

'No. I pinched that blonde bit's arse. You never told us she was the friggin' owner.'

'Cloud Nine?'

'No. They said I was selling drugs. I wasn't. I was giving them away, Esky, it was my birthday.'

'The Well?'

'They give us a vodka and tonic wi' no vodka. I told them. Aye, that was my birthday and all.'

'Slut's?'

'No,' said Mo. 'Not since me and Venus went through the balcony.'

'Leather 'n Lace?'

'Howay! You know that's Doris's.'

'Babes?'

'I can go in that shithole any time. So long as I don't go in wi' Venus. And she can go in and all. Only not if I'm there.'

'Right,' said Esky, shooting a flame at her cigarette tip, 'that just leaves you here. The Howling Wolf.'

'So I had a birthday,' snapped Mighty Mo. 'What are you saying?'

'I'm saying that if you land one on Venus in here, you'll be drinking cans and doing your knitting in front of the telly for the next six months. No bugger'll let you in nowhere, Mo, man, so simmer down.'

'Would I hit Venus?' said Mo, indignant. 'You're off it, Esky, I love her. I don't love her. I idolize her. What would I hit my woman for?'

'It's just a thought,' said Esky. Thank Christ Mo hadn't heard the careless 'little 'un' Venus had thrown her way. Mighty Mo was barely five feet tall and had built a roadblock of biceps and triceps and deltoids to make up for it. The less than welcome entrance of Rose had set the adrenalin storming through every muscle. Eskimo Nell didn't want to lose her best drinking partner again.

'Nah, it's cuz I called you "little 'un",' said Venus fondly. Esky winced, but Mo grinned like a cherub.

'Any other bastard in the universe said that to me, you'd need to call the ambulance, precious,' she said, 'but you can say what you want, Venus. Anything you want, man. Every word that passes your lips is poetry.'

'Is it my round?' said Venus.

'See what I mean, Esky? Poetry.'

At the bar, Venus watched Rose reeling in her catch. Young Peggy was dizzy with it, hoping her friends could see the chat-up, knowing they'd be jealous. She'd already promised to have a look at Rose's washing machine and give her a hand to get the kitchen straight. Rose's eyes lazed over her shoulder and she smiled at Venus and mouthed something.

'What?' said Venus.

Rose leant over and breathed in her ear.

'I cannot say that to her,' said Venus. 'She's my girlfriend.'

'I know,' said Rose, clamping one claw to Peggy's shoulder. 'But she's *my* sister.'

Venus paid for her drinks and shoved her way back to Esky and Mighty Mo.

'What did she say?'

'I can't repeat it,' said Venus.

'Well, I'll tell you,' said Mighty Mo. 'She said tell that fat pig she's getting fatter.'

'How did you know?'

'I was brought up with her, man. I used to go light if she called me fat.'

Last orders came and went; Rose and Peggy vanished in a minicab to Mighty Mo chanting the death march. Christ, I've scored, thought Peggy: Rose was already rehearsing the drawing-room scene: the grandbairn would wake up, her babysitting neighbour would stay for coffee and Peggy would pass out on the sofa. No point in rushing things.

176

Mighty Mo and Venus and Esky stood on the pavement serenading the night.

'Are you coming back, Esky?'

'No. I'm away over to Josie's.'

'You're not still chasing that?'

'Aye,' said Esky. 'I've been forgiven for putting my tab out on the altar. You don't know Josie, Venus, she's a Buddhist or something, and we were lying in bed last week and she went off it. I thought it was an ashtray and she goes, mind my Buddha, I'l have to recharge it now. Friggin' altar at the side of the bed, I'm telling you.'

Venus and Mo started the long uphill walk for home.

'What was she like, Rose, did you ever get on?'

'When we were little,' said Mighty Mo. 'I used to protect her, you know me, Joan of Arc. Then our mam got Bill for our new stepdad and Rose changed. He was always having a go at her. One day she went into the kitchen and wrapped a plate round his lugs. She was about fourteen and she went into care until she was sixteen. She's been mean and lean and fighting ever since. My mam says what did she do to deserve two bent bastards, me she could understand but Rose could get a man if she tried. Well, she had one once and married him. He was another bastard, just like Bill.'

'Rose *married*? That must have been something!'

'It was,' Mighty Mo laughed. 'She thought the sun shone out of his arse. She loved him. Barry. We'd had a bit of a rough time when we were bairns and I think if he'd been all right, she would have been. But he was a pig, no, pigs are nice animals. He was a piece of shit. I think she just gave up on love after him. You know, she'd given it her best shot and it just destroyed her when it went wrong.'

'There's a lot of dykes got married years ago,' said Venus. 'I never thought of it.'

'Pet, in those days it was HARD to be gay. Not glad, not proud. Hard. If you weren't married, well you were strange. People talked about you if your only callers were women. And if you wanted bairns, well, you had to have a man for that. Unmarried mothers – well it's nowt these days. But then!'

'Do you want babies, Mo?'

Mo blushed.

'Well I do and I don't. It's such a decision these days. I mean you'd be pregnant now if I was a fella.'

'Well, you're good. But sometimes I think you'd be pregnant,' Venus snorted. 'One of us would be. Roll on parthenogenesis, I say.'

'Bring on the turkey baster!' said Mo. 'I'm too pissed to talk about babies right now.'

'Mm,' said Venus, feeling all warm and wanted, picturing a baby with Mo's wild blue eyes and crazy smile. 'I'm kind of sorry for Rose, you know. Will you ever speak to her?'

'No. Yes. I don't think so,' said Mighty Mo. 'We've no family, you see, since that bastard Bill showed up. My brothers went in the army and I got a job and a flat as soon as I could. I think of my friends as my family, and Esky's like a sister should be. Your best friend. To have Rose, my flesh and blood sister, treat her that way!'

'So do you love me like a sister, Mo?' Venus said.

'Don't you start on that political shite!' Mighty Mo laughed. 'That would be incest, pet. You're not my sister and I don't love you. I worship you and you're my wife. You could be the mother of our children.'

'I thought you were *my* wife,' Venus put on a John Wayne swagger. 'You'd look really sexy in a maternity dress. Or out of it.'

'I can't see either one of us in a long white frock,' Mo shrieked at the idea. 'You're not my sister, you're not my wife. You're my life.'

'I hope so.' Venus leaned an arm round Mo's neck. 'I really hope so.'

Dyan Sheldon

Day and Night

My sister was laughing when she finally came on the phone. As a rule, she only laughed when my mother wasn't around.

'Carol,' I said. 'Carol, you have to come home.' The house was so quiet that even though I was trying to keep my voice down, it sounded to me as if I were shouting. Bitsy's tail thumped on the floor beside me, like footsteps.

'What?' said Carol. I knew exactly what expression she had on her face. Like she'd just caught me borrowing something of hers. Not clothes or anything like that. I would never wear the stuff she wore. But her radio or her razor or her silver bracelet. 'What? For God's sake, Cheryl, stop whispering, will you? I can't hear what you're saying.'

My mother was always telling everyone how emotional and unstable Carol was, but just the sound of her voice made me feel calmer. There was a lot of chatter and music in the background. I couldn't make out what the song was but it was fast and sounded happy. I raised my own voice slightly. 'Come home,' I said. 'Come home right now.'

'Why should I?'

'Come home, Carol,' I pleaded. I was holding the receiver so tight my hand was sweating. 'Please. I think something's happened to Mom. I'm scared.'

'Jesus,' said my sister. 'You really are a jerk sometimes. She's probably in the A&P, telling everybody on the checkout what a bitch I am. She's probably telling them I have to get married because I'm knocked up.'

It drove my mom nuts when Carol said things like that. Things like Jesus and bitch and knocked up. I would never dare. 'Where

179

do you get your language?' my mom would scream. 'In the gutter? In the gutter with your friends?' But it drove her more nuts when Carol said 'she'. 'Who's *she*?' my mom would shriek. 'Who's *she*? The cat's mother?'

'Come on, Car,' Carol's fiancé, Drew, called out. 'We're ready to eat.'

'Carol,' I said. 'Carol, I have this really bad feeling . . .'

I didn't have to be able to see my sister to know that she was rolling her eyes. 'Nothing's happened to Mom,' said Carol. 'She's too mean.'

My mother yelled and screamed a lot, but she wasn't really mean – not to me. 'You're a gift from God,' my mother had always told me. 'That's what you are, a gift from God.' When I was little, I had an image of the heavens opening just like on the cover of my Illustrated Bible, and the hand of God reaching through on a beam of light and dropping me into my mother's arms. I was wrapped. It was my sister who was her cross to bear.

'But she's not here, Carol.' I could hear Drew mumbling behind her. I talked fast, in case she decided to hang up. 'And she didn't leave a note.' My mother always left a note for me, even if she'd just gone across the street. 'It's after six.'

My sister sighed. 'Jesus Christ,' said Carol. 'Don't be such a baby, will you, Cheryl? You're fifteen, not five. So what if she's not home? She's out on her broomstick somewhere. I'm busy. Go fix yourself a sandwich or something and turn on the tube.'

I grabbed hold of Bitsy's collar. I'd managed to dial Drew's number, but I knew that I wasn't going to be able to turn on the television or open the refrigerator or anything else. I felt like I was in one of those horror movies where if you open a door or touch a knob you trip over a body or something jumps out to grab you. 'I can't,' I said. 'I'm afraid to go into the kitchen. What if she's kneeling on the floor with her head in the oven?'

Carol sighed again. 'Jesus Christ, Cheryl, where do you get this shit from? What's wrong with you?' There was some more mumbling from Drew and then Carol saying, 'It's Cher. She thinks the old bitch has killed herself.' I could hear him laughing, and then Carol said to me, 'Cheryl, you moron, the stove's electric.'

'Please.'

'Drew wants to know if you've been at the painkillers,' said Carol.
'Carol . . .' I said.

They both started to laugh.

My mother always said that Carol and I were like day and night.
'They're like day and night,' she told her friends. 'You wouldn't think
they were sisters if you didn't know.' I was small and fair, like my
mother, and good at school, just as she'd been. Carol was tall and
dark like our father. My mother said it was my father's fault that Carol
was an ingrate and wild and spoiled rotten, because he favoured her. 'I
don't have favourites,' my mother said. 'I love my girls both the same.'
I was the kind of girl who plays the violin in the school orchestra and
wants to be a lawyer, and Carol was the kind of girl who drops out
of school two weeks before graduation and marries a rock guitarist
who thinks Elvis was God.

'Carol, I'm not kidding. I think she's dead.'

'You really are a pain in the ass, you know that?' said my sister.

Carol said that the reason she and my mother fought so much was
because my mother had always hated her. My mother, however,
read *Women's Day* and *McCall's* and she said that the real trouble
between them had started with Carol's period. She said that that was
what happened with some girls. With girls who were wild, spoiled
rotten and unstable. When I was twelve, my mother gave me a box
of sanitary napkins, a pink elastic belt to hold them up with, and
heartfelt advice. 'Don't you change, honey,' my mother warned me.
'Even though you've got all those hormones, don't you change. Don't
you get like your sister got.'

But no matter how many times my mother told me that she'd rather
be dead and buried than see me grow up like Carol, I don't think it
would ever have occurred to me that she might actually kill herself
if it hadn't been for Mrs Wallace.

Mrs Wallace was Betsy Wallace's mother. Betsy and I were in
the orchestra together. Betsy Wallace was small and dark and she
once knocked over her music stand during a performance. She
played the flute. The Christmas before my sister got married, Betsy
Wallace's mother hanged herself in her attic with the clothesline
from the back yard. For some reason, when I thought about this,
I never pictured Mrs Wallace in a noose. I pictured her hanging

on the line with the laundry, as though someone had put her out to dry.

The Wallaces were ordinary, just like we were. I used to see Mrs Wallace at Parents' Nights and fun fairs and waiting in the parking lot for Betsy when she had an appointment with the dentist after school. She was just another mother in her car coat and her knit hat, her lips bright red and her keys jangling as she waited outside the entrance. The kids said she was blue when they cut her down, blue and that her tongue was black and swollen. They said she left a note that said: You know why. When Betsy came back to the orchestra after her mother died, I used to watch her all the time, opening her case and putting her flute together and setting up the music on her stand. And I wondered. I wondered how long it was before they'd found Mrs Wallace. I wondered if Betsy was sitting in front of the television, eating cookies, when they discovered her mother hanging on the line.

Anyway, that night Carmela Spinelli's mother drove me back from practice. Mrs Spinelli and my mother took turns. She stopped the Pontiac in the driveway. Our house was dark. 'Isn't anybody home?' she asked.

I told her that Carol was at Drew's, going over the guest list. Everybody knew that my dad worked nights.

Mrs Spinelli was still looking at the house. It was winter and already dark. The house looked cold. Not even the porch light was on. 'You want to have supper with us?' asked Mrs Spinelli. 'You want to leave a note for your Mom?'

I opened the car door and the overhead light went on. 'Probably my mom's lying down,' I said. My mother would be mad if I went somewhere else when she was expecting me home. It was the kind of thing Carol always did.

Mrs Spinelli nodded. 'Of course she is. She must be exhausted.'

Everybody knew that my mother got headaches. And they all knew why. My mother got headaches because of Carol. Because Carol gave her such a hard time.

'It's the wedding,' Mrs Spinelli was saying. 'There's so much to do ... She'll feel better once it's over.'

I started to climb out. My breath froze in the air. Mrs Spinelli was right. My mother was going to feel great once the wedding was over.

She couldn't wait to get my sister out of the house. 'Everything will be all right then,' she'd tell me. 'It'll be just like when you were little. You won't have your sister setting a bad example.'

Carmela, sitting beside her mother, waved to me as the car backed out of the driveway. When my mother and Carol and I went anywhere, I always sat in the back, because I was the youngest. But after the wedding I wouldn't have to anymore, I'd always be able to sit up front. I waved back.

'Mom!' I called as I opened the front door. 'Mom! I'm home!' I switched on the lamp and put down my violin and threw my books on a chair. Bitsy jumped up on my legs, his tail wagging. 'Mom!' I shouted. 'Mom! Where are you?'

Our house wasn't very big. My sister called it the Cape Cod prison. 'It's got storm doors instead of bars,' my sister said, 'but otherwise we might as well all be in a holding pen.' My parents had one bedroom and Carol and I had the other. If you weren't in your room, then you were in the living-room or the kitchen or the bathroom. Downstairs in the basement was where the washing machine, the boiler, and my father's workbench were. My father had been finishing the basement for six years. Carol said it was just an excuse, so he had someplace to go when he wanted peace and quiet. He went down there a lot. 'Mom!'

I stood there with my coat still on and Bitsy licking my hand, waiting to hear my mother's voice, so sure and sharp, so whole, to shout back, 'Cheryl? Cheryl I'm here!'

I pushed Bitsy away. 'Mom?' I could hear the ticking of the clock over the mantel. Usually when I came home after orchestra practice there were lights on in every room, and supper was cooking in the kitchen, and the television was going or my mother was singing along with the radio. If she wasn't at work or at Drew's, you could hear Carol playing some record my mother hated in her room. A lot of the time, my mother and my sister would be having a fight, or had just had a fight, or my mother would be on the telephone, complaining. Most of the time she was complaining about Carol. If she saw me watching her, listening, she'd lower her voice. 'It's *her*,' she'd say. Her was my sister. 'Now she's trying to turn Cheryl against me too.'

I crossed the living-room and into the hall. The doors to the kitchen, the bedrooms and the bathroom were closed. I tiptoed to my mother's room and knocked softly on the door. 'Mom? Mom, are you sleeping?' I think I knew deep down that she wasn't in there, because I remember getting this clenching in my stomach. I knocked again anyway, though, this time a little louder. 'Mom?'

When she didn't answer, and I couldn't hear her snoring, I opened the door. The room was empty. My mother wasn't lying there in the dark with a compress over her eyes. I didn't step inside. The bed was made, and the blinds were open, and I could see the lights from the Sullivans' house next door and Mrs Sullivan at her kitchen window, doing something at the sink.

My mother, like Betsy Wallace's mother, was a normal, typical, suburban mother. She wore a car coat and a white knit hat with gold spangles on it and her lips were fire-engine red. My mother went shopping and to church and to the Ladies' Home Extension, and once a month she had her hair done in the beauty parlour at the end of Main Street. But she was always home at night. My father worked and Carol ran around, but my mother was home. Where else would she go?

That's what I was thinking as I stood in the doorway. *Where else could she be?* And all of a sudden I thought of Betsy Wallace's mother. I saw her hanging from the clothesline strung across the attic. One of her hands was caught in a white, man's shirt, and there was a pair of knee socks dangling over her shoulder. She was swinging back and forth like the laundry does in a breeze. And then I imagined my mother with her head in the oven, or dangling from the pipes in the basement like one of my father's old rags, or sitting in the car in the garage with the engine running, her purse on her lap and her eyes opened, just like she was waiting to go for a Sunday drive.

I called my sister.

The oil burner hummed, and outside car lights passed like clouds. I sat hunched on the floor of the living-room, the telephone on one side of me and Bitsy on the other, waiting for Carol, just like I used to wait for her to pick me up from Brownies or dance lessons or someone's house when I was a kid. 'Your sister's here!' a voice would shout, and I'd turn around and see her standing in the doorway, her smile like a private joke. 'Hurry up, will you?' my sister would say. 'I don't have all day.'

Drew drove her over in his car. They must have left as soon as she put the phone down, because they were there before I had time to start worrying that she wasn't coming at all. Carol came through the front door first.

'I don't believe you, Cheryl,' she said as she dumped her bag and her jacket on the sofa and started turning on lights. 'We were just sitting down to eat. Drew's parents must think we're all nuts.'

'I'm sorry,' I said. 'I just got scared.'

Drew stepped in behind her. He was carrying a brown paper bag and eating a piece of fried chicken. 'Hey, Cheryl,' winked Drew. 'You better lay off the Coca-Cola. The sugar's making you crazy.'

He held out the bag to me, but I wasn't hungry. All of a sudden I realized how much trouble I was going to be in if my mother wasn't dead and she came home and found us. My mother hated it when Carol and I did anything together. Even if all we were doing was sitting watching television, it drove her nuts. 'What are you laughing at?' she'd want to know. 'What are you talking about?'

Carol gave me a look. 'You really are something,' she said. 'What did you think? That Mom threw herself off a cliff or something?'

Drew turned on the television and flopped into my mother's chair. Bitsy went to sit beside him.

'Sort of,' I said. I stared at my feet. 'You know, like Betsy Wallace's mother.'

My sister gave me another look. 'I don't know where you get your imagination from,' she said. She stepped over my legs. 'I guess I'll check the kitchen.' She came back out almost immediately, with three chocolate bars in her hand. She threw one to me and one to Drew. 'Well she hasn't electrocuted herself in the oven,' she informed us. 'Have you looked in the bathroom?'

'I didn't look anywhere,' I said. 'I didn't want to find her alone.'

'You really are hopeless, you know that?' Carol made a face. 'What's going to happen to you when I'm gone, Cher?' she demanded. 'What's going to happen then?'

I didn't know. I knew that things would be quieter without her around, but I didn't know what would happen to me. I knew that, even though my mother was worried, I would never turn into my sister. I would never dress like she did, or wear my hair like she did, or talk back like she did, or run around and break my mother's heart like she did. But I didn't know what I would do. I wondered if I was going to turn out like my mother.

'Leave her alone,' said Drew, his eyes on the screen. 'Can't you see she's really spooked?'

I stood behind Carol as she peered into the bathroom. 'Well?' I whispered.

'Well, she didn't slit her wrists,' said my sister. She moved aside so I could see the pink tiles and the pink towels and the plastic shower curtain, printed with shells. 'I guess we better check the basement.'

I followed her to the basement door. 'Carol,' I said. 'Carol, what will happen to me if Mom doesn't come back?'

She turned on the light at the top of the stairs. 'You wait here,' she ordered. 'I'll just make sure she hasn't sawed herself in half.'

I counted the steps as my sister walked down them. One, two, three, four ... Besides my father's power saw in the corner, there was a clothesline across one end of the cellar. My sister reached the last step, the thirteenth, and turned to the left. My mother, her lips redder than blood against the blue of her skin and her hand on a pale pink sheet, was hanging from the white cotton rope. From far away, I heard Carol scream, and then I was crying with my arms around my sister and Drew was saying, 'Don't worry, Cheryl. Don't worry, you can come live with us.'

Carol threw the wrapper of her candy bar at me as she came up the stairs. 'She didn't drown herself in the washing machine, if that's what you thought,' said my sister.

My mother came into the house like a stampede. She'd run out of gas on the road between our neighbourhood and town, and she'd had to walk back two miles to the gas station. It wasn't my mother's fault that she'd run out of gas, it was Carol's. Carol had borrowed the car without telling her. Carol had emptied the tank and not filled it up again. Carol's boyfriend was sitting in my mother's chair with his feet on the upholstery, getting fried chicken crumbs all over the rug. Carol and I were playing cards on the coffee table.

My mother didn't even take off her hat or her coat. She turned to my sister. 'You little witch!' she screamed. 'You ungrateful little witch! You did this on purpose, didn't you? You did this on purpose!'

Drew said, 'Mrs Landers –'

I said, 'Mom –'

Carol gave her one of her scornful smiles. 'What the hell's wrong with you now?' she asked.

My mother went for Carol with her handbag.

That night, I lay in my bed, staring over the café curtains at these three tiny stars in the sky. Carol, still shaking long after Drew had pulled my mother off her, had thrown most of her stuff into shopping bags and taken it with her.

'You'll be sorry!' my mother yelled at her from the porch as she got into Drew's car. 'You'll be back!'

'Fuck you!' shouted my sister. 'I'll never step foot in your house again as long as I live! Fuck you!'

'Don't you talk to me like that! I'm your mother!'

'Take a good look!' screamed Carol. 'Take a good look, because you're never going to see me again!'

That night, even though I fell asleep thinking about other nights when my sister stormed out of the house and my mother called up all her friends and cried and told them what Carol had done this time and about Mrs Wallace walking up to the attic with the clothesline in her hands and the note in her pocket – even then, I didn't believe my sister. Even then, I was sure I would see her again.

Louisa May Alcott

~~~

from
Little Women and *Good Wives*

'**G**irls, where are you going!' asked Amy, coming into their room one Saturday afternoon, and finding them getting ready to go out, with an air of secrecy which excited her curiosity.

'Never mind; little girls shouldn't ask questions,' returned Jo sharply.

Now if there *is* anything mortifying to our feelings, when we are young, it is to be told that; and to be bidden to 'run away, dear,' is still more trying to us. Amy bridled up at this insult, and determined to find out the secret, if she teased for an hour. Turning to Meg, who never refused her anything very long, she said coaxingly, 'Do tell me! I should think you might let me go, too; for Beth is fussing over her piano, and I haven't got anything to do, and am *so* lonely.'

'I can't, dear, because you aren't invited, began Meg; but Jo broke in impatiently, 'Now, Meg, be quiet, or you will spoil it all. You can't go, Amy; so don't be a baby, and whine about it.'

'You are going somewhere with Laurie, I know you are; you were whispering and laughing together, on the sofa, last night, and you stopped when I came in. Aren't you going with him.'

'Yes, we are; now do be still, and stop bothering.'

Amy held her tongue, but used her eyes, and saw Meg slip a fan into her pocket.

'I know! I know! you're going to the theatre to see the *Seven Castles*!' she cried; adding resolutely, 'and I *shall* go, for mother said I might see it; and I've got my rag-money, and it was mean not to tell me in time.'

'Just listen to me a minute, and be a good child,' said Meg soothingly. 'Mother doesn't wish you to go this week, because your eyes are not well enough yet to bear the light of this fairy piece. Next week you can go with Beth and Hannah, and have a nice time.'

'I don't like that half as well as going with you and Laurie. Please let me; I've been sick with this cold so long, and shut up, I'm dying for some fun. Do, Meg! I'll be ever so good,' pleaded Amy, looking as pathetic as she could.

'Suppose we take her. I don't believe Mother would mind, if we bundle her up well,' began Meg.

'If *she* goes *I* sha'n't; and if I don't, Laurie won't like it; and it will be very rude, after he invited only us, to go and drag in Amy. I should think she'd hate to poke herself where she isn't wanted,' said Jo crossly, for she disliked the trouble of overseeing a fidgety child, when she wanted to enjoy herself.

Her tone and manner angered Amy, who began to put her boots on, saying, in her most aggravating way, 'I *shall* go; Meg says I may and if I pay for myself, Laurie hasn't anything to do with it.'

'You can't sit with us, for our seats are reserved, and you mustn't sit alone; so Laurie will give you his place, and that will spoil our pleasure; or he'll get another seat for you, and that isn't proper, when you weren't asked. You sha'n't stir a step; so you may just stay where you are,' scolded Jo, crosser than ever, having just pricked her finger in her hurry.

Sitting on the floor, with one boot on, Amy began to cry, and Meg to reason with her, when Laurie called from below, and the two girls hurried down, leaving their sister wailing; for now and then she forgot her grown-up ways, and acted like a spoilt child. Just as the party was setting out, Amy called over the banisters, in a threatening tone, 'You'll be sorry for this, Jo March; see if you ain't.'

'Fiddlesticks!' returned Jo, slamming the door.

They had a charming time, for *The Seven Castles of the Diamond Lake* were as brilliant and wonderful as heart could wish. But, in spite of the comical red imps, sparkling elves, and gorgeous princes and princesses, Jo's pleasure had a drop of bitterness in it; the fairy queen's yellow curls reminded her of Amy; and between the acts she amused herself with wondering what her sister would do to make her 'sorry for it'. She and Amy had had many lively skirmishes in the course of their lives, for both had quick tempers, and were apt to be violent when fairly roused. Amy teased Jo, and Jo irritated

Amy, and semi-occasional explosions occurred, of which both were much ashamed afterward. Although the oldest, Jo had the least self-control, and had hard times trying to curb the fiery spirit which was continually getting her into trouble; her anger never lasted long, and having humbly confessed her fault, she sincerely repented, and tried to do better. Her sisters used to say that they rather liked to get Jo into a fury, because she was such an angel afterward. Poor Jo tried desperately to be good, but her bosom enemy was always ready to flame up and defeat her; and it took years of patient effort to subdue it.

When they got home, they found Amy reading in the parlour. She assumed an injured air as they came in; never lifted her eyes from her book, or asked a single question. Perhaps curiosity might have conquered resentment, if Beth had not been there to inquire, and receive a glowing description of the play. On going up to put away her best hat, Jo's first look was toward the bureau; for, in their last quarrel, Amy had soothed her feelings by turning Jo's top drawer upside down on the floor. Everything was in its place however; and after a hasty glance into her various closets, bags, and boxes, Jo decided that Amy had forgiven and forgotten her wrongs.

There Jo was mistaken; for next day she made a discovery which produced a tempest. Meg, Beth, and Amy were sitting together, late in the afternoon, when Jo burst into the room, looking excited, and demanding breathlessly, 'Has any one taken my book?'

Meg and Beth said 'No,' at once, and looked surprised; Amy poked the fire, and said nothing. Jo saw her colour rise, and was down upon her in a minute.

'Amy, you've got it!'

'No, I haven't.'

'You know where it is then!'

'No, I don't.'

'That's a fib!' cried Jo, taking her by the shoulders, and looking fierce enough to frighten a much braver child than Amy.

'It isn't. I haven't got it, don't know where it is now, and don't care.'

'You know something about it, and you'd better tell at once, or I'll make you,' and Jo gave her a slight shake.

'Scold as much as you like, you'll never see your silly old book again,' cried Amy, getting excited in her turn.

'Why not?'

'I burnt it up.'

'What! My little book I was so fond of, and worked over, and meant to finish before father got home! Have you really burnt it?' said Jo, turning very pale, while her eyes kindled and her hands clutched Amy nervously.

'Yes, I did! I told you I'd make you pay for being so cross yesterday, and I have, so' –

Amy got no farther, for Jo's hot temper mastered her, and she shook Amy till her teeth chattered in her head; crying in a passion of grief and anger –

'You wicked, wicked girl! I never can write it again, and I'll never forgive you as long as I live.'

Meg flew to rescue Amy, and Beth to pacify Jo, but Jo was quite beside herself; and with a parting box on her sister's ear, she rushed out of the room up to the old sofa in the garret, and finished her fight alone.

The storm cleared up below, for Mrs March came home, and, having heard the story, soon brought Amy to a sense of the wrong she had done her sister. Jo's book was the pride of her heart, and was regarded by her family as a literary sprout of great promise. It was only half-a-dozen little fairy-tales, but Jo had worked over them patiently, putting her whole heart into her work, hoping to make something good enough to print. She had just copied them with great care, and had destroyed the old manuscript, so that Amy's bonfire had consumed the loving work of several years. It seemed a small loss to others, but to Jo it was a dreadful calamity, and she felt that it never could be made up to her. Beth mourned as for a departed kitten, and Meg refused to defend her pet; Mrs March looked grave and grieved, and Amy felt that no one would love her till she had asked pardon for the act which she now regretted more than any of them.

When the tea-bell rung, Jo appeared, looking so grim and unapproachable that it took all Amy's courage to say meekly –

'Please forgive me, Jo; I'm very, very sorry.'

'I never shall forgive you,' was Jo's stern answer; and from that moment she ignored Amy entirely.

No one spoke of the great trouble – not even Mrs March – for all had learned by experience that when Jo was in that mood words were wasted; and the wisest course was to wait till some little accident, or her own generous nature, softened Jo's resentment, and healed the breach. It was not a happy evening; for though they sewed as usual, while their mother read aloud from Bremer, Scott, or Edgeworth, something was wanting, and the sweet home-peace was disturbed. They felt this most when singing-time came; for Beth could only play, Jo stood dumb as a stone, and Amy broke down, so Meg and mother sung alone. But, in spite of their efforts to be as cheery as larks, the flutelike voices did not seem to chord as well as usual, and all felt out of tune.

As Jo received her goodnight kiss, Mrs March whispered gently – 'My dear, don't let the sun go down upon your anger; forgive each other, help each other, and begin again tomorrow.'

Jo wanted to lay her head down on that motherly bosom, and cry her grief and anger all away; but tears were an unmanly weakness, and she felt so deeply injured that she really *couldn't* quite forgive yet. So she winked hard, shook her head, and said gruffly, because Amy was listening – 'It was an abominable thing, and she don't deserve to be forgiven.'

With that she marched off to bed, and there was no merry or confidential gossip that night.

Amy was much offended that her overtures of peace had been repulsed, and began to wish she had not humbled herself, to feel more injured than ever, and to plume herself on her superior virtue in a way which was particularly exasperating. Jo still looked like a thunder-cloud, and nothing went well all day. It was bitter cold in the morning; she dropped her precious turn-over in the gutter, Aunt March had an attack of fidgets, Meg was pensive, Beth *would* look grieved and wistful when she got home, and Amy kept making remarks about people who were always talking about being good, and yet wouldn't try, when other people set them a virtuous example.

'Everybody is so hateful, I'll ask Laurie to go skating. He is always kind and jolly, and will put me to rights, I know,' said Jo to herself, and off she went.

Amy heard the clash of skates, and looked out with an impatient exclamation, – 'There! she promised I should go next time, for this is the last ice we shall have. But it's no use to ask such a cross-patch to take me.'

'Don't say that; you *were* very naughty, and it *is* hard to forgive the loss of her precious little book; but I think she might do it now, and I guess she will, if you try her at the right minute,' said Meg. 'Go after them; don't say anything till Jo has got good-natured with Laurie, then take a quiet minute, and just kiss her, or do some kind thing, and I'm sure she'll be friends again with all her heart.'

'I'll try,' said Amy, for the advice suited her; and, after a flurry to get ready, she ran after the friends, who were just disappearing over the hill.

It was not far to the river, but both were ready before Amy reached them. Jo saw her coming, and turned her back; Laurie did not see, for he was carefully skating along the shore, sounding the ice, for a warm spell had preceded the cold snap.

'I'll go on to the first bend, and see if it's all right, before we begin to race,' Amy heard him say, as he shot away, looking like a young Russian, in his fur-trimmed coat and cap.

Jo heard Amy panting after her run, stamping her feet and blowing her fingers, as she tried to put her skates on; but Jo never turned, and went slowly zigzagging down the river, taking a bitter, unhappy sort of satisfaction in her sister's troubles. She had cherished her anger till it grew strong, and took possession of her, as evil thoughts and feelings always do, unless cast out at once. As Laurie turned the bend, he shouted back – 'Keep near the shore; it isn't safe in the middle.'

Jo heard, but Amy was just struggling to her feet, and did not catch a word. Jo glanced over her shoulder, and the little demon she was harbouring said in her ear – 'No matter whether she heard or not, let her take care of herself.'

Laurie had vanished round the bend; Jo was just at the turn, and Amy, far behind, striking out toward the smoother ice in the middle of the river. For a minute Jo stood still, with a strange feeling at her heart; then she resolved to go on, but something held and turned her round, just in time to see Amy throw up her hands and go down, with the sudden crash of rotten ice, the splash of water, and a cry that made Jo's heart stand still with fear. She tried to call Laurie, but her voice was gone; she tried to rush forward, but her feet seemed to have no strength in them; and, for a second, she could only stand motionless, staring, with a terror-stricken face, at the little blue hood above the black water. Something rushed swiftly by her and Laurie's voice cried out – 'Bring a rail; quick, quick!'

How she did it, she never knew; but for the next few minutes she worked as if possessed, blindly obeying Laurie, who was quite self-possessed, and, lying flat, held Amy up by his arm and hockey till Jo dragged a rail from the fence, and together they got the child out, more frightened than hurt.

'Now then, we must walk her home as fast as we can; pile our things on her, while I get off these confounded skates,' cried Laurie, wrapping his coat round Amy, and tugging away at the straps, which never seemed so intricate before.

Shivering, dripping, and crying, they got Amy home; and, after an exciting time of it, she fell asleep, rolled in blankets, before a hot fire. During the bustle Jo had scarcely spoken, but flown about, looking pale and wild, with her things half off, her dress torn, and her hands cut and bruised by ice and rails and refractory buckles. When Amy was comfortably asleep, the house quiet, and Mrs March sitting by the bed, she called Jo to her, and began to bind up the hurt hands.

'Are you sure she is safe?' whispered Jo, looking remorsefully at the golden head, which might have been swept away from her sight for ever under the treacherous ice.

'Quite safe, dear; she is not hurt, and won't even take cold, I think, you were so sensible in covering and getting her home quickly', replied her mother cheerfully.

'Laurie did it all; I only let her go. Mother, if she *should* die, it would be my fault'; and Jo dropped down beside the bed, in a passion of penitent tears, telling all that had happened, bitterly condemning her hardness of heart, and sobbing out her gratitude for being spared the heavy punishment which might have come upon her.

'It's my dreadful temper! I try to cure it; I think I have, and then it breaks out worse than ever. O Mother, what shall I do? what shall I do?' cried poor Jo, in despair.

'Watch and pray, dear; never get tired of trying; and never think it is impossible to conquer your fault,' said Mrs March, drawing the blowzy head to her shoulder, and kissing the wet cheek so tenderly that Jo cried harder than ever.

'You don't know, you can't guess how bad it is! It seems as if I

194

could do anything when I'm in a passion; I get so savage, I could hurt anyone, and enjoy it. I'm afraid I *shall* do something dreadful some day, and spoil my life, and make everybody hate me. O Mother, help me, do help me!'

'I will, my child, I will. Don't cry so bitterly, but remember this day, and resolve, with all your soul, that you will never know another like it. Jo, dear, we all have our temptations, some far greater than yours, and it often takes us all our lives to conquer them. You think your temper is the worst in the world; but mine used to be just like it.'

'Yours, Mother? Why, you are never angry!' and, for the moment, Jo forgot remorse in surprise.

'I've been trying to cure it for forty years, and have only succeeded in controlling it. I am angry nearly every day of my life, Jo; but I have learned not to show it; and I still hope to learn not to feel it, though it may take me another forty years to do so.'

The patience and the humility of the face she loved so well was a better lesson to Jo than the wisest lecture, the sharpest reproof. She felt comforted at once by the sympathy and confidence given her; the knowledge that her mother had a fault like hers, and tried to mend it, made her own easier to bear and strengthened her resolution to cure it; though forty years seemed rather a long time to watch and pray, to a girl of fifteen.

'Mother, are you angry when you fold your lips tight together, and go out of the room sometimes, when Aunt March scolds, or people worry you?' asked Jo, feeling nearer and dearer to her mother than ever before.

'Yes, I've learned to check the hasty words that rise to my lips; and when I feel that they mean to break out against my will, I just go away a minute, and give myself a little shake for being so weak and wicked,' answered Mrs March, with a sigh and a smile, as she smoothed and fastened up Jo's dishevelled hair.

'How did you learn to keep still! That is what troubles me – for the sharp words fly out before I know what I'm about; and the more I say the worse I get, till it's a pleasure to hurt people's feelings, and say dreadful things. Tell me how you do it, Marmee dear.'

'My good mother used to help me' –

'As you do us' – interrupted Jo, with a grateful kiss.

'But I lost her when I was a little older than you are, and for years

195

had to struggle on alone, for I was too proud to confess my weakness to anyone else. I had a hard time, Jo, and shed a good many bitter tears over my failures; for, in spite of my efforts, I never seemed to get on. Then your father came, and I was so happy that I found it easy to be good. But by-and-by, when I had four little daughters round me, and we were poor, then the old trouble began again; for I am not patient by nature, and it tried me very much to see my children wanting anything.'

'Poor Mother! What helped you then?'

'Your father, Jo. He never loses patience – never doubts or complains – but always hopes, and works and waits so cheerfully, that one is ashamed to do otherwise before him. He helped and comforted me, and showed me that I must try to practise all the virtues I would have my little girls possess, for I was their example. It was easier to try for your sakes than for my own; a startled or surprised look from one of you, when I spoke sharply, rebuked me more than any words could have done; and the love, respect, and confidence of my children was the sweetest reward I could receive for my efforts to be the woman I would have them copy.'

'O Mother, if I'm ever half as good as you, I shall be satisfied,' cried Jo, much touched.

'I hope you will be a great deal better, dear; but you must keep watch over your "bosom enemy", as father calls it, or it may sadden, if not spoil your life. You have had a warning; remember it, and try with heart and soul to master this quick temper before it brings you greater sorrow and regret than you have known today.'

'I will try, Mother; I truly will. But you must help me, remind me, and keep me from flying out. I used to see Father sometimes put his finger on his lips, and look at you with a very kind but sober face, and you always folded your lips tight or went away: was he reminding you then?' asked Jo softly.

'Yes; I asked him to help me so, and he never forgot it, but saved me from many a sharp word by that little gesture and kind look.'

Jo saw that her mother's eyes filled and her lips trembled as she spoke; and, fearing that she had said too much, she whispered anxiously, 'Was it wrong to watch you, and to speak of it? I didn't mean to be rude, but it's so comfortable to say all I think to you, and feel so safe and happy here.'

196

'My Jo, you may say anything to your mother, for it is my greatest happiness and pride to feel that my girls confide in me and know how much I love them.'

'I thought I'd grieved you.'

'No, dear; but speaking of Father reminded me how much I miss him, how much I owe him, and how faithfully I should watch and work to keep his little daughters safe and good for him.'

'Yet you told him to go, Mother, and didn't cry when he went and never complain now, or seem as if you needed any help,' said Jo, wondering.

'I gave my best to the country I love, and kept my tears till he was gone. Why should I complain, when we both have merely done our duty and will surely be the happier for it in the end? If I don't seem to need help, it is because I have a better friend, even than Father, to comfort and sustain me. My child, the troubles and temptations of your life are beginning, and may be many; but you can overcome and outlive them all if you learn to feel the strength and tenderness of your Heavenly Father as you do that of your earthly one. The more you love and trust Him, the nearer you will feel to Him, and the less you will depend on human power and wisdom. His love and care never tire or change, can never be taken from you, but may become the source of lifelong peace, happiness, and strength. Believe this heartily, and go to God with all your little cares, and hopes, and sins, and sorrows, as freely and confidingly as you come to your mother.'

Jo's only answer was to hold her mother close, and, in the silence which followed, the sincerest prayer she had ever prayed left her heart without words; for in that sad yet happy hour she had learned not only the bitterness of remorse and despair, but the sweetness of self-denial and self-control; and, led by her mother's hand, she had drawn nearer to the Friend who welcomes every child with a love stronger than that of any father, tenderer than that of any mother.

Amy stirred, and sighed in her sleep; and, as if eager to begin at once to mend her fault, Jo looked up with an expression on her face which it had never worn before.

'I let the sun go down on my anger; I wouldn't forgive her, and today, if it hadn't been for Laurie, it might have been too late! How could I be so wicked?' said Jo, half aloud, as she leaned over her sister, softly stroking the wet hair scattered on the pillow.

As if she heard, Amy opened her eyes, and held out her arms, with a smile that went straight to Jo's heart. Neither said a word, but they hugged one another close, in spite of the blankets, and everything was forgiven and forgotten in one hearty kiss.

* * *

When Jo came home that spring, she had been struck with the change in Beth. No one spoke of it or seemed aware of it, for it had come too gradually to startle those who saw her daily; but to eyes sharpened by absence, it was very plain; and a heavy weight fell on Jo's heart as she saw her sister's face. It was no paler and but little thinner than in the autumn; yet there was a strange, transparent look about it, as if the mortal was being slowly refined away, and the immortal shining through the frail flesh with an indescribably pathetic beauty. Jo saw and felt it, but said nothing at the time, and soon the first impression lost much of its power; for Beth seemed happy, no one appeared to doubt that she was better; and, presently, in other cares, Jo for a time forgot her fear.

But when Laurie was gone, and peace prevailed again, the vague anxiety returned and haunted her. She had confessed her sins and been forgiven; but when she showed her savings and proposed the mountain-trip, Beth had thanked her heartily, but begged not to go so far away from home. Another little visit to the seashore would suit her better, and, as Grandma could not be prevailed upon to leave the babies, Jo took Beth down to the quiet place, where she could live much in the open air, and let the fresh sea breezes blow a little colour into her pale cheeks.

It was not a fashionable place, but even among the pleasant people there, the girls made few friends, preferring to live for one another. Beth was too shy to enjoy society, and Jo too wrapped up in her to care for anyone else; so they were all in all to each other, and came and went, quite unconscious of the interest they excited in those about them, who watched with sympathetic eyes the strong sister and the feeble one, always together, as if they felt instinctively that a long separation was not far away.

They did feel it, yet neither spoke of it; for often between ourselves and those nearest and dearest to us there exists a reserve which it is very hard to overcome. Jo felt as if a veil had fallen between her heart and Beth's; but when she put out her hand to lift it up, there seemed something sacred in the silence, and she waited for Beth to speak. She wondered, and was thankful also, that her parents did not seem to see what she saw; and, during the quiet weeks, when the shadow grew so plain to her, she said nothing of it to those at home, believing that it would tell itself when Beth came back no better. She wondered still more if her sister really guessed the hard truth, and what thoughts were passing through her mind during the long hours when she lay on the warm rocks, with her head in Jo's lap, while the winds blew healthfully over her, and the sea made music at her feet.

One day Beth told her. Jo thought she was asleep, she lay so still; and, putting down her book, sat looking at her with wistfull eyes, trying to see signs of hope in the faint colour on Beth's cheeks. But she could not find enough to satisfy her, for the cheeks were very thin, and the hands seemed too feeble to hold even the rosy little shells they had been gathering. It came to her then more bitterly than ever that Beth was slowly drifting away from her, and her arms instinctively tightened their hold upon the dearest treasure she possessed. For a minute her eyes were too dim for seeing, and when they cleared, Beth was looking up at her so tenderly that there was hardly any need for her to say – 'Jo, dear, I'm glad you know it. I've tried to tell you, but I couldn't.'

There was no answer except her sister's cheek against her own, not even tears; for when most deeply moved, Jo did not cry. She was the weaker, then, and Beth tried to comfort and sustain her, with her arms about her, and the soothing words she whispered in her ear.

'I've known it for a good while, dear, and now I'm used to it, it isn't hard to think of or to bear. Try to see it so, and don't be troubled about me, because it's best; indeed it is.'

'Is this what made you so unhappy in the autumn, Beth? You did not feel it then, and keep it to yourself so long, did you?' asked Jo, refusing to see or say that it *was* best, but glad to know that Laurie had no part in Beth's trouble.

'Yes, I gave up hoping then, but I didn't like to own it. I tried to think it was a sick fancy and would not let it trouble anyone. But when I saw you all so well and strong, and full of happy plans, it was hard to feel that I could never be like you, and then I was miserable, Jo.'

'O Beth, and you didn't tell me, didn't let me comfort and help you! How could you shut me out, and bear it all alone?'

Jo's voice was full of tender reproach, and her heart ached to think of the solitary struggle that must have gone on while Beth learned to say goodbye to health, love, and life, and take up her cross so cheerfully.

'Perhaps it was wrong, but I tried to do right; I wasn't sure, no one said anything, and I hoped I was mistaken. It would have been selfish to frighten you all when Marmee was so anxious about Meg, and Amy away, and you so happy with Laurie – at least, I thought so then.'

'And I thought that you loved him, Beth, and I went away because I couldn't,' cried Jo, glad to say all the truth.

Beth looked so amazed at the idea that Jo smiled in spite of her pain, and added softly – 'Then you didn't, deary! I was afraid it was so, and imagined your poor little heart full of love-lornity all that while.'

'Why, Jo, how could I, when he was so fond of you?' asked Beth, as innocently as a child. 'I do love him dearly! He is so good to me, how can I help it? But he never could be anything to me but my brother. I hope he truly will be, sometime.'

'Not through me,' said Jo decidedly. 'Amy is left for him, and they would suit excellently; but I have no heart for such things, now. I don't care what becomes of anybody but you, Beth. You *must* get well.'

'I want to, oh, so much! I try, but every day I lose a little, and feel more sure that I shall never gain it back. It's like the tide, Jo, when it turns, it goes slowly, but it can't be stopped.'

'It *shall* be stopped, your tide must not turn so soon, nineteen is too young. Beth, I can't let you go. I'll work and pray and fight against it. I'll keep you in spite of everything; there must be ways, it can't be too late. God won't be so cruel as to take you from me,' cried poor Jo rebelliously, for her spirit was far less piously submissive than Beth's.

Simple, sincere people seldom speak much of their piety; it shows itself in acts, rather than in words, and has more influence than homilies or protestations. Beth could not reason upon or explain the faith that gave her courage and patience to give up life, and cheerfully wait for death. Like a confiding child, she asked no questions, but left everything to God and nature, Father and mother of us all, feeling sure that they, and they only, could teach and strengthen heart and spirit for this life and the life to come. She did not rebuke Jo with saintly speeches, only loved her better for her passionate affection, and clung more closely to the dear human love, from which our Father never means us to be weaned, but through which He draws us closer to Himself. She could not say, 'I'm glad to go,' for life was very sweet to her; she could only sob out, 'I try to be willing,' while she held fast to Jo, as the first bitter wave of this great sorrow broke over them together.

By-and-by Beth said, with recovered serenity – 'You'll tell them this when we go home?'

'I think they will see it without words,' sighed Jo; for now it seemed to her that Beth changed every day.

'Perhaps not; I've heard that the people who love best are often blindest to such things. If they don't see it, you will tell them for me. I don't want any secrets, and it's kinder to prepare them. Meg has John and the babies to comfort her, but you must stand by Father and Mother, won't you, Jo?'

'If I can; but, Beth, I don't give up yet; I'm going to believe that it *is* a sick fancy, and not let you think it's true,' said Jo, trying to speak cheerfully.

Beth lay a minute thinking, and then said in her quiet way – 'I don't know how to express myself, and shouldn't try to anyone but you, because I can't speak out, except to my Jo. I only mean to say that I have a feeling that it never was intended I should live long. I'm not like the rest of you; I never made any plans about what I'd do when I grew up; I never thought of being married, as you all did. I couldn't seem to imagine myself anything but stupid little Beth, trotting about at home, of no use anywhere but there. I never wanted to go away, and the hard part now is the leaving you all. I'm not afraid, but it seems as if I should be homesick for you even in heaven.'

Jo could not speak; and for several minutes there was no sound but the sigh of the wind and the lapping of the tide. A white-winged gull flew by, with the flash of sunshine on its silvery breast; Beth watched it till it vanished, and her eyes were full of sadness. A little grey-coated sand-bird came tripping over the beach, 'peeping' softly to itself, as if enjoying the sun and sea; it came quite close to Beth, looked at her with a friendly eye, and sat upon a warm stone, dressing its wet feathers, quite at home. Beth smiled, and felt comforted, for the tiny thing seemed to offer its small friendship, and remind her that a pleasant world was still to be enjoyed.

'Dear little bird! See, Jo, how tame it is. I like peeps better than the gulls: they are not so wild and handsome, but they seem happy, confiding little things. I used to call them my birds, last summer; and Mother said they reminded her of me – busy, quaker-coloured creatures, always near the shore, and always chirping that contented little song of theirs. You are the gull, Jo, strong and wild, fond of the storm and the wind, flying far out to sea, and happy all alone. Meg is the turtle-dove, and Amy is like the lark she writes about, trying to get up among the clouds, but always dropping down into its nest again. Dear little girl! she's so ambitious, but her heart is good and tender; and no matter how high she flies, she never will forget home. I hope I shall see her again, but she seems *so* far away.'

'She is coming in the spring, and I mean that you shall be all ready to see and enjoy her. I'm going to have you well and rosy by that time,' began Jo, feeling that of all the changes in Beth, the talking change was the greatest, for it seemed to cost no effort now, and she thought aloud in a way quite unlike bashful Beth.

'Jo, dear, don't hope anymore; it won't do any good, I'm sure of that. We won't be miserable, but enjoy being together while we wait. We'll have happy times, for I don't suffer much, and I think the tide will go out easily, if you help me.'

Jo leaned down to kiss the tranquil face; and with that silent kiss, she dedicated herself soul and body to Beth.

She was right: there was no need of any words when they got home, for Father and Mother saw plainly, now, what they had prayed to be saved from seeing. Tired with her short journey, Beth went at once to bed, saying how glad she was to be at home; and when Jo went down, she found that she would be spared the hard task of telling Beth's secret. Her father stood leaning his head on the mantelpiece, and did not turn as she came in; but her mother stretched out her arms as if for help, and Jo went to comfort her without a word.

* * *

When the first bitterness was over, the family accepted the inevitable, and tried to bear it cheerfully, helping one another by the increased affection which comes to bind households tenderly together in times of trouble. They put away their grief, and each did his or her part toward making that last year a happy one.

The pleasantest room in the house was set apart for Beth, and in it was gathered everything that she most loved – flowers, pictures, her piano, the little work-table, and the beloved pussies. Father's best books found their way there, Mother's easy-chair, Jo's desk, Amy's finest sketches; and every day Meg brought her babies on a loving pilgrimage, to make sunshine for Aunty Beth. John quietly set apart a little sum, that he might enjoy the pleasure of keeping the invalid supplied with the fruit she loved and longed for; old Hannah never wearied of concocting dainty dishes to tempt a capricious appetite, dropping tears as she worked; and from across the sea came little gifts and cheerful letters, seeming to bring breaths of warmth and fragrance from lands that know no winter.

Here, cherished like a household saint in its shrine, sat Beth, tranquil and busy as ever; for nothing could change the sweet, unselfish nature, and even while preparing to leave life, she tried to make it happier for those who should remain behind. The feeble fingers were never idle, and one of her pleasures was to make little things for the schoolchildren daily passing to and fro – to drop a pair of mittens from her window for a pair of purple hands, a needle-book for some small mother of many dolls, pen-wipers for young penmen toiling through forests of pot-hooks, scrap-books for picture-loving eyes, and all manner of pleasant devices, till the reluctant climbers up the ladder of learning found their way strewn with flowers, as it were, and came to regard the gentle giver as a sort of fairy godmother, who sat above there, and showered down gifts miraculously suited to their tastes and needs. If Beth had wanted any reward, she found it in the bright little faces always turned up to her window, with nods and smiles, and the droll little letters which came to her, full of blots and gratitude.

The first few months were very happy ones, and Beth often used to look round, and say 'How beautiful this is!' as they all sat together in her sunny room, the babies kicking and crowing on the floor, Mother and sisters working near, and Father reading, in his pleasant voice, from the wise old books which seemed rich in good and comfortable words, as applicable now as when written centuries ago; a little chapel, where a paternal priest taught his flock the hard lessons all must learn, trying to show them that hope can comfort love, and faith make resignation possible. Simple sermons, that went straight to the souls of those who listened; for the father's heart was in the minister's religion, and the frequent falter in the voice gave a double eloquence to the words he spoke or read.

It was well for all that this peaceful time was given them as preparation for the sad hours to come; for, by-and-by, Beth said the needle was 'so heavy', and put it down for ever; talking wearied her, faces troubled her, pain claimed her for its own, and her tranquil spirit was sorrowfully perturbed by the ills that vexed her feeble flesh. Ah me! such heavy days, such long, long nights, such aching hearts and imploring prayers, when those who loved her best were forced to see the thin hands stretched out to them beseechingly, to hear the bitter cry, 'Help me, help me!' and to feel that there was no help. A sad eclipse of the serene soul, a sharp struggle of the young life with death; but both were mercifully brief, and then, the natural rebellion over, the old peace returned more beautiful than ever. With the wreck of her frail body, Beth's soul grew strong; and, though she said little, those about her felt that she was ready, saw that the first pilgrim called was likewise the fittest, and waited with her on the shore, trying to see the Shining Ones coming to receive her when she crossed the river.

Jo never left her for an hour since Beth had said, 'I feel stronger when you are here.' She slept on a couch in the room, waking often to renew the fire, to feed, lift, or wait upon the patient creature who seldom asked for anything, and 'tried not to be a trouble'. All day she haunted the room, jealous of any other nurse, and prouder of being chosen then than of any honour her life ever brought her. Precious and helpful hours to Jo, for now her heart received the teaching that it needed; lessons in patience were so sweetly taught her that she could not fail to learn them; charity for all, the lovely spirit that can forgive and truly forget unkindness, the loyalty to duty that makes the hardest easy, and the sincere faith that fears nothing, but trusts undoubtingly.

Often, when she woke, Jo found Beth reading in her well-worn little book, heard her singing softly, to beguile the sleepless night, or saw her lean her face upon her hands, while slow tears dropped through the transparent fingers; and Jo would lie watching her, with thoughts too deep for tears, feeling that Beth, in her simple unselfish way, was trying to wean herself from the dear old life, and fit herself for the life to come, by sacred words of comfort, quiet prayers, and the music she loved so well.

Seeing this did more for Jo than the wisest sermons, the saintliest hymns, the most fervent prayers that any voice could utter; for, with eyes made clear by many tears, and a heart softened by the tenderest sorrow, she recognized the beauty of her sister's life – uneventful, unambitious, yet full of the genuine virtues which 'smell sweet, and blossom in the dust', the self-forgetfulness that makes the humblest on earth remembered soonest in heaven, the true success which is possible to all.

One night, when Beth looked among the books upon her table, to find something to make her forget the mortal weariness that was almost as hard to bear as pain, as she turned the leaves of her old favourite *Pilgrim's Progress*, she found a little paper, scribbled over in Jo's hand. The name caught her eye, and the blurred look of the lines made her sure that tears had fallen on it.

'Poor Jo! she's fast asleep, so I won't wake her to ask leave; she shows me all her things, and I don't think she'll mind if I look at this,' thought Beth, with a glance at her sister, who lay on the rug, with the tongs beside her, ready to wake up the minute the log fell apart.

MY BETH,

Sitting patient in the shadow
　　Till the blessed light shall come,
A serene and saintly presence
　　Sanctifies our troubled home.
Earthly joys and hopes and sorrows
　　Break like ripples on the strand
Of the deep and solemn river
　　Where her willing feet now stand.

O my sister, passing from me,
　　Out of human care and strife,
Leave me, as a gift, those virtues
　　Which have beautified your life.

Dear, bequeath me that great patience
  Which has power to sustain
A cheerful uncomplaining spirit
  In its prison-house of pain.

Give me, for I need it sorely,
  Of that courage wise and sweet,
Which has made the path of duty
  Green beneath your willing feet.
Give me that unselfish nature,
  That with charity divine
Can pardon wrong for love's dear sake
  Meek heart, forgive me mine!

Thus our parting daily loseth
  Something of its bitter pain,
And while learning this hard lesson,
  My great loss becomes my gain.

For the touch of grief will render
  My wild nature more serene,
Give to life new aspirations,
  A new trust in the unseen.

Henceforth, safe across the river,
  I shall see for evermore
A beloved, household spirit
  Waiting for me on the shore.
Hope and faith, born of my sorrow,
  Guardian angels shall become,
And the sister gone before me
  By their hands shall lead me home.

Blurred and blotted, faulty and feeble, as the lines were, they brought
a look of inexpressible comfort to Beth's face, for her one regret had
been that she had done so little; and this seemed to assure her that her
life had not been useless, that her death would not bring the despair
she feared. As she sat with the paper folded between her hands, the
charred log fell asunder. Jo started up, revived the blaze, and crept
to the bedside, hoping Beth slept.

'Not asleep, but so happy, dear. See, I found this and read it; I knew you wouldn't care. Have I been all that to you, Jo?' she asked, with wistful, humble earnestness.

'O Beth, so much, so much!' and Jo's head went down upon the pillow, beside her sister's.

'Then I don't feel as if I'd wasted my life. I'm not so good as you make me, but I *have* tried to do right; and now, when it's too late to begin even to do better, it's such a comfort to know that some one loves me so much, and feels as if I'd helped them.'

'More than anyone in the world, Beth. I used to think I couldn't let you go; but I'm learning to feel that I don't lose you; that you'll be more to me than ever, and death can't part us, though it seems to.'

'I know it cannot, and I don't fear it any longer, for I'm sure I shall be your Beth still, to love and help you more than ever. You must take my place, Jo, and be everything to Father and Mother when I'm gone. They will turn to you, don't fail them; and if it's hard to work alone, remember that I don't forget you, and that you'll be happier in doing that than writing splendid books or seeing all the world; for love is the only thing that we can carry with us when we go, and it makes the end so easy.'

'I'll try, Beth', and then and there Jo renounced her old ambition, pledged herself to a new and better one, acknowledging the poverty of other desires, and feeling the blessed solace of a belief in the immortality of love.

So the spring days came and went, the sky grew clearer, the earth greener, the flowers were up fair and early, and the birds came back in time to say goodbye to Beth, who, like a tired but trustful child, clung to the hands that had led her all her life, as Father and Mother guided her tenderly through the Valley of the Shadow, and gave her up to God.

Seldom, except in books, do the dying utter memorable words, see visions, or depart with beatified countenances; and those who have sped many parting souls know that to most the end comes as naturally and simply as sleep. As Beth had hoped, the 'tide went out easily'; and in the dark hour before the dawn, on the bosom where she had drawn her first breath, she quietly drew her last, with no farewell but one loving look, one little sigh.

With tears and prayers and tender hands, mother and sisters made her ready for the long sleep that pain would never mar again, seeing with grateful eyes the beautiful serenity that soon replaced the pathetic patience that had wrung their hearts so long, and feeling with reverent joy, that to their darling death was a benignant angel, not a phantom full of dread.

When morning came, for the first time in many months the fire was out, Jo's place was empty, and the room was very still. But a bird sang blithely on a budding bough, close by, the snow-drops blossomed freshly at the window, and the spring sunshine streamed in like a benediction over the placid face upon the pillow – a face so full of painless peace that those who loved it best smiled through their tears, and thanked God that Beth was well at last.

*　*　*

IT was easy to promise self-abnegation when self was wrapped up in another, and heart and soul were purified by a sweet example; but when the helpful voice was silent, the daily lesson over, the beloved presence gone, and nothing remained but loneliness and grief, then Jo found her promise very hard to keep. How could she 'comfort Father and Mother', when her own heart ached with a ceaseless longing for her sister; how could she 'make the house cheerful', when all its light and warmth and beauty seemed to have deserted it when Beth left the old home for the new; and where in all the world could she 'find some useful, happy work to do', that would take the place of the loving service which had been its own reward? She tried in a blind, hopeless way to do her duty, secretly rebelling against it all the while, for it seemed unjust that her few joys should be lessened, her burdens made heavier, and life get harder and harder as she toiled along. Some people seemed to get all sunshine, and some all shadow; it was not fair, for she tried more than Amy to be good, but never got any reward, only disappointment, trouble, and hard work.

Poor Jo, these were dark days to her, for something like despair came over her when she thought of spending all her life in that quiet house, devoted to humdrum cares, a few small pleasures, and the duty that never seemed to grow any easier. 'I can't do it. I wasn't meant for a life like this, and I know I shall break away and do something desperate if somebody don't come and help me,' she said

208

to herself, when her first efforts failed, and she fell into the moody, miserable state of mind which often comes when strong wills have to yield to the inevitable.

But some one did come and help her, though Jo did not recognize her good angels at once, because they wore familiar shapes, and used the simple spells best fitted to poor humanity. Often she started up at night, thinking Beth called her; and when the sight of the little empty bed made her cry with the bitter cry of an unsubmissive sorrow, 'O Beth, come back! come back!' she did not stretch out her yearning arms in vain; for, as quick to hear her sobbing as she had been to hear her sister's faintest whisper, her mother came to comfort her, not with words only, but the patient tenderness that soothes by a touch, tears that were mute reminders of a greater grief than Jo's, and broken whispers, more eloquent than prayers, because hopeful resignation went hand-in-hand with natural sorrow. Sacred moments, when heart talked to heart in the silence of the night, turning affliction to a blessing, which chastened grief and strengthened love. Feeling this, Jo's burden seemed easier to bear, duty grew sweeter, and life looked more endurable, seen from the safe shelter of her mother's arms.

When aching heart was a little comforted, troubled mind likewise found help; for one day she went to the study, and, leaning over the good grey head lifted to welcome her with a tranquil smile, she said, very humbly – 'Father, talk to me as you did to Beth. I need it more than she did, for I'm all wrong.'

'My dear, nothing can comfort me like this,' he answered, with a falter in his voice, and both arms round her, as if he, too, needed help, and did not fear to ask it.

Then, sitting in Beth's little chair close beside him, Jo told her troubles – the resentful sorrow for her loss, the fruitless efforts that discouraged her, the want of faith that made life look so dark, and all the sad bewilderment which we call despair. She gave him entire confidence, he gave her the help she needed, and both found consolation in the act; for the time had come when they could talk together not only as father and daughter, but as man and woman, able and glad to serve each other with mutual sympathy as well as mutual love. Happy, thoughtful times there in the old study which Jo called 'the church of one member', and from which she came with fresh courage, recovered cheerfulness, and a more submissive spirit; for the parents who had taught one child to meet death without fear, were trying now to teach another to accept life without despondency or distrust, and to use its beautiful opportunities with gratitude and power.

Other helps had Jo – humble, wholesome duties and delights that would not be denied their part in serving her, and which she slowly learned to see and value. Brooms and dishcloths never could be as distasteful as they once had been, for Beth had presided over both; and something of her housewifely spirit seemed to linger round the little mop and the old brush, that was never thrown away. As she used them, Jo found herself humming the songs Beth used to hum, imitating Beth's orderly ways, and giving the little touches here and there that kept everything fresh and cosy, which was the first step toward making home happy, though she didn't know it, till Hannah said with an approving squeeze of the hand –

'You thoughtful creter, you're determined we sha'n't miss that dear lamb ef you can help it. We don't say much, but we see it, and the Lord will bless you for't, see ef He don't.'

As they sat sewing together, Jo discovered how much improved her sister Meg was; how well she could talk, how much she knew about good, womanly impulses, thoughts, and feelings, how happy she was in husband and children, and how much they were all doing for each other.

'Marriage is an excellent thing, after all. I wonder if I should blossom out half as well as you have, if I tried it?' said Jo, as she constructed a kite for Demi, in the topsy-turvy nursery.

'It's just what you need to bring out the tender, womanly half of your nature, Jo. You are like a chestnut-burr, prickly outside, but silky-soft within, and a sweet kernel, if one can only get at it. Love will make you show your heart some day, and then the rough burr will fall off.'

'Frost opens chestnut-burrs, ma'am, and it takes a good shake to bring them down. Boys go nutting, and I don't care to be bagged by them,' returned Jo, pasting away at the kite which no wind that blows would ever carry up, for Daisy had tied herself on as a bob.

Meg laughed, for she was glad to see a glimmer of Jo's old spirit, but she felt it her duty to enforce her opinion by every argument in her power; and the sisterly chats were not wasted, especially as two of Meg's most effective arguments were the babies, whom Jo loved tenderly. Grief is the best opener for some hearts, and Jo's was nearly ready for the bag: a little more sunshine to ripen the nut, then, not a boy's impatient shake, but a man's hand reached up to pick it gently from the burr, and find the kernel sound and sweet. If she had suspected this, she would have shut up tight, and been more prickly than ever; fortunately she wasn't thinking about herself, so, when the time came, down she dropped.

Now, if she had been the heroine of a moral story-book, she ought at this period of her life to have become quite saintly, renounced the world, and gone about doing good in a mortified bonnet, with tracts in her pocket. But, you see, Jo wasn't a heroine; she was only a struggling human girl, like hundreds of others, and she just acted out her nature, being sad, cross, listless, or energetic, as the mood suggested. It's highly virtuous to say we'll be good, but we can't do it all at once, and it takes a long pull, a strong pull, and a pull all together, before some of us even get our feet set in the right way. Jo had got so far, she was learning to do her duty, and to feel unhappy if she did not; but to do it cheerfully – ah, that was another thing! She had often said she wanted to do something splendid, no matter how hard; and now she had her wish, for what could be more beautiful than to devote her life to Father and Mother, trying to make home as happy to them as they had to her? And, if difficulties were necessary to increase the splendour of the effort, what could be harder for a restless, ambitious girl than to give up her own hopes, plans, and desires, and cheerfully live for others?

Providence had taken her at her word; here was the task, not what she had expected, but better, because self had no part in it: now, could she do it? She decided that she would try; and, in her first attempt, she found the helps I have suggested. Still another was given her, and she took it, not as a reward, but as a comfort, as Christian took the refreshment afforded by the little arbour where he rested, as he climbed the hill called Difficulty.

'Why don't you write? That always used to make you happy,' said her mother once, when the desponding fit overshadowed Jo.

'I've no heart to write, and if I had, nobody cares for my things.'

'We do; write something for us, and never mind the rest of the

211

world. Try it, dear; I'm sure it would do you good, and please us very much.'

'Don't believe I can'; but Jo got out her desk, and began to overhaul her half-finished manuscripts.

An hour afterward her mother peeped in, and there she was, scratching away, with her black pinafore on, and an absorbed expression, which caused Mrs March to smile, and slip away, well pleased with the success of her suggestion. Jo never knew how it happened, but something got into that story that went straight to the hearts of those who read it; for, when her family had laughed and cried over it, her father sent it, much against her will, to one of the popular magazines, and, to her utter surprise, it was not only paid for, but others requested. Letters from several persons, whose praise was honour, followed the appearance of the little story, newspapers copied it, and strangers as well as friends admired it. For a small thing it was a great success; and Jo was more astonished than when her novel was commended and condemned all at once.

'I don't understand it. What *can* there be in a simple little story like that, to make people praise it so?' she said, quite bewildered.

'There is truth in it, Jo, that's the secret; humour and pathos make it alive, and you have found your style at last. You wrote with no thought of fame or money, and put your heart into it, my daughter; you have had the bitter, now comes the sweet. Do your best, and grow as happy as we are in your success.'

'If there *is* anything good or true in what I write, it isn't mine; I owe it all to you and Mother and to Beth,' said Jo, more touched by her father's words than by any amount of praise from the world.

So, taught by love and sorrow, Jo wrote her little stories, and sent them away to make friends for themselves and her, finding it a very charitable world to such humble wanderers; for they were kindly welcomed, and sent home comfortable tokens to their mother, like dutiful children whom good fortune overtakes.

Wajida Tabassum

Hand-me-downs

'Oh no, Allah! I feel shy.'

'Why should you feel shy ... haven't I taken off my clothes too ... ?'

'Hm ...' Chamki shrank back a little further.

'Are you going to take them off or should I call Anna bi ...' yelled Shehzadi Pasha whose veins coursed with the wish to command. Chamki used her small hands with some trepidation to take off her kurta first ... then her pyjama ... On Shehzadi Pasha's orders she jumped into the soapy tub with her.

When they had both bathed Shehzadi Pasha turned to Chamki. With condescending fondness which had in it a large measure of possessive arrogance, she asked, 'Now tell me, what clothes are you going to wear?'

'Clothes,' Chamki said with great seriousness. 'Just these ... my blue kurta-pyjama.'

'These?!' Shehzadi Pasha shrieked and turned up her nose. 'These filthy, stinking ones? Then what's the use of having bathed in water ...'

Chamki asked a question in reply, 'And what are you wearing, Pasha?'

'Me ...', Shehzadi Pasha said with easy pride, 'you know at the time of my bismillah my grandmother had an outfit with *chanak chanak* stitched for me ... but why did you ask?'

Chamki was lost in thought, then she laughed, 'I was thinking ...'

'What?' Shehzadi Pasha asked in some surprise. Just then they heard Anna bi shout, 'No, Pasha! You chased me out of the bathroom, now why are you chattering with this no-good fool? Hurry up, or else I'll tell Bi Pasha right now.'

Chamki spoke quickly, 'Pasha! I was thinking that if you and I exchange our clothes and become *odhni badal** sisters then I could also wear your clothes, no?'

'My clothes . . . ? You mean all those clothes which are lying in my trunks?'

Chamki nodded uncertainly. Shehzadi Pasha was doubled up with laughter, 'Ao, what a foolish girl. You know you are a servant – you wear *my* discarded things. And all your life you'll wear my hand-me-downs.'

Then with infinite love which held more arrogance than any other feeling, Shehzadi Pasha tossed the dress that she had shed for the bath towards Chamki. 'Here, wear this. I have any number of other clothes.'

Chamki was incensed. 'Why should I? You wear *my* dress . . .' she said pointing to her soiled clothes.

Shehzadi Pasha hissed angrily, 'Anna bi, ANNA bi . . .'

Anna bi rattled the door which flew open since it wasn't really shut . . . 'Oh, so both the madams are still standing around naked . . .' She put her finger on her nose and spoke in mock anger.

Shehzadi Pasha immediately took down a soft pink towel and wrapped it around herself. Chamki stood as before. Anna bi glared at her daughter.

'And why did you take a dip in Pasha's bathtub . . . ?'

'Shehzadi Pasha told me to bathe with her.' Anna bi looked around furtively to make sure nobody was around, then she hurriedly pulled her out of the tub and said, 'Get to the servants' rooms . . . quick . . . you might catch a chill . . . wear my clothes . . .' Chamki shrank back a little self-consciously. 'Don't wear these filthy clothes now. There is a kurta-pyjama in the red box which Shehzadi Pasha gave you the other day . . . put that on.'

As she stood there, the little seven-year-old thought deeply and said haltingly, 'Ammavi, if Shehzadi Pasha and I are the same age then why didn't she wear what I took off?'

'Just you wait, I'll go and tell Maina that Chamki said this to me . . .'

Alarmed, Anna bi picked up Pasha and said soothingly, 'You know, Pasha, this whore has gone crazy. Why should you tell your Maina about her ranting? Don't play with her, don't even speak to her. Just be silent and spit on her name, OK?'

---

* Friends so close that, like sisters, they can exchange and share each other's clothes.

Anna bi dressed Shehzadi Pasha up, combed and plaited her hair, served her food, and when she was done with all her chores, she reached her own room to find Chamki still standing unclothed, as naked as the day she was born. Without missing a heartbeat she began slapping her daughter. 'You'll pick up fights with those who feed you, you forward old hag! Now if the bada sarkar throws us out, where will we go, eh? Such a temper!'

According to Anna bi it was a matter of great good fortune that she had been employed as a wet-nurse for Shehzadi Pasha. Her diet was as rich and fastidiously chosen as any begum's because, after all, she suckled the only daughter of the Nawab Sahib. She got lots of clothes too, because it was imperative that the wet-nurse stay absolutely clean. And the best part was that her own daughter got any number of Shehzadi Pasha's hand-me-downs. Getting clothes was usual, but quite often, silver ornaments and toys also came their way. And here was this girl: ever since she had started growing old enough to understand anything at all, her only fixation had been – why should I wear bi Pasha's rejects? Sometimes she'd look at the mirror and wisely state, 'Ammavi, I'm much prettier than bi Pasha, aren't I? *You* make her wear the clothes I discard.'

Anna bi would admonish her all the time. After all the privileged have a lot of power. If somebody got the slightest hint that it was that damned Anna's daughter and not the real daughter of the house who uttered such things, they'd surely cut off our hair and noses and cast us out. As it is, the years of suckling were long past. It was the tradition among such households that the wet-nurse was sent away only on her death. Even so, you can expect to be pardoned only for those faults that are pardonable. Not for this!

Anna bi twisted Chamki's ear and said, 'I don't want to hear any more of this, I promise you. You are to wear bi Pasha's rejects all your life. Have you understood, you child of an ass?!'

The child of an ass stilled her tongue then but the lava continued to boil inside her.

When Shehzadi Pasha turned thirteen it was her first Namaz-e-Kaza. On the eight day was her *gulpashi*. For this occasion her mother got her such a gorgeous, glittering dress that your eye could hardly stay fixed on it. It had pairs of golden bells sewed on so that whenever Pasha walked there was a sound of many anklets – *chunn bunn*. In keeping with tradition even this exquisite, expensive *jora* was given away. Anna bi gleefully gathered up all these gifts and took them to her room. There she found Chamki, who by now was wiser and more self-respecting than her years would suggest. She said unhappily, 'Ammavi, it is one thing to take such gifts because we have little choice, but please don't feel so happy when you take them.'

'Just think, beta', Anna bi whispered, 'even if we were to sell this *jora* it would fetch not less than two hundred rupees. We're lucky to have found a place in such a house.'

With enormous longing Chamki said, 'Ammavi, I wish . . . my heart's desire is that I also give some of my old things to bi Pasha some time.'

Anna bi struck her forehead and wailed, 'Now look, you're getting older – learn what is good for you. What will I do if anybody hears you say such things? Have pity on my old bones at least.'

Seeing her mother weep, Chamki fell silent.

Maulvi Sahib started both bi Pasha and Chamki on their Quran Sharif lessons and the Urdu alphabet. Chamki showed much greater intelligence and interest than bi Pasha did. When both of them completed their first recital of the Quran, the senior Pasha got Chamki a new set of clothes of ordinary material, as a mark of favour. Though Chamki later got bi Pasha's heavy set, she treasured her own clothes more than her life. She felt no hint of slight in them. A pale orange dress was much better than numerous glittering clothes.

Now that Shehzadi Pasha was as educated as was desirable, and was the right age, appropriately enough there was talk of her marriage. The house became the hub for goldsmiths, tailors and traders. All Chamki could think of was that even on the day of the biggest celebration, the wedding, she would wear only those clothes which were her own, not somebody's rejects.

The senior Pasha was a woman of great virtue and compassion; she always considered the welfare of her servants as she did that of her own children. So she was just as concerned about Chamki's marriage as she was about Shehzadi Pasha's. Finally, after nagging Nawab Sahib, she found a suitable groom for Chamki, too. In the general hubbub of Shehzadi Pasha's wedding, Chamki's nikah could also be managed, she thought.

That day, a day before Shehzadi Pasha's nikah, the house was packed with guests. A large gaggle of girls made the whole place

216

gay and noisy. Shehzadi Pasha sat among her friends with henna on her feet and said to Chamki, 'When you go to your husband's house, I'll put henna on yours.'

'Oh, God forbid!' said Anna bi fondly. 'May your enemies only have to touch her feet. That you said such a thing is good enough. Just pray that the boy she marries turns out to be as good and kind as yours.'

'But when is she getting married?' asked one of the young girls.

Shehzadi Pasha laughed the same arrogant laugh that she had as a child. 'There will be so many of my used things that her dowry is as good as ready.'

Rejects, discards, used goods . . . it was as if a thousand needles pierced Chamki's heart. She swallowed her tears and lay quietly in her room. As the sun went down the girls picked up the dholak again. Songs loaded with double entendre were sung. The previous night had been a *ratjaga* – an all-night celebration – and there was to be one tonight as well. In the courtyard at the back, the cooks were cooking various delicacies on a battery of fires. It seemed like broad daylight in the middle of the night, in the house.

Chamki's tearful beauty appeared even more attractive in her pale orange outfit. This was one dress which could lift her from the depths of her inferiority and reach her to the very skies. These were nobody's old clothes. This new dress, made of new material, had come her way but once in her life. The rest of it had been spent wearing Shehzadi Pasha's old things. And because her trousseau also consisted of Shehzadi Pasha's clothes she would have to use them for the rest of her life. *But Bi Pasha, a daughter of Sayyads can be pushed only so far and no further – you'll see. You gave me one old thing after another. Now you see.*

She entered the house of the groom with a large plate of *malida*. The house was decorated with rows of lamps, and bustled with as much gaiety as the bride's. After all, the wedding was to take place the next morning.

In the huge house and general confusion nobody took any notice of Chamki. After enquiring here and there she reached the groom's chambers. Tired out after all the ceremonies of haldi and henna, the groom lay sprawled on his bed. As the curtain moved, he looked around and was transfixed.

A knee-length pale orange kurta, tight pyjamas stretched over rounded calves, a lightly embroidered, silver-dotted orange dupatta. Eyes which swam a little, soft, firm arms emerging from short sleeves, hair adorned with garlands of white flowers and a dangerously attractive smile playing on her lips! None of this was new, but a man who has spent the past several nights fantasizing about a woman can be quite explosively susceptible, however respectable and well brought up he may be.

Night is an invitation to sin. Loneliness is what gives strength to transgression. Chamki looked at him in such a way that he felt his very bones turn brittle. She turned her face away with calculated swiftness. He stood up agitatedly and planted himself before her. Chamki sent him such a look from the corner of her eye that he felt he was going to pieces.

'Your name . . . ?' he swallowed.

'Chamki,' and a lustrous smile lit up the moonlike loveliness of her face.

'How could you have had any other name . . . ? You shine so . . . you could only be Chamki.' He put his hands on her shoulders with a tremor. His attitude was not that of the usual male who chats up girls to seduce them. His hands shook as he took hers and said, 'What do you have in this plate?'

Chamki replied encouragingly, 'I brought some *malida* for you. There was a *ratjaga* . . . at night.' She cut him to the quick as she smiled with inviting slowness '. . . to sweeten your tongue.'

'I don't want any *malida* to sweeten my tongue. I . . . we . . . yes . . .' and he brought his mouth close to hers for a taste of honey. Chamki gave herself up to his embrace. To rob him of his purity, to lose her own, to plunder all of them.

On the second day, the day of the bride's departure, Shehzadi Pasha went to give her bridal costume to her foster mother's daughter, according to the convention of the family. Chamki smiled and said, 'Pasha, all my life I lived with your used things, but now you, too . . .' She laughed like one possessed '. . . all your life something that I have used is for you . . .' Her manic laughter wouldn't stop.

Everyone thought the sorrow of parting from her childhood playmate had temporarily unhinged Chamki.

Translated by Manisha Chaudhry

Elizabeth Gaskell

from
Cranford

In the first place, Cranford is in possession of the Amazons; all the holders of houses, above a certain rent, are women. If a married couple come to settle in the town, somehow the gentleman disappears; he is either fairly frightened to death by being the only man in the Cranford evening parties, or he is accounted for by being with his regiment, his ship, or closely engaged in business all the week in the great neighbouring commercial town of Drumble, distant only twenty miles on a railroad. In short, whatever does become of the gentlemen, they are not at Cranford. What could they do if they were there? The surgeon has his round of thirty miles, and sleeps at Cranford; but every man cannot be a surgeon. For keeping the trim gardens full of choice flowers without a weed to speck them; for frightening away little boys who look wistfully at the said flowers through the railings; for rushing out at the geese that occasionally venture into the gardens if the gates are left open; for deciding all questions of literature and politics without troubling themselves with unnecessary reasons or arguments; for obtaining clear and correct knowledge of everybody's affairs in the parish; for keeping their neat maid-servants in admirable order; for kindness (somewhat dictatorial) to the poor, and real tender good offices to each other whenever they are in distress, the ladies of Cranford are quite sufficient. 'A man', as one of them observed to me once, 'is *so* in the way in the house!' Although the ladies of Cranford know all each other's proceedings, they are exceedingly indifferent to each other's opinions. Indeed, as each has her own individuality, not to say eccentricity, pretty strongly developed, nothing is so easy as verbal retaliation; but, somehow, good-will reigns among them to a considerable degree.

The Cranford ladies have only an occasional little quarrel, spirted out in a few peppery words and angry jerks of the head; just enough to prevent the even tenor of their lives from becoming too flat. Their dress is very independent of fashion; as they observe, 'What does it signify how we dress here at Cranford, where everybody knows us?' And if they go from home, their reason is equally cogent, 'What does it signify how we dress here, where nobody knows us?' The materials of their clothes are, in general, good and plain, and most of them are nearly as scrupulous as Miss Tyler, of cleanly memory; but I will answer for it, the last gigot, the last tight and scanty petticoat in wear in England, was seen in Cranford – and seen without a smile.

I can testify to a magnificent family red silk umbrella, under which a gentle little spinster, left alone of many brothers and sisters, used to patter to church on rainy days. Have you any red silk umbrellas in London? We had a tradition of the first that had ever been seen in Cranford; and the little boys mobbed it, and called it 'a stick in petticoats.' It might have been the very red silk one I have described, held by a strong father over a troop of little ones; the poor little lady – the survivor of all – could scarcely carry it.

Then there were rules and regulations for visiting and calls; and they were announced to any young people, who might be staying in the town, with all the solemnity with which the old Manx laws were read once a year on the Tinwald Mount.

'Our friends have sent to inquire how you are after your journey tonight, my dear' (fifteen miles, in a gentleman's carriage); 'they will give you some rest tomorrow, but the next day, I have no doubt, they will call; so be at liberty after twelve – from twelve to three are our calling-hours.'

Then, after they had called,

'It is the third day; I dare say your mamma has told you, my dear, never to let more than three days elapse between receiving a call and returning it; and also, that you are never to stay longer than a quarter of an hour.'

'But am I to look at my watch? How am I to find out when a quarter of an hour has passed?'

'You must keep thinking about the time, my dear, and not allow yourself to forget it in conversation.'

As everybody had this rule in their minds, whether they received or paid a call, of course no absorbing subject was ever spoken about. We kept ourselves to short sentences of small talk, and were punctual to our time.

I imagine that a few of the gentlefolks of Cranford were poor, and had some difficulty in making both ends meet; but they were like the Spartans, and concealed their smart under a smiling face. We none of us spoke of money, because that subject savoured of commerce and trade, and though some might be poor, we were all aristocratic. The Cranfordians had that kindly *esprit de corps* which made them overlook all deficiencies in success when some among them tried to conceal their poverty. When Mrs Forrester, for instance, gave a party in her baby-house of a dwelling, and the little maiden disturbed the ladies on the sofa by a request that she might get the tea-tray out from underneath, everyone took this novel proceeding as the most natural thing in the world, and talked on about household forms and ceremonies as if we all believed that our hostess had a regular servants' hall, second table, with housekeeper and steward, instead of the one little charity-school maiden, whose short ruddy arms could never have been strong enough to carry the tray upstairs, if she had not been assisted in private by her mistress, who now sat in state, pretending not to know what cakes were sent up, though she knew, and we knew, and she knew that we knew, and we knew that she knew that we knew, she had been busy all the morning making tea-bread and sponge cakes.

There were one or two consequences arising from this general but unacknowledged poverty, and this very much acknowledged gentility, which were not amiss, and which might be introduced into many circles of society to their great improvement. For instance, the inhabitants of Cranford kept early hours, and clattered home in their pattens, under the guidance of a lantern-bearer, about nine o'clock at night; and the whole town was abed and asleep by half-past ten. Moreover, it was considered 'vulgar' (a tremendous word in Cranford) to give anything expensive, in the way of eatable or drinkable, at the evening entertainments. Wafer bread-and-butter and sponge-biscuits were all that the Honourable Mrs Jamieson gave; and she was sister-in-law to the late Earl of Glenmire, although she did practise such 'elegant economy'.

221

'Elegant economy!' How naturally one falls back into the phrase-
ology of Cranford! There, economy was always 'elegant', and money-
spending always 'vulgar and ostentatious'; a sort of sour grapeism
which made us very peaceful and satisfied. I never shall forget the
dismay felt when a certain Captain Brown came to live at Cranford,
and openly spoke about his being poor – not in a whisper to an
intimate friend, the doors and windows being previously closed, but
in the public street! in a loud military voice! alleging his poverty as
a reason for not taking a particular house. The ladies of Cranford
were already rather moaning over the invasion of their territories
by a man and a gentleman. He was a half-pay captain, and had
obtained some situation on a neighbouring railroad, which had been
vehemently petitioned against by the little town; and if, in addition
to his masculine gender, and his connection with the obnoxious
railroad, he was so brazen as to talk of being poor – why, then,
indeed, he must be sent to Coventry. Death was as true and as
common as poverty; yet people never spoke about that, loud out in
the streets. It was a word not to be mentioned to ears polite. We had
tacitly agreed to ignore that any with whom we associated on terms
of visiting equality could ever be prevented by poverty from doing
anything that they wished. If we walked to or from a party, it was
because the night was *so* fine, or the air *so* refreshing, not because
sedan-chairs were expensive. If we wore prints, instead of summer
silks, it was because we preferred a washing material; and so on, till
we blinded ourselves to the vulgar fact that we were, all of us, people
of very moderate means. Of course, then, we did not know what to
make of a man who could speak of poverty as if it was not a disgrace.
Yet, somehow, Captain Brown made himself respected in Cranford,
and was called upon, in spite of all resolutions to the contrary. I was
surprised to hear his opinions quoted as authority at a visit which I
paid to Cranford about a year after he had settled in the town. My
own friends had been among the bitterest opponents of any proposal
to visit the captain and his daughters, only twelve months before;
and now he was even admitted in the tabooed hours before twelve.
True, it was to discover the cause of a smoking chimney, before the
fire was lighted; but still Captain Brown walked upstairs, nothing
daunted, spoke in a voice too large for the room, and joked quite
in the way of a tame man about the house. He had been blind to

all the small slights, and omissions of trivial ceremonies, with which he had been received. He had been friendly, though the Cranford ladies had been cool; he had answered small sarcastic compliments in good faith; and with his manly frankness had overpowered all the shrinking which met him as a man who was not ashamed to be poor. And, at last, his excellent masculine common sense, and his facility in devising expedients to overcome domestic dilemmas, had gained him an extraordinary place as authority among the Cranford ladies. He himself went on in his course, as unaware of his popularity as he had been of the reverse; and I am sure he was startled one day when he found his advice so highly esteemed as to make some counsel which he had given in jest to be taken in sober, serious earnest.

It was on this subject: An old lady had an Alderney cow, which she looked upon as a daughter. You could not pay the short quarter-of-an-hour call without being told of the wonderful milk or wonderful intelligence of this animal. The whole town knew and kindly regarded Miss Betsy Barker's Alderney; therefore great was the sympathy and regret when, in an unguarded moment, the poor cow tumbled into a lime-pit. She moaned so loudly that she was soon heard and rescued; but meanwhile the poor beast had lost most of her hair, and came out looking naked, cold, and miserable, in a bare skin. Everybody pitied the animal, though a few could not restrain their smiles at her droll appearance. Miss Betsy Barker absolutely cried with sorrow and dismay; and it was said she thought of trying a bath of oil. This remedy, perhaps, was recommended by some one of the number whose advice she asked; but the proposal, if ever it was made, was knocked on the head by Captain Brown's decided 'Get her a flannel waistcoat and flannel drawers, ma'am, if you wish to keep her alive. But my advice is, kill the poor creature at once.'

Miss Betsy Barker dried her eyes, and thanked the Captain heartily; she set to work, and by-and-by all the town turned out to see the Alderney meekly going to her pasture, clad in dark grey flannel. I have watched her myself many a time. Do you ever see cows dressed in grey flannel in London?

Captain Brown had taken a small house on the outskirts of the town, where he lived with his two daughters. He must have been upwards of sixty at the time of the first visit I paid to Cranford after I had left it as a residence. But he had a wiry, well-trained, elastic

223

figure, a stiff military throw-back of his head, and a springing step, which made him appear much younger than he was. His eldest daughter looked almost as old as himself, and betrayed the fact that his real was more than his apparent age. Miss Brown must have been forty; she had a sickly, pained, careworn expression on her face, and looked as if the gaiety of youth had long faded out of sight. Even when young she must have been plain and hard-featured. Miss Jessie Brown was ten years younger than her sister, and twenty shades prettier. Her face was round and dimpled. Miss Jenkyns once said, in a passion against Captain Brown (the cause of which I will tell you presently), 'that she thought it was time for Miss Jessie to leave off her dimples, and not always to be trying to look like a child'. It was true there was something childlike in her face; and there will be, I think, till she dies, though she should live to a hundred. Her eyes were large blue wondering eyes, looking straight at you; her nose was unformed and snub, and her lips were red and dewy; she wore her hair, too, in little rows of curls, which heightened this appearance. I do not know whether she was pretty or not; but I liked her face, and so did everybody, and I do not think she could help her dimples. She had something of her father's jauntiness of gait and manner; and any female observer might detect a slight difference in the attire of the two sisters – that of Miss Jessie being about two pounds per annum more expensive than Miss Brown's. Two pounds was a large sum in Captain Brown's annual disbursements.

Such was the impression made upon me by the Brown family when I first saw them all together in Cranford church. The captain I had met before – on the occasion of the smoky chimney, which he had cured by some simple alteration in the flue. In church, he held his double eye-glass to his eyes during the Morning Hymn, and then lifted up his head erect and sang out loud and joyfully. He made the responses louder than the clerk – an old man with a piping feeble voice, who, I think, felt aggrieved at the captain's sonorous bass, and quavered higher and higher in consequence.

On coming out of church, the brisk captain paid the most gallant attention to his two daughters. He nodded and smiled to his acquaintances; but he shook hands with none until he had helped Miss Brown to unfurl her umbrella, had relieved her of her prayer book, and had waited patiently till she, with trembling nervous hands, had taken up her gown to walk through the wet roads.

I wondered what the Cranford ladies did with Captain Brown at their parties. We had often rejoiced, in former days, that there was no gentleman to be attended to, and to find conversation for, at the card-parties. We had congratulated ourselves upon the snugness of the evenings; and, in our love for gentility, and distaste of mankind, we had almost persuaded ourselves that to be a man was to be 'vulgar'; so that when I found my friend and hostess, Miss Jenkyns, was going to have a party in my honour, and that Captain and the Miss Browns were invited, I wondered much what would be the course of the evening. Card-tables, with green-baize tops, were set out by daylight, just as usual; it was the third week in November, so the evenings closed in about four. Candles, and clean packs of cards were arranged on each table. The fire was made up; the neat maid-servant had received her last directions; and there we stood, dressed in our best, each with a candle-lighter in our hands, ready to dart at the candles as soon as the first knock came. Parties in Cranford were solemn festivities, making the ladies feel gravely elated as they sat together in their best dresses. As soon as three had arrived, we sat down to 'Preference', I being the unlucky fourth. The next four comers were put down immediately to another table; and presently the tea-trays, which I had seen set out in the store-room as I passed in the morning, were placed each on the middle of a card-table. The china was delicate egg-shell; the old-fashioned silver glittered with polishing; but the eatables were of the slightest description. While the trays were yet on the tables, Captain and the Miss Browns came in; and I could see that, somehow or other, the captain was a favourite with all the ladies present. Ruffled brows were smoothed, sharp voices lowered at his approach. Miss Brown looked ill, and depressed almost to gloom. Miss Jessie smiled as usual, and seemed nearly as popular as her father. He immediately and quietly assumed the man's place in the room; attended to every one's wants, lessened the pretty maid-servant's labour by waiting on empty cups and bread-and-butterless ladies; and yet did it all in so easy and dignified a manner, and so much as if it were a matter of course for the strong to attend to the weak, that he was a true man throughout. He played for three-penny points with as grave an interest as if they had been pounds; and yet, in all his attention to strangers, he had an eye on his suffering daughter – for suffering I was sure she was, though to many eyes she might only appear to be irritable. Miss Jessie could not play cards: but she talked to the sitters-out, who, before her coming, had been rather inclined to be cross. She sang, too, to an old cracked piano, which I think had been a spinnet in its youth. Miss Jessie sang, 'Jock of Hazeldean' a little out of tune; but we were none of us musical, though Miss Jenkyns beat time, out of time, by way of appearing to be so.

It was very good of Miss Jenkyns to do this; for I had seen that, a little before, she had been a good deal annoyed by Miss Jessie Brown's unguarded admission (*à propos* of Shetland wool) that she had an uncle, her mother's brother, who was a shopkeeper in Edinburgh. Miss Jenkyns tried to drown this confession by a terrible cough – for the Honourable Mrs Jamieson was sitting at the card-table nearest Miss Jessie, and what would she say or think if she found out she was in the same room with a shopkeeper's niece! But Miss Jessie Brown (who had no tact, as we all agreed the next morning) *would* repeat the information, and assure Miss Pole she could easily get her the identical Shetland wool required, 'through my uncle, who has the best assortment of Shetland goods of any one in Edinbro'.' It was to take the taste of this out of our mouths, and the sound of this out of our ears, that Miss Jenkyns proposed music; so I say again, it was very good of her to beat time to the song.

When the trays reappeared with biscuits and wine, punctually at a quarter to nine, there was conversation, comparing of cards, and talking over tricks; but by-and-by Captain Brown sported a bit of literature.

'Have you seen any numbers of *The Pickwick Papers*?' said he. (They were then publishing in parts.) 'Capital thing!'

Now Miss Jenkyns was daughter of a deceased rector of Cranford; and, on the strength of a number of manuscript sermons, and a pretty good library of divinity, considered herself literary, and looked upon any conversation about books as a challenge to her. So she answered and said, 'Yes, she had seen them; indeed, she might say she had read them.'

'And what do you think of them?' exclaimed Captain Brown. 'Aren't they famously good?'

226

So urged, Miss Jenkyns could not but speak.

'I must say, I don't think they are by any means equal to Dr Johnson. Still, perhaps, the author is young. Let him persevere, and who knows what he may become if he will take the great Doctor for his model.' This was evidently too much for Captain Brown to take placidly; and I saw the words on the tip of his tongue before Miss Jenkyns had finished her sentence.

'It is quite a different sort of thing, my dear madam,' he began.

'I am quite aware of that,' returned she. 'And I make allowances, Captain Brown.'

'Just allow me to read you a scene out of this month's number,' pleaded he. 'I had it only this morning, and I don't think the company can have read it yet.'

'As you please,' said she, settling herself with an air of resignation. He read the account of the 'swarry' which Sam Weller gave at Bath. Some of us laughed heartily. *I* did not dare, because I was staying in the house. Miss Jenkyns sat in patient gravity. When it was ended, she turned to me, and said, with mild dignity,

'Fetch me *Rasselas*, my dear, out of the book-room.'

When I brought it to her, she turned to Captain Brown.

'Now allow *me* to read you a scene, and then the present company can judge between your favourite, Mr Boz, and Dr Johnson.'

She read one of the conversations between Rasselas and Imlac, in a high-pitched majestic voice; and when she had ended, she said, 'I imagine I am now justified in my preference of Dr Johnson as a writer of fiction.' The captain screwed his lips up, and drummed on the table, but he did not speak. She thought she would give a finishing blow or two.

'I consider it vulgar, and below the dignity of literature, to publish in numbers.'

'How was the *Rambler* published, ma'am?' asked Captain Brown, in a low voice, which I think Miss Jenkyns could not have heard.

'Dr Johnson's style is a model for young beginners. My father recommended it to me when I began to write letters – I have formed my own style upon it; I recommend it to your favourite.'

'I should be very sorry for him to exchange his style for any such pompous writing,' said Captain Brown.

Miss Jenkyns felt this as a personal affront, in a way of which the captain had not dreamed. Epistolary writing she and her friends considered as her *forte*. Many a copy of many a letter have I seen written and corrected on the slate, before she 'seized the half-hour just previous to post-time to assure' her friends of this or of that; and Dr Johnson was, as she said, her model in these compositions. She drew herself up with dignity, and only replied to Captain Brown's last remark by saying, with marked emphasis on every syllable, 'I prefer Dr Johnson to Mr Boz.'

It is said – I won't vouch for the fact – that Captain Brown was heard to say, *sotto voce*, 'D–n Dr Johnson!' If he did, he was penitent afterwards, as he showed by going to stand near Miss Jenkyns's armchair, and endeavouring to beguile her into conversation on some more pleasing subject. But she was inexorable. The next day she made the remark I have mentioned about Miss Jessie's dimples.

It was impossible to live a month at Cranford and not know the daily habits of each resident; and long before my visit was ended I knew much concerning the whole Brown trio. There was nothing new to be discovered respecting their poverty; for they had spoken simply and openly about that from the very first. They made no mystery of the necessity for their being economical. All that remained to be discovered was the captain's infinite kindness of heart, and the various modes in which, unconsciously to himself, he manifested it. Some little anecdotes were talked about for some time after they occurred. As we did not read much, and as all the ladies were pretty well suited with servants, there was a dearth of subjects for conversation. We therefore discussed the circumstance of the captain taking a poor old woman's dinner out of her hands one very slippery Sunday. He had met her returning from the bakehouse as he came from church, and noticed her precarious footing; and, with the grave dignity with which he did everything, he relieved her of her burden, and steered along the street by her side, carrying her baked mutton and potatoes safely home. This was thought very eccentric; and it was rather expected that he would pay a round of calls, on the Monday morning, to explain and apologize to the Cranford sense of propriety: but he did no such thing; and then it was decided that he was ashamed, and was keeping out of sight. In a kindly pity for him, we began to say, 'After all, the Sunday morning's occurrence showed great goodness of heart', and it was resolved that he should be comforted on his next appearance amongst us; but, lo! he came down upon us, untouched by any sense of shame, speaking loud and bass as ever, his head thrown back, his wig as jaunty and well-curled as usual, and we were obliged to conclude he had forgotten all about Sunday.

Miss Pole and Miss Jessie Brown had set up a kind of intimacy on the strength of the Shetland wool and the new knitting stitches; so it happened that when I went to visit Miss Pole I saw more of the Browns than I had done while staying with Miss Jenkyns, who had never got over what she called Captain Brown's disparaging remarks upon Dr Johnson as a writer of light and agreeable fiction. I found that Miss Brown was seriously ill of some lingering, incurable complaint, the pain occasioned by which gave the uneasy expression to her face that I had taken for unmitigated crossness. Cross, too, she was at times, when the nervous irritability occasioned by her disease became past endurance. Miss Jessie bore with her at these times, even more patiently than she did with the bitter self-upbraidings by which they were invariably succeeded. Miss Brown used to accuse herself, not merely of hasty and irritable temper, but also of being the cause why her father and sister were obliged to pinch, in order to allow her the small luxuries which were necessaries in her condition. She would so fain have made sacrifices for them and have lightened their cares, that the original generosity of her disposition added acerbity to her temper. All this was borne by Miss Jessie and her father with more than placidity – with absolute tenderness. I forgave Miss Jessie her singing out of tune, and her juvenility of dress, when I saw her at home. I came to perceive that Captain Brown's dark Brutus wig and padded coat (alas! too often threadbare) were remnants of the military smartness of his youth, which he now wore unconsciously. He was a man of infinite resources, gained in his barrack experience. As he confessed, no one could black his boots to please him, except himself: but, indeed, he was not above saving the little maid-servant's labours in every way – knowing, most likely, that his daughter's illness made the place a hard one.

He endeavoured to make peace with Miss Jenkyns, soon after the memorable dispute I have named, by a present of a wooden fire-shovel (his own making), having heard her say how much the grating of an iron one annoyed her. She received the present with cool gratitude, and thanked him formally. When he was gone, she bade me put it away in the lumber-room; feeling, probably, that no present from a man who preferred Mr Boz to Dr Johnson could be less jarring than an iron fire-shovel.

Such was the state of things when I left Cranford and went to Drumble. I had, however, several correspondents who kept me *au fait* as to the proceedings of the dear little town. There was Miss Pole, who was becoming as much absorbed in crochet as she had been once in knitting, and the burden of whose letter was something like, 'But don't you forget the white worsted at Flint's' of the old song; for at the end of every sentence of news came a fresh direction as to some crochet commission which I was to execute for her. Miss Matilda Jenkyns (who did not mind being called Miss Matty when Miss Jenkyns was not by) wrote nice, kind, rambling letters, now and then venturing into an opinion of her own; but suddenly pulling herself up, and either begging me not to name what she had said, as Deborah thought differently, and *she* knew, or else putting in a postscript to the effect that, since writing the above, she had been talking over the subject with Deborah, and was quite convinced that, &c. – (here probably followed a recantation of every opinion she had given in the letter). Then came Miss Jenkyns – Debōrah, as she liked Miss Matty to call her, her father having once said that the Hebrew name ought to be so pronounced. I secretly think she took the Hebrew prophetess for a model in character; and, indeed, she was not unlike the stern prophetess in some ways, making allowance, of course, for modern customs and difference in dress. Miss Jenkyns wore a cravat, and a little bonnet like a jockey-cap, and altogether had the appearance of a strong-minded woman; although she would have despised the modern idea of women being equal to men. Equal, indeed! she knew they were superior. But to return to her letters. Everything in them was stately and grand, like herself. I have been looking them over (dear Miss Jenkyns, how I honoured her!), and I will give an extract, more especially because it relates to our friend Captain Brown: –

'The Honourable Mrs Jamieson has only just quitted me; and, in the course of conversation, she communicated to me the intelligence that she had yesterday received a call from her revered husband's quondam friend, Lord Mauleverer. You will not easily conjecture what brought his lordship within the precincts of our little town. It was to see Captain Brown, with whom, it appears, his lordship was acquainted in the "plumed wars", and who had the privilege of averting destruction from his lordship's head, when some great peril was impending over it, off the misnomered Cape of Good Hope. You know our friend the Honourable Mrs Jamieson's deficiency in the spirit of innocent curiosity; and you will therefore not be so much surprised when I tell you she was quite unable to disclose to me the exact nature of the peril in question. I was anxious, I confess, to ascertain in what manner Captain Brown, with his limited establishment, could receive so distinguished a guest; and I discovered that his lordship retired to rest, and, let us hope, to refreshing slumbers, at the Angel Hotel; but shared the Brunonian meals during the two days that he honoured Cranford with his august presence. Mrs Johnson, our civil butcher's wife, informs me that Miss Jessie purchased a leg of lamb; but, besides this, I can hear of no preparation whatever to give a suitable reception to so distinguished a visitor. Perhaps they entertained him with "the feast of reason and the flow of soul"; and to us, who are acquainted with Captain Brown's sad want of relish for "the pure wells of English undefiled", it may be matter for congratulation that he has had the opportunity of improving his taste by holding converse with an elegant and refined member of the British aristocracy. But from some mundane failings who is altogether free?'

Miss Pole and Miss Matty wrote to me by the same post. Such a piece of news as Lord Mauleverer's visit was not to be lost on the Cranford letter-writers: they made the most of it. Miss Matty humbly apologized for writing at the same time as her sister, who was so much more capable than she to describe the honour done to Cranford; but, in spite of a little bad spelling, Miss Matty's account gave me the best idea of the commotion occasioned by his lordship's visit, after it had occurred; for, except the people at the Angel, the Browns, Mrs Jamieson, and a little lad his lordship had sworn at for driving a dirty hoop against the aristocratic legs, I could not hear of anyone with whom his lordship had held conversation.

My next visit to Cranford was in the summer. There had been

neither births, deaths, nor marriages since I was there last. Everybody lived in the same house, and wore pretty nearly the same well-preserved, old-fashioned clothes. The greatest event was, that Miss Jenkynses had purchased a new carpet for the drawing-room. Oh the busy work Miss Matty and I had in chasing the sunbeams, as they fell in an afternoon right down on this carpet through the blindless window! We spread newspapers over the places, and sat down to our book or our work; and, lo! in a quarter of an hour the sun had moved, and was blazing away on a fresh spot; and down again we went on our knees to alter the position of the newspapers. We were very busy, too, one whole morning, before Miss Jenkyns gave her party, in following her directions, and in cutting out and stitching together pieces of newspaper so as to form little paths to every chair set for the expected visitors, lest their shoes might dirty or defile the purity of the carpet. Do you make paper paths for every guest to walk upon in London?

Captain Brown and Miss Jenkyns were not very cordial to each other. The literary dispute, of which I had seen the beginning, was a 'raw', the slightest touch on which made them wince. It was the only difference of opinion they had ever had; but that difference was enough. Miss Jenkyns could not refrain from talking *at* Captain Brown; and, though he did not reply, he drummed with his fingers, which action she felt and resented as very disparaging to Dr Johnson. He was rather ostentatious in his preference of the writings of Mr Boz; would walk through the streets so absorbed in them that he all but ran against Miss Jenkyns; and though his apologies were earnest and sincere, and though he did not, in fact, do more than startle her and himself, she owned to me she had rather he had knocked her down, if he had only been reading a higher style of literature. The poor, brave captain! he looked older, and more worn, and his clothes were very threadbare. But he seemed as bright and cheerful as ever, unless he was asked about his daughter's health.

'She suffers a great deal, and she must suffer more; we do what we can to alleviate her pain; – God's will be done!' He took off his hat at these last words. I found, from Miss Matty, that everything had been done, in fact. A medical man, of high repute in that country neighbourhood, had been sent for, and every injunction he had given was attended to, regardless of expense. Miss Matty was sure they denied themselves many things in order to make the invalid comfortable; but they never spoke about it; and as for Miss Jessie! – 'I really think she's an angel,' said poor Miss Matty, quite overcome. 'To see her way of bearing with Miss Brown's crossness, and the bright face she puts on after she's been sitting up a whole night and scolded above half of it, is quite beautiful. Yet she looks as neat and as ready to welcome the captain at breakfast-time as if she had been asleep in the Queen's bed all night. My dear! you could never laugh at her prim little curls or her pink bows again if you saw her as I have done.' I could only feel very penitent, and greet Miss Jessie with double respect when I met her next. She looked faded and pinched; and her lips began to quiver, as if she was very weak, when she spoke of her sister. But she brightened, and sent back the tears that were glittering in her pretty eyes, as she said:

'But, to be sure, what a town Cranford is for kindness! I don't suppose any one has a better dinner than usual cooked but the best part of all comes in a little covered basin for my sister. The poor people will leave their earliest vegetables at our door for her. They speak short and gruff, as if they were ashamed of it; but I am sure it often goes to my heart to see their thoughtfulness.' The tears now came back and overflowed; but after a minute or two she began to scold herself, and ended by going away the same cheerful Miss Jessie as ever.

'But why does not this Lord Mauleverer do something for the man who saved his life?' said I.

'Why, you see, unless Captain Brown has some reason for it, he never speaks about being poor; and he walked along by his lordship looking as happy and cheerful as a prince; and as they never called attention to their dinner by apologies, and as Miss Brown was better that day, and all seemed bright, I daresay his lordship never knew how much care there was in the background. He did send game in the winter pretty often, but now he is gone abroad.'

I had often occasion to notice the use that was made of fragments and small opportunities in Cranford; the rose-leaves that were gathered ere they fell to make into a pot-pourri for some one who had no garden; the little bundles of lavender-flowers sent to strew the drawers of some town-dweller, or to burn in the chamber of some invalid. Things that many would despise, and actions which it seemed scarcely worthwhile to perform, were all attended to in Cranford. Miss Jenkyns stuck an apple full of cloves, to be heated and smell pleasantly in Miss Brown's room; and as she put in each clove she uttered a Johnsonian sentence. Indeed, she never could think of the Browns without talking Johnson; and, as they were seldom absent from her thoughts just then, I heard many a rolling, three-piled sentence.

Captain Brown called one day to thank Miss Jenkyns for many little kindnesses, which I did not know until then that she had rendered. He had suddenly become like an old man; his deep bass voice had a quavering in it, his eyes looked dim, and the lines on his face were deep. He did not – could not – speak cheerfully of his daughter's state, but he talked with manly, pious resignation, and not much. Twice over he said, 'What Jessie has been to us, God only knows!' and after the second time, he got up hastily, shook hands all round without speaking, and left the room.

That afternoon we perceived little groups in the street, all listening with faces aghast to some tale or other. Miss Jenkyns wondered what could be the matter for some time before she took the undignified step of sending Jenny out to inquire.

Jenny came back with a white face of terror. 'Oh, ma'am! oh, Miss Jenkyns, ma'am! Captain Brown is killed by them nasty cruel railroads!' and she burst into tears. She, along with many others, had experienced the poor Captain's kindness.

'How? – where – where? Good God! Jenny, don't waste time in crying, but tell us something.' Miss Matty rushed out into the street at once, and collared the man who was telling the tale.

'Come in – come to my sister at once, – Miss Jenkyns, the rector's daughter. Oh, man, man! – say it is not true,' she cried, as she brought the affrighted carter, sleeking down his hair, into the drawing-room, where he stood with his wet boots on the new carpet, and no one regarded it.

'Please, mum, it is true. I seed it myself,' and he shuddered at the recollection. 'The Captain was a-reading some new book as he was deep in, a-waiting for the down train; and there was a little lass as wanted to come to its mammy, and gave its sister the slip, and came toddling across the line. And he looked up sudden, at the sound of the train coming, and seed the child, and he darted on the line and cotched it up, and his foot slipped, and the train came over him in no time. Oh Lord, Lord! Mum, it's quite true – and they've come over to tell his daughters. The child's safe, though, with only a bang on its shoulder, as he threw it to its mammy. Poor Captain would be glad of that, mum, wouldn't he? God bless him!' The great rough carter puckered up his manly face, and turned away to hide his tears. I turned to Miss Jenkyns. She looked very ill, as if she were going to faint, and signed to me to open the window.

'Matilda, bring me my bonnet. I must go to those girls. God pardon me, if ever I have spoken contemptuously to the Captain!'

Miss Jenkyns arrayed herself to go out, telling Miss Matilda to give the man a glass of wine. While she was away, Miss Matty and I huddled over the fire, talking in a low and awestruck voice. I know we cried quietly all the time.

Miss Jenkyns came home in a silent mood, and we durst not ask her many questions. She told us that Miss Jessie had fainted, and that she and Miss Pole had had some difficulty in bringing her round; but that, as soon as she recovered, she begged one of them to go and sit with her sister.

'Mr Hoggins says she cannot live many days, and she shall be spared this shock,' said Miss Jessie, shivering with feelings to which she dared not give way.

'But how can you manage, my dear?' asked Miss Jenkyns; 'you cannot bear up, she must see your tears.'

'God will help me – I will not give way – she was asleep when the news came; she may be asleep yet. She would be so utterly miserable, not merely at my father's death, but to think of what would become of me; she is so good to me.' She looked up earnestly in their faces with her soft true eyes, and Miss Pole told Miss Jenkyns afterwards she could hardly bear it, knowing, as she did, how Miss Brown treated her sister.

However, it was settled according to Miss Jessie's wish. Miss Brown was to be told her father had been summoned to take a short journey on railway business. They had managed it in some way – Miss Jenkyns could not exactly say how. Miss Pole was to stop with Miss Jessie. Mrs Jamieson had sent to inquire. And this was all we heard that night; and a sorrowful night it was. The next day a full account of the fatal accident was in the county paper which Miss

Jenkyns took in. Her eyes were very weak, she said, and she asked me to read it. When I came to the 'gallant gentleman was deeply engaged in the perusal of a number of *Pickwick*, which he had just received,' Miss Jenkyns shook her head long and solemnly, and then sighed out, 'Poor, dear, infatuated man!'

The corpse was to be taken from the station to the parish church, there to be interred. Miss Jessie had set her heart on following it to the grave; and no dissuasives could alter her resolve. Her restraint upon herself made her almost obstinate; she resisted all Miss Pole's entreaties and Miss Jenkyns's advice. At last Miss Jenkyns gave up the point; and after a silence, which I feared portended some deep displeasure against Miss Jessie, Miss Jenkyns said she should accompany the latter to the funeral.

'It is not fit for you to go alone. It would be against both propriety and humanity were I to allow it.'

Miss Jessie seemed as if she did not half like this arrangement; but her obstinacy, if she had any, had been exhausted in her determination to go to the interment. She longed, poor thing, I have no doubt, to cry alone over the grave of the dear father to whom she had been all in all, and to give way, for one little half-hour, uninterrupted by sympathy and unobserved by friendship. But it was not to be. That afternoon Miss Jenkyns sent out for a yard of black crape, and employed herself busily in trimming the little black silk bonnet I have spoken about. When it was finished she put it on, and looked at us for approbation – admiration she despised. I was full of sorrow, but, by one of those whimsical thoughts which come unbidden into our heads, in times of deepest grief, I no sooner saw the bonnet than I was reminded of a helmet; and in that hybrid bonnet, half-helmet, half-jockey cap, did Miss Jenkyns attend Captain Brown's funeral, and, I believe, supported Miss Jessie with a tender, indulgent firmness which was invaluable, allowing her to weep her passionate fill before they left.

Miss Pole, Miss Matty, and I, meanwhile, attended to Miss Brown: and hard work we found it to relieve her querulous and never-ending complaints. But if we were so weary and dispirited, what must Miss Jessie have been! Yet she came back almost calm, as if she had gained a new strength. She put off her mourning dress, and came in, looking pale and gentle, thanking us each with a soft long pressure of the hand. She could even smile – a faint, sweet, wintry smile – as if to reassure us of her power to endure; but her look made our eyes fill suddenly with tears, more than if she had cried outright.

It was settled that Miss Pole was to remain with her all the watching livelong night; and that Miss Matty and I were to return in the morning to relieve them, and give Miss Jessie the opportunity for a few hours of sleep. But when the morning came, Miss Jenkyns appeared at the breakfast-table, equipped in her helmet-bonnet, and ordered Miss Matty to stay at home, as she meant to go and help to nurse. She was evidently in a state of great friendly excitement, which she showed by eating her breakfast standing, and scolding the household all round.

No nursing – no energetic strong-minded woman could help Miss Brown now. There was that in the room as we entered which was stronger than us all, and made us shrink into solemn awestruck helplessness. Miss Brown was dying. We hardly knew her voice, it was so devoid of the complaining tone we had always associated with it. Miss Jessie told me afterwards that it, and her face too, were just what they had been formerly, when her mother's death left her the young anxious head of the family, of whom only Miss Jessie survived.

She was conscious of her sister's presence, though not, I think, of ours. We stood a little behind the curtain: Miss Jessie knelt with her face near her sister's, in order to catch the last soft awful whispers.

'Oh, Jessie! Jessie! How selfish I have been! God forgive me for letting you sacrifice yourself for me as you did! I have so loved you – and yet I have thought only of myself. God forgive me!'

'Hush, love! hush!' said Miss Jessie, sobbing.

'And my father! my dear, dear father! I will not complain now, if God will give me strength to be patient. But, oh, Jessie! tell my father how I longed and yearned to see him at last, and to ask his forgiveness. He can never know now how I loved him – oh! if I might but tell him, before I die! What a life of sorrow his has been, and I have done so little to cheer him!'

A light came into Miss Jessie's face. 'Would it comfort you, dearest, to think that he does know? – would it comfort you, love, to know that his cares, his sorrows –' Her voice quivered, but she steadied it into calmness, – 'Mary! he has gone before you to the place where the weary are at rest. He knows now how you loved him.'

A strange look, which was not distress, came over Miss Brown's face. She did not speak for some time, but then we saw her lips form the words, rather than heard the sound – 'Father, Mother, Harry, Archy'; – then, as if it were a new idea throwing a filmy shadow over her darkened mind – 'But you will be alone, Jessie!'

Miss Jessie had been feeling this all during the silence, I think; for the tears rolled down her cheeks like rain, at these words, and she could not answer at first. Then she put her hands together tight, and lifted them up, and said – but not to us –

'Though He slay me, yet will I trust in Him.'

In a few moments more Miss Brown lay calm and still – never to sorrow or murmur more.

After this second funeral, Miss Jenkyns insisted that Miss Jessie should come to stay with her rather than go back to the desolate house, which, in fact, we learned from Miss Jessie, must now be given up, as she had not wherewithal to maintain it. She had something above twenty pounds a year, besides the interest of the money for which the furniture would sell; but she could not live upon that: and so we talked over her qualifications for earning money.

'I can sew neatly,' said she, 'and I like nursing. I think, too, I could manage a house, if any one would try me as housekeeper; or I would go into a shop, as saleswoman, if they would have patience with me at first.'

Miss Jenkyns declared, in an angry voice, that she should do no such thing; and talked to herself about 'some people having no idea of their rank as a captain's daughter', nearly an hour afterwards, when she brought Miss Jessie up a basin of delicately-made arrowroot, and stood over her like a dragoon until the last spoonful was finished: then she disappeared. Miss Jessie began to tell me some more of the plans which had suggested themselves to her, and insensibly fell into talking of the days that were past and gone, and interested me so much I neither knew nor heeded how time passed. We were both startled when Miss Jenkyns reappeared, and caught us crying. I was afraid lest she would be displeased, as she often said that crying hindered digestion, and I knew she wanted Miss Jessie to get strong; but, instead, she looked queer and

238

excited, and fidgeted round us without saying anything. At last she spoke.

'I have been so much startled – no, I've not been at all startled – don't mind me, my dear Miss Jessie – I've been very much surprised – in fact, I've had a caller, whom you knew once, my dear Miss Jessie –'

Miss Jessie went very white, then flushed scarlet, and looked eagerly at Miss Jenkyns.

'A gentleman, my dear, who wants to know if you would see him.'

'Is it? – it is not –' stammered out Miss Jessie – and got no farther.

'This is his card,' said Miss Jenkyns, giving it to Miss Jessie; and while her head was bent over it, Miss Jenkyns went through a series of winks and odd faces to me, and formed her lips into a long sentence, of which, of course, I could not understand a word.

'May he come up?' asked Miss Jenkyns, at last.

'Oh, yes! certainly!' said Miss Jessie, as much as to say, this is your house, you may show any visitor where you like. She took up some knitting of Miss Matty's and began to be very busy, though I could see how she trembled all over.

Miss Jenkyns rang the bell, and told the servant who answered it to show Major Gordon upstairs; and, presently, in walked a tall, fine, frank-looking man of forty or upwards. He shook hands with Miss Jessie; but he could not see her eyes, she kept them so fixed on the ground. Miss Jenkyns asked me if I would come and help her to tie up the preserves in the store-room; and, though Miss Jessie plucked at my gown, and even looked up at me with begging eye, I durst not refuse to go where Miss Jenkyns asked. Instead of tying up preserves in the store-room, however, we went to talk in the dining-room; and there Miss Jenkyns told me what Major Gordon had told her; – how he had served in the same regiment with Captain Brown, and had become acquainted with Miss Jessie, then a sweet-looking, blooming girl of eighteen; how the acquaintance had grown into love on his part, though it had been some years before he had spoken; how, on becoming possessed, through the will of an uncle, of a good estate in Scotland, he had offered and been refused, though with so much agitation and evident distress that he was sure she was not indifferent to him; and how he had discovered that the obstacle was the fell disease which was, even then, too surely threatening her sister. She had mentioned that the surgeons foretold intense suffering; and there was no one but herself to nurse her poor Mary, or cheer and comfort her father during the time of illness. They had had long discussions; and on her refusal to pledge herself to him as his wife when all should be over, he had grown angry, and broken off entirely, and gone abroad, believing that she was a cold-hearted person whom he would do well to forget. He had been travelling in the East, and was on his return home when, at Rome, he saw the account of Captain Brown's death in *Galignani*.

Just then Miss Matty, who had been out all the morning, and had only lately returned to the house, burst in with a face of dismay and outraged propriety.

'Oh, goodness me!' she said. 'Deborah, there's a gentleman sitting in the drawing-room with his arm round Miss Jessie's waist!' Miss Matty's eyes looked large with terror.

Miss Jenkyns snubbed her down in an instant.

'The most proper place in the world for his arm to be in. Go away, Matilda, and mind your own business.' This from her sister, who had hitherto been a model of feminine decorum, was a blow for poor Miss Matty, and with a double shock she left the room.

The last time I ever saw poor Miss Jenkyns was many years after this. Mrs Gordon had kept up a warm and affectionate intercourse with all at Cranford. Miss Jenkyns, Miss Matty, and Miss Pole had all been to visit her, and returned with wonderful accounts of her house, her husband, her dress, and her looks. For, with happiness, something of her early bloom returned; she had been a year or two younger than we had taken her for. Her eyes were always lovely, and, as Mrs Gordon, her dimples were not out of place. At the time to which I have referred, when I last saw Miss Jenkyns, that lady was old and feeble, and had lost something of her strong mind. Little Flora Gordon was staying with the Misses Jenkyns, and when I came in she was reading aloud to Miss Jenkyns, who lay feeble and changed on the sofa. Flora put down the *Rambler* when I came in.

'Ah!' said Miss Jenkyns, 'you find me changed, my dear. I can't see as I used to do. If Flora were not here to read to me, I hardly know how I should get through the day. Did you ever read the *Rambler*? It's a wonderful book – wonderful! and the most improving reading for

Flora' (which I dare say it would have been, if she could have read half the words without spelling, and could have understood the meaning of a third), 'better than that strange old book, with the queer name, poor Captain Brown was killed for reading – that book by Mr Boz, you know – '*Old Poz*; when I was a girl – but that's a long time ago – I acted Lucy in *Old Poz*.' She babbled on long enough for Flora to get a good long spell at the *Christmas Carol*, which Miss Matty had left on the table.

I thought that probably my connection with Cranford would cease after Miss Jenkyns's death; at least, that it would have to be kept up by correspondence, which bears much the same relation to personal intercourse that the books of dried plants I sometimes see ('*Hortus Siccus*', I think they call the thing) do to the living and fresh flowers in the lanes and meadows. I was pleasantly surprised, therefore, by receiving a letter from Miss Pole (who had always come in for a supplementary week after my annual visit to Miss Jenkyns) proposing that I should go and stay with her; and then, in a couple of days after my acceptance, came a note from Miss Matty, in which, in a rather circuitous and very humble manner, she told me how much pleasure I should confer if I could spend a week or two with her, either before or after I had been at Miss Pole's; 'for', she said, 'since my dear sister's death I am well aware I have no attractions to offer; it is only to the kindness of my friends that I can owe their company.'

Of course I promised to come to dear Miss Matty as soon as I had ended my visit to Miss Pole; and the day after my arrival at Cranford I went to see her, much wondering what the house would be like without Miss Jenkyns, and rather dreading the changed aspect of things. Miss Matty began to cry as soon as she saw me. She was evidently nervous from having anticipated my call. I comforted her as well as I could; and I found the best consolation I could give was the honest praise that came from my heart as I spoke of the deceased. Miss Matty slowly shook her head over each virtue as it was named and attributed to her sister; and at last she could not restrain the tears which had long been silently flowing, but hid her face behind her handkerchief, and sobbed aloud.

'Dear Miss Matty!' said I, taking her hand – for indeed I did not know in what way to tell her how sorry I was for her, left deserted in the world. She put down her handkerchief, and said:

'My dear, I'd rather you did not call me Matty. *She* did not like it; but I did many a thing she did not like, I'm afraid – and now she's gone! If you please, my love, will you call me Matilda?'

I promised faithfully, and began to practise the new name with Miss Pole that very day; and, by degrees, Miss Matilda's feeling on the subject was known through Cranford, and we all tried to drop the more familiar name, but with so little success that by and by we gave up the attempt.

My visit to Miss Pole was very quiet. Miss Jenkyns had so long taken the lead in Cranford that, now she was gone, they hardly knew how to give a party. The Honourable Mrs Jamieson, to whom Miss Jenkyns herself had always yielded the post of honour, was fat and inert, and very much at the mercy of her old servants. If they chose that she should give a party, they reminded her of the necessity for so doing: if not, she let it alone. There was all the more time for me to hear old-world stories from Miss Pole, while she sat knitting, and I making my father's shirts. I always took a quantity of plain sewing to Cranford; for, as we did not read much, or walk much, I found it a capital time to get through my work. One of Miss Pole's stories related to a shadow of a love affair that was dimly perceived or suspected long years before.

Presently, the time arrived when I was to remove to Miss Matilda's house. I found her timid and anxious about the arrangements for my comfort. Many a time, while I was unpacking, did she come backwards and forwards to stir the fire, which burned all the worse for being so frequently poked.

'Have you drawers enough, dear?' asked she. 'I don't know exactly how my sister used to arrange them. She had capital methods. I am sure she would have trained a servant in a week to make a better fire than this, and Fanny has been with me four months.'

This subject of servants was a standing grievance, and I could not wonder much at it; for if gentlemen were scarce, and almost unheard of in the 'genteel society' of Cranford, they or their counterparts – handsome young men – abounded in the lower classes. The pretty neat servant-maids had their choice of desirable 'followers'; and their mistresses, without having the sort of mysterious dread of men and matrimony that Miss Matilda had, might well feel a little anxious lest the heads of their comely maids should be turned by the joiner, or the butcher, or the gardener, who were obliged, by their callings, to come to the house, and who, as ill-luck would have it, were generally handsome and unmarried. Fanny's lovers, if she had any – and Miss Matilda suspected her of so many flirtations that, if she had not been very pretty, I should have doubted her having one – were a constant anxiety to her mistress. She was forbidden, by the articles of her engagement, to have 'followers'; and though she had answered, innocently enough, doubling up the hem of her apron as she spoke, 'Please, ma'am, I never had more than one at a time,' Miss Matty prohibited that one. But a vision of a man seemed to haunt the kitchen. Fanny assured me that it was all fancy, or else I should have said myself that I had seen a man's coat-tails whisk into the scullery once, when I went on an errand into the store-room at night; and another evening, when, our watches having stopped, I went to look at the clock, there was a very odd appearance, singularly like a young man squeezed up between the clock and the back of the open kitchen door: and I thought Fanny snatched up the candle very hastily, so as to throw the shadow on the clock-face, while she very positively told me the time half an hour too early, as we found out afterwards by the church clock. But I did not add to Miss Matty's anxieties by naming my suspicions, especially as Fanny said to me, the next day, that it was such a queer kitchen for having odd shadows about it, she really was almost afraid to stay; 'for you know, miss,' she added, 'I don't see a creature from six o'clock tea, till Missus rings the bell for prayers at ten.'

However, it so fell out that Fanny had to leave; and Miss Matilda begged me to stay and 'settle her' with the new maid; to which I consented, after I had heard from my father that he did not want me at home. The new servant was a rough, honest-looking country-girl, who had only lived in a farm place before; but I liked her looks when she came to be hired; and I promised Miss Matilda to put her in the ways of the house. The said ways were religiously such as Miss Matilda thought her sister would approve. Many a domestic rule and regulation had been a subject of plaintive whispered murmur to me during Miss Jenkyns's life; but now that she was gone, I do not think that even I, who was a favourite, durst have suggested an alteration. To give an instance: we constantly adhered to the forms which were observed, at meal times, in 'my father, the rector's house'. Accordingly, we had always wine and dessert; but the decanters were only filled when there was a party, and what remained was seldom touched, though we had two wine glasses apiece every day after dinner, until the next festive occasion arrived, when the state of the remainder wine was examined into in a family council. The dregs were often given to the poor: but occasionally, when a good deal had been left at the last party (five months ago, it might be), it was added to some of a fresh bottle, brought up from the cellar. I fancy poor Captain Brown did not much like wine, for I noticed he never finished his first glass, and most military men take several. Then, as to our dessert, Miss Jenkyns used to gather currants and gooseberries for it herself, which I sometimes thought would have tasted better fresh from the trees; but then, as Miss Jenkyns observed, there would have been nothing for dessert in summertime. As it was, we felt very genteel with our two glasses apiece, and a dish of gooseberries at the top, of currants and biscuits at the sides, and two decanters at the bottom. When oranges came in, a curious proceeding was gone through. Miss Jenkyns did not like to cut the fruit; for, as she observed, the juice all ran out nobody knew where; sucking (only I think she used some more recondite word) was in fact the only way of enjoying oranges; but then there was the unpleasant association with a ceremony frequently gone through by little babies; and so, after dessert, in orange season, Miss Jenkyns and Miss Matty used to rise up, possess themselves each of an orange in silence, and withdraw to the privacy of their own rooms to indulge in sucking oranges.

I had once or twice tried, on such occasions, to prevail on Miss Matty to stay, and had succeeded in her sister's lifetime. I held up a screen, and did not look, and, as she said, she tried not to make the noise very offensive; but now that she was left alone, she seemed quite horrified when I begged her to remain with me in the warm dining-parlour, and enjoy her orange as she liked best. And so it was in everything. Miss Jenkyns's rules were made more stringent than ever, because the framer of them was gone where there could be no appeal. In all things else Miss Matilda was meek and undecided to a fault. I have heard Fanny turn her round twenty times in a morning about dinner, just as the little hussy chose; and I sometimes fancied she worked on Miss Matilda's weakness in order to bewilder her, and to make her feel more in the power of her clever servant. I determined that I would not leave her till I had seen what sort of a person Martha was; and, if I found her trustworthy, I would tell her not to trouble her mistress with every little decision.

Martha was blunt and plain-spoken to a fault; otherwise she was a brisk, well-meaning, but very ignorant girl. She had not been with us a week before Miss Matilda and I were astounded one morning by the receipt of a letter from a cousin of hers, who had been twenty or thirty years in India, and who had lately, as we had seen by the 'Army List', returned to England, bringing with him an invalid wife who had never been introduced to her English relations. Major Jenkyns wrote to propose that he and his wife should spend a night at Cranford, on his way to Scotland – at the inn, if it did not suit Miss Matilda to receive them into her house; in which case they should hope to be with her as much as possible during the day. Of course, it *must* suit her, as she said; for all Cranford knew that she had her sister's bedroom at liberty; but I am sure she wished the major had stopped in India and forgotten his cousins out and out.

'Oh! how must I manage?' asked she, helplessly. 'If Deborah had been alive she would have known what to do with a gentleman-visitor. Must I put razors in his dressing-room? Dear! dear! and I've got none. Deborah would have had them. And slippers, and coat-brushes?' I suggested that probably he would bring all these things with him. 'And after dinner, how am I to know when to get up and leave him to his wine? Deborah would have done it so well; she would have been quite in her element. Will he want coffee, do you think?' I undertook the management of the coffee, and told her I would instruct Martha in the art of waiting – in which it must be owned she was terribly deficient – and that I had no doubt Major and Mrs Jenkyns would understand the quiet mode in which a lady lived by herself in a country town. But she was sadly fluttered. I made her empty her decanters and bring up two fresh bottles of wine. I wished I could have prevented her from being present at my instructions to Martha, for she frequently cut in with some fresh direction, muddling the poor girl's mind, as she stood open-mouthed, listening to us both.

'Hand the vegetables round,' said I (foolishly, I see now – for it was aiming at more than we could accomplish with quietness and simplicity); and then, seeing her look bewildered, I added, 'Take the vegetables round to people, and let them help themselves.'

'And mind you go first to the ladies,' put in Miss Matilda. 'Always go to the ladies before gentlemen when you are waiting.'

'I'll do it as you tell me, ma'am,' said Martha; 'but I like lads best.'

We felt very uncomfortable and shocked at this speech of Martha's, yet I don't think she meant any harm; and, on the whole, she attended very well to our directions, except that she 'nudged' the major when he did not help himself as soon as she expected to the potatoes, while she was handing them round.

The major and his wife were quiet, unpretending people enough when they did come; languid, as all East Indians are, I suppose. We were rather dismayed at their bringing two servants with them, a Hindoo body-servant for the major, and a steady elderly maid for his wife; but they slept at the inn, and took off a good deal of the responsibility by attending carefully to their master's and mistress's comfort. Martha, to be sure, had never ended her staring at the East Indian's white turban and brown complexion, and I saw that Miss Matilda shrunk away from him a little as he waited at dinner. Indeed, she asked me, when they were gone, if he did not remind me of Blue Beard? On the whole, the visit was most satisfactory, and is a subject of conversation even now with Miss Matilda; at the time, it greatly excited Cranford, and even stirred up the apathetic and Honourable Mrs Jamieson to some expression of interest, when I went to call and thank her for the kind answers she had vouchsafed to Miss Matilda's inquiries as to the arrangement of a gentleman's dressing-room – answers which I must confess she had given in the wearied manner of the Scandinavian prophetess –

Leave me, leave me to repose.

And *now* I come to the love affair.

It seems that Miss Pole had a cousin, once or twice removed, who had offered to Miss Matty long ago. Now this cousin lived four or five miles from Cranford on his own estate; but his property was not large enough to entitle him to rank higher than a yeoman; or rather, with something of the 'pride which apes humility', he had refused to push himself on, as so many of his class had done, into the ranks of the squires. He would not allow himself to be called Thomas Holbrook, *Esq.*; he even sent back letters with this address, telling the postmistress at Cranford that his name was *Mr* Thomas Holbrook, yeoman. He rejected all domestic innovations; he would have the house door stand open in summer and shut in winter, without knocker or bell to summon a servant. The closed fist or the knob of the stick did this office for him if he found the door locked. He despised every refinement which had not its root deep down in humanity. If people were not ill, he saw no necessity for moderating his voice. He spoke the dialect of the country in perfection, and constantly used it in conversation; although Miss Pole (who gave me these particulars) added, that he read aloud more beautifully and with more feeling than any one she had ever heard, except the late rector.

'And how came Miss Matilda not to marry him?' asked I.

'Oh, I don't know. She was willing enough, I think; but you know cousin Thomas would not have been enough of a gentleman for the rector and Miss Jenkyns.'

'Well! but they were not to marry him,' said I, impatiently.

'No; but they did not like Miss Matty to marry below her rank. You know she was the rector's daughter, and somehow they are related to Sir Peter Arley: Miss Jenkyns thought a deal of that.'

'Poor Miss Matty!' said I.

'Nay, now, I don't know anything more than that he offered and was refused. Miss Matty might not like him – and Miss Jenkyns might never have said a word – it is only a guess of mine.'

'Has she never seen him since?' I inquired.

'No, I think not. You see Woodley, cousin Thomas's house, lies halfway between Cranford and Misselton; and I know he made Misselton his market-town very soon after he had offered to Miss Matty; and I don't think he has been into Cranford above once or twice since – once, when I was walking with Miss Matty, in High Street, and suddenly she darted from me, and went up Shire Lane. A few minutes after I was startled by meeting cousin Thomas.'

'How old is he?' I asked, after a pause of castle-building.

'He must be about seventy, I think, my dear,' said Miss Pole, blowing up my castle, as if by gunpowder, into small fragments.

247

Very soon after – at least during my long visit to Miss Matilda – I had the opportunity of seeing Mr Holbrook; seeing, too, his first encounter with his former love, after thirty or forty years' separation. I was helping to decide whether any of the new assortment of coloured silks which they had just received at the shop would do to match a grey and black mousseline-de-laine that wanted a new breadth, when a tall, thin, Don Quixote-looking old man came into the shop for some woollen gloves. I had never seen the person (who was rather striking) before, and I watched him rather attentively while Miss Matty listened to the shopman. The stranger wore a blue coat with brass buttons, drab breeches, and gaiters, and drummed with his fingers on the counter until he was attended to. When he answered the shop-boy's question, 'What can I have the pleasure of showing you today, sir?' I saw Miss Matilda start, and then suddenly sit down; and instantly I guessed who it was. She had made some inquiry which had to be carried round to the other shopman.

'Miss Jenkyns wants the black sarsenet two-and-twopence the yard'; and Mr Holbrook had caught the name, and was across the shop in two strides.

'Matty – Miss Matilda – Miss Jenkyns! God bless my soul! I should not have known you. How are you? how are you?' He kept shaking her hand in a way which proved the warmth of his friendship; but he repeated so often, as if to himself, 'I should not have known you!' that any sentimental romance which I might be inclined to build was quite done away with by his manner.

However, he kept talking to us all the time we were in the shop; and then waving the shopman with the unpurchased gloves on one side, with 'Another time, sir! another time!' he walked home with us. I am happy to say my client, Miss Matilda, also left the shop in an equally bewildered state, not having purchased either green or red silk. Mr Holbrook was evidently full with honest, loud-spoken joy at meeting his old love again; he touched on the changes that had taken place; he even spoke of Miss Jenkyns as 'Your poor sister! Well, well! we all have our faults', and bade us goodbye with many a hope that he should soon see Miss Matty again. She went straight to her room, and never came back till our early tea-time, when I thought she looked as if she had been crying.

A few days after, a note came from Mr Holbrook, asking us – impartially asking both of us – in a formal, old-fashioned style, to spend a day at his house – a long June day – for it was June now. He named that he had also invited his cousin, Miss Pole; so that we might join in a fly, which could be put up at his house.

I expected Miss Matty to jump at this invitation; but, no! Miss Pole and I had the greatest difficulty in persuading her to go. She thought it was improper; and was even half annoyed when we utterly ignored the idea of any impropriety in her going with two other ladies to see her old lover. Then came a more serious difficulty. She did not think Deborah would have liked her to go. This took us half a day's good hard talking to get over; but, at the first sentence of relenting, I seized the opportunity, and wrote and dispatched an acceptance in her name – fixing day and hour, that all might be decided and done with.

The next morning she asked me if I would go down to the shop with her; and there, after much hesitation, we chose out three caps to be sent home and tried on, that the most becoming might be selected to take with us on Thursday.

She was in a state of silent agitation all the way to Woodley. She had evidently never been there before; and, although she little dreamt I knew anything of her early story, I could perceive she was in a tremor at the thought of seeing the place which might have been her home, and round which it is probable that many of her innocent girlish imaginations had clustered. It was a long drive there, through paved jolting lanes. Miss Matilda sat bolt upright, and looked wistfully out of the windows as we drew near the end of our journey. The aspect of the country was quiet and pastoral. Woodley stood among fields; and there was an old-fashioned garden where roses and currant-bushes touched each other, and where the feathery asparagus formed a pretty background to the pinks and gilly-flowers; there was no drive up to the door. We got out at a little gate, and walked up a straight box-edged path.

'My cousin might make a drive, I think,' said Miss Pole, who was afraid of ear-ache, and had only her cap on.

'I think it is very pretty,' said Miss Matty, with a soft plaintiveness in her voice, and almost in a whisper, for just then Mr Holbrook appeared at the door, rubbing his hands in very effervescence of hospitality. He looked more like my idea of Don Quixote than ever, and yet the likeness was only external. His respectable housekeeper stood modestly at the door to bid us welcome; and, while she led the elder ladies upstairs to a bedroom, I begged to look about the garden. My request evidently pleased the old gentleman, who took me all round the place, and showed me his six-and-twenty cows, named after the different letters of the alphabet. As we went along, he surprised me occasionally by repeating apt and beautiful quotations from the poets, ranging easily from Shakespeare and George Herbert to those of our own day. He did this as naturally as if he were thinking aloud, and their true and beautiful words were the best expression he could find for what he was thinking or feeling. To be sure he called Byron 'my Lord Byrron', and pronounced the name of Goethe strictly in accordance with the English sound of the letters – 'As Goethe says, "Ye ever-verdant palaces",' &c. Altogether, I never met with a man, before or since, who had spent so long a life in a secluded and not impressive country, with ever-increasing delight in the daily and yearly change of season and beauty.

When he and I went in, we found that dinner was nearly ready in the kitchen – for so I suppose the room ought to be called, as there were oak dressers and cupboards all round, all over by the side of the fireplace, and only a small Turkey carpet in the middle of the flag-floor. The room might have been easily made into a handsome dark oak dining-parlour by removing the oven and a few other appurtenances of a kitchen, which were evidently never used, the real cooking-place being at some distance. The room in which we were expected to sit was a stiffly-furnished, ugly apartment; but that in which we did sit was what Mr Holbrook called the counting-house, when he paid his labourers their weekly wages at a great desk near the door. The rest of the pretty sitting-room – looking into the orchard, and all covered over with dancing tree-shadows – was filled with books. They lay on the ground, they covered the walls, they strewed the table. He was evidently half-ashamed and half-proud of his extravagance in this respect. They were of all kinds – poetry and wild weird tales prevailing. He evidently chose his books in accordance with his own tastes, not because such and such were classical or established favourites.

'Ah!' he said, 'we farmers ought not to have much time for reading; yet somehow one can't help it.'

250

'What a pretty room!' said Miss Matty, *sotto voce*.

'What a pleasant place!' said I, aloud, almost simultaneously.

'Nay! if you like it,' replied he; 'but can you sit on these great black leather three-cornered chairs? I like it better than the best parlour; but I thought ladies would take that for the smarter place.'

It was the smarter place, but, like most smart things, not at all pretty, or pleasant, or homelike; so, while we were at dinner, the servant-girl dusted and scrubbed the counting-house chairs, and we sat there all the rest of the day.

We had pudding before meat; and I thought Mr Holbrook was going to make some apology for his old-fashioned ways, for he began:

'I don't know whether you like new-fangled ways.'

'Oh, not at all!' said Miss Matty.

'No more do I,' said he. 'My housekeeper *will* have these in her new fashion; or else I tell her that, when I was a young man, we used to keep strictly to my father's rule, "No broth, no ball; no ball, no beef"; and always began dinner with broth. Then we had suet puddings, boiled in the broth with the beef, and then the meat itself. If we did not sup our broth, we had no ball, which we liked a deal better; and the beef came last of all, and only those had it who had done justice to the broth and the ball. Now folks begin with sweet things, and turn their dinners topsy-turvy.'

When the ducks and green peas came, we looked at each other in dismay; we had only two-pronged, black-handled forks. It is true the steel was as bright as silver; but what were we to do? Miss Matty picked up her peas, one by one, on the point of the prongs, much as Aminé ate her grains of rice after her previous feast with the Ghoul. Miss Pole sighed over her delicate young peas as she left them on one side of her plate untasted, for they *would* drop between the prongs. I looked at my host: the peas were going wholesale into his capacious mouth, shovelled up by his large, round-ended knife. I saw, I imitated, I survived! My friends, in spite of my precedent, could not muster up courage enough to do an ungenteel thing; and, if Mr Holbrook had not been so heartily hungry, he would probably have seen that the good peas went away almost untouched.

After dinner, a clay pipe was brought in, and a spittoon; and, asking us to retire to another room, where he would soon join us, if we disliked tobacco-smoke, he presented his pipe to Miss

251

Matty, and requested her to fill the bowl. This was a compliment to a lady in his youth; but it was rather inappropriate to propose it as an honour to Miss Matty, who had been trained by her sister to hold smoking of every kind in utter abhorrence. But if it was a shock to her refinement, it was also a gratification to her feelings to be thus selected so she daintily stuffed the strong tobacco into the pipe, and then we withdrew.

'It is very pleasant dining with a bachelor,' said Miss Matty softly, as we settled ourselves in the counting-house. 'I only hope it is not improper; so many pleasant things are!'

'What a number of books he has!' said Miss Pole, looking round the room. 'And how dusty they are!'

'I think it must be like one of the great Dr Johnson's rooms,' said Miss Matty. 'What a superior man your cousin must be!'

'Yes!' said Miss Pole, 'he's a great reader; but I am afraid he has got into very uncouth habits with living alone.'

'Oh! uncouth is too hard a word. I should call him eccentric; very clever people always are!' replied Miss Matty.

When Mr Holbrook returned, he proposed a walk in the fields; but the two elder ladies were afraid of damp, and dirt, and had only very unbecoming calashes to put on over their caps; so they declined, and I was again his companion in a turn which he said he was obliged to take to see after his men. He strode along, either wholly forgetting my existence, or soothed into silence by his pipe – and yet it was not silence exactly. He walked before me, with a stooping gait, his hands clasped behind him; and, as some tree or cloud, or glimpse of distant upland pastures, struck him, he quoted poetry to himself, saying it out loud in a grand, sonorous voice with just the emphasis that true feeling and appreciation give. We came upon an old cedar-tree, which stood at one end of the house –

The cedar spreads his dark-green layers of shade.

'Capital term – "layers!" Wonderful man!' I did not know whether he was speaking to me or not; but I put in an assenting 'wonderful', although I knew nothing about it, just because I was tired of being forgotten, and of being consequently silent.

He turned sharp round. 'Ay! you may say "wonderful". Why, when I saw the review of his poems in *Blackwood*, I set off within an hour, and walked seven miles to Misselton (for the horses were not in the way) and ordered them. Now, what colour are ash-buds in March?'

Is the man going mad? thought I. He is very like Don Quixote.

'What colour are they, I say?' repeated he, vehemently.

'I am sure I don't know, sir,' said I, with the meekness of ignorance.

'I knew you didn't. No more did I – an old fool that I am! – till this young man comes and tells me. Black as ash-buds in March. And I've lived all my life in the country; more shame for me not to know. Black: they are jet-black, madam.' And he went off again, swinging along to the music of some rhyme he had got hold off.

When we came back, nothing would serve him but he must read us the poems he had been speaking of; and Miss Pole encouraged him in his proposal, I thought, because she wished me to hear his beautiful reading, of which she had boasted; but she afterwards said it was because she had got to a difficult part of her crochet, and wanted to count her stitches without having to talk. Whatever he had proposed would have been right to Miss Matty; although she did fall sound asleep within five minutes after he had begun a long poem, called 'Locksley Hall', and had a comfortable nap, unobserved, till he ended; when the cessation of his voice wakened her up, and she said, feeling that something was expected, and that Miss Pole was counting –

'What a pretty book!'

'Pretty, madam! it's beautiful! Pretty, indeed!'

'Oh yes! I meant beautiful!' said she, fluttered at his disapproval of her word. 'It is so like that beautiful poem of Dr Johnson's my sister used to read – I forget the name of it; what was it, my dear?' turning to me.

'Which do you mean, ma'am? What was it about?'

'I don't remember what it was about, and I've quite forgotten what the name of it was; but it was written by Dr Johnson, and was very beautiful, and very like what Mr Holbrook has just been reading.'

'I don't remember it,' said he, reflectively. 'But I don't know Dr Johnson's poems well. I must read them.'

As we were getting into the fly to return, I heard Mr Holbrook say he should call on the ladies soon, and inquire how they got home; and this evidently pleased and fluttered Miss Matty at the time he said it; but after we had lost sight of the old house among the trees her sentiments towards the master of it were gradually absorbed into a distressing wonder as to whether Martha had broken her word, and seized on the opportunity of her mistress's absence to have a 'follower'. Martha looked good, and steady, and composed enough, as she came to help us out; she was always careful of Miss Matty, and tonight she made use of this unlucky speech:

'Eh! dear ma'am, to think of your going out in an evening in such a thin shawl! It's no better than muslin. At your age, ma'am, you should be careful.'

'My age!' said Miss Matty, almost speaking crossly, for her, for she was usually gentle – 'My age! Why, how old do you think I am, that you talk about my age?'

'Well, ma'am, I should say you were not far short of sixty: but folks' looks is often against them – and I'm sure I meant no harm.'

'Martha, I'm not yet fifty-two!' said Miss Matty, with grave emphasis; for probably the remembrance of her youth had come very vividly before her this day, and she was annoyed at finding that golden time so far away in the past.

But she never spoke of any former and more intimate acquaintance with Mr Holbrook. She had probably met with so little sympathy in her early love, that she had shut it up close in her heart; and it was only by a sort of watching, which I could hardly avoid since Miss Pole's confidence, that I saw how faithful her poor heart had been in its sorrow and its silence.

She gave me some good reason for wearing her best cap every day, and sat near the window, in spite of her rheumatism, in order to see, without being seen, down into the street.

He came. He put his open palms upon his knees, which were far apart, as he sat with his head bent down, whistling, after we had replied to his inquiries about our safe return. Suddenly, he jumped up:

'Well, madam! have you any commands for Paris? I am going there in a week or two.'

'To Paris!' we both exclaimed.

'Yes, madam! I've never been there, and always had a wish to go; and I think if I don't go soon, I mayn't go at all; so as soon as the hay is got in I shall go, before harvest time.'

We were so much astonished that we had no commissions.

Just as he was going out of the room, he turned back, with his favourite exclamation:

'God bless my soul, madam! but I nearly forgot half my errand. Here are the poems for you you admired so much the other evening at my house.' He tugged away at a parcel in his coat-pocket. 'Goodbye, miss,' said he; 'goodbye, Matty! take care of yourself.' And he was gone. But he had given her a book, and he had called her Matty, just as he used to do thirty years ago.

'I wish he would not go to Paris,' said Miss Matilda, anxiously. 'I don't believe frogs will agree with him; he used to have to be very careful what he ate, which was curious in so strong-looking a young man.'

Soon after this I took my leave, giving many an injunction to Martha to look after her mistress, and to let me know if she thought that Miss Matilda was not so well; in which case I would volunteer a visit to my old friend, without noticing Martha's intelligence to her.

Accordingly I received a line or two from Martha every now and then; and, about November, I had a note to say her mistress was 'very low and sadly off her food'; and the account made me so uneasy that, although Martha did not decidedly summon me, I packed up my things and went.

I received a warm welcome, in spite of the little flurry produced by my impromptu visit, for I had only been able to give a day's notice. Miss Matilda looked miserably ill; and I prepared to comfort and cosset her.

I went down to have a private talk with Martha.

'How long has your mistress been so poorly?' I asked, as I stood by the kitchen fire.

'Well! I think it's better than a fortnight; it is, I know; it was one Tuesday, after Miss Pole had been, that she went into this moping way. I thought she was tired, and it would go off with a night's rest; but no! she has gone on and on ever since, till I thought it my duty to write to you, ma'am.'

'You did quite right, Martha. It is a comfort to think she has so faithful a servant about her. And I hope you find your place comfortable?'

'Well, ma'am, missus is very kind, and there's plenty to eat and drink, and no more work but what I can do easily, – but –' Martha hesitated.

'But what, Martha?'

'Why, it seems so hard of missus not to let me have any followers; there's such lots of young fellows in the town; and many a one has as much as offered to keep company with me; and I may never be in such a likely place again, and it's like wasting an opportunity. Many a girl as I know would have 'em unbeknownst to missus; but I've given my word, and I'll stick to it; or else this is just the house for missus never to be the wiser if they did come: and it's such a capable kitchen – there's such good dark corners in it – I'd be bound to hide anyone. I counted up last Sunday night – for I'll not deny I was crying because I had to shut the door in Jem Hearn's face, and he's a steady young man, fit for any girl; only I had given missus my word.' Martha was all but crying again; and I had little comfort to give her, for I knew, from old experience, of the horror with which both the Miss Jenkynses looked upon 'followers'; and in Miss Matty's present nervous state this dread was not likely to be lessened.

I went to see Miss Pole the next day, and took her completely by surprise, for she had not been to see Miss Matilda for two days.

'And now I must go back with you, my dear, for I promised to let her know how Thomas Holbrook went on; and, I'm sorry to say, his housekeeper has sent me word today that he hasn't long to live. Poor Thomas! that journey to Paris was quite too much for him. His housekeeper says he has hardly ever been round his fields since, but just sits with his hands on his knees in the counting-house, not reading or anything, but only saying what a wonderful city Paris was! Paris has much to answer for if it's killed my cousin Thomas, for a better man never lived.'

'Does Miss Matilda know of his illness?' asked I – a new light as to the cause of her indisposition dawning upon me.

'Dear! to be sure, yes! Has not she told you? I let her know a fortnight ago, or more, when first I heard of it. How odd she shouldn't have told you!'

Not at all, I thought; but I did not say anything. I felt almost guilty of having spied too curiously into that tender heart, and I was not going to speak of its secrets – hidden, Miss Matty believed, from all the world. I ushered Miss Pole into Miss Matilda's little drawing-room, and then left them alone. But I was not surprised when Martha came to my bedroom door, to ask me to go down to dinner alone, for that missus had one of her bad headaches. She came into the drawing-room at tea-time, but it was evidently an effort to her; and, as if to make up for some reproachful feeling against her late sister, Miss Jenkyns, which had been troubling her all the afternoon, and for which she now felt penitent, she kept telling me how good and how clever Deborah was in her youth; how she used to settle what gowns they were to wear at all the parties (faint, ghostly ideas of grim parties, far away in the distance, when Miss Matty and Miss Pole were young!); and how Deborah and her mother had started the benefit society for the poor, and taught girls cooking and plain sewing; and how Deborah had once danced with a lord; and how she used to visit at Sir Peter Arley's, and try to remodel the quiet rectory establishment on the plans of Arley Hall, where they kept thirty servants; and how she had nursed Miss Matty through a long, long illness, of which I had never heard before, but which I now dated in my own mind as following the dismissal of the suit of Mr Holbrook. So we talked softly and quietly of old times through the long November evening.

The next day Miss Pole brought us word that Mr Holbrook was dead. Miss Matty heard the news in silence; in fact, from the account of the previous day, it was only what we had to expect. Miss Pole kept calling upon us for some expression of regret, by asking if it was not sad that he was gone, and saying:

'To think of that pleasant day last June, when he seemed so well! And he might have lived this dozen years if he had not gone to that wicked Paris, where they are always having revolutions.'

She paused for some demonstration on our part. I saw Miss Matty could not speak, she was trembling so nervously; so I said what I really felt: and after a call of some duration – all the time of which I have no doubt Miss Pole thought Miss Matty received the news very calmly – our visitor took her leave.

Miss Matty made a strong effort to conceal her feelings – a concealment she practised even with me, for she has never alluded to Mr Holbrook again, although the book he gave her lies with her Bible on the little table by her bedside. She did not think I heard her when she asked the little milliner of Cranford to make her caps something like the Honourable Mrs Jamieson's, or that I noticed the reply –

'But she wears widows' caps, ma'am?'

'Oh? I only meant something in that style; not widows', of course, but rather like Mrs Jamieson's.'

This effort at concealment was the beginning of the tremulous motion of head and hands which I have seen ever since in Miss Matty.

The evening of the day on which we heard of Mr Holbrook's death, Miss Matilda was very silent and thoughtful; after prayers she called Martha back, and then she stood, uncertain what to say.

'Martha!' she said, at last, 'you are young' – and then she made so long a pause that Martha, to remind her of her half-finished sentence, dropped a curtsey, and said –

'Yes, please, ma'am; two-and-twenty last third of October, please, ma'am.'

'And perhaps, Martha, you may some time meet with a young man you like, and who likes you. I did say you were not to have followers; but if you meet with such a young man, and tell me, and I find he is respectable, I have no objection to his coming to see you once a week. God forbid!' said she, in a low voice, 'that I should grieve any young hearts.' She spoke as if she were providing for some distant contingency, and was rather startled when Martha made her ready eager answer.

'Please, ma'am, there's Jem Hearn, and he's a joiner making three-and-sixpence a day, and six foot one in his stocking-feet, please, ma'am; and if you'll ask about him tomorrow morning, every one will give him a character for steadiness; and he'll be glad enough to come tomorrow night, I'll be bound.'

Though Miss Matty was startled, she submitted to Fate and Love.

Georgina Hammick

Tales from the Spare Room

Whenever they are invited to, they play cards with the maids in the maids' sitting-room.

Alice has got the Queen, Barbara says, pointing a finger at Alice who retreats into the sofa clutching her cards close to her face, so that Barbara shan't see them.

Barbara leans across and tweaks a card from Alice's hand. She looks at it and pouts and pulls her bottom lip and then raises her eyes to the ceiling in what seems to be despair; and then she slots the card into her own hand and spreads the cards into a fan. Mollie and Lucy, on the other side of the table, and on chairs, snigger. Hee hee, Barbara's got it now, Lucy says. Hee hee hee.

Fooled yer, Barbara says. She whips two cards from her fan and slaps them face up on the oilcloth, and sure enough she has a pair – two threes, hearts and spades.

Barbara is always fooling them. She is the sharp one of the maids, and as unlike Mollie, her sister and elder by two years, as it's possible to be. Barbara is short, not more than five foot. She has a round, pimply face and small features; her eyes are grey and sly, her no-colour hair is scraped back from her forehead. Because of her sharpness and her grating and sarcastic remarks, her singing voice comes as a surprise. She sings 'Open the door, Richard' (her young man's name is Dick) and 'Give Me Five Minutes More' and 'I Surrender, Dear' very sweetly when she cleans the bathrooms and the stairs.

Mollie is perhaps two inches taller. She hasn't got a young man (which is strange because she is prettier than Barbara), and she hasn't got spots. Her dark hair waves and curls round her oval face; her cheeks are red, her eyes brown. Mollie's eyes fill easily with tears. A sad song, a baby in a pram, a bunch of primroses

259

– and Mollie's eyes brim and she dabs them with a drenched handkerchief.

More embarrassing even than her tears is her habit of hugging and kissing them. Each time they come to stay at Grandmother's house, she is waiting in the hall when they arrive – hands clasped together, lips parted, face pink and radiant in its halo of curls. Oooh, aren't they lovely, aren't they grand, Mollie says in a sort of gasp; and she grabs them in turn and lifts them off the ground and covers their eyes, their cheeks, their mouths, with kisses and tears. She presses their faces to her bosom so they can't breathe; she murmurs Darling, Sweetheart, My Love into their hair. It is terrible, but there is no way of avoiding it.

Even though experience has taught them she is not to be trusted, they prefer Barbara and Barbara's style. She takes no part in the welcome ceremony. If she happens to be in the hall, she stands on her own by the stairs, hand on hip, tapping a black shoe and looking the other way. When she does look at them, her expression is cool; if she does speak, her words are brief and uncomplimentary:

What a great fat thing you are now, Lucy – couldn't get me arms round you if I wanted. Which I don't. Look at Alice, dressed up to kill. Quite the little London lady, aren't we – eh?

Barbara calls them Southern Spivs and Foreigners. She mimics the way they pronounce bath and path. When she's in a bate she says they're toffee-nosed. If either of them unthinkingly begins a sentence 'I really think' or 'Actually, I', Barbara will pounce: Oh I *rarely* think, don't yoou? *A*ctually, my deah – and she blows smoke rings at the ceiling, transferring her cigarette from its normal position (between index finger and thumb) to the one (between index finger and second) film stars and nobs use. When Barbara mocks them, Mollie's eyes fill and she touches her sister's arm: Don't Barb – it's not their fault, poor loves – and then she turns to them and chats about her and Barb's mother who is a widow and lives in a terraced cottage down by the railway line; or she asks about London, where she and Barb have never been. Is it much bigger than Liverpule? What are the shops like, like? Is there a Marshall's? Bigger than the one in Lord Street?

They do not love the maids, but they are fascinated by them, especially Barbara. They do not love their grandmother, whose house this is and has always seemed to be though their grandfather bought it, and though until two years ago he was alive and going daily on the train to his sack business in Bootle. When they think of him they think of his pipes and wiry hair and middle parting, his habit of changing red bedroom slippers for black shoes in the dining-room after breakfast; they remember the way he – sitting at the head of the table beneath his boardroom likeness on the wall – ate that breakfast; chomping so hard they feared he might dislocate his jaw, while grease from his bacon and egg ran in shiny, interesting rivulets down his navy blue chin; blotting his chin with a stiff-as-card napkin, before chomping his toast and marmalade. Grandfather left early and returned late, and in the evenings and at weekends was protected from them by Grandmother (Don't disturb your grandfather!) so they never saw much of him at all. Grandfather is dead, and they miss him, but they feel he can't have gone far: his check caps and smelly mackintoshes – so long they almost graze the slopped water from the dogs' drinking bowls on the tiled floor – still hang in the porch; his walking-sticks and canes and golf clubs still clutter the stick rack.

They do not love their grandmother. There is only one person in her house they love: Edie, who came to look after their own mother when she was a baby and never got away. Edie is housekeeper, cook (since Kate left in a huff), chauffeur (since Thomas left in the war) and slave to Grandmother's whims. And she does everything for them. She washes and irons their clothes, she gets them up and puts them to bed. She takes them on the train to the cinema in Southport and to the theatre in Liverpool. She drives them to the Village and buys them sweets and comics and drawing paper and pencils; she walks them to the shore, and on the endless journey back (between grey asparagus fields and wind-bitten pines), she carries their wet bathing things. She reads to them by the hour, although they are, as Grandmother says, great girls of eight and nearly ten and can read for themselves. When she dozes off, which she always does (her head falls on her chest, her spectacles mist up, she snores), they prod her awake and make her carry on.

Edie is tall and big-boned. She has a high, receding forehead, a big nose, big eyes – very dark brown behind her specs – a big mouth and big teeth. Her hands (the gloves they gave her one

Christmas wouldn't pull on at all) and feet are man-sized, her bosom a pillow whose weight of feathers collects just above the waist. Edie wears pale silky blouses with tucks and pleated fronts and little collars, under which she pins a cameo or pearl tie-pin. Even when the weather's boiling, she wears a cardigan – voluminous, and buttoned below the pillow with three buttons. She wears loose skirts of soft wool and elasticated knickers that reach almost to the knee; thick stockings, through which, when she sits down (not often, she's always on the go) they can see the ridge of her support bandages. For Church and for expeditions to Town, Edie wears a hat – felt, with a wide brim and a bow at the side, secured by a hat pin. Surprisingly for an unfrivolous person, she loves hats. Sometimes she says to them: Do you like my new hat, dears? and they stand on tiptoe and examine it from all sides and say, Yes we do, but the new hat is the same as her old one, the same as all her other hats. When Edie wakes them in the morning she wears her old dressing-gown, which is a man's and thick and heavy as a carpet.

Edie never alters – how old is Edie? If they ask, she is ninety-nine next birthday, dear. Has Edie ever been in love? That would be telling, Duck. Edie does everything that servants do, but she is not a servant. She never has a day off. Also, she calls Grandmother Mummy, though she is not Grandmother's daughter, and not young enough to be. Grandmother calls Edie Nurse, a cold starched title that does not suit her, and treats her badly, bullying her at mealtimes and bossing her. Edie never answers back. While Grandmother's blows fall, she sits in silence, staring out through the thick glass of her spectacles and the window, or at her plate. If Lucy asks, Why is Granny so horrible to you? Edie says, Oh I don't know, Duck – she has her problems, I daresay, and changes the subject and gets out the ironing board.

Edie gossips about no one, has no small talk, keeps her thoughts to herself. She talks to the cocker spaniels, she calls them Old Dear, Old Darling, Old Lady while she defleas their coats and untangles their ears with a steel comb. After breakfast she feeds the spaniels with Radio malt kept for that purpose in the nursery on a curtained-off shelf. The malt falls from the spoon on to the first finger of Edie's left hand, she spins the spoon and the malt winds round the finger like a bandage. The dogs have a finger of malt each. With their tongues they pull and tug at the bandage, and the malt enters their mouths in long strings, like rubber bands. This happens every morning, after bedmaking, after going to the lavatory, and it is very interesting to watch.

It is now, just about now, that Grandmother comes to the nursery. She huffs and puffs through the door; she blows out her cheeks; she sits heavily in the rocking chair; she leans back and rocks; she stares around her in disapproval. She has come to order the shopping. Edie makes a list and Grandmother huffs and puffs and blows out her cheeks. Grandmother is ugly and her ugliness is made worse by all the huffing and puffing. Does she know she does it? If she could see herself, would she? She leans back in her chair and crosses and recrosses her legs, examining her ankles, twisting them round. She is proud of her ankles and her calves and her small feet. Her clothes cupboard contains hundreds of pairs of shoes, all from Raynes, all new-looking, all with tissue paper crushed into their toes. Grandmother judges people by their extremities. If asked her opinion of so-and-so, she will answer: Pretty ankles – i.e., Yes – or Ugly calves – i.e., No. It is as well she doesn't judge people by their stomachs. Her own is a barrel that gurgles and heaves as she rocks.

What are the girls going to do today, Nurse? Grandmother asks Edie, puffing and rocking. If she addresses them directly, it's You girls, if indirectly, The girls. Grandmother doesn't like girls. Men (sons-in-law are the exception) are gods, boys heroes, girls nothing and good for nothing. Girls have no brains, no talents, no virtues. Grandmother has two sons and four daughters, four grandsons and six granddaughters, but you would never guess this from the snapshots of curly-headed heroes she keeps by her bed, or from the studio portraits of uniformed gods that stand on the piano. Grandmother doesn't conceal her prejudice or bother to defend it. Example: Alice and Lucy are good at drawing and painting; they do it all the time, they've won prizes, they fill a drawing book a week. If they take their drawing books to Grandmother for her inspection, she flips the pages without looking or stopping. Handing them back without comment, she then praises the efforts of their cousin Robert who, as everyone knows, can't draw for toffee. (Once, when their drawing books were full, and Edie busy in the kitchen, they went to Grandmother and asked her for threepence each for a new one; and Grandmother said, Why should I pay out good money for your scribbles? and turned on her Raynes high heel.)

Example 2: On one occasion, when Robert – at that time a shaven-headed thug of six – was over for tea, he hit Alice on the head with one of Grandfather's golf clubs he'd taken from the porch. The blow was intentional; it knocked Alice out and produced a large bump on her temple, but it was Robert who cried. While Alice was left for dead (until Edie came, summoned from the fruit cage by Lucy), Grandmother took the bellowing hero on to her lap and kissed and comforted him and fed him liquorice allsorts from a paper bag.

Grandmother must, presumably, have been a girl herself once. So why doesn't she like girls?

When Grandmother asks Edie in that snide way (which implies they are lazy good-for-nothings) what the girls are going to do today, they want to ask: What are *you* going to do today, Granny? They know what they will be doing. Shopping with Edie, drawing, reading (the bound volumes of *Little Folks* and *The Girls' Own Annual*; the Red, Green and Violet Fairy Books); walking the dogs; quick-stepping to Geraldo and Jack Payne and Roy Fox (on the radiogram in the Big Room); lining up lead soldiers and lead nurses and stretcher-bearers; staging a drama in the toy theatre (a model of the Liverpool Playhouse, with working lights and scenery and an orchestra pit): staging a drama in the dolls' house (a model of Grandmother's house, even to the motor cars in the garage and the petrol pump outside it); dressing up – as pirates (clothes and jewels from the dressing-up chest on the landing); building card houses and brick houses; playing snakes and ladders and ludo (with Edie); playing Old Maid (with the maids). And in summer the list is longer. In summer they can add riding the cranky bikes that belonged to their aunts when they were young; knocking up on the red tennis court; paddling and bathing in the sea. (Or, if the sea is too far out, which it very often is – a thin smear between the sand and the sky – shrimping in pools on the ribbed sand). They will be plunging their hands for frogs in any one of five lily ponds; jumping off the stone balls that surmount the terrace wall; eating their way through hot houses and vegetable gardens and plum orchards. They know what they will be doing. What will Grandmother be doing?

Grandmother will be sitting and rocking, if not in the nursery upstairs, in the drawing-room downstairs, if not in the drawing-room, in the morning-room, if not in the morning-room, in the summerhouse. Or, should the day be really hot and sunny, she will be found under the awning of the swing seat on the terrace, swinging and perhaps reading. (And that – apart from loading the bird table and feeding the red squirrels and the goldfish – is all Grandmother seems to do.) When Grandmother reads, she holds the book like a shield in front of her face and moves her head from side to side and mutters the words aloud. She reads the same books over and over again – *A Little Green World* is the title of one of them. As Edie coaxes the tea trolley over the crazy paving (the maids are off duty till six) and unstacks the brown-spotty tea service cups and plates, Grandmother goes on reading. Alice drags a teak table to the swing seat, Lucy jumps to with a cup of tea and a plate of sandwiches, but Grandmother doesn't say thank you. She stretches a hand for a sandwich without looking up from the page, and goes on muttering. Grandmother is rude.

Grandmother is mad. It must be madness that brings her, in corsets and petticoat, into the spare room where they sleep. (They don't sleep; they lie awake till early light, reading and discussing the madness of Grandmother.) She comes at bedtime, or after lunch when they are resting on their beds. She huffs into the room and leans against the clothes cupboard, or on her elbows over the mahogany foot of the nearest bed. She massages the back of her left hand with the fingertips of her right. Her shoulders are grooved with pink shoulder straps, three or four to each shoulder. Edie comes to the spare room to tuck them up (they lock their arms round her neck; they won't let her go) and draw back their curtains in the morning; to say, Sweet dreams, darlings, or Time to get up, Lucy old duck; Edie comes to take away their dirty clothes or bring them clean ones, to help them make their beds. Grandmother comes for one purpose only: to tell lies about her eldest daughter (their mother) and her daughter's husband (their father). Grandmother tells them their mother is a hussy and irresponsible; that she has abandoned them and gone off to America because she does not love them and can't be bothered to look after them. She says their father is a fortune hunter who married their mother for her money; that he is idle; that he is dull; that he is too clever by half; that there is bad blood in his family; and that she could tell them a thing or two . . .

If they lie still and shut their eyes and ears and say nothing, she eventually goes away, banging the door behind her. But she is always back. They count to twenty and watch the doorknob and it turns, and there she is again, in the doorway, huffing. And another thing – she begins, and goes on and on and on. She may leave and return half-a-dozen times to tell more and worse lies about their parents; or she may stand huffing but without speaking, just inside the door, one hand on the doorknob. If one of them (Lucy is the braver) sits up and shouts, How dare you say such wicked lies about our parents? How dare you? Why do you do it? Why? Grandmother closes her puffy eyes and smiles a secret, horrible smile. Or she shakes her fist at them and turns on her heel.

Can witches ever be fat? If so, Grandmother is a witch. Her loathing of cats, which amounts almost to fear (she will not have one in the house; the stray kitten Lucy found on the shore was banished within the hour), would seem to discount this, but there's a tiger on the wall of the main staircase, and a leopard stretched out on the carpet in the hall. And the terrace reeks of catmint, it grows between the paving and in every crevice of the wall. In any case, Grandmother does have a familiar of sorts – a Maltese terrier called Clarence. Clarence is a shivering whingeing piece of fluff, but the worst aspect of him is his smell. He smells, he stinks, of wee. This is because, when he widdles, he balances on both front legs in a handstand, so that his body and back legs go vertically into the air. Naturally the wee runs down his stomach, and as he wees a lot his underside is permanently yellow. Grandmother doesn't seem to notice the stain or the smell, or the dark and damp twist of hair at the end of his thing. She keeps him with her, on her lap in a rocking chair, or nestled beside her in the cushions of the swing seat. She hand-feeds him his dinner, a sickening mess of boiled rabbit and chicken and sodden, baked bread. He is fussy, of course, and shivers and turns his nose away, and she has to coax and beg him. If he dares to escape, she huffs from room to room looking and calling: Clarrie, Clarrie, Clarrie, come to Mother, precious boy.

Grandmother has no taste. She worships the disgusting Clarence and ignores the spaniels who, if anyone leaves a gate open, risk no dinner and a beating to spend the day rabbiting in the pinewoods beyond the golf course.

Grandmother has no taste, but she is always talking about Taste.

Taste is to do with shoes and dress stuffs, and also with carpets and curtains and chair covers. Grandmother is houseproud, she likes everything just so, and she has a thing about loose covers. Loose covers? Loose covers may be all right in their way, nothing wrong with loose covers, but not something to get worked up about. Grandmother gets very worked up about them. She leans back in the drawing-room sofa (blue-grey roses, green leaves on a white ground) and strokes its loose-covered arm. Come here, girls, she says, and feel these beeauuutiful loose covers – She does the same thing with curtains – flowered chintz in every room of Grandmother's house. Look, girls, she says, holding them out like skirts from the window, They're lined and interlined, beeauutifully made. You'll go a long way before you see curtains as beautiful as these. Or she bends down (not an easy feat for her) and pats the carpet. Puuure wool Wilton, she says. Come and feel it girls, puure puure wool ... Grandmother's obsession brings her into the nursery where they are drawing or playing ludo, where Edie is washing their pants in the marble basin beside the window. She huffs and puffs through the door with a roll of something under her arm, and unravels it on to their drawing books or the ludo board. This material is very expensive, she declares, holding a corner of it to her cheek. Look at it, girls, feel it. (She makes them pinch and stroke it.) One day – she says with an important pause – You may be lucky enough to own material of this quality ... After she's gone (very suddenly and huffily, bored perhaps with their lack of enthusiasm), Lucy will lift a corner of the tablecloth and hold it to her cheek. Look at this, girls, she'll say, it's puure, puure gingham. One day you may be lucky enough to own ... Very naughty, Duck, Edie says, straightening up from the basin, her arms soapy to the elbows. *Very* naughty. But when they shriek and roll around and clutch themselves, Edie laughs too. There's no malice in Edie's laughter. It's the best noise in the world.

Grandmother is unfair. Don't tell tales, she says, should they complain that one of their hero cousins (over for tea) has pinched or punched or hit them on the head with a croquet mallet. But should the hero tell tales on them, they're sent supperless to the spare room. That'll teach you to bully your dear little cousin, Grandmother says. It's not fair, they grumble, but Grandmother has an answer to everything. Life isn't fair, she says. Whoever said it was?

Grandmother breaks all the rules, the rules for living and behaviour that she has laid down. You can't get out of life what you don't put in, she's always telling them, but what does she put in, exactly? Let your meat stop your mouth, she orders when they chatter at lunch, yet she herself talks incessantly, and with her mouth full, a muttered monologue of complaint, addressed to everyone and no one. Sitting in silence while Grandmother mutters on, they may catch Barbara's eye (the maids wait at table and between courses stand either side the fireplace) and if they do, Barbara will wink and pull faces at them. When Grandmother isn't looking, she pulls faces at Grandmother, and sticks her tongue out before resuming a demure posture, eyes cast down, hands folded on her apron.

Grandmother is superstitious. Stop that Cornishman drowning! she barks if anyone accidentally knocks a glass at table; and the culprit hastily touches the rim to silence the ring and save the Cornishman from his fate.

Grandmother is mean. Get me a quarter of pontefract cakes and a quarter of liquorice allsorts, will you, Nurse, she orders as they leave for the Village, but she keeps her sweet ration in her bedroom and never shares it.

Once a week Grandmother accompanies them on the shopping trip. She wears a hat (velour, veiled) and sits in the passenger seat of the Hillman with a basket of empty cider bottles on her knee. Stop at Dean's, Nurse, she orders, which is where Edie is going anyway. At Dean's, which is the grocers, Edie gets out and they get out, and Grandmother stays in the car with her basket. Dean's smells of bacon and coffee. Edie stands at the counter reading out her list, and Mrs Dean finds all the items from the shelves and licks her pencil to make it blacker and writes everything down in the invoice book. As soon as Edie enters the shop, Mr Dean peers through the window, and if he sees Grandmother in the car he drops whatever he's doing and abandons whoever he's serving and hurries out to her. Grandmother winds down the window and Mr Dean bows before her, his hands clasped to the chest of his green button-through overall. How are you today, Mrs Moss? he says, and Grandmother's puffy face explodes in smiles. She nods and chats and tosses her head. She laughs in a girlish way. This performance is repeated everywhere they go. Grandmother stays in the car, and Mr Taylor, Mr Cross, Mr Bower and Mr Darbyshire all leave their businesses to pay court to her. And she is charming to them all.

Only at the wine merchants is this pattern broken. Rimmer's is not in the High Street, and does not look like a shop. It's a tall brick house in an ordinary road of tall brick houses. The Hillman jerks to a halt outside the gate, and Edie goes round and opens the passenger door for Grandmother, and then Grandmother, on her own with the basket, huffs and puffs up the path and the steps and vanishes through the front door. They wait in the car for what feels like an hour (Edie taps the steering wheel and looks at her watch), and eventually Grandmother reappears all smiles, with Mr Rimmer beside her carrying the basket which is heavy now because the cider bottles are full.

Shopping is quicker when Grandmother doesn't come, and more enjoyable. They can chew their way from shop to shop because Edie buys them peppermint lumps at Darbyshires, and they are treated like royalty everywhere they go. These are Mrs Moss's little granddaughters from the big house, Mrs Dean or Mrs Darbyshire will announce to the other customers, and the other customers gasp and stare and pass admiring remarks, as though Alice and Lucy were the Princesses Elizabeth and Margaret Rose.

Why is Grandmother so important? Is it because she was married to Grandfather, who was a very rich man? Or because her house is so large? It is enormous, but there are other large houses in that very long road. It does have special features: it is the only one with a hard tennis court and orchards; and it is the nearest to the shore. Outside Grandmother's gate the metalled road gives up and a flatly cobbled, cindered and sandy track takes over. Day-trippers from Liverpool to the sea stop here, and put down their spades and nets and hoist themselves on to the wall or the stone balls of the gateposts to get a view – for Grandmother's garden is the most splendid for miles. If the gate is, unusually, open, the trippers may even venture inside and stand on the white gravel and gaze at the blazing borders and ornamental trees and striped lawns, at the terrace where the lady of the house and her family are (self-consciously, for they feel like a tableau) having tea. Shut the gate now, girls, Grandmother orders when the day-trippers at last back out of the drive, still gazing and exclaiming. (Surprisingly, Grandmother never tells the trippers to go away. She calls out Good afternoon, and waves graciously from the swing seat and beams at them from under her sun hat).

Not many invited visitors come to Grandmother's house. Perhaps it's because she doesn't like women that Grandmother has so few friends. Once in a blue moon a visitor does come (for tea always, never for lunch or dinner), but whatever it is between them, it doesn't seem like friendship. The visitor is always very polite to Grandmother and agrees with everything she says in a way friends generally don't, and calls her Mrs Moss and not Dilys, which is Grandmother's first name.

Is Grandmother lonely? Does she miss the time (the photograph albums in the morning-room record) when the terrace steps were ranked with young men waving cricket bats, and girls with tennis racquets and frizzy perms (can that one in the eyeshade be their mother?), when the drive was chock-a-block with Morgans and MGs?

Does she miss her children after all?

Does she, after all, miss Grandfather?

Sometimes when they come across Grandmother rocking and muttering, they find the muttering is weeping. If they can, they creep away before she's seen them – if not, she collars them. Come here darlings, she says – darling a word normally reserved for grandsons and for Clarence. She makes them sit at her knee. She imprisons their hands. She tells them their Grandfather was a great and good man, a wonderful man, a brilliant man. He was the best husband, the best father, the best grandfather who ever lived. Their grandfather was – they must remember this, they must never forget it – a saint. There aren't many saints in this world, but he was one of them. A saint, do they understand? Their grandfather was a SAINT.

What is all this? Grandfather was a kind man, kind to them when they saw him, kind to Grandmother so far as they could tell; and his children had all loved him, so he must have been kind to them. He was hard-working and good at cricket, and he had an interesting way of chomping his bacon and egg and talking while chewing his pipe. But they'd known him to lose his temper, and he sometimes made unsaintly remarks about Jews and Roman Catholics. Does Grandmother believe what she says? Does she believe they will believe it? Can it be she's forgotten how she treated Grandfather

270

after his stroke? After his stroke Grandfather couldn't talk or feed himself or shave. He dribbled and coughed and his nose ran. Long strings of saliva fell unchecked down his shirt or pyjama jacket; if he leaned forward they collected in his lap. It must have been terrible for Grandfather, who'd always taken pride in his appearance, and who not long ago had been bowling to his grandsons and running to the net to smash a volley, but Grandmother mocked and jeered. While he sat slumped in his wheelchair, his eyes sunk and staring, she talked about him as though he wasn't there. Give it a rest, Mummy, Edie would say, very sharply for her. Leave Daddy alone. Let him be. But Grandmother would go on and on. What does it matter? she'd say, he's only a carcass. What does it matter?

Grandfather couldn't speak, or feed himself, or wash or go to the lavatory – but could he hear? What if he could understand? They discuss this possibility in bed at night, in the spare room; they decide that Grandmother is at her most awful when she sanctifies Grandfather. Of all her moods, this one, in which no word of remorse or regret ever interrupts the tearful listing of his virtues, is the worst.

When they can escape her, they run (through the hall, down the passage, past the pantry and the store-room, through the kitchen) to the maids' sitting-room, a place where Grandmother almost never goes.

The maids' sitting-room smells of smoke and armpits. The smoke of a million Wills' Whiffs and Woodbines has tanned the once-cream walls and ceiling and worked its way into the uncut moquette of the sofa and the stringy rug that lies on the lino in front of the gas fire. To step into this room, to sit on the smoked sofa and lean elbows on the oilclothed table-top, is to enter a different house. It is dingily lit (by a cone-shaped enamel light, dangling from a chancy flex); bereft of ornament (two plaster alsatians, merely, and an oak half-moon clock on the shelf above the fire); devoid of comfort (apart from the sofa, two hard kitchen chairs). The room is an odd shape, triangular, and has only one, very small, window, too high up to see out of and always closed.

The room is dangerous. Grandmother may not come here, but when Barbara shuts the door they risk, they are sure, never returning to Edie and safety again. The conversation is dangerous. As Barbara,

271

fag hanging from her mouth, deals the cards – so old and smoked they stick together when she tries to shuffle them – as they pick them up and sort them into suits, she gossips about Grandmother. Mrs M. is a silly old cow, Barbara says, a right bitch, and what she pays her and Mollie is laffable, not mind you that she's laffing. Come here, Clarrie, Barbara says in Grandmother's voice – and she gets up and hunts round the room and under the table for Clarence, walking bow-legged like Grandmother, bending down and patting the inside of her right knee, as Grandmother does: Come to mother, darling, precious boykin ... (They don't like Grandmother; they fear her and talk about her in bed in the spare room. So why does Barbara's performance – which is accurate and very funny – make them anxious?)

When Barbara has said all she has to say on the subject of Grandmother, they talk Smut. Barbara is the leader, but they all do it, even Mollie, though it makes her more than usually pink-faced. Through round after round of Old Maid (invariably Alice) and Rumblebelly and Strip Jack Naked and Seven of Diamonds and Snap, they talk of bosoms and bottoms, bras and knickers, lavs and chamber pots. Eyes, nose, mouth and chin, Barbara says, touching these features with a small grey hand, all the way down to Uncle Jim (she sticks the hand between her legs); Uncle Jim makes lemonade (Pssssssssss – to indicate wee), round the corner (hand goes round the back, to Barbara's bottom) chocolate's made (plop plop plop plop – to indicate number twos). Red, white and blue, Dirty Kangaroo, went behind the dustbin, and did his number two (fart noises; more plops). My Uncle Billy had a ten foot willy, he showed it to the lady next door – Eee, don't, Barb, Mollie interrupts, you musn't, they're too young.

When Barbara leans across the table to tweak a card from Lucy, her underarm smell fills the room. They know she washes, they've seen her in the maids' bathroom stripped to the waist, bent over the tiny corner basin. She soaps herself with sour yellow soap. Under each arm is a pelt of black fur, like the false moustaches in the dressing-up chest on the landing. Grown-up women don't put soap on their faces, they use Ardena Deep Cleansing Cream, but Barbara works the yellow bar between her hands and lathers her face into bubbles all over, screwing her eyes tight and blowing out her cheeks as though she were inflating a balloon. If invited, they follow her along the passage to the maids' bedroom and watch her change. (The maids wear green dresses and white aprons in day time; black dresses with frillier aprons and cuffs and caps in the evening.) The rooms in Grandmother's house are painted cream or pastel shades of blue or grey, but the maids' bedroom is wallpapered with roses, red, yellow and blue, giant blooms, and the door and skirtings are an outdoor green. It's a dark room because the one window looks on to the wash-house wall, and it smells – of smoke and of the contents of the chamber pots, one under each brass bed. (Once, when Alice, for some reason in the maids' bedroom without Lucy, caught sight of Barbara's po and smelt its sickly-sweetish smell, its contents were red – like water beetroot's boiled in, she told Lucy afterwards: Perhaps Barbara had cut her bottom? Lucy suggested.)

The maids wear black stockings in the evening when they change, but in daytime, even in winter, their legs are bare and sore-looking, descending to red ankles and black lace-up shoes. Their legs are bare when they go off on their bikes on Thursday afternoons. In winter they ride away in belted coats and headscarves and high-heeled shoes; in summer they put on shiny rayon dresses which have shoulder pads and ruched sleeves, and they squeeze their feet into tiny sling-backs with peep toes. Grandmother doesn't allow make-up on duty, but on Thursday afternoons when they pedal off, their eyebrows are black and arched, their eyelids mauvey purple, their mouths a hard dark red.

Where do the maids go on Thursday afternoons? MYOB, Barbara says, as she and Mollie wheel their bikes down the path between the tennis court and the holly hedge to the back gate. To see a man about a dog, she says, unlatching the gate, or, Wouldn't you like to know?

But one time when they ask, Mollie says they can come next time, if they like; they'll go shopping in the High Street, and then have tea at home. Our mother's heard a lot about you two, she says. Better ask your Grandma, Barb calls over her shoulder, Better ask Mrs M.

They won't ask Grandmother, they'll ask Edie. I don't see why not, Duck, Edie says, If you behave yourselves.

Grandmother hears about it, of course. What do you want to do that for? she asks, puffing out her cheeks. It isn't suitable. Gentlefolk don't shop in the afternoon.

Later in the week Grandmother comes to the spare room and leans over the end of Alice's bed. Behind her on the wall, muddy clouds gather above a horse-drawn plough. You can't go on your bicycles, anyway, she says, as though adding to a conversation that has just taken place. It's too far and too dangerous, you'll have to walk.

What's all this? They ride their bikes every day, up Larkhill Lane as far as the Army Camp, along College Avenue, down Shireburn Road, all over the place and she never asks questions. Bike riding has never been dangerous before. But Grandmother won't listen to their pleas or change her mind. Don't go, then, she says. Take it or leave it; walk or don't go.

Next Thursday they're dressed in cotton frocks and cardigans, ankle socks and sandals. Let's have a look at you, Barbara says. Well . . . and Mollie squeezes the breath out of them and says, Aren't they lovely, aren't they grand? It's a hot day, and a long walk to the Village, which is not a village like the ones at home are – set among fields with a pub and a shop and a school and a church. The Village is mile upon mile of criss-crossing roads of shiny brick houses, in the middle of which is a High Street of shops. By the time they get there, the maids are wilting in their rayon, and they've got blisters on their heels because their socks have gone to sleep in their sandals.

What happens next, whatever it is, they will try to make sense of in the spare room tonight, and tomorrow night, and weeks of nights to come. What happens, what happened (or did not happen – but it was the same for both of them) was this: They were in the High Street, but it was not the High Street they knew. No, it had to be the High Street they knew, because there at the end of it was the Post Office with its clock and chain railing.

Try again. They were in the High Street they knew, but the shops were not the same shops. The shops they visit daily with Edie were not there; had vanished; did not exist. In their place were other shops that Barbara and Mollie knew well and kept popping into – for knitting wool; for 'a pound of tripe for our mother, Jack love'; for black stockings; for 'necessaries'; for a tired-looking cabbage.

Everywhere they went, the shopkeepers greeted the maids with: 'Lo Barb love, is yer fellar still at sea, then? or How's my Mollie? Be a love and take this packet of lard, yer Mam left it behind last Tuesday – while they were ignored. Even when Barb – in answer

274

to a baker they'd never seen before's, You've bin keeping these kids very quiet, I must say – said, They're Mrs M.'s grandchildren from the big house, no one seemed interested. The baker said, Oh yeh, without looking up, and put five buns in a paper bag and swung the bag by the corners and handed it to Barb.

Where were they? Outside, the pavement, the shops, the cherry trees, the parked bicycles and prams, swam in the heat. They looked at each other in panic.

Where were they? Lucy tugged Barbara's arm. Where are we?

We're in the High Street, that's where, don't be daft, Barbara said.

They're hot, poor loves, Mollie said, they'll be wanting an ice.

There is only one place for ices – Darbyshires, where Edie buys their drawing books and peppermint lumps, and the pontefract cakes Grandmother never shares. Mrs Darbyshire will be pleased to see them. They will be safe in Darbyshires.

This way, Barbara said. A blistered door shimmered before them. She pushed it open and a bell jangled. They waited in the dark till a woman in hair curlers came out of the back and leant her bosom on the counter. Two wafers, two cones, Marge, Barbara said. And don't forget me Woodbines –

Out on the pavement the margarine ices turned to sticky rivers that trickled over their wrists. Alice can't eat vanilla I'm afraid, Lucy said to Barb before Alice could stop her. It makes her sick. Oh, my lady can't eat vanilla – Barbara dropped a curtsey – Well, there's some of us as can – and she took the cornet from Alice's hand and finished it off with three sharp bites.

Where are they? Why isn't Edie here? Why doesn't she save them? Where *are* they?

They are in an alleyway between high brick walls.

One minute they were in the High Street, the maids' High Street, and the next they were following Barb through a brick arch, into an alleyway. There is no brick arch, and no alleyway in Edie's High Street.

Nearly there now loves, Mollie said, as the walls crumbled to iron railings and spiky grass, through which they could see snippets of back gardens and washing-lines and the backs of dark houses. Our mother'll give us a nice cup of tea. Barb's and Mollie's mother will give them a nice cup of tea, and they will be able to go to the lavatory. Lucy was already crossing her legs.

In front of them the alley ended in a bank of pale grasses, dotted with willow trees and rising steeply to the railway line. Just before they reached it, Barbara opened a gate on the right, and they followed her up a brick path.

A witch was sitting on the doorstep, shelling peas into a basin. Her knees were wide apart and the tin basin, full of peas, rested between them on the step. She was bent forward and her long hair fell in front of her face and over her knotted arms. The step, her worn skirt and the path at her feet were littered with pea pods.

'Lo Mum, Barbara shouted above the noise of a train, rattling past on the embankment. How's tricks, our Mother? The witch parted her hair, and when she saw them she threw back her head and cackled. She had no teeth. Her mouth was a black cave. She was a hundred years old. So these are Mrs M.'s girls, she whispered in a gummy lisp, and she stretched out her arms and pulled them to her as Mollie does, and kissed and squeezed them as Mollie kisses and squeezes them, and her hair went in their mouths and noses. Then she pushed them away and poked their stomachs with a knobby finger. Fat, she said, pinching Lucy's arm above the elbow. Fat, both of them. Fat as butter. And the black cave opened again and she laughed and laughed and laughed.

Never again, Barbara said on the endless walk back to Grandmother's house, Never again, Misses High-and-Mighty. Too grand to say a word to our mother. Not a peep, not a smile, not a please or a thank you out of the pair of you.

But it wasn't their fault they couldn't speak or eat, or drink their tea. The witch had cast a spell on them; she'd turned them to stone. It wasn't their fault. They looked at Mollie, but Mollie, who always defends them, pursed her mouth and said nothing.

On the way back Lucy wet her knickers (and her legs and her socks and her sandals). Having been turned to stone she couldn't, of course, follow Barbara to the wooden hut at the end of the witch's garden.

Grandmother was in the swing seat when they turned in the drive. Clarence yapped and whined, but Grandmother didn't look up as they climbed the terrace steps; she went on puffing and muttering and turning the pages. At the entrance to the porch the maids left

276

them without saying goodbye, and went round the side of the terrace and down the side steps – past the hen run and the first vegetable garden – to the back door.

Did you have a nice time, dears? Edie said when they ran at her. They wanted to tell her, but they couldn't. What could they tell?

Barbara sent them to Coventry for a fortnight. If they met her on the stairs she looked the other way and hummed under her breath. In the dining-room she stared through them or over the tops of their heads. Mollie didn't speak either, but she gazed at them sorrowfully, pink in the face.

It's months before they're invited to the maids' sitting-room to play cards. When they do, Barbara doesn't gossip about Grandmother, and she doesn't pretend to hunt for Clarence, and nobody talks smut. Alice had got the Queen – as per, Barbara says in a bored voice, blowing smoke rings at the ceiling; and she winks – at Mollie, not at them.

They spend less time with the maids now, more time with Edie, more time by themselves.

Most mornings they go shopping with Edie in the Hillman. They go to Taylor's and Cross's and Bower's, they go to Dean's and Darbyshire's. If Grandmother comes, she sits in the passenger seat with a basket of empties on her knee, and all the shopkeepers leave their customers to pay court to her.

As they follow Edie from shop to familiar shop, they fear that at any moment they will find themselves in that other High Street they visited with the maids; the street where there is a greengrocer with tired vegetables, the blistered door of a tobacconist that sells ices and a brick arch that leads to a terraced cottage under the railway line.

Marjorie Barnard

Habit

iss Jessie Biden was singing in a high plangent voice as she made the beds. It was a form of self-expression she allowed herself only when there were no guests in the house, and she mingled the hymns and sentimental songs of her girlhood with a fine impartiality. She made the beds with precision, drawing the much washed marcella quilts, with spiky fringes, up over the pillows so that the black iron bedsteads had an air of humility and self-respect. The sheets, though not fine, smelt amiably of grass, and the blankets were honest, if a little hard with much laundering. With the mosquito nets hanging from a hoop which in its turn, was suspended from a cup hook screwed into the wooden ceiling, the beds looked like virtuous but homely brides.

Jessie stopped singing for a minute as she pulled the green holland blind to the exact middle of the window, and surveyed the room to see if all were in order. She had very strict notions about the exact degree of circumspection to which paying guests were entitled. Yesterday everything washable in the rooms had been washed, the floor, the woodwork, the heavy florid china on the rather frail, varnished wooden washstands. The rooms smelled of soap, linoleum polish and wood. The lace curtains were stiff with starch. Indeed, there was more starch than curtain, and without it they would have been draggled and pitiful wisps.

As every door in the house was open and it was a light wooden shell of a place, old as Australian houses go, and dried by many summers, Jessie could quite comfortably talk to Catherine, who was cooking in the kitchen, from wherever she happened to be working. But presently, the rooms finished, she came to stand in the kitchen doorway with a list of the guests they were expecting for Easter, in her hand.

The kitchen was a pleasant room looking on to the old orchard, a row of persimmon trees heavy with pointed fruit turning golden in the early autumn, squat, round, guava bushes, their plump, red-coronetted fruit hidden in their glossy dark leaves, several plum and peach trees, one old wide-spreading apple tree and a breakwind of loquats and quinces. Beyond again was the bush, blue-green, shimmering a little in the morning sunshine.

Catherine Biden, too, was pleasant, and in keeping with the warm autumn landscape. Her red-gold hair, fine, heavy and straight, made a big bun on her plump white neck, her milky skin was impervious to the sun and her arms, on which her blue print sleeves were rolled up, were really beautiful. In the parlance of the neighbours, neither of the sisters would see forty again, which somehow sounded duller and more depressing than to say that Catherine was forty-two and Jessie forty-six.

'I'm putting the Adamses in the best room,' Jessie was saying, 'because they don't mind sharing a bed. And Miss Dickens and her friend in the room with the chest of drawers. Mrs Holles says she must have a room to herself, so it will have to be the little one. The Thompsons and Miss George'll sleep on the verandah and dress together in the other room. The old lady and her niece next the dining-room. That leaves only the verandah room this side, for Mr Campbell.'

'It's quite all right while the weather is cool,' said Catherine, in her placid way, rolling dough.

Jessie looked at her list with disfavour. 'We know everyone but Mr Campbell. It's rather awkward having just one man and so many women.'

'Perhaps he'll like it,' Catherine suggested.

'I don't think so. His name's Angus. He's probably a man's man.'

'Oh, if he's as Scotch as all that he won't mind. He'll fish all the time.'

'Well, all I hope is he doesn't take fright and leave us with an empty room.' The Easter season was so short, they couldn't afford an empty room.

'I hope', said Catherine, 'we don't get a name for having only women. We do get more teachers every year and fewer men, don't we?'

279

'Yes, we do. I think we'd better word the advertisement differently.'

She sighed. Jessie, growing stout, with high cheek bones and a red skin, was the romantic one. She had always taken more kindly to this boarding-house business than Catherine, because of its infinite possibilities – new people, new chances of excitement and romance. Although perhaps she no longer thought of romance, the habit of expecting something to happen remained with her.

Their father had married late. This house beside the lagoon had come to him with his wife and he had spent his long retirement in it, ministered to by his daughters. When he and his pension had died together, he had not, somehow, been able to leave them anything but the house, the small orchard and the lovely raggedy slope of wild garden running down to the water. Jessie, in a mood of tragic daring, advertised accommodation for holiday guests, carefully copying other advertisements she found in the paper. This expedient would, they hoped, tide them over. That was twelve years ago. A makeshift had become a permanency. In time, with the instrumentality of the local carpenter, they had added a couple of rooms and put up some almost paper-thin partitions. It looked as if they had developed the thing as far as they could.

They both still looked on their home as something different from their guest house. It was vested in that company of lares and penates now in bondage to mammon, but some day to be released. 'Our good things,' the sisters called them, the original furniture of the house, the bits and pieces that their mother had cherished. The big brass bed that had been their parents' was still in the best bedroom, though the cedar chest of drawers with pearl buttons sunk in its knobs and the marble topped washstand had gone to raise the tone of other rooms. The dining-room was very much as it had always been. The sideboard with the mirrors and carved doors took up the best part of one wall, and set out on it was the old lady's brightly polished but now unused silver coffee service. The harmonium, with its faded puce silk, filled an inconvenient amount of room by the window. The old people's enlarged portraits, an ancient, elaborate work-table with dozens of little compartments, and other intimate treasures not meant for paying guests, but impossible to move out of their way, gave the room a genteel but overcrowded appearance. In the dining-room in the off season it was almost as if nothing had ever happened.

In twelve years Jessie's hopefulness had worn a little thin and Catherine's gentle placid nature had become streaked with discontent, as marble is veined with black. Sometimes she asked herself where it was all leading, what would happen to them by and by and if this was all life had in store? She began in a slow blind way to feel cheated, and to realize how meaningless was the pattern of the years with their alternations of rush and stagnation, of too much work and too little money. Of their darker preoccupations the sisters did not speak to one another. In self-defence they looked back rather than forward.

The guests began to arrive at lunchtime. Angus Campbell was the last to come, by the late train, long after dark. Catherine went up to the bus stop with a lantern to meet him. He saw her for the first time with the light thrown upward on her broad fair face, and he thought how kind and simple and good she looked. His tired heart lifted, and he felt reassured.

Undressing in the small stuffy room they shared, next to the kitchen, Jessie asked her sister, 'Do you think he'll fit in all right?'

'I think so,' Catherine answered. 'He seems a nice, quiet man.'

'Young?' asked Jessie with the last flicker of interest in her tired body.

'About our age.'

'Oh well . . .'

They kissed one another goodnight as they had every night since they were children, and lay down side by side to sleep.

The shell of a house was packed with sleeping people, all known and all strangers.

Angus Campbell evidently did not find his position of solitary man very trying, for on Easter Monday he asked, rather diffidently, if he might stay another week. He was taking his annual holidays. When the other guests departed, he remained. One week grew into two, then he had to return to Sydney.

He was a tall, gaunt, slightly stooped man with a weather-beaten complexion – the kind of Scots complexion that manages to look weather-beaten even in a city office – and a pair of clear, under-standing, friendly, hazel eyes. His manner was very quiet and at first he seemed rather a negligible and uninteresting man. But presently you discovered in him a steadfast quality that was very likeable. You missed him when he went away.

When he was alone with the sisters, life settled inevitably into a more intimate rhythm. They ate their meals together on a rickety table on the verandah, where they could look over the garden to the lagoon. He would not let the sisters chop wood or do the heavy outdoor work that they were accustomed to, and he even came into the kitchen and helped Jessie wash up while Catherine put away. He did it so simply and naturally that it seemed right and natural to them.

One day he began digging in the garden, and, from taking up the potatoes they wanted, went on to other things. 'You oughtn't to be doing this,' Jessie said. 'It's your holiday.'

'You don't know how I enjoy it,' he answered, and his eyes, travelling over the upturned loamy earth to the blazing persimmon trees and the bush beyond, had in them a look of love and longing. She knew that he spoke the truth.

He went out fishing and brought back strings of fish for their supper with pride and gusto, and then had to watch Catherine cook them. There seemed to be something special about Catherine cooking the fish he caught.

He helped Catherine pick fruit for jam and she was aware that for all he was thin and stooped he was much stronger than she, and it gave her a curious, pleased feeling. Jessie, alone in the house, could hear their voices in the orchard, a little rarefied and idealized, in the still warm air.

One day it rained, great gusts of thick fine rain that blotted out the lagoon, and Angus, kept in, took his book on to the verandah. Passing to and fro doing the work, Catherine saw that he was not reading, but looking out into the rain. Then he went and stood by the verandah rail for a long time. She came and stood beside him.

He said, 'If you listen you can just hear the rain on the grass and among the leaves – and smell the earth. It's good, isn't it? The trees are more beautiful looming through the mist – the shape of them.'

Marvelling, she saw that he was half in love with the beauty that she had lived with all her life.

A magpie flew through the rain, calling. He laid his hand on her shoulder and she was a little shaken by that warm and friendly touch. The eyes he turned on her still held the reflection of a mystery she had not seen.

Angus Campbell told them about himself. He was a clerk in a secure job and for years he had looked after his invalid mother, coming home from the office to sit with her, getting up in the night to tend her, his money going in doctor's bills. She had often been querulous and exacting. 'The pain and the tedium were so hard for her to bear, and there was so little I could do for her. Of course I remember her very different. No one could have had a better mother. She was very ambitious for me, and made great sacrifices when I was a boy, so that I should have a good education and get on. But I never did — not very far.' It was evident that he thought he owed her something for that disappointment. Two months ago she had died and he missed her bitterly. 'She had become my child,' he said. He felt, too, the cruelty of her life that had been hard and unsatisfied, and had ended in pain. Now there was no hope of ever retrieving it.

'He is very good,' said Jessie to her sister when they were alone that night.

'And kind,' said Catherine. 'The kindest man I've ever known.'

Neither of them thought how few men they'd known.

Jessie raised herself on her elbow to look at Catherine as she slept in the faint moonlight, and thought how comely she was, sweet and wholesome.

When Angus had, at last, to go, he said he would be back for the weekend. They kissed him. He was to arrive on the Friday by the late train again, and Catherine prepared supper for him before the fire, for it was getting cold now. She took the silver coffee pot, the sacred silver coffee pot that had been their mother's, and put it to warm above the kitchen stove. She cast a half defiant glance at Jessie as she did so, but Jessie went and took the silver sugar bowl too, and the cream jug, filled them, and set them on the table.

Angus asked Catherine to go out in the boat with him or to go walking, and then he paid Jessie some little attention. But they both knew. One Sunday, perhaps it was the fourth weekend he had come, the autumn was now far advanced, he and Catherine went for a long walk and he asked her to marry him. He took her in his arms and kissed her. She felt very strange, for she had never been kissed before, not by a man who was in love with her. They walked home hand in hand as if they were still very young, and when Catherine saw Jessie waving to them from the verandah she stood still and the unaccountable tears began to flow down her cheeks.

They said, everybody said, that there was no reason why they should wait, meaning they had better hurry up. The wedding was fixed for three months ahead.

It was a curious three months for Catherine. When Angus came for the weekend they would not let him pay his board, and that made a little awkwardness. Even calling him Angus seemed a trifle strange. He did not come every weekend now. Once he said, 'It seems wrong to take you away from all this beauty and freedom and shut you up in a little suburban house among a lot of other little houses just the same. Do you think you'll fret, my darling?'

Catherine had never thought very much about the beauties of nature. So she just shook her head where it rested against his shoulder. Still, her heart sank a little when she saw his house with its small windows, dark stuff hangings and many souvenirs of the late Mrs Campbell. It seemed as if sickness and death had not yet been exorcized from it.

Catherine and Jessie sewed the trousseau. 'We must be sensible,' they said to one another, and bought good stout cambric and flannelettes, though each secretly hankered after the pretty and the foolish. Catherine could not quite forget that she was going to be a middle-aged bride, and that that was just a little ridiculous. Neighbours, meaning to be kind, teased her about her wedding and were coy, sly and romantic in a heavy way, so that she felt abashed.

A subtle difference had taken place in the relationship of the sisters. Jessie felt a new tenderness for Catherine. She was the younger sister who was going to be married. Jessie's heart burned with love and protectiveness. She longed, she didn't know why, to protect Catherine, to do things for her. 'Leave that to me,' she would say when she saw Catherine go to clean the stove or perform some other dirty job. 'You must take care of your hands now.'

But Catherine always insisted on doing the roughest work. 'He's not marrying me for my beauty,' she laughed.

Catherine too thought more of her sister and of how good and unselfish she was, and her little peculiarities that once rather irritated her, now almost brought the tears to her eyes. One night she broached what was always on her mind.

'What will you do when I've gone?' she asked in a low voice.

'I'll get Ivy Thomas to help me in the busy times,' Jessie answered in a matter of fact voice, 'and in between, I'll manage.'

'But it will be lonely,' said Catherine weakly.

Jessie cast a reproachful glance at her. 'I'll manage,' she said.

Catherine was no longer discontented and weighed down with a sense of futility. Another emotion had taken its place, something very like homesickness.

As she did her jobs about the place she thought now, 'It is for the last time,' and there was a little pain about her heart. She looked at her world with new eyes. Angus's eyes perhaps. Going down to the fowlyard in the early morning with the bucket of steaming bran and pollard mash, she would look at the misty trees and the water like blue silk under the milk-pale sky; at the burning autumn colours of the persimmon trees, and the delicate frosty grass, and her heart would tremble with its loveliness.

One evening, coming in with the last basket of plums – ripe damsons with a thick blue bloom upon them – she stopped to rest, her back to the stormy sunset, and she saw thin, blue smoke like tulle winding among the quiet trees where a neighbour was burning leaves. She thought that she would remember this all her life. Picking nasturtiums under the old apple tree she laid her cheek for a moment against the rough silvery bark, and closed her eyes. 'My beloved old friend,' she thought but without words, 'I am leaving you for a man I scarcely know.'

It would seem as if the exaltation of being loved, of that one ripe and golden Sunday when she thought she could love too, had become detached from its object and centred now about her home. She even became aware of a rhythm in her daily work. Objects were dear because her hands were accustomed to them from childhood. And now life had to be imagined without them.

'Wherever I am, I shall have to grow old,' she thought, 'and it

285

would be better to grow old here where everything is kind and open, than in a strange place.' It was as if the bogy she had feared, meaningless old age, had revealed itself a friend at the last moment, too late.

Jessie lit the porcelain lamp with the green shade and set it in the middle of the table among the litter of the sewing. She stood adjusting the wick, her face in shadow, and said:

'We'll have to have a serious talk about the silver and things, Cathy. We'd better settle it tonight before we get too busy.'

'What about them?' Catherine asked, biting off a thread.

'You must have your share. We'll have to divide them between us.' Jessie's voice was quite steady and her tone matter of fact.

'Oh, no,' cried Catherine, with a sharp note of passion in her voice. 'I don't want to take anything away.'

'They are as much yours as mine.'

'They belong here.'

'They belong to both of us, and I'm not going to have you go away empty-handed.'

'But, Jessie, I'll come back often. The house wouldn't seem the same without Mother's things. Don't talk as if I were going away for ever.'

'Of course you'll come back, but it won't be the same. You'll have a house of your own.'

'It won't be the same,' echoed Catherine very low.

'I specially want you to have Mother's rings. I've always wanted you to wear them. You've got such pretty hands and now you won't have to work so hard . . . and the pendant. Father gave that to Mother for a wedding present so as you're the one getting married it is only fit you should wear it on your wedding day too. I'll have the cameos. I'm sort of used to them. And the cat's-eye brooch that I always thought we ought to have given Cousin Ella when Mother died.' Jessie drew a rather difficult breath.

'You're robbing yourself,' said Catherine, 'giving me all the best. You're the eldest daughter.'

'That has nothing to do with it. We must think of what is suitable. I think you ought to have the silver coffee things. They've seemed specially yours since that night – you remember – when Angus came. Perhaps they helped . . .'

286

Catherine made a funny little noise.

'I don't want the silver coffee set.'

'Yes, you do. They're heaps too fine for guests. They're good. What fair puzzles me is the work-table. You ought to have it because after all I suppose I'll be keeping all the big furniture, but this room wouldn't be the same without it.'

'No,' cried Catherine. 'Oh, Jessie, no. Not the work-table. I couldn't bear it.' And she put her head down among the white madapolam and began to cry, a wild, desperate weeping.

'Cathy, darling, what is it? Hush, Petie, hush. We'll do everything just as you want.'

'I won't strip our home. I won't.'

'No, darling, no, but you'll want some of your own friendly things with you.'

Jessie was crying a little too, but not wildly. 'You're overwrought and tired. I've let you do too much.' Her heart was painfully full of tenderness for her sister.

Catherine's sobs grew less at last, and she said in a little gasping, exhausted voice, 'I can't do it.'

'I won't make you. It can stay here in its old place and you can see it when you come on a visit.'

'I mean I can't get marired and go away. It's harder than anything is worth.'

Jessie was aghast. They argued long and confusedly. Once Catherine said: 'I wish it had been you, Jessie.'

Jessie drew away. 'You don't think that I . . .'

'No, dear, only on general grounds. You'd have made such a good wife and,' with a painful little smile, 'you were always the romantic one.'

'Not now,' said Jessie staunchly.

'I'll write to Angus now, tonight,' Catherine declared.

She wanted to be rid of this intolerable burden at once, although Jessie begged her to sleep on it. Neither of them had considered Angus, nor did they now. She got out the bottle of ink, and the pen with the cherry wood handle, which they shared, and began the letter. She was stiff and inarticulate on paper, and couldn't hope to make him understand. It was a miserable, hopeless task but she had to go through with it.

287

While she bent over the letter, Jessie went out into the kitchen and relit the fire. She took the silver coffee pot, the sugar basin and the cream jug, and set them out on the tray with the best worked traycloth. From the cake tin she selected the fairest of the little cakes that had been made for the afternoon tea of guests arriving tomorrow. Stinting nothing, she prepared their supper. When she heard Catherine sealing the letter, thumping the flap down with her fist to make the cheap gum stick, she carried in the tray.

Although she felt sick with crying, Catherine drank her coffee and ate a cake. The sisters smiled at one another with shaking lips and stiff reddened eyelids.

'He won't come again now,' said Jessie regretfully, but each added in her heart, 'He was a stranger, after all.'

Katherine Mansfield

The Daughters of the Late Colonel

The week after was one of the busiest weeks of their lives. Even when they went to bed it was only their bodies that lay down and rested; their minds went on, thinking things out, talking things over, wondering, deciding, trying to remember where . . .

Constantia lay like a statue, her hands by her sides, her feet just overlapping each other, the sheet up to her chin. She stared at the ceiling.

'Do you think Father would mind if we gave his top-hat to the porter?'

'The porter?' snapped Josephine. 'Why ever the porter? What a very extraordinary idea!'

'Because,' said Constantia slowly, 'he must often have to go to funerals. And I noticed at – at the cemetery that he only had a bowler.' She paused. 'I thought then how very much he'd appreciate a top-hat. We ought to give him a present, too. He was always very nice to Father.'

'But,' cried Josephine, flouncing on her pillow and staring across the dark at Constantia, 'Father's head!' And suddenly, for one awful moment, she nearly giggled. Not, of course, that she felt in the least like giggling. It must have been habit. Years ago, when they had stayed awake at night talking, their beds had simply heaved. And now the porter's head, disappearing, popped out, like a candle, under Father's hat . . . The giggle mounted, mounted; she clenched her hands; she fought it down; she frowned fiercely at the dark and said 'Remember' terribly sternly.

'We can decide tomorrow,' she said.

Constantia had noticed nothing; she sighed.

'Do you think we ought to have our dressing-gowns dyed as well?'

'Black?' almost shrieked Josephine.

'Well, what else?' said Constantia. 'I was thinking – it doesn't seem quite sincere, in a way, to wear black out of doors and when we're fully dressed, and then when we're at home –'

'But nobody sees us,' said Josephine. She gave the bed-clothes such a twitch that both her feet became uncovered, and she had to creep up the pillows to get them well under again.

'Kate does,' said Constantia. 'And the postman very well might.'

Josephine thought of her dark-red slippers, which matched her dressing-gown, and of Constantia's favourite indefinite green ones which went with hers. Black! Two black dressing-gowns and two pairs of black woolly slippers, creeping off to the bathroom like black cats.

'I don't think it's absolutely necessary,' said she.

Silence. Then Constantia said, 'We shall have to post the papers with the notice in them tomorrow to catch the Ceylon mail . . . How many letters have we had up till now?'

'Twenty-three.'

Josephine had replied to them all, and twenty-three times when she came to 'We miss our dear father so much' she had broken down and had to use her handkerchief, and on some of them even to soak up a very light-blue tear with an edge of blotting-paper. Strange! She couldn't have put it on – but twenty-three times. Even now, though, when she said over to herself sadly 'We miss our dear father *so* much,' she could have cried if she'd wanted to.

'Have you got enough stamps?' came from Constantia.

'Oh, how can I tell?' said Josephine crossly. 'What's the good of asking me that now?'

'I was just wondering,' said Constantia mildly.

Silence again. There came a little rustle, a scurry, a hop.

'A mouse,' said Constantia.

'It can't be a mouse because there aren't any crumbs,' said Josephine.

'But it doesn't know there aren't,' said Constantia.

A spasm of pity squeezed her heart. Poor little thing! She wished she'd left a tiny piece of biscuit on the dressing-table. It was awful to think of it not finding anything. What would it do?

'I can't think how they manage to live at all,' she said slowly.

'Who?' demanded Josephine.

And Constantia said more loudly than she meant to, 'Mice.'

Josephine was furious. 'Oh, what nonsense, Con!' she said. 'What have mice got to do with it? You're asleep.'

'I don't think I am,' said Constantia. She shut her eyes to make sure. She was.

Josephine arched her spine, pulled up her knees, folded her arms so that her fists came under her ears, and pressed her cheek hard against the pillow.

Another thing which complicated matters was they had Nurse Andrews staying on with them that week. It was their own fault; they had asked her. It was Josephine's idea. On the morning – well, on the last morning, when the doctor had gone, Josephine had said to Constantia, 'Don't you think it would be rather nice if we asked Nurse Andrews to stay on for a week as our guest?'

'Very nice,' said Constantia.

'I thought,' went on Josephine quickly, 'I should just say this afternoon, after I've paid her, "My sister and I would be very pleased, after all you've done for us, Nurse Andrews, if you would stay on for a week as our guest." I'd have to put that in about being our guest in case –'

'Oh, but she could hardly expect to be paid!' cried Constantia.

'One never knows,' said Josephine sagely.

Nurse Andrews had, of course, jumped at the idea. But it was a bother. It meant they had to have regular sit-down meals at the proper times, whereas if they'd been alone they could just have asked Kate if she wouldn't have minded bringing them a tray wherever they were. And mealtimes now that the strain was over were rather a trial.

Nurse Andrews was simply fearful about butter. Really they couldn't help feeling that about butter, at least, she took advantage of their kindness. And she had that maddening habit of asking for just an inch more bread to finish what she had on her plate, and then, at the last mouthful, absent-mindedly – of course it wasn't absent-mindedly – taking another helping. Josephine got very red when this happened, and she fastened her small, beadlike eyes on the tablecloth as if she saw a minute strange insect creeping through the web of it. But

291

Constantia's long, pale face lengthened and set, and she gazed away
– away – far over the desert, to where that line of camels unwound
like a thread of wool . . .

'When I was with Lady Tukes,' said Nurse Andrews, 'she had such
a dainty little contrayvance for the buttah. It was a silvah Cupid
balanced on the – on the bordah of a glass dish, holding a tayny
fork. And when you wanted some buttah you simply pressed his foot
and he bent down and speared you a piece. It was quite a gayme.'

Josephine could hardly bear that. But 'I think those things are very
extravagant' was all she said.

'But whey?' asked Nurse Andrews, beaming through her eye-
glasses. 'No one, surely, would take more buttah than one wanted
– would one?'

'Ring, Con,' cried Josephine. She couldn't trust herself to reply.

And proud young Kate, the enchanted princess, came in to see
what the old tabbies wanted now. She snatched away their plates
of mock something or other and slapped down a white, terrified
blancmange.

'Jam, please, Kate,' said Josephine kindly.

Kate knelt and burst open the sideboard, lifted the lid of the
jam-pot, saw it was empty, put it on the table, and stalked off.

'I'm afraid,' said Nurse Andrews a moment later, 'there isn't any.'

'Oh, what a bother!' said Josephine. She bit her lip. 'What had we
better do?'

Constantia looked dubious. 'We can't disturb Kate again,' she
said softly.

Nurse Andrews waited, smiling at them both. Her eyes wandered,
spying at everything behind her eye-glasses. Constantia in despair
went back to her camels. Josephine frowned heavily – concentrated.
If it hadn't been for this idiotic woman she and Con would, of course,
have eaten their blancmange without. Suddenly the idea came.

'I know,' she said. 'Marmalade. There's some marmalade in the
sideboard. Get it, Con.'

'I hope,' laughed Nurse Andrews – and her laugh was like a
spoon tinkling against a medicine-glass – 'I hope it's not very bittah
marmalayde.'

But, after all, it was not long now, and then she'd be gone for good.

And there was no getting over the fact that she had been very kind to Father. She had nursed him day and night at the end. Indeed, both Constantia and Josephine felt privately she had rather overdone the not leaving him at the very last. For when they had gone in to say goodbye Nurse Andrews had sat beside his bed the whole time, holding his wrist and pretending to look at her watch. It couldn't have been necessary. It was so tactless, too. Supposing Father had wanted to say something – something private to them. Not that he had. Oh, far from it! He lay there, purple, a dark, angry purple in the face, and never even looked at them when they came in. Then, as they were standing there, wondering what to do, he had suddenly opened one eye. Oh, what a difference it would have made, what a difference to their memory of him, how much easier to tell people about it, if he had only opened both! But no – one eye only. It glared at them a moment and then . . . went out.

It had made it very awkward for them when Mr Farolles, of St John's, called the same afternoon.

'The end was quite peaceful, I trust?' were the first words he said as he glided towards them through the dark drawing-room.

'Quite,' said Josephine faintly. They both hung their heads. Both of them felt certain that eye wasn't at all a peaceful eye.

'Won't you sit down?' said Josephine.

'Thank you, Miss Pinner,' said Mr Farolles gratefully. He folded his coat-tails and began to lower himself into father's armchair, but just as he touched it he almost sprang up and slid into the next chair instead.

He coughed. Josephine clasped her hands; Constantia looked vague.

'I want you to feel, Miss Pinner,' said Mr Farolles, 'and you, Miss Constantia, that I'm trying to be helpful. I want to be helpful to you both, if you will let me. These are the times,' said Mr Farolles, very simply and earnestly, 'when God means us to be helpful to one another.'

'Thank you very much, Mr Farolles,' said Josephine and Constantia.

'Not at all,' said Mr Farolles gently. He drew his kid gloves through his fingers and leaned forward. 'And if either of you would like a little Communion, either or both of you, here *and* now, you have only to tell me. A little Communion is often very help – a great comfort,' he added tenderly.

But the idea of a little Communion terrified them. What! In the drawing-room by themselves – with no – no altar or anything! The piano would be much too high, thought Constantia, and Mr Farolles could not possibly lean over it with the chalice. And Kate would be sure to come bursting in and interrupt them, thought Josephine. And supposing the bell rang in the middle? It might be somebody important – about their mourning. Would they get up reverently and go out, or would they have to wait . . . in torture?

'Perhaps you will send round a note by your good Kate if you would care for it later,' said Mr Farolles.

'Oh yes, thank you very much!' they both said.

Mr Farolles got up and took his black straw hat from the round table.

'And about the funeral,' he said softly. 'I may arrange that – as your dear father's old friend and yours, Miss Pinner – and Miss Constantia?'

Josephine and Constantia got up too.

'I should like it to be quite simple,' said Josephine firmly, 'and not too expensive. At the same time, I should like –'

'A good one that will last,' thought dreamy Constantia, as if Josephine were buying a nightgown. But, of course, Josephine didn't say that. 'One suitable to our father's position.' She was very nervous.

'I'll run round to our good friend Mr Knight,' said Mr Farolles soothingly. 'I will ask him to come and see you. I am sure you will find him very helpful indeed.'

Well, at any rate, all that part of it was over, though neither of them could possibly believe that Father was never coming back. Josephine had had a moment of absolute terror at the cemetery, while the coffin was lowered, to think that she and Constantia had done this thing without asking his permission. What would Father say when he found out? For he was bound to find out sooner or later. He always did. 'Buried. You two girls had me *buried*!' She heard his stick thumping. Oh, what would they say? What possible excuse could they make? It sounded such an appallingly heartless thing to do. Such a wicked advantage to take of a person because he happened to be helpless at the moment. The other people seemed to treat it all as a matter of course. They were strangers; they couldn't be expected to understand that Father was the very last person for such a thing to happen to. No, the entire blame for it all would fall on her and Constantia. And the expense, she thought, stepping into the tight-buttoned cab. When she had to show him the bills. What would he say then?

She heard him absolutely roaring. 'And do you expect me to pay for this gimcrack excursion of yours?'

'Oh,' groaned poor Josephine aloud, 'we shouldn't have done it, Con!'

And Constantia, pale as a lemon in all that blackness, said in a frightened whisper, 'Done what, Jug?'

'Let them bu-bury Father like that,' said Josephine, breaking down and crying into her new, queer-smelling mourning handkerchief.

'But what else could we have done?' asked Constantia wonderingly. 'We couldn't have kept him, Jug – we couldn't have kept him unburied. At any rate, not in a flat that size.'

Josephine blew her nose; the cab was dreadfully stuffy.

'I don't know,' she said forlornly. 'It is all so dreadful. I feel we ought to have tried to, just for a time at least. To make perfectly sure. One thing's certain' – and her tears sprang out again – 'Father will never forgive us for this – never!'

Father would never forgive them. That was what they felt more than ever when, two mornings later, they went into his room to go through his things. They had discussed it quite calmly. It was even down on Josephine's list of things to be done. *Go through Father's things and settle about them*. But that was a very different matter from saying after breakfast:

'Well, are you ready, Con?'

'Yes, Jug – when you are.'

'Then I think we'd better get it over.'

It was dark in the hall. It had been a rule for years never to disturb Father in the morning, whatever happened. And now they were going to open the door without knocking even ... Constantia's eyes were enormous at the idea; Josephine felt weak in the knees.

'You – you go first,' she gasped, pushing Constantia.

But Constantia said, as she always had said on those occasions, 'No, Jug, that's not fair. You're eldest.'

Josephine was just going to say – what at other times she wouldn't have owned to for the world – what she kept for her very last weapon, 'But you're tallest,' when they noticed that the kitchen door was open, and there stood Kate . . .

'Very stiff,' said Josephine, grasping the door-handle and doing her best to turn it. As if anything ever deceived Kate!

It couldn't be helped. That girl was . . . Then the door was shut behind them, but – but they weren't in Father's room at all. They might have suddenly walked through the wall by mistake into a different flat altogether. Was the door just behind them? They were too frightened to look. Josephine knew that if it was it was holding itself tight shut; Constantia felt that, like the doors in dreams, it hadn't any handle at all. It was the coldness which made it so awful. Or the whiteness – which? Everything was covered. The blinds were down, a cloth hung over the mirror, a sheet hid the bed; a huge fan of white paper filled the fireplace. Constantia timidly put out her hand; she almost expected a snowflake to fall. Josephine felt a queer tingling in her nose, as if her nose was freezing. Then a can klop-klopped over the cobbles below, and the quiet seemed to shake into little pieces.

'I had better pull up a blind,' said Josephine bravely.

'Yes, it might be a good idea,' whispered Constantia.

They only gave the blind a touch, but it flew up and the cord flew after, rolling round the blind-stick, and the little tassel tapped as if trying to get free. That was too much for Constantia.

'Don't you think – don't you think we might put it off for another day?' she whispered.

'Why?' snapped Josephine, feeling, as usual, much better now that she knew for certain that Constantia was terrified. 'It's got to be done. But I do wish you wouldn't whisper, Con.'

'I didn't know I was whispering,' whispered Constantia.

'And why do you keep on staring at the bed?' said Josephine, raising her voice almost defiantly. 'There's nothing *on* the bed.'

'Oh, Jug, don't say so!' said poor Connie. 'At any rate, not so loudly.'

Josephine felt herself that she had gone too far. She took a wide

296

swerve over to the chest of drawers, put out her hand, but quickly drew it back again.

'Connie!' she gasped, and she wheeled round and leaned with her back against the chest of drawers.

'Oh, Jug – what?'

Josephine could only glare. She had the most extraordinary feeling that she had just escaped something simply awful. But how could she explain to Constantia that Father was in the chest of drawers? He was in the top drawer with his handkerchiefs and neckties, or in the next with his shirts and pyjamas, or in the lowest of all with his suits. He was watching there, hidden away – just behind the door-handle – ready to spring.

She pulled a funny old-fashioned face at Constantia, just as she used to in the old days when she was going to cry.

'I can't open,' she nearly wailed.

'No, don't, Jug,' whispered Constantia earnestly. 'It's much better not to. Don't let's open anything. At any rate, not for a long time.'

'But – but it seems so weak,' said Josephine, breaking down.

'But why not be weak for once, Jug?' argued Constantia, whispering quite fiercely. 'If it is weak.' And her pale stare flew from the locked writing-table – so safe – to the huge glittering wardrobe, and she began to breathe in a queer, panting way. 'Why shouldn't we be weak for once in our lives, Jug? It's quite excusable. Let's be weak – be weak, Jug. It's much nicer to be weak than to be strong.'

And then she did one of those amazingly bold things that she'd done about twice before in their lives: she marched over to the wardrobe, turned the key, and took it out of the lock. Took it out of the lock and held it up to Josephine, showing Josephine by her extraordinary smile that she knew what she'd done, she'd risked deliberately Father being in there among his overcoats.

If the huge wardrobe had lurched forward, had crashed down on Constantia, Josephine wouldn't have been surprised. On the contrary, she would have thought it the only suitable thing to happen. But nothing happened. Only the room seemed quieter than ever, and bigger flakes of cold air fell on Josephine's shoulders and knees. She began to shiver.

'Come, Jug,' said Constantia, still with that awful callous smile, and

Josephine followed just as she had that last time, when Constantia had pushed Benny into the round pond.

But the strain told on them when they were back in the dining-room. They sat down, very shaky, and looked at each other.

'I don't feel I can settle to anything,' said Josephine, 'until I've had something. Do you think we could ask Kate for two cups of hot water?'

'I really don't see why we shouldn't,' said Constantia carefully. She was quite normal again. 'I won't ring. I'll go to the kitchen door and ask her.'

'Yes, do,' said Josephine, sinking down into a chair. 'Tell her, just two cups, Con, nothing else – on a tray.'

'She needn't even put the jug on, need she?' said Constantia, as though Kate might very well complain if the jug had been there.

'Oh no, certainly not! The jug's not at all necessary. She can pour it direct out of the kettle,' cried Josephine, feeling that would be a labour-saving indeed.

Their cold lips quivered at the greenish brims. Josephine curved her small red hands round the cup; Constantia sat up and blew on the wavy steam, making it flutter from one side to the other.

'Speaking of Benny,' said Josephine.

And though Benny hadn't been mentioned Constantia immediately looked as though he had.

'He'll expect us to send him something of Father's, of course. But it's so difficult to know what to send to Ceylon.'

'You mean things get unstuck so on the voyage,' murmured Constantia.

'No, lost,' said Josephine sharply. 'You know there's no post. Only runners.'

Both paused to watch a black man in white linen drawers running through the pale fields for dear life, with a large brown-paper parcel in his hands. Josephine's black man was tiny; he scurried along glistening like an ant. But there was something blind and tireless about Constantia's tall, thin fellow, which made him, she decided, a very unpleasant person indeed ... On the verandah, dressed all

298

in white and wearing a cork helmet, stood Benny. His right hand shook up and down, as Father's did when he was impatient. And behind him, not in the least interested, sat Hilda, the unknown sister-in-law. She swung in a cane rocker and flicked over the leaves of the *Tatler*.

'I think his watch would be the most suitable present,' said Josephine.

Constantia looked up; she seemed surprised.

'Oh, would you trust a gold watch to a native?'

'But, of course, I'd disguise it,' said Josephine. 'No one would know it was a watch.' She liked the idea of having to make a parcel such a curious shape that no one could possibly guess what it was. She even thought for a moment of hiding the watch in a narrow cardboard corset-box that she'd kept by her for a long time, waiting for it to come in for something. It was such beautiful, firm cardboard. But, no, it wouldn't be appropriate for this occasion. It had lettering on it: *Medium Women's 28. Extra Firm Busks*. It would be almost too much of a surprise for Benny to open that and find Father's watch inside.

'And, of course, it isn't as though it would be going – ticking, I mean,' said Constantia, who was still thinking of the native love of jewellery. 'At least,' she added, 'it would be very strange if after all that time it was.'

Josephine made no reply. She had flown off on one of her tangents. She had suddenly thought of Cyril. Wasn't it more usual for the only grandson to have the watch? And then dear Cyril was so appreciative, and a gold watch meant so much to a young man. Benny, in all probability, had quite got out of the habit of watches; men so seldom wore waistcoats in those hot climates. Whereas Cyril in London wore them from year's end to year's end. And it would be so nice for her and Constantia, when he came to tea, to know it was there. 'I see you've got on Grandfather's watch, Cyril.' It would be somehow so satisfactory.

Dear boy! What a blow his sweet, sympathetic little note had been! Of course they quite understood; but it was most unfortunate.

'It would have been such a point, having him,' said Josephine.

'And he would have enjoyed it so,' said Constantia, not thinking what she was saying.

However, as soon as he got back he was coming to tea with his aunties. Cyril to tea was one of their rare treats.

'Now, Cyril, you mustn't be frightened of our cakes. Your Aunty Con and I bought them at Buszard's this morning. We know what a man's appetite is. So don't be ashamed of making a good tea.'

Josephine cut recklessly into the rich dark cake that stood for her winter gloves or the soling and heeling of Constantia's only respectable shoes. But Cyril was most unmanlike in appetite.

'I say, Aunt Josephine, I simply can't. I've only just had lunch, you know.'

'Oh, Cyril, that can't be true! It's after four,' cried Josephine. Constantia sat with her knife poised over the chocolate-roll.

'It is, all the same,' said Cyril. 'I had to meet a man at Victoria, and he kept me hanging about till ... there was only time to get lunch and to come on here. And he gave me – phew' – Cyril put his hand to his forehead – a terrific blow-out,' he said.

It was disappointing – today of all days. But still he couldn't be expected to know.

'But you'll have a meringue, won't you, Cyril?' said Aunt Josephine. 'These meringues were bought specially for you. Your dear father was so fond of them. We were sure you are, too.'

'I *am*, Aunt Josephine,' cried Cyril ardently. 'Do you mind if I take half to begin with?'

'Not at all, dear boy; but we mustn't let you off with that.'

'Is your dear father still so fond of meringues?' asked Aunty Con gently. She winced faintly as she broke through the shell of hers.

'Well, I don't quite know, Aunty Con,' said Cyril breezily.

At that they both looked up.

'Don't know?' almost snapped Josephine. 'Don't know a thing like that about your own father, Cyril?'

'Surely,' said Aunty Con softly.

Cyril tried to laugh it off. 'Oh, well,' he said, 'it's such a long time since –' He faltered. He stopped. Their faces were too much for him.

300

'Even *so*,' said Josephine.

And Aunty Con looked.

Cyril put down his teacup. 'Wait a bit,' he cried. 'Wait a bit, Aunt Josephine. What am I thinking of?'

He looked up. They were beginning to brighten. Cyril slapped his knee.

'Of course,' he said, 'it was meringues. How could I have forgotten? Yes, Aunt Josephine, you're perfectly right. Father's most frightfully keen on meringues.'

They didn't only beam. Aunt Josephine went scarlet with pleasure; Aunty Con gave a deep, deep sigh.

'And now, Cyril, you must come and see Father,' said Josephine. 'He knows you were coming today.'

'Right,' said Cyril, very firmly and heartily. He got up from his chair; suddenly he glanced at the clock.

'I say, Aunty Con, isn't your clock a bit slow? I've got to meet a man at – at Paddington just after five. I'm afraid I shan't be able to stay very long with Grandfather.'

'Oh, he won't expect you to stay *very* long!' said Aunt Josephine.

Constantia was still gazing at the clock. She couldn't make up her mind if it was fast or slow. It was one or the other, she felt almost certain of that. At any rate, it had been.

Cyril still lingered. 'Aren't you coming along, Aunty Con?'

'Of course,' said Josephine, 'we shall all go. Come on, Con.'

They knocked at the door, and Cyril followed his aunts into Grandfather's hot, sweetish room.

'Come on,' said Grandfather Pinner. 'Don't hang about. What is it? What've you been up to?'

He was sitting in front of a roaring fire, clasping his stick. He had a thick rug over his knees. On his lap there lay a beautiful pale yellow silk handkerchief.

'It's Cyril, Father,' said Josephine shyly. And she took Cyril's hand and led him forward.

'Good afternoon, Grandfather,' said Cyril, trying to take his hand out of Aunt Josephine's. Grandfather Pinner shot his eyes at Cyril in the way he was famous for. Where was Aunty Con? She stood on the other side of Aunt Josephine; her long arms hung down in

301

front of her; her hands were clasped. She never took her eyes off Grandfather.

'Well,' said Grandfather Pinner, beginning to thump, 'what have you got to tell me?'

What had he, what had he got to tell him? Cyril felt himself smiling like a perfect imbecile. The room was stifling, too.

But Aunt Josephine came to his rescue. She cried brightly, 'Cyril says his father is still very fond of meringues, Father dear.'

'Eh?' said Grandfather Pinner, curving his hand like a purple meringue-shell over one ear.

Josephine repeated, 'Cyril says his father is still very fond of meringues.'

'Can't hear,' said old Colonel Pinner. And he waved Josephine away with his stick, then pointed with his stick to Cyril. 'Tell me what she's trying to say,' he said.

(My God!) 'Must I?' said Cyril, blushing and staring at Aunt Josephine.

'Do, dear,' she smiled. 'It will please him so much.'

'Come on, out with it!' cried Colonel Pinner testily, beginning to thump again.

And Cyril leaned forward and yelled, 'Father's still very fond of meringues.'

At that Grandfather Pinner jumped as though he had been shot.

'Don't shout!' he cried. 'What's the matter with the boy? *Meringues!* What about 'em?'

'Oh, Aunt Josephine, must we go on?' groaned Cyril desperately.

'It's quite all right, dear boy,' said Aunt Josephine, as though he and she were at the dentist's together. 'He'll understand in a minute.' And she whispered to Cyril, 'He's getting a bit deaf, you know.' Then she leaned forward and really bawled at Grandfather Pinner, 'Cyril only wanted to tell you, Father dear, that *his* father is still very fond of meringues.'

Colonel Pinner heard that time, heard and brooded, looking Cyril up and down.

'What an esstrordinary thing!' said old Grandfather Pinner. 'What an esstrordinary thing to come all this way here to tell me!'

And Cyril felt it *was*.

'Yes, I shall send Cyril the watch,' said Josephine.

'That would be very nice,' said Constantia. 'I seem to remember last time he came there was some little trouble about the time.'

They were interrupted by Kate bursting through the door in her usual fashion, as though she had discovered some secret panel in the wall.

'Fried or boiled?' asked the bold voice.

Fried or boiled? Josephine and Constantia were quite bewildered for the moment. They could hardly take it in.

'Fried or boiled what, Kate?' asked Josephine, trying to begin to concentrate.

Kate gave a loud sniff. 'Fish.'

'Well, why didn't you say so immediately?' Josephine reproached her gently. 'How could you expect us to understand, Kate? There are a great many things in this world, you know, which are fried or boiled.' And after such a display of courage she said quite brightly to Constantia, 'Which do you prefer, Con?'

'I think it might be nice to have it fried,' said Constantia. 'On the other hand, of course, boiled fish is very nice. I think I prefer both equally well ... Unless you ... In that case –'

'I shall fry it,' said Kate, and she bounced back, leaving their door open and slamming the door of her kitchen.

Josephine gazed at Constantia; she raised her pale eyebrows until they rippled away into her pale hair. She got up. She said in a very lofty, imposing way, 'Do you mind following me into the drawing-room, Constantia? I've something of great importance to discuss with you.'

For it was always to the drawing-room they retired when they wanted to talk over Kate.

Josephine closed the door meaningly. 'Sit down, Constantia,' she said, still very grand. She might have been receiving Constantia for the first time. And Con looked round vaguely for a chair, as though she felt indeed quite a stranger.

'Now the question is,' said Josephine, bending forward, 'whether we shall keep her or not.'

'That is the question,' agreed Constantia.

'And this time,' said Josephine firmly, 'we must come to a definite decision.'

Constantia looked for a moment as though she might begin going over all the other times, but she pulled herself together and said, 'Yes, Jug.'

'You see, Con,' explained Josephine, 'everything is so changed now.' Constantia looked up quickly. 'I mean,' went on Josephine, 'we're not dependent on Kate as we were.' And she blushed faintly. 'There's not Father to cook for.'

'That is perfectly true,' agreed Constantia. 'Father certainly doesn't want any cooking now whatever else –'

Josephine broke in sharply, 'You're not sleepy, are you, Con?'

'Sleepy, Jug?' Constantia was wide-eyed.

'Well, concentrate more,' said Josephine sharply, and she returned to the subject. 'What it comes to is, if we did' – and this she barely breathed, glancing at the door – 'give Kate notice' – she raised her voice again – 'we could manage our own food.'

'Why not?' cried Constantia. She couldn't help smiling. The idea was so exciting. She clasped her hands. 'What should we live on, Jug?'

'Oh, eggs in various forms!' said Jug, lofty again. 'And, besides, there are all the cooked foods.'

'But I've always heard,' said Constantia, 'they are considered so very expensive.'

'Not if one buys them in moderation,' said Josephine. But she tore herself away from this fascinating bypath and dragged Constantia after her.

'What we've got to decide now, however, is whether we really do trust Kate or not.'

Constantia leaned back. Her flat little laugh flew from her lips.

'Isn't it curious, Jug,' said she, 'that just on this one subject I've never been able to quite make up my mind?'

She never had. The whole difficulty was to prove anything. How did one prove things, how could one? Suppose Kate had stood in front of her and deliberately made a face. Mightn't she very well have been in pain? Wasn't it impossible, at any rate, to ask Kate if she was making a face at her? If Kate answered 'No' – and, of course, she would say 'No' – what a position! How undignified! Then, again, Constantia suspected, she was almost certain that Kate went to her

304

chest of drawers when she and Josephine were out, not to take things but to spy. Many times she had come back to find her amethyst cross in the most unlikely places, under her lace ties or on top of her evening Bertha. More than once she had laid a trap for Kate. She had arranged things in a special order and then called Josephine to witness.

'You see, Jug?'

'Quite, Con.'

'Now we shall be able to tell.'

But, oh dear, when she did go to look, she was as far off from a proof as ever! If anything was displaced, it might so very well have happened as she closed the drawer; a jolt might have done it so easily.

'You come, Jug, and decide. I really can't. It's too difficult.'

But after a pause and a long glare Josephine would sigh, 'Now you've put the doubt into my mind, Con, I'm sure I can't tell myself.'

'Well, we can't postpone it again,' said Josephine. 'If we postpone it this time –'

But at that moment in the street below a barrel-organ struck up. Josephine and Constantia sprang to their feet together.

'Run, Con,' said Josephine. 'Run quickly. There's sixpence on the –'

Then they remembered. It didn't matter. They would never have to stop the organ-grinder again. Never again would she and Constantia be told to make that monkey take his noise somewhere else. Never would sound that loud, strange bellow when Father thought they were not hurrying enough. The organ-grinder might play there all day and the stick would not thump.

> It never will thump again,
> It never will thump again,

played the barrel-organ.

What was Constantia thinking? She had such a strange smile; she looked different. She couldn't be going to cry.

'Jug, Jug,' said Constantia softly, pressing her hands together. 'Do you know what day it is? It's Saturday. It's a week today, a whole week.'

A week since father died,
A week since father died,

cried the barrel-organ. And Josephine, too, forgot to be practical and sensible; she smiled faintly, strangely. On the Indian carpet there fell a square of sunlight, pale red; it came and went and came – and stayed, deepened – until it shone almost golden.

'The sun's out, said Josephine, as though it really mattered.

A perfect fountain of bubbling notes shook from the barrel-organ, round, bright notes, carelessly scattered.

Constantia lifted her big, cold hands as if to catch them, and then her hands fell again. She walked over to the mantelpiece to her favourite Buddha. And the stone and gilt image, whose smile always gave her such a queer feeling, almost a pain and yet a pleasant pain, seemed today to be more than smiling. He knew something; he had a secret. 'I know something that you don't know,' said her Buddha. Oh, what was it, what could it be? And yet she had always felt there was . . . something.

The sunlight pressed through the windows, thieved its way in, flashed its light over the furniture and the photographs. Josephine watched it. When it came to Mother's photograph, the enlargement over the piano, it lingered as though puzzled to find so little remained of Mother, except the ear-rings shaped like tiny pagodas and a black feather boa. Why did the photographs of dead people always fade so? wondered Josephine. As soon as a person was dead their photograph died too. But, of course, this one of Mother was very old. It was thirty-five years old. Josephine remembered standing on a chair and pointing out that feather boa to Constantia and telling her that it was a snake that had killed their mother in Ceylon . . . Would everything have been different if Mother hadn't died? She didn't see why. Aunt Florence had lived with them until they had left school, and they had moved three times and had their yearly holiday and . . . and there'd been changes of servants, of course.

Some little sparrows, young sparrows they sounded, chirped on the window-ledge. *Yeep – eyeep – yeep*. But Josephine felt they were not sparrows, not on the window-ledge. It was inside her, that queer little crying noise. *Yeep – eyeep – yeep*. Ah, what was it crying, so weak and forlorn?

If Mother had lived, might they have married? But there had been nobody for them to marry. There had been Father's Anglo-Indian friends before he quarrelled with them. But after that she and Constantia never met a single man except clergymen. How did one meet men? Or even if they'd met them, how could they have got to know men well enough to be more than strangers? One read of people having adventures, being followed, and so on. But nobody had ever followed Constantia and her. Oh yes, there had been one year at Eastbourne a mysterious man at their boarding house who had put a note on the jug of hot water outside their bedroom door! But by the time Connie had found it the steam had made the writing too faint to read; they couldn't even make out to which of them it was addressed. And he had left next day. And that was all. The rest had been looking after Father and at the same time keeping out of Father's way. But now? But now? The thieving sun touched Josephine gently. She lifted her face. She was drawn over to the window by gentle beams . . .

Until the barrel-organ stopped playing Constantia stayed before the Buddha, wondering, but not as usual, not vaguely. This time her wonder was like longing. She remembered the times she had come in here, crept out of bed in her nightgown when the moon was full, and lain on the floor with her arms outstretched, as though she was crucified. Why? The big, pale moon had made her do it. The horrible dancing figures on the carved screen had leered at her and she hadn't minded. She remembered too how, whenever they were at the seaside, she had gone off by herself and got as close to the sea as she could, and sung something, something she had made up, while she gazed all over that restless water. There had been this other life, running out, bringing things home in bags, getting things on approval, discussing them with Jug, and taking them back to get more things on approval, and arranging Father's trays and trying not to annoy Father. But it all seemed to have happened in a kind of tunnel. It wasn't real. It was only when she came out of the tunnel into the moonlight or by the sea or into a thunderstorm that she really felt herself. What did it mean? What was it she was always wanting? What did it all lead to? Now? Now?

She turned away from the Buddha with one of her vague gestures.

She went over to where Josephine was standing. She wanted to say something to Josephine, something frightfully important, about – about the future and what . . .

'Don't you think perhaps –' she began.

But Josephine interrupted her. 'I was wondering if now –' she murmured. They stopped; they waited for each other.

'Go on, Con,' said Josephine.

'No, no, Jug; after you,' said Constantia.

'No, say what you were going to say. You began,' said Josephine.

'I . . . I'd rather hear what you were going to say first,' said Constantia.

'Don't be absurd, Con.'

'Really, Jug.'

'Connie!'

'Oh, *Jug*!'

A pause. Then Constantia said faintly, 'I can't say what I was going to say, Jug, because I've forgotten what it was . . . that I was going to say.'

Josephine was silent for a moment. She stared at a big cloud where the sun had been. Then she replied shortly, 'I've forgotten too.'

Christina Rossetti

Goblin Market

Morning and evening
Maids heard the goblins cry:
'Come buy our orchard fruits,
Come buy, come buy:
Apples and quinces,
Lemons and oranges,
Plump unpecked cherries,
Melons and raspberries,
Bloom-down-cheeked peaches,
Swart-headed mulberries,
Wild free-born cranberries,
Crab-apples, dewberries,
Pine-apples, blackberries,
Apricots, strawberries; –
All ripe together
In summer weather, –
Morns that pass by,
Fair eves that fly;
Come buy, come buy:
Our grapes fresh from the vine,
Pomegranates full and fine,
Dates and sharp bullaces,
Rare pears and greengages,
Damsons and bilberries,
Taste them and try:
Currants and gooseberries,
Bright-fire-like barberries,
Figs to fill your mouth,
Citrons from the South,

Sweet to tongue and sound to eye;
Come buy, come buy.'

Evening by evening
Among the brookside rushes,
Laura bowed her head to hear,
Lizzie veiled her blushes:
Crouching close together
In the cooling weather,
With clasping arms and cautioning lips,
With tingling cheeks and finger tips.
'Lie close,' Laura said,
Pricking up her golden head:
'We must not look at goblin men,
We must not buy their fruits:
Who knows upon what soil they fed
Their hungry thirsty roots?'
'Come buy,' call the goblins
Hobbling down the glen.
'Oh,' cried Lizzie, 'Laura, Laura,
You should not peep at goblin men.'
Lizzie covered up her eyes,
Covered close lest they should look;
Laura reared her glossy head,
And whispered like the restless brook:
'Look, Lizzie, look, Lizzie,
Down the glen tramp little men.
One hauls a basket,
One bears a plate,
One lugs a golden dish
Of many pounds' weight.
How fair the vine must grow
Whose grapes are so luscious;
How warm the wind must blow
Through those fruit bushes.'
'No,' said Lizzie: 'No, no, no;
Their offers should not charm us,
Their evil gifts would harm us.'

She thrust a dimpled finger
In each ear, shut eyes and ran:
Curious Laura chose to linger
Wondering at each merchant man.
One had a cat's face,
One whisked a tail,
One tramped at a rat's pace,
One crawled like a snail,
One like a wombat prowled obtuse and furry,
One like a ratel tumbled hurry skurry.
She heard a voice like voice of doves
Cooing all together:
They sounded kind and full of loves
In the pleasant weather.

Laura stretched her gleaming neck
Like a rush-imbedded swan,
Like a lily from the beck,
Like a moonlit poplar branch,
Like a vessel at the launch
When its last restraint is gone.

Backwards up the mossy glen
Turned and trooped the goblin men,
With their shrill repeated cry,
'Come buy, come buy.'
When they reached where Laura was
They stood stock still upon the moss,
Leering at each other,
Brother with queer brother;
Signalling each other,
Brother with sly brother.
One set his basket down,
One reared his plate;
One began to weave a crown
Of tendrils, leaves, and rough nuts brown
(Men sell not such in any town);

One heaved the golden weight
Of dish and fruit to offer her:
'Come buy, come buy,' was still their cry.
Laura stared but did not stir,
Longed but had no money:
The whisk-tailed merchant bade her taste
In tones as smooth as honey,
The cat-faced purr'd,
The rat-paced spoke a word
Of welcome, and the snail-paced even was heard;
One parrot-voiced and jolly
Cried 'Pretty Goblin' still for 'Pretty Polly'; –
One whistled like a bird.

But sweet-tooth Laura spoke in haste:
'Good folk, I have no coin;
To take were to purloin:
I have no copper in my purse,
I have no silver either,
And all my gold is on the furze
That shakes in windy weather
Above the rusty heather.'
'You have much gold upon your head,'
They answered all together:
'Buy from us with a golden curl.'
She clipped a precious golden lock,
She dropped a tear more rare than pearl,
Then sucked their fruit globes fair or red:
Sweeter than honey from the rock,
Stronger than man-rejoicing wine,
Clearer than water flowed that juice;
She never tasted such before,
How should it cloy with length of use?
She sucked and sucked and sucked the more
Fruits which that unknown orchard bore;
She sucked until her lips were sore;
Then flung the emptied rinds away
But gathered up one kernel-stone,

312

And knew not was it night or day
As she turned home alone.

Lizzie met her at the gate
Full of wise upbraidings:
'Dear, you should not stay so late,
Twilight is not good for maidens;
Should not loiter in the glen
In the haunts of goblin men.
Do you not remember Jeanie,
How she met them in the moonlight,
Took their gifts both choice and many,
Ate their fruits and wore their flowers
Plucked from bowers
Where summer ripens at all hours?
But ever in the noonlight
She pined and pined away;
Sought them by night and day,
Found them no more, but dwindled and grew
   grey;
Then fell with the first snow,
While to this day no grass will grow
Where she lies low:
I planted daisies there a year ago
That never blow.
You should not loiter so.'
'Nay, hush,' said Laura:
'Nay, hush, my sister:
I ate and ate my fill,
Yet my mouth waters still;
To-morrow night I will
Buy more': and kissed her:
'Have done with sorrow;
I'll bring you plums to-morrow
Fresh on their mother twigs,
Cherries worth getting;
You cannot think what figs
My teeth have met in,

313

What melons icy-cold
Piled on a dish of gold
Too huge for me to hold,
What peaches with a velvet nap,
Pellucid grapes without one seed:
Odorous indeed must be the mead
Whereon they grow, and pure the wave they drink
With lilies at the brink,
And sugar-sweet their sap.'

Golden head by golden head,
Like two pigeons in one nest,
Folded in each other's wings,
They lay down in their curtained bed:
Like two blossoms on one stem,
Like two flakes of new-fall'n snow,
Like two wands of ivory
Tipped with gold for awful kings.
Moon and stars gazed in at them,
Wind sang to them lullaby,
Lumbering owls forbore to fly,
Not a bat flapped to and fro
Round their nest:
Cheek to cheek and breast to breast
Locked together in one nest.

Early in the morning
When the first cock crowed his warning,
Neat like bees, as sweet and busy,
Laura rose with Lizzie:
Fetched in honey, milked the cows,
Aired and set to rights the house,
Kneaded cakes of whitest wheat,
Cakes for dainty mouths to eat,
Next churned butter, whipped up cream,
Fed their poultry, sat and sewed;
Talked as modest maidens should:

314

Lizzie with an open heart,
Laura in an absent dream,
One content, one sick in part;
One warbling for the mere bright day's delight,
One longing for the night.

At length slow evening came:
They went with pitchers to the reedy brook;
Lizzie most placid in her look,
Laura most like a leaping flame.
They drew the gurgling water from its deep;
Lizzie plucked purple and rich golden flags,
Then turning homeward, said: 'The sunset flushes
Those furthest loftiest crags;
Come, Laura, not another maiden lags,
No wilful squirrel wags,
The beasts and birds are fast asleep.'
But Laura loitered still among the rushes
And said the bank was steep.

And said the hour was early still,
The dew not fall'n, the wind not chill:
Listening ever, but not catching
The customary cry,
'Come buy, come buy,'
With its iterated jingle
Of sugar-baited words:
Not for all her watching
Once discerning even one goblin
Racing, whisking, tumbling, hobbling;
Let alone the herds
That used to tramp along the glen,
In groups or single,
Of brisk fruit-merchant men.

Till Lizzie urged, 'O Laura, come;
I hear the fruit-call, but I dare not look:

You should not loiter longer at this brook:
Come with me home.
The stars rise, the moon bends her arc,
Each glowworm winks her spark,
Let us get home before the night grows dark:
For clouds may gather
Though this is summer weather,
Put out the lights and drench us through;
Then if we lost our way what should we do?'

Laura turned cold as stone
To find her sister heard that cry alone,
That goblin cry,
'Come buy our fruits, come buy.'
Must she then buy no more such dainty fruit?
Must she no more such succous pasture find,
Gone deaf and blind?
Her tree of life drooped from the root:
She said not one word in her heart's sore ache;
But peering thro' the dimness, naught discerning,
Trudged home, her pitcher dripping all the way;
So crept to bed, and lay
Silent till Lizzie slept;
Then sat up in a passionate yearning,
And gnashed her teeth for baulked desire, and
    wept
As if her heart would break.

Day after day, night after night,
Laura kept watch in vain
In sullen silence of exceeding pain.
She never caught again the goblin cry:
'Come buy, come buy'; –
She never spied the goblin men
Hawking their fruits along the glen:
But when the moon waxed bright
Her hair grew thin and grey;

316

She dwindled, as the fair full moon doth turn
To swift decay and burn
Her fire away.

One day remembering her kernel-stone
She set it by a wall that faced the south;
Dewed it with tears, hoped for a root,
Watched for a waxing shoot,
But there came none;
It never saw the sun,
It never felt the trickling moisture run:
While with sunk eyes and faded mouth
She dreamed of melons, as a traveller sees
False waves in desert drouth
With shade of leaf-crowned trees,
And burns the thirstier in the sandful breeze.

She no more swept the house,
Tended the fowls or cows,
Fetched honey, kneaded cakes of wheat,
Brought water from the brook:
But sat down listless in the chimney-nook
And would not eat.

Tender Lizzie could not bear
To watch her sister's cankerous care
Yet not to share.
She night and morning
Caught the goblins' cry:
'Come buy our orchard fruits,
Come buy, come buy': –
Beside the brook, along the glen,
She heard the tramp of goblin men,
The voice and stir
Poor Laura could not hear;
Longed to buy fruit to comfort her,
But feared to pay too dear.

She thought of Jeanie in her grave,
Who should have been a bride;
But who for joys brides hope to have
Fell sick and died
In her gay prime,
In earliest Winter time,
With the first glazing rime,
With the first snow-fall of crisp Winter time.

Till Laura dwindling
Seemed knocking at Death's door:
Then Lizzie weighed no more
Better and worse;
But put a silver penny in her purse,
Kissed Laura, crossed the heath with clumps of
    furze
At twilight, halted by the brook:
And for the first time in her life
Began to listen and look.

Laughed every goblin
When they spied her peeping:
Came towards her hobbling,
Flying, running, leaping,
Puffing and blowing,
Chuckling, clapping, crowing,
Clucking and gobbling,
Mopping and mowing,
Full of airs and graces,
Pulling wry faces,
Demure grimaces,
Cat-like and rat-like,
Ratel- and wombat-like,
Snail-paced in a hurry,
Parrot-voiced and whistler,
Helter skelter, hurry skurry,
Chattering like magpies,
Fluttering like pigeons,

Gliding like fishes, –
Hugged her and kissed her,
Squeezed and caressed her:
Stretched up their dishes,
Panniers, and plates:
'Look at our apples
Russet and dun,
Bob at our cherries,
Bite at our peaches,
Citrons and dates,
Grapes for the asking,
Pears red with basking
Out in the sun,
Plums on their twigs;
Pluck them and suck them,
Pomegranates, figs.' –

'Good folk,' said Lizzie,
Mindful of Jeanie:
'Give me much and many': –
Held out her apron,
Tossed them her penny.
'Nay, take a seat with us,
Honour and eat with us,'
They answered grinning:
'Our feast is but beginning.
Night yet is early,
Warm and dew-pearly,
Wakeful and starry:
Such fruits as these
No man can carry;
Half their bloom would fly,
Half their dew would dry,
Half their flavour would pass by.
Sit down and feast with us,
Be welcome guest with us,
Cheer you and rest with us.' –
'Thank you,' said Lizzie: 'But one waits

At home alone for me:
So without further parleying,
If you will not sell me any
Of your fruits though much and many,
Give me back my silver penny
I tossed you for a fee.' –
They began to scratch their pates,
No longer wagging, purring,
But visibly demurring,
Grunting and snarling.
One called her proud,
Cross-grained, uncivil;
Their tones waxed loud,
Their looks were evil.
Lashing their tails
They trod and hustled her,
Elbowed and jostled her,
Clawed with their nails,
Barking, mewing, hissing, mocking,
Tore her gown and soiled her stocking,
Twitched her hair out by the roots,
Stamped upon her tender feet,
Held her hands and squeezed their fruits
Against her mouth to make her eat.

White and golden Lizzie stood,
Like a lily in a flood, –
Like a rock of blue-veined stone
Lashed by tides obstreperously, –
Like a beacon left alone
In a hoary roaring sea,
Sending up a golden fire, –
Like a fruit-crowned orange-tree,
White with blossoms honey-sweet,
Sore beset by wasp and bee, –
Like a royal virgin town
Topped with gilded dome and spire
Close beleaguered by a fleet

Mad to tug her standard down.

One may lead a horse to water,
Twenty cannot make him drink.
Though the goblins cuffed and caught her.
Coaxed and fought her,
Bullied and besought her,
Scratched her, pinched her black as ink,
Kicked and knocked her,
Mauled and mocked her,
Lizzie uttered not a word;
Would not open lip from lip
Lest they should cram a mouthful in:
But laughed in heart to feel the drip
Of juice that syruped all her face,
And lodged in dimples of her chin,
And streaked her neck which quaked like curd.
At last the evil people
Worn out by her resistance
Flung back her penny, kicked their fruit
Along whichever road they took,
Not leaving root or stone or shoot;
Some writhed into the ground,
Some dived into the brook
With ring and ripple,
Some scudded on the gale without a sound,
Some vanished in the distance.

In a smart, ache, tingle,
Lizzie went her way;
Knew not was it night or day;
Sprang up the bank, tore thro' the furze,
Threaded copse and dingle;
And heard her penny jingle
Bouncing in her purse, –
Its bounce was music to her ear.
She ran and ran
As if she feared some goblin man

Dogged her with gibe or curse
Or something worse:
But not one goblin skurried after,
Nor was she pricked by fear;
The kind heart made her windy-paced
That urged her home quite out of breath with
    haste
And inward laughter.

She cried, 'Laura,' up the garden,
'Did you miss me?
Come and kiss me.
Never mind my bruises,
Hug me, kiss me, suck my juices
Squeezed from goblin fruits for you,
Goblin pulp and goblin dew.
Eat me, drink me, love me;
Laura, make much of me:
For your sake I have braved the glen
And had to do with goblin merchant men.'

Laura started from her chair,
Flung her arms up in the air,
Clutched her hair:
'Lizzie, Lizzie, have you tasted
For my sake the fruit forbidden?
Must your light like mine be hidden,
Your young life like mine be wasted,
Undone in mine undoing
And ruined in my ruin,
Thirsty, cankered, goblin-ridden?' –
She clung about her sister,
Kissed and kissed and kissed her:
Tears once again
Refreshed her shrunken eyes,
Dropping like rain
After long sultry drouth;
Shaking with aguish fear, and pain,

She kissed and kissed her with a hungry mouth.

Her lips began to scorch,
That juice was wormwood to her tongue,
She loathed the feast:
Writhing as one possessed she leaped and sung,
Rent all her robe, and wrung
Her hands in lamentable haste,
And beat her breast.
Her locks streamed like the torch
Borne by a racer at full speed,
Or like the mane of horses in their flight,
Or like an eagle when she stems the light
Straight toward the sun,
Or like a caged thing freed,
Or like a flying flag when armies run.

Swift fire spread through her veins, knocked at
    her heart,
Met the fire smouldering there
And overbore its lesser flame;
She gorged on bitterness without a name:
Ah! fool, to choose such part
Of soul-consuming care!
Sense failed in the mortal strife:
Like the watch-tower of a town
Which an earthquake shatters down
Like a lightning-stricken mast,
Like a wind-uprooted tree
Spun about,
Like a foam-topped waterspout
Cast down headlong in the sea,
She fell at last;
Pleasure past and anguish past,
Is it death or is it life?

Life out of death.
That night long Lizzie watched by her,

Counted her pulse's flagging stir,
Felt for her breath,
Held water to her lips, and cooled her face
With tears and fanning leaves:
But when the first birds chirped about their eaves,
And early reapers plodded to the place
Of golden sheaves,
And dew-wet grass
Bowed in the morning winds so brisk to pass,
And new buds with new day
Opened of cup-like lilies on the stream,
Laura awoke as from a dream,
Laughed in the innocent old way,
Hugged Lizzie but not twice or thrice;
Her gleaming locks showed not one thread of
   grey,
Her breath was sweet as May
And light danced in her eyes.

Days, weeks, months, years,
Afterwards, when both were wives
With children of their own;
Their mother-hearts beset with fears,
Their lives bound up in tender lives;
Laura would call the little ones
And tell them of her early prime,
Those pleasant days long gone
Of not-returning time:
Would talk about the haunted glen,
The wicked quaint fruit-merchant men,
Their fruits like honey to the throat
But poison in the blood;
(Men sell not such in any town:)
Would tell them how her sister stood
In deadly peril to do her good,
And win the fiery antidote:
Then joining hands to little hands
Would bid them cling together,

'For there is no friend like a sister
In calm or stormy weather;
To cheer one on the tedious way,
To fetch one if one goes astray,
To lift one if one totters down,
To strengthen whilst one stands.'

Notes on the Authors

~~~~~~~~~~

LOUISA MAY ALCOTT (1832–88) was born in Philadelphia, the eldest daughter of the philosopher Bronson Alcott. She was educated chiefly by her father but her other teachers included Thoreau, Emerson and Theodore Park. After the failure of her father's school and their vegetarian community, 'Fruitlands', the family lived in great poverty and Louisa contributed to the family income by sewing, teaching and domestic work. She wrote for publication from the age of sixteen, mostly romance and revenge thrillers for magazines. Her first book, *Flower Fables*, appeared in 1855. *Hospital Sketches* (1863), based on her experiences as an army nurse, brought her a national reputation. *Little Women* (1868) was an instant success. Louisa worked prodigiously hard, producing novels, stories, articles and poems as the family's sole breadwinner and was a vehement supporter of Black rights and women's suffrage. She died in Boston on the day of her father's funeral.

ANJANA APPACHANA graduated from Delhi and Jawaharlal Nehru Universities. In 1984 she left India to live in the United States where she obtained an MFA in English from Pennsylvania State University. Her stories have been widely published in journals and magazines in India and the United States; one of them 'Her Mother', included in *Incantations and Other Stories* (1991), won an O. Henry Festival prize in 1989. She lives in Tempe, Arizona with her husband and daughter, and is working on a novel.

MARJORIE BARNARD (1897–1987) was born in Australia. She graduated with Honours from the University of Sydney but felt that parental duty prevented her from taking up an Oxford Graduate Scholarship and became a librarian. She collaborated with Flora Eldershaw, under the joint pseudonym M. Barnard Eldershaw, to write several novels from 1929, including *Tomorrow and Tomorrow and Tomorrow* (1947), and other works, including *Essays in Australian Fiction* (1938). Barnard's collection of short stories, *The Persimmon Tree*, appeared in 1943; she also wrote stories for children, historical studies and literary criticism, including a study of Miles Franklin. Marjorie Barnard was awarded the Patrick White Award in 1983, the New South Wales Special Medal in 1984 and an Honorary Doctorate of

Letters from the University of Sydney in 1986. She also received the Order of Australia.

BANI BASU was born in Calcutta in 1939. The author of many poems, essays and short stories, she began publishing seriously only in 1980. She has published three novels and several stories in Bengali and has translated stories by Somerset Maugham into Bengali. She lives and works in Calcutta. 'Aunty' is translated by Shampa Bannerjee from the Bengali.

MERLE COLLINS is Grenadian and was a member of Grenada's National Women's Organization until 1983. Her poetry has appeared in a number of anthologies and she has published two collections: *Because the Dawn Breaks* (1985) and *Rotten Pomerack* (1992). She co-edited and contributed to *Watchers and Seekers: Creative Writing by Black Women in Britain* (1987) and is the author of *Angel* (1987), an outstanding first novel centred on the lives of three Grenadian women, and *Rain Darling* (1990), a collection of short stories. She is currently a lecturer in Caribbean Studies at the Polytechnic of North London.

FIONA COOPER was born in Bristol. Her novels are *Rotary Spokes* (1988), *Heartbreak on the High Sierra* (1989), *Jay Loves Lucy* (1991) and *Not the Swiss Family Robinson* (1991). She has published numerous short stories and written journalistic satire. Her latest novel, *The Empress of the Seven Oceans*, appeared in 1992. Fiona Cooper lives on Tyneside.

MARILYN DUCKWORTH, OBE was born in Auckland, New Zealand and grew up in England. Her first novel, *A Gap in the Spectrum* (1959), was published when she was twenty-three; her fifth novel, *Disorderly Conduct*, won the New Zealand Book Award for fiction in 1984. She has been awarded the Scholarship in Letters twice, the Katherine Mansfield Fellowship in 1980 and a Fulbright Scholarship in 1987. In the same year she received the OBE for services to literature. Her collection of short stories, *Explosions on the Sun*, appeared in 1989; her tenth novel, *Unlawful Entry*, was published in 1992. Marilyn Duckworth lives in Wellington.

MARY FLANAGAN was born and grew up in New Hampshire. She was educated by the Sisters of Mercy, attended the local High School and received a degree in History of Art from Brandeis University, after which she worked in publishing in New York for three years. Her collection of short stories, *Bad Girls*, was published in 1984 and she has written two novels, *Trust* (1987) and *Rose Reason* (1991). Mary Flanagan lives in London where she is working on a new novel.

JANET FRAME, CBE was born in Dunedin, New Zealand in 1924. Her works include ten novels, among them *Living in the Maniototo* (1980), which won the Fiction Prize, New Zealand Book Awards, *Owls Do Cry* (1957), *Faces in the Water* (1961) and *Scented Gardens for the Blind* (1963). Patrick White called her 'the most considerable New Zealand novelist yet', and she has been awarded all the major New Zealand literary prizes, and was the 1989 winner of The Commonwealth Writers Prize. Her three volumes of autobiography, *To the Is-Land* (1983), *An Angel at my Table* (1984) and *The Envoy from Mirror City* (1985) (published in one volume as *An Autobiography*, 1990) were filmed as *An Angel at my Table*, directed by Jane Campion. Janet Frame was awarded a CBE in 1983.

ELIZABETH CLEGHORN GASKELL (1810–65), the daughter of a Unitarian Minister and keeper of the Treasury Records, was brought up by an aunt in Knutsford, Cheshire, the original of *Cranford* (1853) and of Hollingford in *Wives and Daughters* (1866). Her first novel *Mary Barton* (1848), based on industrial troubles, was criticized as being hostile to the employers but was highly popular. Her works include *Ruth* (1853), *North and South* (1855), and her controversial *Life of Charlotte Bronte* (1857). She also contributed to Dickens' *Household Words* and *All The Year Round*. Elizabeth Gaskell was very happily married to William Gaskell, a Unitarian minister.

GEORGINA HAMMICK's first collection of stories *People For Lunch* was published in 1987, and its title story was a winner of *Stand* magazine's Short Story Competition of 1985. She has contributed to a number of literary journals and story anthologies, including *The Listener*, *Critical Quarterly* and *Winter's Tales*, and her work appears in the *Best Short Stories* collections of 1987, 1988 and 1991. Her second volume of stories, *Spoilt*, was published in 1992. She is also the editor of *The Virago Book of Love and Loss* (1992). Georgina Hammick has three grown-up children, and lives in Wiltshire.

ELIZABETH JOLLEY trained as a nurse and wrote for twenty years before publishing her first novel. Her books include *Miss Peabody's Inheritance* (1983), *Mr Scobie's Riddle* (1983), *Five Acre Virgin* (1976), *The Travelling Entertainer* (1979) (story collections), and *The Well* (1986) which won the Miles Franklin Award. Elizabeth Jolley lives with her husband, a retired university librarian, in Western Perth and devotes much of her time to a farm where she raises geese and grows fruit.

KATHERINE MANSFIELD (1888–1923) was born Kathleen Mansfield Beauchamp in Wellington, New Zealand and was educated there and in London, to which she travelled in 1903. She spent most of her life in Europe, writing stories, and seeking higher standards in her art while battling against constant ill-health. Her work includes *In a German Pension* (1911), *Bliss and Other Stories* (1920), *The Garden Party* (1922) and *The Dove's Nest* (1923) and *Something Childish* (1924), both published posthumously. Her collected *Stories*, edited by Antony Alpers, were published in 1984. Katherine Mansfield died tragically young, of tuberculosis, leaving a legacy of some of the greatest, original and groundbreaking stories ever written, and her wonderful *Journal* which, like her letters, was edited by her husband John Middleton Murry.

NANN MORGENSTERN was born in New York and brought up and educated in Queens before graduating from Wells College. She came to London in 1964 and worked first in publishing and then trained as a teacher. After six years' teaching she returned to publishing, where she works now. Nann Morgenstern has published previous work under a pseudonym. She has two grown-up sons and lives in London.

EDNA O'BRIEN was born in County Clare in 1932 and graduated from the Pharmaceutical College of Dublin. She practised pharmacy briefly before becoming a writer. Her novels include *The Country Girls Trilogy* (1960–64), *August is a Wicked Month* (1965), *Casualties of Peace* (1966) and *A Pagan Place* (1970). She has also published collections of stories, including *A Scandalous Woman and Other Stories* (1974), *Mrs Rheinhardt and Other Stories* (1978), *A Fanatic Heart* (1984), and *Lantern Slides* (1990) and has written plays. Her latest novel, *Time and Tide,* appeared in 1992.

CYNTHIA RICH is the author, with Barbara Macdonald, of *Look Me in the Eye: Old Women, Aging, and Ageism*. Her most recent book, *Desert Years: Undreaming the American Dream*, is based on her life in a trailer on the Anza-Borrego Desert, where she and Barbara Macdonald have lived for some years.

CHRISTINA GEORGINA ROSSETTI (1830–94) was the sister of Dante Gabriel Rossetti. Her work ranged from poems of fantasy and verses for the young to religious poetry, which constituted the greater part of it. Her first work in book form, *Goblin Market and Other Poems*, appeared in 1862; other works include *The Prince's Progress* (1866), *Sing-Song* (juvenile, 1872) and *A Pageant and Other Poems* (1881), and she contributed to the short-lived Pre-Raphaelite periodical *The Germ* under a pseudonym. *Time Flies, a Reading Diary* (1885) with a poem or thought for each day was published in 1883. *Monna Innominata* is a series of sonnets about unhappy love. A volume of *New Poems* appeared posthumously in 1896.

DYAN SHELDON was born in Brooklyn and raised on Long Island. She is the author of three novels, *Victim of Love* (1982), *Dreams of an Average Man* (1985) and *My Life as a Whale* (1992), as well as several books for children. One of these, *Whale Song* (1990), won the Kate Greenaway Award. Her short stories have appeared in various publications. She also writes as

Serena Gray, under which name she has published five titles, including *Life's a Bitch And Then You Diet* (1990), *The Alien's Survival Manual* (1991) and *The Frog Factor* (1993). Dyan Sheldon has one daughter and divides her time between New York and London.

JEAN STAFFORD (1915–79) was born in California. She was awarded a Masters Degree by the University of Colorado in 1936. She married three times, the first time, in 1940, to the poet Robert Lowell. They divorced in 1948. Her novels are *Boston Adventure* (1944), *Mountain Lion* (1947) and *Catherine Wheel* (1952). She also worked on the *Southern Review* and taught at Flushing College, as well as writing short stories, children's books and interviews. 'A Mother in History', an interview with the mother of Lee Harvey Oswald, appeared in 1966. Jean Stafford was awarded the Pulitzer Prize for her *Collected Stories* in 1970.

WAJIDA TABASSUM (b. 1935) was born and brought up in Amravati and Hyderabad, and is the author of twenty-seven books of fiction and poetry. Her story, *Utran*, was written in 1975 and has been translated into all major Indian languages. In 1988, it was made into a television programme and has proved to be one of her most controversial stories. Widely travelled, Wajida Tabassum now lives and works in Bombay. 'Hand-me-downs' is translated by Manisha Chaudhry who has translated many stories by prominent women writers from Hindi into English.

SYLVIA TOWNSEND WARNER (1893–1978) lived most of her life with the writer Valentine Ackland, and the two women's joint commitment to the resistance of European Fascism gave an important context to Warner's writing. She had studied music, and was one of the four editors of the ten-volume *Tudor Church Music* (1923–9). Sylvia Townsend Warner published four volumes of poetry, essays and eight volumes of short stories, many of which first appeared in the *New Yorker*. Her seven novels include *Lolly Willowes* (1926), *Mr Fortune's Maggot* (1927), *Summer Will Show* (1936) and *The Corner That Held Them* (1948).